Neville Peat (right) with Sir Tim Wallis.

NEVILLE PEAT has written extensively about the geography and natural history of southern New Zealand, the setting for many of Sir Tim Wallis's business operations and adventures. Neville's books describe areas such as Fiordland, Mount Aspiring and Rakiura (Stewart Island) National Parks, and the Wanaka and West Coast regions.

Each year Neville is contracted to be the study leader for American educational tours of New Zealand in the expedition ship, *Clipper Odyssey*. For his series of photographic souvenir books on Dunedin, as well as for his work in the environmental field, he was awarded the inaugural Dunedin Citizen of the Year title in 1994.

An Otago Regional Councillor, Neville is a fifth-generation descendant of Scottish pioneers in Otago. He lives on Otago Peninsula with his wife, Mary, and their daughter, Sophora.

D0905544

Tim Wallis with a stag he shot in 1960 up the Okuru Valley, South Westland. Robert Wilson

Also by Neville Peat:

Winging it!

THE ADVENTURES OF TIM WALLIS

A book for 11- to 14-year-olds based on *Hurricane Tim*.

HURRICANE TIM

The Story of Sir TIM WALLIS

NEVILLE PEAT

Longacre Press

Reid Jackson – Friend and Mentor

I could not have accomplished the business initiatives and research-and-development described here without the advice of Reid Jackson, my Dunedin accountant. Reid was not only a brilliant accountant and business adviser; he also became a close friend of mine. For our first meeting in the mid-1960s I brought two apple boxes, containing all my records, to his office in a building near the old Chief Post Office in Dunedin. Reid grilled me about what I wanted to achieve. At a follow-up meeting next day he agreed to accept me as a client providing I was always completely open and honest with him. It was my job, he said, to create a cash flow for the business and he would advise where and how to invest the money. His advice was invaluable to me. It was a tragedy for his family and me when he died in 1987 at the early age of 52.

Tim Wallis

Photography credits: all photographs are from the Alpine Deer Group collection unless otherwise acknowledged.

Robin Carr's quote, used on the front cover, is from the *Marlborough Express.*

ISBN 1 877361 70 4

First published in hardback by Longacre Press 2005
Reprinted 2005, 2006
This paperback edition published by Longacre Press 2006
30 Moray Place, Dunedin, New Zealand.
www.longacre.co.nz

A catalogue record for this book is available from the National Library of New Zealand.

Book and cover design by Christine Buess.
Back cover photo: Tim Wallis flying his Spitfire Mk XVI over Wanaka. *Phil Makanna.*
Map on page 17 from *Pick of the Bunch: New Zealand Wildflowers* by Peter Johnson, Longacre Press, 1997.
Maps on pages 186 and 196 reproduced with permission from Lonely Planet Publications ©2005.
Printed by Everbest Printing Company Ltd, China.

Contents

Robert Wilson

THE WALLIS and Wilson families have been great friends for almost four generations. Tim and I have complementary godfather roles to one another's eldest sons. We grew up together as boys with a special interest in the outdoors. He remains my greatest friend, hunting companion and long-time close business associate.

Tim's early attraction to the bush, mountains and deer hunting led to his first challenge and great dream – an industry based on New Zealand red deer. With Tim as a driving force, that industry succeeded beyond all expectations. It is easy to dream but to follow and drive those dreams to reality you need to be a special person. From the 1970s to the 1990s, Tim actively encouraged and inspired many others to follow their own dreams. He helped finance and train pilots, encouraged the expansion of deer farming, actively promoted and developed markets and was involved in dozens of entrepreneurial adventures.

Tim has always been able to be at one with all levels of society, humble or great. He recognizes the goodness or potential in individuals, and has often become a mentor. He is a born leader. At the height of his career, he instigated close team-work and instilled in his workmates and associates the spirit of comradeship and trust. Faced with danger and great stress, Tim thought of others ahead of his own perils. When all seemed stacked against him, he not only survived but pushed on – and often succeeded. This kind of determination is very special.

Surviving a horrific aircraft accident, Tim has demonstrated an ability to take on a new life. He has had to disregard impediments and handicaps that would have been insurmountable to most. This is a story in itself.

In Tim we see great courage, not the least the courage of his convictions. New Zealand is certainly a better place for having experienced the calibre and the unique abilities of Hurricane Tim. He has been a positive force across multiple levels – individual, community, industry and the economy. For Tim, life and its opportunities are not just a waiting game. He has lived a vision, which is that life is for living and that living with others is life. His story is inspiring.

Mark Acland

TIM WALLIS has many friends. I am one of them. Over the years, I have teamed up with Tim on many expeditions and projects, both in New Zealand and overseas.

Adventure and thrill have been major aspects of our friendship, which goes back to school days when we were the only boys fresh from State country schools, flung into the very different world of Christ's College. I have enjoyed his larger-than-life personality, his zest for challenges, and his absolutely one-track mind approach to all projects. In return, I hope I have been a sounding board and someone to turn to in the down times that accompany the kind of vivid, remarkable life he has led. He has always been an incredibly generous and loyal friend. I admire him hugely for his courage and leadership.

During the busiest phases of his life, he kept calm in all situations. In work, when all around him was 'full on', he never lost sight of his goals. He also kept remarkably calm in bad flying conditions: such as the time we were involved in a helicopter crash. I well recall his first words, 'Are you all right, Mark?' after which he took firm charge of the situation. Tim's passion for flying meant that in the air he really was larger than life. He pushed boundaries but when flying with him you had confidence that you were with one of the very best mountain pilots in the business.

Tim is a compassionate person. In the risky game of helicopter deer recovery and live capture, crew lost their lives. Tim always took this very personally and would do all he could to help the affected families.

Whether it is entertaining royalty or waiting in an airport in Northern China, Tim's presence and charm are always felt. He gets on with all nationalities and finds language no barrier. In business, he employed people from varied backgrounds whom he would guide and encourage, whatever their role within his companies.

A remarkable innovator and leader in business and community affairs, his determination, self-confidence, and foresight, have been his greatest assets. Yet he is also respected – and loved – by his friends and employees for his loyalty.

Author's Note

In the wild mountain environment of Southwest New Zealand, a land known to breed characters, Tim Wallis attained 'character' status in his twenties for his enterprising, daring, swashbuckling approach to life. Never still, he liked to be on the front foot. He flew helicopters close to their limits and pushed boundaries in business as well.

Today, Tim – Sir Tim in formal settings – is a legendary figure in aviation, the deer industry, business enterprise and the collection and display of vintage warplanes. He founded the phenomenally successful vintage fighter aircraft pageant, Warbirds Over Wanaka, held biennially at Easter. In earlier decades he dazzled the deer industry with his innovative use of helicopters for venison and live deer recovery, his leading-edge developments in deer farming, and his promotion of velvet in addition to venison as an important export opportunity for deer farmers.

He was a pathfinder in what has been described as 'New Zealand's Last Great Adventure', the intensive helicopter shooting and netting of red deer from the mountains of Southern New Zealand in the 1960s and 1970s. Despite breaking his back in a helicopter crash in 1968, and walking with a limp thereafter, he ventured into business in regions as far away as Siberia and Canada. He also looked at setting up commercial enterprises based on beef in tropical Vanuatu and spider crabs and wild pigs in the subantarctic Auckland Islands.

Tim liked nothing better than to be creating new opportunities during those days. He lived life like he flew helicopters – boldly, directly, hurriedly. He had more than his fair share of crashes, and in business some of his ideas were wrecked as well. Tim is a survivor. His rehabilitation after a near-fatal Spitfire crash at Wanaka in January 1996 that left him brain injured is testament to that – his toughest challenge in a life full of challenges.

When I met Tim in 2003 to discuss the writing of his life story, I envisaged a tale filled with adventure, innovation, even heroism. In New Zealand heroes are generally found in sporting arenas or among those who provide emergency services in remote and difficult settings. Tim Wallis is a hero of a different kind, admired the length of the land. The most telling evidence of this is found in the 3,000 cards and letters that poured into Dunedin Public Hospital after his Spitfire crash, his last crash. One outsized card carries the signatures of 700 scouts who had seen him perform a Spitfire aerobatic routine over their jamboree camp near Manapouri the day before his Wanaka crash.

Life has changed for Tim since the 1996 crash. That he is no longer the energetic aviator and businessman he once was does not stop him from travelling around New Zealand and overseas, and plugging away at his ideas. He remains a public figure, somewhat larger than life.

Neville Peat
Broad Bay, June 2005

Writing the life story of a man like Tim Wallis calls for some innovative ways to express his dynamism and the full force of his personality. As an entrée into Tim's world I have chosen the year 1968 because it provides an insight into his dynamic approach to business, his exuberant character and adventurous lifestyle. In 1968, he caught red deer live for experimental farming, he incorporated coastal vessels into his Fiordland venison harvesting venture and he met Prue Hazledine, who would become his wife a few years later. It was also the year he broke his back.

On hurricanes ...

In the early 1990s, a New Zealand television documentary maker asked Prue Wallis to describe what it was like being married to Tim Wallis. She replied: 'It's like living with a hurricane roaring around on all sides. Sometimes it feels like the boys and I are the eye of the hurricane.'

hurricane *n.* Storm with violent wind ... violent commotion.
The Concise Oxford Dictionary

HAWKER HURRICANE Mark IIA, serial number P3351, was built in England in 1940 for the Royal Air Force. It participated in the Battle of Britain. In 1942, the aircraft joined the Russian Air Force but crashed the following year in tundra near the Arctic Circle city of Murmansk. Fifty years later, the plane was acquired by Tim Wallis and it had its first flight after restoration in the millennium year. At the Warbirds Over Wanaka 2000 airshow, the Hurricane was a star.

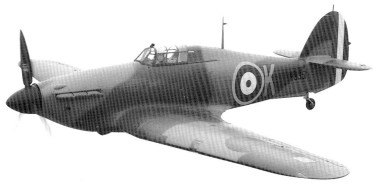

Chapter 1

Sixty-eight

*Snow and ice ... helicopters to the rescue ...
a mothership in Fiordland ... live capture ...
Queenstown Hill crash ... Christchurch Hospital*

IT WAS A WINTER worthy of an ice age. Through June and July of 1968, snow lay across much of southern New Zealand, closing country schools, disrupting transport and causing farmers to declare the winter the worst in a decade –the worst ever, some said. The Otago region was badly hit. With hundreds of sheep trapped in snow drifts, stock losses were mounting. As the snow froze in Otago's harbour capital, Dunedin, driving conditions in the city became chaotic. Temperatures dipped below zero 24 days in a row – a frost record for the city.

Notwithstanding the extreme cold, a rugby football match between Otago and the touring French team at Carisbrook went ahead on the first Saturday in July. The French, victors by 12 points to six, were accused of 'dirty rucking'. Four Otago players retired from the game injured. Newspapers at the time also accused France of foul play in the South Pacific. That same weekend the first hydrogen bomb was detonated at a remote atoll in French Polynesia. Also in the news – renewed annihilation of North Vietnam villages by massive B-52 Stratofortress bombers of the United States Air Force. On the local aviation scene, the first Boeing 737 jet service into Dunedin was announced, starting in October.

As snow and ice gripped the land that weekend, Tim Wallis and the other pilots of Luggate Game Packers Ltd – Russell Gutschlag, Roy McIvor and Bill Black – were creating news of their own. From the company's base at Luggate, near the quiet lakeside town of Wanaka, they were rescuing people stranded in the mountains and farm animals trapped in the snow. A helicopter flown by Russell Gutschlag had been called to Mount Cook National Park to lift out two shooters stuck in a high-alpine hut for a week. Other jobs involved carrying bales of hay to snow-bound mobs of sheep and cattle, and ferrying farm hands assigned to 'snow raking'. It was

Opposite: Tim refuelling a Hiller 12E helicopter in the East Matukituki Valley in 1967.
Robert Wilson

the task of the farm hands to lead stock back to safety by trampling trails through the snow. Snow raking was tough work. Helicopter access to the stock removed a lot of the grunt. Although much of Otago was affected, the snowfalls had been especially heavy around Wanaka, the Cardrona Valley and the Crown Range overlooking the tourist resort of Queenstown and Lake Wakatipu. Hundreds of sheep were trapped, most of them hardy merinos. Government subsidies through the 1960s helped farmers cope financially with extreme weather events like this. During the Big Chill of '68 the farmers turned to a relatively new tool in their midst – helicopters.

Luggate Game Packers had the largest fleet of helicopters in the south – four American-made Hillers. The Hiller UH 12E was a robust, versatile three-seater that could cruise at 130 kilometres per hour and lift up to about 400 kilograms. At the age of 29, Tim Wallis was the company's managing director – a boss more interested in flying than in running an office. He did most of his thinking and planning in the air and inevitably returned to base brimming with ideas that needed active follow-up through phone calls, letters or a personal visit. He hit the ground running, a big man in a hurry. Tim's physique mirrored the tall, broad-shouldered landscape of Southwest New Zealand. Having explored parts of the back-country on foot, he both loved the landscape and pretty much had the measure of it. He knew how it could amaze anyone venturing into it – and how it could change abruptly. There were river gorges too deep for the sun to penetrate, broad glaciated valleys where the cold rivers flaunted their braids, formidable rock walls and rippling slopes of snow tussock. It was a powerful landscape that suited his powerful frame. And its airspace he knew intimately, from the reasonably defined 'grain' of the land east of the main divide in Mount Aspiring National Park to the confusing jumble of mountains and valleys that constitute Fiordland. He revelled in the landscape as much as he did the business of flying helicopters. Yet whereas the landscape was almost everywhere rugged, Tim Wallis had a pronounced softer side, expressed in his smooth, boyish face and a warm smile that set his eyes asparkle.

Tim was from a West Coast background, but had settled in the Luggate-Wanaka area seven years before. He bought his first helicopter in 1965. He also owned and flew a fixed-wing Cessna 180, a four-seater with tail wheel. Complementing this inland air force was a navy of sorts comprising two ships, the *Ranginui* and *Hotunui*, which were formerly engaged in the New Zealand coastal trade but destined now for new frontiers.

In July of '68 the *Ranginui*, 32 metres long and 158 tons gross, was in Fiordland's remote steep-sided waterways, carrying out an extraordinary role. Tim had bought her to act as a floating, mobile refrigerator and

The Ranginui, *a former coastal trader, at a mooring at the head of Milford Sound, Fiordland.* Janice Wallis

staging post for deer recovery in Fiordland National Park. Neither New Zealand nor the world had ever seen the likes of her. The *Ranginui*'s chiller space could hold up to 600 red deer carcasses. A motherlode of venison.

THE *RANGINUI* had first steamed into the narrows of Bradshaw Sound, an inner arm of Doubtful Sound, five months earlier, in February 1968. On that day, two Luggate Game Packers helicopters made rendezvous with her. Tim Wallis flew one of the Hillers, Te Anau-based pilot Bill Black the other. Fresh from a conversion at a Port Chalmers shipyard near Dunedin, the *Ranginui* had a helicopter pad amidships, where the main mast had once stood. Skipper Dave Henigan slowed the ship from her cruising speed of nine knots to allow the machines to use her flight deck, one at a time – a stately mothership a long way from anywhere civilised, with two lively white offspring circling around her.

Not unused to novelty, Tim would remember the *Ranginui*'s first day in Fiordland as something special. So would Bill Black. As they set out on

Kingi Keha organising the storage of deer carcasses in the chiller hold of the Ranginui.

the day's hunting, each pilot had a deer shooter on one side of him and a gutter on the other. It was the gutter's job to leap out; trim the dead animals into gutted carcasses and then hook them on to the helicopter when the pile was big enough. Tim had told Blackie to take one side of Bradshaw Sound while he worked the other side. Blackie noted wryly, once airborne, that he had been allotted the steeper, more rugged side; nonetheless, he and his team got cracking with a will and without complaint. The adrenalin was already pumping.

Above the beech forest that clung precariously to the lower sides of the fiord, tussocklands, herbfields and stunted shrubland provided good habitat for red deer. The mountains here bulged above the winding fiords to heights over 1,400 metres. It was Fiordland at its most rugged and secluded, with not a road, bridge nor hut to be seen, and no trails apart from deer tracks. From high up, the *Ranginui* looked smaller than a toy boat, and from down at the water the helicopters, when visible, appeared as white dragonflies, buzzing mutedly, and flitting, darting, diving, backtracking and only occasionally pausing.

In no time the helicopters were dropping deer, five or six at a time, on to the *Ranginui's* flight deck. The ship's crew were soon knee-deep in carcasses and complaining about how the two teams seemed to be competing to see who could deliver more deer.

During the afternoon Tim had to fly out to Te Anau to collect a part for the chiller equipment. Cheekily, he picked up a few of Blackie's deer before leaving for Te Anau and landed them on the *Ranginui* to boost his own tally. By the day's end, 330 deer were hanging in the dim chiller spaces. At this rate the *Ranginui* could be filled in only two good days' shooting. Then she would have to sail north to Milford Sound – six or seven hours steaming from the Doubtful Sound area – to offload the carcasses into trucks bound for processing plants inland.

By the time the *Ranginui* had been afloat in its new role for four months, the arrival of the first snow in June that year, and a consequent lull in venison recovery, triggered a burst of activity of a different sort in Tim. In the space of a few weeks he flew between Stewart Island in the south and the Bay of Islands in the north.

At Stewart Island he did an aerial survey of the island's burgeoning and enviromentally damaging herds of white-tailed and red deer, to see if helicopter deer harvesting would work there in the future. Next stop was the Port Chalmers shipyard of Sims Engineering, where his other ship, the *Hotunui*, was getting a makeover more extensive than the *Ranginui*'s. Considerably larger than the *Ranginui*, at 50 metres long and 594 tons gross, the *Hotunui* was having her derricks removed, a flight deck installed and holds converted as freezer space. Fiordland deer were again the target. Refitted, the *Hotunui* would be able to load 2,500 deer at a time. From Port Chalmers, Tim travelled north to the Bay of Islands for a week's yachting with friends before returning to Port Chalmers to check on progress with his ship, said to be the largest privately-owned vessel in New Zealand. Officers and crew numbered ten. A commissioning ceremony was planned for mid-July. It would be a big day, and the planning for it, involving a Cabinet Minister, was already well advanced.

Tim wanted the day to be a statement of where he was going with his

Deer carcasses barged ashore from the Ranginui *at Milford Sound are loaded on to trucks for the journey out to a processing plant. The tractor was fitted with a special boom so it could lift the carcasses off the pontoon.*

helicopters and ships and the harvesting of deer. These things were his business, his recreation, his life. But a good deer was not necessarily a dead deer.

ON THE FIRST SATURDAY OF JULY, 1968, when much of Otago was under snow and ice, Tim set out to fulfil some work and recreational commitments. The day looked promising, with clear skies, little wind and rising day temperatures forecast. He had made arrangements to capture up to ten red deer for an unusual experiment planned at Lincoln College (now Lincoln University) near Christchurch. Drugging this number of red deer then plucking them live from the wild was something that defied the odds. Tim believed it could be done. In a day. In the right conditions, it might take just a few hours.

Live capture was his commitment for the first Saturday in July. Sunday was going to be different. He had invited girlfriend Prue Hazledine to join him from Dunedin for some skiing at Coronet Peak on the Sunday. After a series of southerly storms, the snow lay delightfully deep over the Queenstown skifield, New Zealand's best. He expected to be busy in the morning, flying in support of sheep rescue and feeding out on the grassy tops of the 'Queenstown Hill' farm between Queenstown and Arrowtown. By midday he and Prue, together with his sister, Josephine, and her Dunedin boyfriend, would be enjoying the Coronet Peak powder.

For months, Tim had been discussing the live deer project with Colin Murdoch of the Timaru company, Paxarms. Colin was a chemist by training with several years' experience capturing wild animals in Australia and New Zealand. He had manufactured a long-barrelled pistol that could shoot a dart into a deer's body from a helicopter. The darts carried a syringe loaded with a paralysing slug of muscle relaxant prepared by Colin.

D-day arrived. Red deer running wild on the Criffel Range near Wanaka were the target, and Tim judged conditions to be near-perfect. With visibility good, deer tracks would stand out in the snow – as would the deer themselves. Under the snow the vegetation comprised mainly tussock grasses. On this dry mountain range there were only scrappy remnants of forest for the deer to hide in.

All three seats in the Hiller were filled. Colin Murdoch was in the right seat, which suited a right-hander firing a pistol. Tim had the pilot's seat in the middle, and on his left was Lin Herron, a good friend of Tim's who ran Branches Station, a backblocks sheep and cattle farm which sprawled across 45,000 hectares of the upper Shotover region behind Queenstown. Tim had invited Lin to assist with the stranded stock operations of recent

Fiordland

Fiordland is a bewildering and awesomely wild expanse of steep-walled valleys, ice-carved fiords, snowy peaks, tussocky ranges, and, everywhere, water features – lakes, rivers, waterfalls, and the fiords themselves, with their curiously dark, tannin-stained surface waters, more fresh than salt. Eighty percent of the land area is under wet-footed forest, comprising mostly southern beech. Rain, measured in metres per year, fuels the ecology. This is one of the world's wettest areas, a reception centre for a procession of moist, often stormy weather systems radiating out of the vast Southern Ocean. Weather-wise, Fiordland is a testing place for any airborne or seaborne operation, not the least one engaged in deer recovery. Only two roads traverse the region – the Milford Sound highway via the Homer Tunnel and an unsealed road crossing from Lake Manapouri to Deep Cove, Doubtful Sound, via Wilmot Pass. The rest of the region remains a preserve of nature.

The bulk of the region became a national park in 1952. In 1986, Fiordland's unique natural features were recognised in its listing as a World Heritage Area.

Tim flying his Hughes 500D helicopter ZK-HOT in the 'Campbell's Kingdom' gorge near Doubtful Sound, Fiordland.

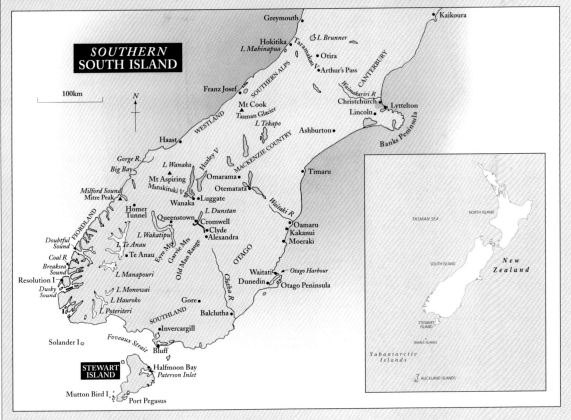

SOUTHERN SOUTH ISLAND

100km

N

days. The two of them worked well together.

A minute or two after take-off the Hiller came upon deer tracks in the snow in the upper reaches of Luggate Creek. Then a mob of four or five appeared higher up. Colin readied his pistol as Tim began herding the deer. The Hiller drew closer, jinking in tune with the quarry. Tim was used to driving them like this and he could generally rely on the deer to run together at a steady pace. After each darting, Tim drew the Hiller away, knowing that the drug, called Paximmo A, would take a few minutes to work. Lin's job, when the helicopter returned to the scene, was to jump from the skid, strap the legs of the deer and place them in nets for underslinging back to base.

Tim knew a thing or two about close encounters with snow in a chopper. His first scare ever was in snow, in September 1965. He had just acquired a new Bell 47 G4 helicopter, the type featured in the *Mash* television series about United States involvement in the Korean War. Within days of flying it home to Luggate, he was working with shooters in the Mill Creek catchment of the Matukituki Valley. He attempted to land in snow beside a pile of newly-gutted deer. The skids sank, almost causing

Lin Herron with tranquillised deer bound for Lincoln College. The deer were captured live on the Criffel Range in July 1968. Lin, then owner of Branches Station in the Shotover area, assisted Colin Murdoch and Tim with the capture.

the tail rotor to strike the snow. It was a lesson. Since then he had clocked up about 1,000 hours' flying in helicopters.

On this Saturday, after about four hours on the Criffel Range, the live-capture team had drugged and delivered eight deer, including a stag with an impressive rack of antlers: a 14-pointer. Tim decided to call it a day. The deer were loaded into a Reid's Transport truck. Next stop, Lincoln College.

The day was a dream come true for Tim: work on developing a syringe dart had been going on for more than a year and he had fielded enquiries from various New Zealand zoos about whether he might be able to supply chamois and tahr as well as red deer. 'The idea,' he wrote to his mother, Janice, 'is a real beauty.'

At Lincoln, a university experimental farm, Professor Ian Coop was setting out to study the potential for farming red deer. The Wallis deer, featured on the front page of the Christchurch *Press*, such was their novelty, joined a group of five tame animals in the Lincoln paddocks. The feral ones, which spent much of the day running up and down the fence lines, proved a handful to manage.

Deer farming on any scale was but a twinkle in the eye.

SUNDAY, 7 JULY 1968, was a sparkling winter's day in the Wanaka-Queenstown region, the sort of day that made the mountains look alluringly close. Mirror images of them bounced off silvery glacial lakes. The landscape was dazzlingly white, its edges softened by the snow reaching down to the valley floors. At his cottage at the foot of an old river terrace on the margins of the township of Luggate, Tim was up before dawn, as usual, but with an urgent request weighing on his mind.

Queenstown Hill's owner, Arnold Middleton, had been in touch about the pressing need to feed out his merino sheep on the summit crests before they succumbed to the cold. He told Tim a 'stinker of a storm' had brought the latest snowfall, the heaviest to date. On parts of the 1,160 hectare farm, the drifts were well over a sheep's head. A helicopter would be a godsend.

They departed in the Hiller soon after breakfast – Tim, Prue and Lin Herron. Tim had met Prue, a tall, slim 24-year-old blonde, a few months earlier when they were both guests at an Easter wedding at East Taieri (near Mosgiel, a short drive from Dunedin). Tim's smooth complexion, tanned and radiant, and his generous smile, wide as a circus clown's, spoke of a life outdoors, and one filled with fun if not excitement. Prue's miniskirt caught Tim's eye. He and Prue got talking. Tim recognised in Prue an engaging, lively personality, and a sharp wit and intelligence. (A production

Drugging deer

For Tim Wallis's live capture of red deer in the winter of 1968, a drug called Paximmo A, formulated by Colin Murdoch of Paxarms, was loaded into the syringes. A muscle relaxant in the drug immobilised the limbs and neck of the darted animal and a powerful sedative was incorporated in the formula to calm it. At the correct dose, Paximmo A worked well but if the dosages were not precise it could fatally affect a deer's heart muscle and breathing. The paralysing component of it wore off after about 15 to 20 minutes. Other drugs, with wider tolerances, were used in live recovery of deer in the 1970s.

The Paxarms pistol, dart syringes and other equipment used in the tranquillising of feral red deer in the 1960s.

Prue Hazledine (left) and Tim's sister, Josephine, on holiday at Queenstown.

secretary assigned to magazine programmes at the Dunedin television studios of DNTV2, Prue, like so many New Zealanders in their early twenties, at the time was saving for an overseas working holiday.)

Prue knew something of Tim's world. Her family used to holiday at Wanaka; her parents were friendly with the Wilson family, whose son, Robert, had been associated with Tim and his business for years; and while at dinner at the Wilsons' Maori Hill home a week or two earlier she had viewed a cine film taken by Robert of his and Tim's latest business trip to Hong Kong. Since the East Taieri wedding, she and Tim had met as frequently as possible. She sometimes flew with him in his helicopter on TV filming trips in Central Otago.

Approaching Queenstown Hill, Tim diverted to nearby Arthurs Point where his sister Josephine was based for the weekend at her boyfriend's A-frame holiday cottage overlooking the Shotover Canyon. The cottage was owned by Bob Berry and his brother, George. Also at the cottage that weekend was Dick Burton, seafood manager for the Dunedin exporting firm, Wilson Neill Ltd, whose executive director, Robert Wilson, was an old school mate of Tim's. Dick had come up for the skiing but had hurt his ankle. On the helicopter's arrival at Arthurs Point Prue offered Dick her seat. He accepted. As Tim flew out from Arthurs Point, he told Prue to expect him back about lunchtime.

During the next couple of hours, the Hiller carted hay on its skid-mounted racks to high points on Queenstown Hill – three trips in all.

A hay barn not far from the homestead at the end of Tuckers Beach Road was the staging point, and each time Tim took off he passed over the homestead, climbing steeply. Away to his right as he departed with each load was the gravel-laden Tuckers Beach bend of the Shotover River. On one trip, Tim transported Arnold Middleton and two assistants to a point high up on the property to see that the sheep were fed and to create escape routes for them through the snow. The trio had agreed they would walk home in the afternoon.

Back at the barn after the last of the hay had been distributed, Tim signalled to Lin and Dick to reboard the Hiller for a flight out to the township of Frankton, where Lin and his wife, Alexa, had a house they used in winter when the road to their farm was blocked by snow. It was almost 11a.m. Alexa had hot soup ready – yet Tim's mind was not on food; it was on an afternoon's skiing. The mountains were bathed in sunshine. He longed to get out into the snow, having flown over so much of it. He wondered, too, whether Bill Black had finished another feeding-out job that morning in the Cardrona Valley.

Tim's passengers were still fastening their lap belts as he scanned the instruments in front of him, lifted the collective – the lever at his left side – and simultaneously wound on power through the twist-grip throttle at the end of the collective. The twin-bladed main rotor gripped the air, bringing the Hiller to a hover. Between his two long legs, his right hand twitched the cyclic: the stick that directed the machine in any direction: forwards, backwards or sideways. The Lycoming engine roared to meet the demands of rotor pitch and torque as the Hiller lifted away from the area of the barn and towards Frankton. This time, instead of passing the homestead, the flightpath would take them in almost the opposite direction, over Lake Johnson, a glacial finger lake perched in a gap in the hills above them.

Tim did not see the power lines. No one on board did. There was no warning.

Three 33,000 volt lines formed the main feed into Queenstown from a substation at Frankton. Near the Queenstown Hill hay barn they sagged between two distant spurs.

Each wire, 12 millimetres in diameter, comprised a steel core wrapped by six aluminium strands.

In the blinding light, against the snow, they were all but invisible. The pole supporting them on the spur near Lake Johnson where the Hiller was headed, which might have given Tim a clue to the presence of wires, was partly obscured by trees. Although Tim had flown over the lines further along their route several times during the morning, they were not conspicuous on his flightpath now. Further along, the lines ran close to the steep slopes and were not a hazard.

As the main rotor blades snapped the lines, lengths of wire began wrapping around the rotor head and the rods controlling the pitch of the blades. It was a sickening sound above the noise of engine and rotors. The strangling of the control rods had the effect of increasing pitch. Ironically, for a few moments, the helicopter continued climbing, with its engine screaming in response to extreme torque.

Instantly, the helicopter was out of control. The collective was useless, the cyclic ineffective, and autorotation not an option.

The Hiller began plummeting. It fell over 50 metres and crashed more or less on its skids on a flat paddock between the spurs. The 20 centimetres of snow on the paddock did little to cushion the impact. The skids disintegrated, the tail crumpled.

Dick Burton was hurled halfway out the broken right door. Lin Herron was thrown forward violently through the Perspex bubble. Restrained by his lap strap (shoulder harnesses were not used then), Tim remained upright in his seat – unable to move, unable to feel his legs. All three men were conscious. Tim knew he had suffered a serious back injury and suspected Dick was also paralysed. Lin was the only one who could move. Unbeknown to Tim, who thought his friend had probably broken a few ribs on the alloy bar reinforcing the bubble, Lin had suffered vertebrae damage as well. But he could walk.

A tough back-country farmer undaunted by the wintry conditions, Lin hobbled off through the snow to get help from the homestead about 600 metres away. He tried to take a short-cut but encountered a bank which proved too much for him to climb, so he doubled back to the road and followed it up to the house.

Isabelle Middleton (the wife of the farmer, Arnold, who knew nothing of the crash until he arrived home from the summit crests about 4.30), was at home with her two infant children. She answered an urgent knocking at the door and was on the phone immediately, summoning an ambulance from town. Next she gathered up the baby and some blankets, made sure the older child would be safe in its cot, and got Lin to show her the crash site in the family car, which had chains fitted to the wheels.

The ambulance was quickly on the scene, closely followed by a tractor driven by a neighbouring farmer, Reg Hansen. The tractor towed the ambulance through the snow over the last few hundred metres – right to the wreckage.

AT CORONET PEAK, the main chairlift was doing a roaring trade on this sublime Sunday morning. Just on 11 o'clock, it stopped abruptly, leaving dozens of skiers swinging in their chairs. Right across Queenstown, in hotels and homes, tourist shops and cafes, the power failed.

Josephine Wallis, skiing at the time, saw the chairlift stop – and remain still. Eventually she made her way down to the main buildings, puzzled by how long it was taking to get the chairlift working again. She joined a long queue in the cafe for food and a hot drink. Someone answered a phone call. Then she heard her name: 'It's a call for a Jo Wallis.'

Jo was very fond of her older brother. A physiotherapist, she had in fact returned from a working holiday in England and Canada to help out Tim with his venison-recovery operations by managing the camps and supply lines for his shooters in places as far flung as Manapouri and Haast.

Wreckage of the Hiller 12E, ZK-HBF, that struck power lines at Queenstown Hill station. The helicopter is lying on its side with the remains of the instrument panels protruding.

In the Cardrona Valley, pilot Bill Black had been feeding out hay to stranded stock. He had completed the bulk of the job when his Hiller developed a fuel problem. He put it down to a sticky throttle, caused possibly by the cold conditions. By late morning, he was over at Queenstown Airport seeking repairs. Then the lights went out.

That afternoon he would fly to the crash site and cover it. Next day he would bring out the remains of Tim's helicopter, slinging it beneath his own. The Hiller registered as ZK-HBF was a total wreck, good only for spare parts for the remaining three Hillers in the fleet. At least it was insured.

At the A-frame cottage at Arthurs Point, Prue Hazledine became impatient as morning slipped into afternoon and she had not heard from Tim. As there was no phone at the crib, she decided to walk to the local hotel and try to contact Alexa Herron. The hotel was closed – it was a Sunday in the 1960s – but a woman there asked if Prue was from an A-frame cottage up the hill. There was a message from Frankton Hospital, reporting an accident without any details of how serious it was, and asking the hotel owners to give the news to the A-frame. She had not known which one they meant.

The ambulance had taken the three crash victims to the hospital at Frankton. In no time at all staff there judged the injuries to be rather more serious than they could cope with. Kew Hospital at Invercargill was alerted. By the time Prue arrived at Frankton Hospital, Tim and his injured companions had left for Invercargill. She hired a car from Queenstown and made her way to Invercargill as fast as she could over roads made hazardous by snow and ice.

The coaster Hotunui *on commissioning day at Port Chalmers, July 1968. Two Luggate Game Packers helicopters demonstrated the loading of deer carcasses on to the ship's helipad.* Otago Daily Times

Josephine, Tim's brother George (who lived in Haast), and his god-mother, Aunt Betsy from Queenstown, also made their way to Invercargill, where Tim and the others were receiving treatment.

The *Otago Daily Times* ran the story on the front page next morning. Queenstown, it said, was without power for three hours – at a time when the district was experiencing some of its coldest weather in 40 years.

On Wednesday, three days after the crash, Tim was transferred to Christchurch Public Hospital and admitted to Ward 13B, the spinal injury unit. He had the worst injuries. Dick Burton suffered a crushed sternum and ribs. Lin's vertebrae damage was expected to heal reasonably well. But Tim had suffered crush injuries to the lowest two of five lumbar vertebrae, L1 and L2: the most vulnerable to vertical impact.

Tim never entertained the thought he might end up disabled. He had survived the physical demands of the back country and the rough and tumble of interprovincial rugby. Mentally, he was tough as well – tough, determined and ambitious. It would take more than a few crushed vertebrae to put him off his stride. The hospital staff attending him discerned fortitude of a rare kind. In that first week, all he worried about was whether he would be out of hospital in time to attend the commissioning of the *Hotunui* at Port Chalmers. 'I've bust my back,' he told family and friends, 'but I've got to be right by next Wednesday.'

Tim at his mother's home following his discharge from Christchurch Hospital. He is holding his catheter bottle. A calliper was fitted to his paralysed left leg later.

THE COMMISSIONING of the *Hotunui* went ahead on 17 July as planned. It could not be delayed. For one thing, the refit had taken two months longer than expected. For another, it was 50 percent over budget. Equipped with venison processing facilities, the *Hotunui* became a fully licensed game packing house, GPH 19. At the commissioning and blessing of the ship, the Minister of Lands and Forests, Duncan MacIntyre, spoke of the need for effective deer control in the national parks and wilderness areas of New Zealand. Driving rain forced him to curtail his speech. Despite the conditions, a Luggate Game Packers Hiller demonstrated the landing of deer carcasses on the ship's helicopter pad, just as Tim had planned it. But Tim was not there to see it. He faced weeks – if not months – in hospital.

In Christchurch, Tim's back was operated on. Steel plates were bolted to opposite sides of the L1 and L2 spinus processes, which protrude from the vertebrae as the 'back bone'. The purpose of these 20 millimetre plates was to support healing of the damaged vertebrae by immobilising them.

Commonly the nerves right across the spinal canal are permanently damaged by the crushing of L1 and L2. But in Tim's case, the damage was predominantly on the left side. The likely outcome was that his left leg would be floppy forever. A question mark remained over the use of his right leg.

For the time being, Tim was immobilised, but he never let that interrupt his thinking about his business operations – not for a moment. His physical world had narrowed down to the environs of a hospital bed but he could still talk, read and write, he could still champ at the bit about business imperatives, still be exuberant and express his creativity. By hook or by crook, he would turn that small temporary setting into a bustling office. All he needed was a telephone at his bedside so he could communicate with his Luggate office, dictate letters, provide direction. He also wanted a radio telephone at arm's reach, to keep in touch with his field bases at Te Anau and Haast as well as his ships. Nursing staff in Ward 13B had never had to deal with such requests. Phones and radio sets in the ward? Not likely. It was illegal, was it not? Tim persisted. He put it to the staff bluntly: lives were at risk. He was in charge of a complex helicopter business that operated in the wild south-west corner of New Zealand, and the pilots, shooters, gutters and field staff depended on his advice and direction. He simply had to keep in touch with them. The medical consultants attending Tim, including senior urologist Bill Utley, realised that he would 'add to the safety of his pilots and helicopter crews'. Tim got his radio equipment and a phone. In the sixties, hospitals were run along rigid lines; the concept of patients' rights had yet to emerge. Tim broke through the formality with his persistence, force of personality and powers of persuasion.

George Wallis had a spare radio-telephone at Haast and promptly sent it to Christchurch Hospital. The aerial wire was fed out the ward window and attached to the adjacent nurses' home. Tim even asked if some of the electrical gear in the ward could be moved in order to improve RT reception. That request met a professional brick wall. Personality could stretch hospital rules only so far.

There was a continuous stream of visitors – family, friends and workmates. Tim's mother, Janice, lived not too far away, in Beverley Street, St Albans. She had moved there from the family home at Greymouth after Tim's father, Arthur, died in 1961. Sister Josephine came to live in Christchurch for a time to be near Tim.

Each of his pilots also visited Ward 13B in turn. Russell Gutschlag latched on quickly to the medical staff's instruction to Tim: drink plenty; the more fluids going through your system, the better. A visit to a local pub seemed the best way to achieve that. The Grenadier was just down the road from the hospital. At reasonably frequent intervals, Tim was wheeled several hundred metres to the local. Pilots Gutchslag and Black took him. So did Robert Wilson and Mark Acland, a farmer from Mt Peel Station in mid-Canterbury.

With the permission of the ward staff, Mark and Robert wheeled him to the Grenadier one evening on the kind of table used in an operating theatre. With his back still recovering from the implant of the steel plates, Tim lay face down on the table, with a urine bottle hanging underneath it. They pushed him along the road, mixing in with the traffic, which, sympathetic to the appearance of an operating table on a main street, if not a little bemused, kept well clear. Tim revelled in the spectacle of it all. It reminded him of the pranks they got up to at school: for Robert, Mark and Tim had been contemporaries at Christ's College (itself not too far from the hospital).

In the Grenadier, they lined Tim up at the bar. Clad in a hospital gown and lying face down, he had to lift his head off the pillow to drink. Nearby, an older woman, a glass of beer on the bar and cigarette in hand (and who looked like she spent a lot of time in just that pose), could not resist commenting:

'What have you done, my dear?'

'Broken my back,' said Tim. 'Here, see for yourself.' And with that he untied the gown at the back and threw it open, baring not only a 20 centimetre-long scar on his back, but also his buttocks.

The startled woman spilt her beer.

In a bizarre coincidence, Tim shared some time in the ward with another Christ's College contemporary, Simon Chaffey, who had suffered a spinal injury as a passenger in a tourist plane that crashed on the Tasman Glacier beneath Aoraki/Mt Cook. Amid the lighter moments of life in 13B – recalling boarding school experiences with Simon – Tim worried about how his business was doing. He liked to lead by example. A broken back had put paid to that for the moment. Yet already Tim's fighting spirit was inspiring a strong brand of loyalty. Immediately following his accident, Tim's accountant and business adviser, Reid Jackson, accompanied by his wife, Pat, drove to Invercargill and Kew Hospital from Dunedin. Tim was clearly going to be out of action for some time even though he insisted otherwise. Next morning the Jacksons travelled to Luggate to see to any paperwork that needed attention. A stabilising influence in Tim's life since he became involved in the Luggate Game Packers operation in 1966, Reid would do all he could to help keep the business on an even keel. Over the next couple of months he flew to Christchurch to have business meetings with Tim. Reid sounded a few warnings. Tim had invested a small fortune in ships, aircraft, buildings, bases and equipment.

A fresh-faced, 29-year-old Tim at a function at Glenfalloch Woodland Gardens near Dunedin in 1968, a few months before his crash in July that year.
Ken & David Lloyd

He needed to go carefully. Reid mentioned the B word – bankruptcy.

Between business calls and social visits, Tim worked on his rehabilitation. Early on, he had been told to expect the worst. He was told he might not walk again and that he might not be able to have children. He took little notice of this grim prognosis. He would get back to Luggate, helicopters and the mountains. No question.

Before the end of 1968 things would get worse for Tim and Luggate Game Packers. But adversity seemed only to incite in Tim a stronger will to succeed. He believed implicitly in what he was doing. Combine that level of self-belief with other character strengths – chiefly a fighting spirit and boundless energy – wrap them up in a powerful physical presence and you have a picture of a man of steel ready to take on the world. From 1968, in order to get around, he wore a metal calliper on his left leg. To Tim it was a minor impediment – of little concern compared to life in a wheelchair – but to his friends and associates it became a symbol of his passion to succeed in aviation, in business, in whatever challenge he took on. By the time of the back-breaking Queentown crash Tim was well known for pushing limits. He appeared to be cast in a leadership mould – a latter-day pioneer entrusted with taming a new frontier. From where did he get this focussed energy? Was it instilled in him from an early age? There are some clues in his upbringing and schooling, to which we turn next.

Tim Wallis in Hiller helicopter at Makarora, 1967. Dave Osmers

Chapter 2

Young and Daring

1950s–1960s
A rifle for Christmas ... Wallis and Blunden families ...
Grey Main ... Kopara sawmill ... adventures at
Queenstown ... Christ's College ... Harry Reginald
Hornsby ... cold baths, bombs and a car ... vintage
rugby ... University Entrance

THE FIRST PISTOL was a prototype only; the second was much improved. It was for keeps. In a workshop beside the chemistry lab at Christ's College, Tim Wallis made the .22-calibre pistols during his fifth form year, 1955. He collaborated with another student on this project. First Tim drew plans for the pistol, then a model was produced out of wood. The barrel was a cut-down .22 rifle barrel. Much thought went into the manufacture and function of the firing pin. In the workshop there were metal-working tools, but parts that required lathing or welding had to be manufactured in the city. A pistol butt fashioned out of wood was taken to a Christchurch moulder for a moulding to be cast in aluminium. Finally, Tim made a leather holster.

For target practice, he would go to a friend's farm on a Sunday and have a crack at rabbits and an occasional hare. Hitting live targets was not what he built the pistol for, however; he simply wanted to produce a functional pistol.

Tim had grown up with firearms. His father, a member of the Christ's College shooting team in his day, went hunting at times, and encouraged the Wallis children to become familiar with guns. His mother could also handle a rifle.

For his ninth birthday, Tim received a spring-loaded BSA air gun from his parents. He took it into his bed the first few nights and scarcely slept. During the Christmas holidays that year, 1947, Tim took the gun to his Aunt Betsy's place at Queenstown, where the Wallis family often spent summer holidays. Aunt Betsy and her husband, Bob Ensor, ran a small-

Choir boys: Tim (left) and his brother, Adrian, were members of the local Anglican Church choir during their primary school years.

boat hire business for visitors in Queenstown Bay, next to the Steamer Wharf. It was on the Ensors' jetty that Tim met Robert Wilson, a Dunedin boy of similar age, for the first time. Although their fathers had attended Christ's College at the same time, the sons hadn't encountered each other till now. As Tim described his new air gun to Robert, he thought up the idea of a competition back at his aunt's place. They would line up boxes of waxhead matches on a fence as targets.

Back at the Ensor house, on the lower slopes of Queenstown Hill, the two boys took turns at knocking over the little boxes. When that proved easy enough, they competed to see who could light the matches. To do this, the slug had to strike the match-heads very exactly. At some stage Tim set up the boxes so their match-head end was upside down, which foiled Robert's chances of lighting them up. Tim Wallis the trickster, even at the age of nine.

When he turned 17, in his second-to-last year at Christ's College, Tim acquired a .303 Lee Enfield rifle. His parents paid for half the cost of it, he paid the rest. Tim wrote home inviting his father to go deer-stalking with him during the next round of school holidays. In addition to his interest in guns and how they worked Tim was developing a feel for hunting game, primarily the red deer that roamed the Westland mountains, the foothills of the Southern Alps. Success at deer-stalking required knowledge of how deer lived and moved. You needed bush skills, an appreciation of teamwork if you went with a mate, the right gear and, most important of all, an instinct for tracking. The sport was called deer-stalking for good reason – not deer killing, although a fine head was what motivated many hunters. The pull of the trigger was but the end of an experience, not necessarily the finest moment of it. Tim learnt all aspects of the hunt. It became a passion.

TIMOTHY WILLIAM WALLIS was born in Christchurch to a West Coast family on 9 September 1938. His mother, Janice, had grown up on a farm near Oxford, North Canterbury. At Christchurch she was near her family in the last stages of pregnancy. Tim acquired a name derived from a character created by Beatrix Potter, the English children's writer and illustrator who invented the likes of Peter Rabbit and Jemima Puddle-Duck. Another favourite was Timmy Willie, the Country Mouse, who lived happily in a quiet, simple garden setting. Tim's parents liked the combination of names, which had a ring to it, especially when you added the surname – thus Timothy William Wallis. But Tim's life was never destined to become confined to a rural backwater.

Tim's father, Arthur Trevor Wallis, was born at Invercargill in 1898. He was in the timber and sawmilling business all his working his life. In this he had been encouraged by his father, Alexander, who co-owned the 40,000 hectare Morton Mains estate in Southland as part of a syndicate. Alexander founded the Invercargill-based sawmilling firm of A.R. Wallis Ltd. Although involved in the Southland timber industry, he saw potential in the vast areas of native forest on the West Coast and bought cutting rights to a number of substantial blocks.

The Wallis home in Geraldine Street, Greymouth. The family's 1947 Chevrolet car is parked in the street.

The Kopara sawmill in the mid-1930s as it appeared to water-colourist Olivia Spencer-Bower. The mill was managed by Tim's father, Arthur Wallis.

In December 1917, at the age of 19, Arthur motorbiked through Arthurs Pass and the Otira Gorge between Canterbury and the Coast. His mission was to investigate the prospects for timber milling on the West Coast. In a ten-page letter home from Hokitika he recounted aspects of the journey. The road, traversed mainly by horse-drawn coaches and drays, was in a rough state. He told of crossing creeks, placing rocks in some of them to create a ford or riding over narrow planks. He pushed his motor-cycle in places, including one stretch of 'about a mile, up a hill as steep as the side of a house'. Approaching a sharp bend while riding the bike, he came upon the regular Cobb & Co. coach just ahead of him, bound for the Coast from Christchurch. The horses, unused to motor traffic, shied and left the road. The driver expressed 'great wrath' and said he would be asking the Government to ban motor vehicles from this difficult moun-tain road.

In fact, the writing was on the wall for the horse-and-carriage era. Coaches disappeared with the opening of the Otira rail tunnel in 1923. When Arthur travelled across the alpine road, construction of the tunnel was fairly well advanced. He could see how a rail link – the Midland Line – with Christchurch would boost the timber trade on the Coast.

By the time Arthur married Tim's mother in 1934, he and his brother

Norman were operating several sawmills on the Coast from a base at Greymouth. The mills were spread from Inangahua Landing north of Reefton to Whataroa in South Westland. There had been an A.R. Wallis Ltd mill by the Midland Line at Rotomanu, east of Lake Brunner, that operated in the 1920s. The locality was known as Wallis Siding. Having the family name on the map was an acknowledgement of the enterprising nature of Tim's father and uncle and specifically their achievements in the sawmilling business. In fact, on both sides of Tim's family, there was a history of achievement in the primary-production sector, and no doubt some of it rubbed off on Tim when he was a schoolboy.

Tim's mother, Janice Mildred Blunden, was born in Christchurch in 1908, the elder daughter in a family of two girls and four boys. They grew up on a farm at Bennetts, North Canterbury. Janice's father, Arthur Reginald Blunden, became an auctioneer for the stock-and-station company, Dalgety's. Janice and her sister, Betty, who was known as Betsy from an early age, both attended Amberley House, a private boarding school whose students were mainly the daughters of Canterbury farmers. Betsy was just on two years younger than Janice. All of her brothers had their secondary schooling at Christ's College. Their mother, Nora (nee Shand), came from a pioneering Canterbury family whose members included Tom Shand, the Minister of Labour in the National Government in the 1960s.

After leaving school, Janice went to work at the office of a well-known Christchurch architect, Cecil Woods, where she managed accounts and traced drawings. She also did some driving for him. At Christmas 1933, she drove the architect and his wife to Wanaka for a holiday. Arthur Wallis happened to be staying at the Wanaka Hotel on a fishing holiday at that time. With two friends, he had travelled from Greymouth. On New Year's Eve, he and Janice met. It was 'love at first sight', according to Janice. In four months they were married in a little church at Cust, North Canterbury.

In March 1935, the first son, George, was born. Tim arrived three and a half years later, in 1938. He gained two godparents – Aunt Betsy and Janice's brother, Peter, who was five years younger than Janice. There were two more children – Adrian and Josephine. Their ages spanned eight years.

Greymouth was their home town. The newly-wed Arthur and Janice lived at Heaphy Street, where George was born, then South Beach, where Adrian was born, before moving to the Wallis family home at 66 Marsden Road. It was an elegant old four-bedroom home which had a drawing room where family treasures were kept, a smoking room for the men, and a tennis court in the grounds. During the Second World War, Arthur was in the Home Guard. Because of his prominence in the timber trade, he was deemed to have an important role in an 'essential industry' at home

A financial shock

In 1940, a financial disaster hit A.R. Wallis Ltd. Norman Wallis and his mother, Freda, had invested in a goldmining venture in the Grey Valley area in the 1930s – on the back of the Great Depression. Norman had a reputation for being more entrepreneurial than Arthur. When the gold venture went broke, the losses rocked the parent company and the main Kopara and Whataroa mills were liquidated.

Although Tim's generation was never briefed on what exactly happened, the upshot was that Arthur maintained an interest in the reformed Kopara Sawmilling Company, which was now run by a syndicate, by buying a quarter-share. The other quarter shares were held by two Christchurch-based timber merchants and the Timaru firm of Desmond Unwin Ltd. Arthur's competent management of the Kopara business was recognised by his appointment as managing director of the new company. The Whataroa mill was sold to a Christchurch company.

Butter-box timber

Kahikatea, New Zealand's tallest native tree species, was more commonly known as white pine during the heyday of milling on the Coast. Rimu, another native podocarp species and the main one for timber, was called red pine. Much of the white pine timber was exported from Greymouth or Hokitika to Australia to be used in the manufacture of butter boxes, pallets for frozen meat or staves for tallow barrels. It was valued as a timber that did not taint produce.

and did not take part in military service overseas. The Greymouth Home Guard met and exercised regularly. Greymouth looked out to the Tasman Sea, and on the other side of it was Australia, under threat of a Japanese invasion. Greymouth was a long way from the main centres of New Zealand, a long way from military resources.

From Marsden Road the Wallises moved to 2 Geraldine Street, where Tim spent the bulk of his childhood. Uncle Norman and his family took over the Marsden Road home. The stylish two-storeyed Geraldine Street house, clad in stucco with a gabled roof line, was on the edge of Greymouth's southern outskirts, about 1.5 km south of the town centre. There was about half an acre of bush on one side of the property. A small stream, Grandjeans Creek, ran near the house, more or less bisecting the property. It flowed into a larger stream, Sawyers Creek, which formed the southern boundary. There was a bush reserve across the street, crowded with ferns and supplejack and other vines. It was like a jungle to the Wallis children. They often explored it.

More suitable for an expanding family, Geraldine Street had three bedrooms upstairs. Just inside the arched front entrance, there was a sitting room on the right, with a sun porch off it. Family treasures on display in the house included an Indian tiger skin, complete with taxidermied head, shot by a great uncle of Tim's. The skin had a bullet hole about the region of the animal's heart. Family folklore said the tiger clawed the shooter's arm as it died.

To accommodate 'Grandad', Janice's father, a room was built at the rear of the house. He came to live in Greymouth in 1939 after Nora died. He stayed with the family on and off for 20 years, a keen home gardener and card player.

Buildings in the garden included a glasshouse, henhouse and woodshed down by Sawyers Creek. Tim's mother loved gardening. She created paths through the bush areas and mingled rhododendrons with tree ferns. Greymouth had a moist, mild climate – the southern limit for nikau palms and other native plants. The glasshouse, with Grandad's help, was crowded with tomatoes, mushrooms and other produce. From the leafy surroundings of Geraldine Street and his mother's interest in gardening, the young Tim saw how native bush and people could live side by side. In his last year at primary school he would write about the need to conserve native forest.

Most days Arthur would be away attending to his timber business. He was renowned for striking a firm but fair bargain. He was constantly on the road. He and his brother, Norman, managed a number of mills. Some were permanently established but most were relocatable 'spot' mills that operated for a short time only while the local supply of logs lasted. Arthur

managed the northern region, with many of the mills located in the Grey Valley and out towards Reefton. The largest was the Kopara sawmill in the Haupiri district, where a road off the Grey Valley was completed to open up a back-country area in the direction of the Southern Alps. Built in 1934 after the closure of Wallis Siding and the relocation of plant to Haupiri, the Kopara mill worked kahikatea logs from the river flats and rimu, matai and miro from the terraces and surrounding slopes.

The Wallis mills provided a lot of employment. Arthur had dozens of men working for him. Every fortnight he would deliver their pay – and sometimes groceries and other supplies – to the mill sites.

In the 1930s and during the war years he drove a Buick car; in the late 1940s and 1950s he had a Chevrolet, which he was able to buy because of his 'essential industry' status. In the school holidays, some of his children would come for the ride. At the Kopara mill, Tim and his brothers often rode the locomotive that hauled logs out of the bush. On the car trips, there were usually many stops on the way to and from Haupiri to buy or deliver supplies, or do business. During these trips Arthur might stop at Tom Crofts' trucking business at Stillwater; Nelson Creek for groceries and bread, including a store run by the two Miss Fishers; the butchery at Nelson Creek; the railway depot at Ngahere to see about timber consign-ments; a hermit's hut belonging to a retired bushman, 'Peter the Pirate', beside the Haupiri River bridge; a pub here and there. The managing director was not too proud to go into a pub and have a beer with his men, although he drank in moderation. If he had any of the children with him, he would tell them to wait in the car and bring them lemonade drinks,

Above: Janice and Arthur Wallis with the children at Geraldine Street, Greymouth.

Above right: Tim as a pre-schooler, with his younger brother, Adrian.

reddened with raspberry or sarsaparilla essence. Occasionally a bushman would squeeze into the car with them for a ride somewhere.

During the working week, if he were going to be home late, Arthur would phone Janice, who would have the children fed, bathed and in their dressing gowns by 7 o'clock. Dad would read them a story and after they had headed off to bed, Arthur would relax with a tot of whisky and a cigarette. Then he and Janice would eat dinner together. Like so many women of her generation, Janice was highly resourceful. She made all the children's clothes and most of her own, even though she never sewed before she was married. She taught herself. When it came to housekeeping matters and the children's health and appearance, she generally had the last say.

Janice looked on Arthur as kind and considerate and not prone to angry outbursts. If Janice, more high-spirited than her husband, expressed some contrary view or had something decisive to say about anyone or any issue, Arthur would turn to her and say: 'Do you think so, my dear?'

Politically, Arthur was on the conservative side. He supported the National Party, as did Janice's family. In a Labour stronghold like Greymouth and the surrounding districts (the Labour Party of today originated in Blackball up the Grey Valley), a 'Tory' inclination was liable to count against you. But Arthur was generally well liked in the community. Brought up in Victorian times, he had a formal dress sense. His boys were taught to dress for Sunday dinner in jacket and tie and stand up when a woman entered the room. Table manners were essential. Tim absorbed this role modelling and carried basic courtesy, if not his father's more formal manners, into his adult life.

At the same time, Arthur had a sense of humour – and a hearty laugh. That laugh would announce Arthur's presence in a crowded room. He was also known for his bold, almost road-hoggish driving style. He drove fast. If you saw broad-chested Arthur Wallis driving towards you, with a hat on and dressed as if he meant business, you might want to pull over or at least keep well left. On the narrow back roads, with forest pressing in on both sides, you definitely had to pull over. Seat belts were unknown then. The Wallises, as a family, were very mobile. They would drive long distances when it was not really the thing to do. Picnic destinations included Punakaiki, 50 km from home.

Despite his hearty laugh and the gregarious nature of his work, Tim's father was socially rather quiet. Tim, on the other hand, was not at all shy as a pre-schooler. On train trips to Christchurch with his mother, the blue-eyed little boy with his shock of fair hair parted on the right and swept back thickly over his ears, would walk along the aisle of the carriage trying to chat to everyone. At home, too, he was always on the go, even at night, when he was prone to bouts of sleep-walking.

At the age of four and a-half, Tim went to stay with the Coates family, who had a farm at Haupiri. Arthur had been at Christ's College with Paddy Coates. His son, Richard, was about the same age as Tim, and the two families often socialised. When Richard's mother, Vi, who was a doctor with a local GP's practice, tried to bath Tim, the Wallis boy took exception to it. One day, in the early afternoon, he ran away while Vi was having a nap. Paddy Coates was busy on the farm burning gorse. Richard raised the alarm. Paddy and Vi were very concerned and set off in their car to look for Tim, calling first at the Kopara sawmill. Staff there said they had not seen him – and told them to try the Ensor place down the road. Betsy and Bob Ensor were caretaking a farm for Malcolm Wallace, another friend of Arthur's, who was away at the war. And there they found him.

Tim had walked over ten kilometres from the Coates farm to where

Holiday time at Queenstown. From left are Adrian, Josephine, Belinda Wilson, her brother Robert Wilson, and Tim. Photographed by the Steamer Wharf boat-hire business run by Tim's godmother Aunt Betsy and her husband.

the Ensors lived. He passed by the sawmill without stopping and cut across a few paddocks. From the house, Betsy caught sight of a small figure running over the paddocks to the house, where Tim promptly burst into tears.

Vi Coates told him that he was a naughty boy to run away like that, and that the cows could have gored him. Tim nodded. Through tears, he said, 'I had to shut a gate in a bull's face.'

TIM STARTED PRIMARY SCHOOL, Grey Main, in 1943, in the fourth year of a world war. There were air-raid shelters in the school grounds – and a large red cross on the roof of the local hospital – in case of an attack by Japanese warplanes. Marching was a form of exercise for school children then and an acknowledgement of the war effort. The children would be lined up to march out the school gates and around the block. In the vicinity of the school, to help them keep in step, they had brass-band music blaring from a wind-up gramophone. There were about 300 pupils at Grey Main – 30 to a class.

Tim, his brothers and sister biked about one kilometre to school. They biked home for lunch. In their spare time and often with childhood friends they cycled to other parts of town – down to the wharf to see the ships working cargoes, to the signal station at the end of the breakwater, to the aerodrome. The Wallis boys wanted to do newspaper deliveries for pocket money but their father said their involvement would have taken work away from local lads who really needed the money. He wanted them to do chores for the elderly in the community, like lawn mowing, and not mind if they received nothing for it.

The Wallis kids built tree huts at Geraldine Street. They explored Sawyers Creek to its source in the forested hills inland of their home. A boy from across the road, David Wilson, often joined them on these explorations. Sawyers Creek got a new name – the Wil-Wal River. Eels from the creek were caught, cooked and fed to the hens. Some eels were subject to dissection. They would be kept in the washhouse tubs at home while the boys, demonstrating an early interest in delving into natural history, rounded up their grandfather's veterinary instruments. Using chloroform, Tim and his brothers or their friends would anaesthetise the eels at the backdoor step then cut them open to inspect their internal organs. A beating heart was what they mainly wanted to see.

Tim would also take part in possum-trapping expeditions in the company of school mates, including Geoff Taylor. The Aorangi Reserve near Bodytown was a favourite haunt.

Arthur Wallis insisted on the children doing their homework when they came in from school and before they headed out to play. By the end of his Standard One year, aged eight, Tim was described in a school report as 'a good worker' with top marks in arithmetic. The report went on to say he was 'very quick but must improve in neatness'.

He got his air rifle the next year. It was the highlight of the Christmas holidays at Queenstown that year. A few blackbirds and thrushes around Geraldine Street also stared down the barrel of it.

Christmas Day at Geraldine Street started with the opening of gifts, which were wrapped in plain brown paper and placed on the beds of the children overnight. By 7 a.m., the family would leave for the local Anglican church, Holy Trinity, for a Christmas service. Later in the morning, friends would arrive for a Christmas drink and when the Salvation Army band turned up in the street, playing carols from the back of a truck, Arthur would 'shout' for them with bottles of beer. A typical Christmas dinner consisted of roast chicken and roast vegetables, with pavlova to follow. The adults drank sparkling wine, which was rarely seen at the table any other time.

Presents from outside the family had to be acknowledged through 'bread and butter' letters, and the children were made to write these in the afternoon of Christmas Day. This command from parents to communicate thanks would stick with Tim all his life.

On Boxing Day, the family usually packed up their car and departed for a holiday at Queenstown, to where the Ensors had moved, or Dublin Bay, Wanaka, where the Wilsons also holidayed. Arthur's friends, the Burdons, were also at Wanaka, owning Mt Burke Station. Sometimes the family went to Nelson. The Wallises often put up tents and camped. For the trips south they had to go by way of Arthur's Pass as the Haast Pass was not open then. The road south stopped at Lake Paringa, south of the glacier town of Fox.

Holidays with Aunt Betsy were action-packed. Not only did she and husband Bob have boats to mess around in; Tim's godmother was also keen on tramping and climbing.

Betsy Blunden became a mountain guide based at The Hermitage, Mount Cook village, in 1928, when she was 18. At that time it was unusual for a woman to hold such a job. Indeed, Betsy was said to be the world's first female alpine guide. She was a professional guide for three years but continued to climb after that. At 21, she had a first ascent to her name – Mt Oates (2,009 metres) in Arthur's Pass National Park, which she climbed with the legendary John Pascoe and another mountaineer, Bryan Barrer. They all belonged to the Canterbury Mountaineering Club. Mt Oates overlooks Goat Pass, used as the mountain-run leg of the

A young, fair-haired Tim Wallis with his godmother, Betsy, and Dr Ray Kirk, who had a holiday home next to Betsy and Bob Ensor's house. The Kirk children played with the Wallises.

An essay on native forest

At 12 years old, in his last year at primary school, Tim wrote an essay titled, 'Why We Must not Destroy our Native Forest'. Forest protected river banks from erosion, he wrote, but mostly it provided habitat and food for native birds, including the kiwi 'which is not yet called extinct'. He discussed the loss of birds like the huia and orange-wattled crow [kokako]. Sawmillers cut down trees that provided their habitat. He raised another issue – the impact of introduced animals. 'Some animals mainly deer and oppusums destroy our young trees ... so deer cullers and oppusum trappers help keep them down.' Nonetheless, the forest produced timber, which was 'very essential' for building houses.

He filled his school exercise book with numerous stories. Topics included Marconi, of wireless fame, Hiawatha, and an argument in favour of retaining 'manual' subjects such as woodwork and cooking at primary school. He did have a criticism of the woodwork and cooking equipment, however, claiming it was 'far too old for the speedy work done nowadays'.

modern Coast-to-Coast events. Besides climbing, Betsy was keen on skiing. She was a member of the national team in 1950.

She inspired Tim and his siblings in the value of outdoor recreation and the ability of women to explore new vocational frontiers. Tim admired the strength of her personality, which was similar to his mother's, and her tenaciousness in the midst of a world dominated by men. She didn't have children of her own but took Tim and the others on walks short and long. They tramped the Routeburn Track in 1948, when Tim was ten, and they climbed through tussock grasslands to the top of Ben Lomond, at 1,748 metres the highest peak close to Queenstown. In January 1951, Betsy's husband, Bob Ensor, led a group of boys including Tim and Adrian, to the summit of The Remarkables, the iconic mountain wall overlooking Lake Wakatipu and Queenstown. The boys averaged 12 years of age. After camping overnight at the foot of the range, they climbed up past the blue-green waters of alpine Lake Alta, in its armchair cirque, to reach the 2,324 metre summit, Double Cone, in the early afternoon. On the final pitch they scrambled over slabby, sharp-edged rocks of the south-east ridge. In the steepest places, Bob instructed them to use ropes.

From the top of Double Cone, the boys stood in wonder at the great white wedge of Mt Aspiring away to the north, at 3,027 metre the highest mountain outside Aoraki/Mt Cook National Park and the outstanding peak of the southern region of the Southern Alps. Away to the left, they could also see Mt Earnslaw (2,819 metres), the second highest peak in Mt Aspiring National Park. Tim asked about doing that next.

Back home, Tim's mother worked on their cultural side. She encouraged their musical abilities. Her mother, Nora, who died four months after Tim's birth, had been very musical and Janice had inherited an interest in music. She thought she would pass it on to her children, and at one time thought they might form a small orchestra. George, Adrian and Josephine learnt piano; Tim took flute lessons. Tim and Adrian joined the choir at church, practising once a week. At church services they wore white cassocks. Their mother used to give the boys a shilling for the plate. If it was in two sixpences they would put one in the plate and use the other to buy sweets.

In addition to his cultural side, Tim worked at his experimental and scientific proclivities. With school mate Ron Johnson he played around with chemicals that converted coal into something that looked like coral. By the back door at Geraldine Street, the scene of many such activities, the boys would place chunks of coal in a large basin and douse them with chemicals until the coal – true-blue West Coast coal – turned pink and white and, yes, even blue. They likened the end product to a tropical coral reef.

Approaching his teenage years, Tim would also experiment with explosives. They could buy the chemicals, including Condy's crystals and sulphur, from the pharmacy in town. During the summer school holidays one year, Tim and his brother Adrian, who was only 18 months younger, asked their mother if there was anything they could do or construct in the garden. Janice said they could fix the broken concrete steps down to Sawyers Creek if they liked. No sooner said than done, Mum, was the boys' reaction. The next thing she heard was an explosion. Then the phone rang. It was a near neighbour and he was distressed. He said he had nearly been hit on the head by a piece of concrete. It landed right beside him in the garden.

Janice rushed down to see what the boys were doing. They had been trying to dislodge the old concrete steps using explosives. Telling them to take greater care, Janice said the fall-out from the explosion had almost struck a neighbour.

'Good,' said an undeterred Tim, 'that experiment was a success then.' Here, in one simple sentence, Tim articulated the entrepreneurial confidence and self-belief that would soon become hallmarks of his character.

The last report on Timothy William Wallis from his primary school, Grey Main, in 1951 read: '…needs confidence in himself building up.'

CHRIST'S COLLEGE was a rude awakening for a new boarder in the 1950s. Tim joined the class of '52. In Spartan dormitories the boys of School House, two floors up, were out of bed at 6.30 a.m. and making their way down a well-worn wooden staircase in dressing gowns to the bathroom and changing room on the ground floor, where the lockers were. The bathroom floor was concrete. Colder still was the 'bath', a small communal pool with water flowing continuously into it. The water overflowed to drain away over the concrete floor. In winter the experience was punishingly cold – some would say, character building.

After the morning bath, the boys dressed in their school uniforms and made their way to the school's wood-panelled dining hall, where they ate breakfast from heavy wooden tables that reeked of history. The stone exterior of the dining hall, featuring a row of buttresses topped by ornate finials, looked austerely Victorian – the kind of architecture that could have been the model for Harry Potter's Hogwarts. Most of the buildings surrounding the school's quadrangle had stone facades. Before school started they proceeded next door to the chapel for a 15-minute service, taken by the college chaplain. There were readings from the Bible and a hymn or two. The chapel had an array of stained-glass windows beneath an impressive timbered ceiling. There were chapel services six times a week and twice on Sundays. Like the cold bath in the morning, you had no choice.

Christ's College was founded in Christchurch in 1850, the year of Canterbury's settlement by English immigrants. Its imposing stone gates opened on to Rolleston Avenue, a kilometre from Cathedral Square, the city centre. The buildings, including the various houses for boarders, the classrooms blocks, dining hall, chapel and office block, surrounded a grassed quadrangle. Behind the school, the Avon River flowed sedately between willow-lined banks, and beyond the river, the woodland expanses of Hagley Park made the college appear rural and part of the Canterbury Plains.

The school accepted students from all over New Zealand, although most hailed from Canterbury, and they were often the sons of families with roots going back to Canterbury's 'First Four Ships'. The English settlers set up a private, Church of England boarding school for boys, which was based firmly on an English traditional model. Christ's had masters and tutors rather than teachers, and the boys wore a charcoal-grey suit or black blazer with vertical white stripes, a narrow black-and-white striped tie, starched collar and boaters. There were strict rules, and canings for breaches of them. The school motto, *Bene tradita Bene servanda*, on the college coat-of-arms, stood for 'A good tradition well kept'.

Both sides of Tim's family had attended the college – his father and his uncles on his mother's side. On his mother's side, Tim and his brothers were the fourth generation to go to Christ's. His brother, George, preceded him by three years (George's last year was Tim's first), and Adrian was a year behind. His sister Josephine attended Craighead, a boarding school for girls at Timaru, from the age of 11, beginning in 1954. At Christ's, family tradition chose the house for Tim. School House took boys from families with two or more generations at the college. It had a stone frontage with an arched entrance and brick walls on the sides and back. Less than 50 paces from the back door was the Avon River, with Hagley Park stretching invitingly into the distance on the other side of the river.

The house master was also the headmaster – Harry Reginald Hornsby, 'Reg' to his colleagues. The boys called him 'Harry', although not to his face. He became a significant figure in their lives.

In Tim's year there were about 400 students, 230 of them boarders. Tim adapted to college life very quickly. He made friends easily. Some of the other third-formers in his dormitory were not so happy, and cried at nights. Unlike today, there were no partitions between the beds. Notwithstanding the austerity expressed at Christ's College, these were prosperous times, the fifties. The New Zealand economy feasted on farming (wool in the fifties was worth 'a pound a pound' at one point) as well as on forestry and the timber industry, with many of the boys' families contributing directly and substantially to the country's gross domestic product. New Zealanders in this period generally enjoyed one of the highest standards of living in the world.

Tim tackled the academic side of college with mixed success. His best subject was biology, in which he topped the class most years. His geography marks were also consistently high. One term report noted 'a natural ability' at these subjects. When it came to mathematics, however, a fourth-form report described him as 'capable but rather slapdash' and his maths teacher in a later year reported 'a slackening off of effort'. In physics his practical work was described as good but the theory part 'only fair'.

Tim was in an academic stream that had two years in the fifth form and sat School Certificate after four years at college.

If his practical work in physics was assessed by his teachers to be good, outside the classroom it was outstanding. He made pistols, for a start. He also fixed things – first, a worn-out old chainsaw, which he acquired from his father's mill at Kopara and got working again. Suddenly, he had an asset worth trading. A nascent business instinct kicked in. He wanted a motorbike. During school holidays he advertised in the *Greymouth Evening Star*: 'Wanted to swap: chainsaw for a motorbike'. A man came around to

Headmaster Hornsby

Reg Hornsby arrived at Christ's College in 1951, aged 44. Born in England, he led a Ghurkha unit when the Second World War interrupted his teaching career. Tim's intake was his first at Christ's. By 1952, Reg Hornsby was familiar enough with the school to begin making changes. More liberal than his predecessors, he introduced new subjects and challenged the boys to read more widely and become interested in international affairs and politics. He referred them to news magazines like the *New Statesman* and *The Economist*.

School House, of which he was head, underwent something of a culture change under his leadership. It became less narrow in its traditions and outlook. Many of the boys, including Tim and his West Coast friend Richard Coates, found Mr Hornsby inspiring. A famous figure in New Zealand agriculture, Peter Elworthy, who was three years ahead of Tim's intake, said the headmaster had 'a profound influence' on the school and many of its students. He brought out the best in them.

Reg Hornsby remained headmaster of Christ's until 1963. He had no children of his own. At his funeral, his pallbearers included Tim, Mark Acland and Peter Elworthy. To Tim, he bequeathed a silver-handled walking stick.

Geraldine Street with a Royal Enfield 350 cc bike, worth about £60. It was a deal – a straight swap. Tim soon learnt to maintain it.

Later that year, 1955, about the time he was preparing to sit School Certificate, the motorbike was sold – by his brother, George, on his behalf – for £65.

Tim had seen a 1931 Austin car for sale. It needed work done on the body. He was confident, with the help of schoolmates, he could manage the work in his spare time. He offered £45 and ended up with £20 change from the motorbike sale. In a letter home outlining the succession of deals, he said with intense satisfaction: '. . . after all, it all came from the chainsaw.'

Tim and his mates, including one with welding gear, got to work on the Austin. They took it to bits and put it back again, and drove it up Cashmere Hill for test runs. When the school year ended, it was parked in the street outside a friend's house in Christchurch. Someone reported it to the police as possibly a stolen car now abandoned. Halfway through the holidays a policeman arrived at 2 Geraldine Street saying the car's registration had that address and did Mr and Mrs Wallis know anything about it. As Tim told his college mates in the New Year, 'Mum and Dad needed an explanation.'

But his enterprising spirit was not confined to cars. With the support of other students, and tapping into the adventurous spirit Christ's College students seemed to have in abundance, Tim combined chemistry and physics knowledge to produce explosives. Towards the end of the third term in 1955, a couple of days before he was due to go home on holiday, Tim and a friend made a bomb. They had access to tubes of white blasting powder and researched how to make a bomb using a steel soda siphon pressure cartridge as a container and a two-minute length of fuse.

In a letter home, Tim proudly announced to his parents that they took the bomb down to the school swimming pool and lit the fuse. 'There was a tremendous explosion,' Tim wrote. 'We didn't wait to see the results . . . we were in the [botanic] gardens in no time at all.' At the evening meal, schoolmates said they had seen 'a column of white smoke'.

In another escapade, about two o'clock one morning Tim and his friend, Peter Williams, set off an empty Nescafé coffee tin filled with a bomb mixture and flashing powder that consisted mainly of aluminium powder. It was thrown into the college quadrangle from an upstairs window. The bang awoke most of the boys and not a few masters. In the morning, at assembly, those responsible were asked to come forward. Tim and his friend were lined up for caning. For being the instigator, Tim got six strokes – six of the best, as they used to say then. His friend got four whacks.

Tim was also caned for other misdemeanours, such as writing a letter

home during a 'prep' session or, in his early years at college, sneaking around the dormitory after lights-out. But he rarely complained about the punishments.

The boys were directed to write home once a week. Time was set aside on Sundays after church, and the letter made the Monday post. Tim wrote his letters with a fountain pen, signing them, in the first year, 'Your loving son, T.W. Wallis' – a formality that seemed to imitate the way his father signed letters to his parents in Invercargill when he was young, 'From your loving son, A.T. Wallis'. In subsequent years he signed off, 'I remain, Tim' or simply, 'Love, Tim'.

The letters were often about his involvement in sport and other recreational things. He described visits to his Great Aunt Beab's home in Bryndwr. Aunt Beab (Rebie) was a surrogate grandmother for Tim and Adrian and much loved by the family at large. At her home Tim and Adrian might do some gardening or hedge trimming.

Tim sometimes also described visits to Port Levy on Banks Peninsula to see his godfather, Uncle Peter, and Peter's Greek wife, Thalia. The couple had a farm there. Uncle Peter, a prisoner-of-war in Greece during the Second World War, was captured in Crete but escaped from northern Greece and made his way back to Egypt to resume service with the New

Tim (centre with headgear and striped jersey) in action for the Christ's College rugby First XV against Otago Boys' High School at the Otago Boys' ground, Dunedin, 1956. Lock Tom Hutchinson is catching the ball. Christ's won 11–3. Otago Daily Times

Zealand forces in the North Africa and Italian campaigns. He later married Thalia, who had associations with the people who helped Peter escape, after she agreed to come and live in New Zealand. Tim's uncle and aunt were colourful people, whose war connection fascinated Tim.

In his letters Tim also discussed rifles, movies, planes, cars, clothes and equipment, especially ski gear in winter – and food, always important for a boy growing quickly to manhood. References to food were generally requests for treats such as mum's jams, cakes and cordial drinks, or grateful thanks for the last consignment. Invariably, he wrote in a bright, optimistic, upbeat tone.

Movies were another good talking point. He would let his parents know if there were any good movies showing in the city that they should see on their next visit to Christchurch. War films were popular with him. They included *The Dam Busters* (May 1955), which recounted a Royal Air Force bomber squadron's use of a bouncing bomb to destroy German hydro-electric dams during the Second World War. (Tim's uncle, Neil Blunden, served in the RAF Bomber Command and died during the war.)

His parents paid fairly regular visits to Christchurch to see Tim and Adrian or, in Arthur's case, to do business. Arthur and Janice stayed at the United Service Hotel, and they would invite Tim and Adrian, who caught up with Tim in the fifth form, to join them for dinner. United Service was a top hotel, located in Cathedral Square. At times like this, Tim used to think his parents, if not especially wealthy, were comfortably well off. Naturally enough, his parents covered the college fees, uniforms and other clothing, and Tim had an account at Ballantyne's, the city's smartest department store. But Tim also had his own bank account, out of which he bought books, sweets and model planes. He flew his model planes in Hagley Park's grass expanses, sometimes with his flute teacher, who was a fan of model aircraft.

Tim and his brothers regularly sought holiday jobs so they could pay for extras. Tim worked at Montieths Brewery in Greymouth, washing empty bottles, and also at the Wallis mills, packing up firewood from the offcuts; Adrian got a job spraying ragwort for the Grey County Council and tarsealing with Council road gangs.

Holidays were fun times as well. Fishing and horse trekking were favourite activities at Port Levy, where Uncle Peter and Aunt Thalia kept a former packhorse called Coster, a huge hack, measuring over 17 hands, that they had bought for £8. A great climber, Coster would carry the Wallis youngsters, one or two at a time, on treks up to pillar-shaped Acropolis Peak overlooking Port Levy. Coster was a gentle horse but knew how to let anyone know he had had enough walking for the day. As the next hopeful rider lifted a foot into the stirrup, Coster would trip up the supporting leg with his back leg.

Peter used to take Tim and the others fishing in the milky blue waters of Port Levy in a small boat that leaked rather a lot. They caught flounder and trevally. They also collected paua and mussels. On the 330 hectare property, which Peter and Thalia acquired as a post-war 'rehab' farm, they went shooting rabbits and possums. There were goats on the farm, and when he was younger, on holidays from Greymouth, Tim liked to cuddle the baby goats and even took one to bed once.

Winter, to Tim, was for skiing at the Mt Cheeseman field in the Canterbury mountains between Springfield and Arthur's Pass. He took every weekend opportunity. Introduced to skiing at Coronet Peak as a youngster by Aunt Betsy, who at first worried about the risks he took then became used to his antics, Tim quickly proved good enough to be in the college ski team.

In a letter home after a weekend at Mt Cheeseman, Tim told of ' … going very fast out of control … did an eggbeater into the snow. It's good doing a decent spill, it's all in the game.' Not even a broken bone in his right hand, a rugby injury, would put him off a ski trip. Skiing also meant the welcome company of girls, a contrast to the relentlessly male environment of college.

In college sports, Tim was an all-rounder. He played golf, squash and tennis, he rowed, swam and boxed. To meet his weight class in one boxing tournament he had to lose seven and a half pounds. Skiing and rugby, the latter commonly called 'football' then, were his top sports. At rugby he started off playing in the backs but in 1955 switched to being a loose forward, a flanker (called 'breakaway' then) or No. 8, in which position he packed down at the back of the scrum.

Tim, meanwhile, won a school prize in mathematics in 1955, and continued to do well in biology and geography. His first term report in 1955 placed him at the top of his class for biology ('thoroughly deserves his position,' said his teacher). Headmaster Hornsby wrote: 'As usual, cheerful and busy'. The headmaster was especially pleased about Tim's flute playing. In an end-of-term concert, Tim performed in a chamber quartet.

That year he knuckled down academically, and passed School Certificate. His younger brother, Adrian, was in a stream that sat School Certificate after three years, and when Adrian also passed the examination, he joined Tim in the sixth form in 1956. Adrian was more studious. Chemistry was his forte. His mother would tell her friends that he read chemistry texts as if they were novels. Adrian would go on to excel at chemistry at the University of Canterbury, where he gained a Ph.D. in organic chemistry. He left soon afterwards to pursue a research career in Canada and Australia.

It was a full-on year, 1955. Tim and his mates were 15 or 16 – an age for pushing limits. The boys were opportunists knocking on the doors of adulthood. Risks were part and parcel of the age. They amounted to rites of passage.

Mark Acland, a friend who would later assist Tim with his deer farming initiatives, had his father's car, and was licensed to drive. After a school dance in Christchurch one evening, Tim asked Mark if he would drive him to the railway station. Tim was due home at the weekend on the railcar that ran overnight between Christchurch and Greymouth through the Otira Tunnel and the Alps. There were only minutes to go before the railcar was due to depart. Mark drove the 1952 Chevrolet as fast as he dared down Colombo Street, faster than the speed limit. A policeman on the beat saw the car racing towards him and stepped out with his torch, flagging them down. Tim wound down his window and explained they were dreadfully late for the railcar.

'Then you'll have to hurry, sonny,' was the policeman's reply.

They did, but the railcar was pulling out as they arrived at the station.

'Okay,' said Tim, 'Let's get ahead of it.' Mark sped along Moorhouse Avenue, a multi-laned city artery running parallel to the railway line, and passed the railcar after a couple of blocks. A few blocks further on Tim told Mark to turn left sharply and let him out at the level crossing a short distance from Moorhouse Avenue.

Tim ran with his bag to the tracks. Standing in the middle of them, illuminated by the railcar's lights, he waved his arms madly. The driver slammed on the brakes, recognising Tim as one of the West Coast students who often used to get home by rail.

Tim was standing on the railway one second, gone the next. To Mark, it was just another close shave. They had had another one in a school study, involving Tim and his pistol. Tim fired a shot at a brick wall through an open window. The next thing, there was a knock at the door. It was the new house master, Pat Williams. He came in and sniffed the air.

'Everything all right in here, boys?'

They nodded. The master went out. Between the master's knocking and entering, Tim had quietly slipped the gun behind a desk.

In his last year at college, 1956, Tim was appointed a prefect. 'I don't enjoy being a school prefect very much,' he reported home, 'but I suppose I will get over that.' Despite his misgivings, his housemaster, with whom he interacted a lot as a prefect, considered he was fulfilling the role. He described Tim as 'reliable and active' in a term report.

Tim presumed his fifth year at college would be his last, and that one way or the other – through examination or accreditation – he would leave with a University Certificate qualification. He studied hard but was not at all confident of getting UE accredited.

His maths slipped and his essays in current affairs – a subject newly introduced by Headmaster Hornsby – were 'below standard due to faulty English.'

In other ways, though, he was having a great year. In biology, he was again the top student in his class, and on the rugby field, he was a loose forward in the school's First XV.

The team had an excellent year, inspired perhaps by the 3–1 series win by the All Blacks over the touring South African team, the 1956 Springboks – the first New Zealand tour by the All Blacks' arch rivals in almost 20 years. By now Tim was a strapping lad. He weighed in at about 80 kilograms and stood 1.83 metres (6 feet) tall. In his five years at college he had put on 25 kilograms (4 stone) and gained 29 centimetres (1 foot 7 inches). The Christ's First XV won every game that year except for a draw with Christchurch Boys' High. Hosting the quadrangular tournament with Nelson College, Wanganui Collegiate and Wellington College in 1956, Christ's triumphed for the eighth time in the event, run annually since 1925.

The coach, Zane Dalzell, who was also house tutor for School House at the time, played Tim as the open-side flanker, one of the game's taller players in that position. Tim stood out in the loose and at lineout time. Coach Dalzell taught the boys two basic things – 1) tackle around the

Fagging

In the 1950s, fagging was still a tradition at Christ's College. Fags were juniors who performed chores for the senior students. The juniors might clean shoes, make beds or go to the tuck-shop to buy something for the senior boy they were assigned to. Tim had been a fag in his early days at college. By the sixth form, he had his own fags. He wrote home: 'My fags are fairly efficient, and I get my bed made just like you do in a hotel.' With Harry Hornsby in charge, the practice of fagging was on the way to being phased out.

The Wallis quartet – George, Tim, Adrian and Josephine.

ankles and 2) never lose sight of the ball. He summed up Tim's performance on and off the field that year: 'He'd give everything a go.'

Tim was accredited University Entrance. It was a surprise to him that his teachers would assess his academic performance during the year as worthy of the qualification, when all along he felt he would have to sit the exam. He wrote home immediately. 'Both Adrian and I have got UE accredited, and am I pleased, because I don't think I deserved it.'

Earlier in the year he had signalled to his parents his intention not to pursue academic studies. He was not cut out for an 'indoors life', he said. He thought he would rather go farming. His father had other ideas, saying to Tim's mother that the boy would be better off in the timber industry. Janice, meanwhile, was encouraging Tim to go to medical school. By the middle of his last year at college, Tim was planning to get a microscope. 'I will need one when I am a doctor,' he wrote home.

With UE under his belt and summer holidays looming, Tim's time at Christ's College drew to a close. Christ's had given him fulfilment, friends and adventure, to which he had added a fair dollop of daring.

'We will miss him very much,' wrote his house master in his final report, to which Reg Hornsby added, 'He possesses an independent mind.'

Chapter 3

In Transition

Late 1950s–1960s
Burnham ... Medical School ... 'whistle boy' ... first
deer ... Timaru ... Lancaster Park ... Hamilton firewood
merchant ... Haast Timbers ... Luggate sawmill ...
venison export samples ... Arthur Wallis dies ...
a helicopter experiment

FRESH FROM PREFECT and First XV status at secondary school, where the world seemed orderly and rewarding, Tim plunged into a period of uncertainty and change, starting with compulsory military training at Burnham camp, south of Christchurch, in early January 1957. His was one of the last compulsory intakes before the Labour Government introduced balloting by birthday. Enrolled as Private 826168, he became a gunner despite having had thoughts of joining the air force at one time. His Christ's College and West Coast mate, Richard ('Mo') Coates, was part of the same intake. To enlist, they drove over Arthurs Pass from the Coast in Tim's Austin 7 car, which ran out of power at the top of the steep zig-zag beyond Otira. Tim turned the little car around and, backing up in the super-low reverse gear with Richard pushing, they made it. In his artillery unit at Burnham, Tim got to fire 25-pounder field guns and drive up to six different vehicle types in a day. Already familiar with boarding school discipline, he made the most of the Burnham environment, although, as he told his family at home, the discipline was 'so strict in parts it becomes stupid'. In the interest of fitness, he decided to quit cigarette smoking, which he had only recently taken up in a minor way.

After ten weeks at Burnham he enrolled in another institution – as a medical student at the University of Canterbury. His mother was sure he wanted to be a doctor; his father was not so sure, although went along with the idea, perhaps believing he would return to the timber industry sooner or later. At university, Tim had Richard Coates for company again and they boarded at College House in Rolleston Avenue. After only a few

Tim (left) and Sam Satterthwaite were part of the 21st Compulsory Military Training (CMT) intake at the Burnham camp, south of Christchurch.

weeks at his studies, Tim was sounding less than confident. 'Still finding the work pretty tough,' he wrote home.

His university studies lasted two terms. He left at the end of August.

Now it was his father's turn to influence his career path. Arthur organised a job for him at the Kopara Sawmilling Company's mill at Haupiri. Tim was under his father's direction, although he lived at the mill's boarding house, run by a Mrs Harper. The single men lived there, and Mrs Harper produced meals for about 12 boarders. He started at the bottom – 'whistle boy'. It was the best place to start, his father told him. Tim was 18. The job involved communicating between the snigger, who roped up the newly fallen logs, and the winchman. The felling and hauling work was conducted under the experienced eye of Doug Wratt, head bushman. They hauled mainly rimu logs out of the bush. The stands of kahikatea were dwindling. Matai, miro and tawhai raunui (red beech logs were also in the mix.

From whistle boy Tim became a 'slabbie', whose job it was to manage the waste wood and clean up the mill at the end of the eight-hour day. From there, Tim could graduate to operating the skids and docking saw. A lot of the time he dreamed about deer hunting.

All his spare time was devoted to hunting. He teamed up, at various times and in various combinations, with Ron Hartill, Ron Lawton, Trevor Hingston and the Gosling brothers, Pat and Lou. Often he hunted alone, after work. He would head up through the forested country east of the Haupiri district to the tussock tops, locally known as the Coates' Hill, around Mt Mason and Mt Newcombe, which were both over 1,200 m. On warm summer nights he sometimes camped out in the tussock and made it back to the mill in the morning for the start of a new working day.

He was strong and fit, a shade over 6 foot tall and, like his father, broad across the chest. His hunting mates envied his ability to race uphill with a light pack and .303 rifle. He told Paddy Coates one day that he stalked his first kill in the Haupiri rangelands so closely he could hear the deer munching just before it died. Deer-stalking was about honing your senses and physical strength, and pitching these against a quarry you knew could hear and smell – and possibly see – better than you. Tim revelled in it. He also loved the setting, a mix of bush and mountain range whose remoteness required a hunter to be self-sufficient and look out for his safety. Help was a long way off if anything went wrong.

After each successful trip, Tim and his mates boned out the carcasses on the river flats, wrapped the meat in stockingette, cheese cloth or similar material and sold it to Fensons Butchery in Stillwater. They got a shilling a pound for it or meat and smallgoods instead of money. Venison was

First deer

Tim shot his first deer on a Haupiri logging road. He was motorbiking along the road when a spiker (a young stag with only two points on its antlers) walked out of the bush in front of him. He slammed on the brakes, swung around, grabbed his rifle, a .303, and fired. Down went the deer, shot in the shoulder area. Tim was quivering with excitement. He hardly knew what to do next – gutting and dressing a deer were beyond his experience. He placed the spiker across the petrol tank and off he went with it to the Kopara mill, proud as Punch.

Tim deer-stalking at the head of a South Westland valley in the 1960s.

blended into Fensons' sausages, which were a favourite on the Coast, although few customers probably realised deer meat was involved. Tim delighted in knowing he was contributing, if anonymously, to a popular product. Another outlet for the venison in 1958 was a Christchurch export firm, Maddren Bros. The carcasses were loaded on to the train at Greymouth for the trip 'over the hill'. Besides venison, Tim also sold tails and velvet on occasion, to the South Seas Trading Company in Christchurch or George Ting, of Ashburton. Ting wrote back once, complaining of tails arriving 'very stink' in summer.

The mill job led on to a posting with the New Zealand Forest Service, measuring and cataloguing native trees for their timber value in areas of state forest around Haupiri – a task known as 'cruising'. He had a motorbike for transport between Haupiri and Greymouth, about 60 kilometres away. He also continued the hunting of what he called 'redskins' – red deer – in the mountain hinterland.

The Forest Service was seriously interested in tails. As the government agency responsible for deer control, it paid in ammunition for tails at the rate of three rounds a tail. Tim considered this bounty killing an utter waste of a venison resource.

IN APRIL 1959, Arthur Wallis travelled with his oldest son, George, on a reconnaissance visit to the Haast area, where Arthur introduced him to farming families who owned areas of native forest subject to cutting rights. They drove through the Haast Pass between Otago and South Westland by way of a road that was not yet officially open – and would not open officially until November the following year. The road, started as a job-creation scheme during the Great Depression of the 1930s, was still a mess in places. Father and son travelled in an International pick-up truck, which had to be towed across the Haast River at Pleasant Flat. The bridge there had not yet been built. Out at the coast, in the Turnbull River area south of Haast, they talked to landowner families such as the Buchanans and the Nolans about starting logging in the near future.

This expansion into South Westland by the Wallises provided further impetus for Tim to advance his skills in the timber industry, encouraged by his father. Arthur arranged for him to get experience in a timber merchants' business at the Timaru firm of Desmond Unwin Ltd. Des Unwin, a close friend of Arthur's, had a shareholding in the Kopara mill, and some of the Kopara lumber ended up passing through his Timaru yard, which was located close enough to the turquoise sea off Timaru for the sound of surf and a whiff of salt spray to be in the air some days.

Accommodated at a cottage owned by the Unwin family, Tim became absorbed in the laborious side of the timber trade. He unloaded timber from railway wagons, some of which had come from the Coast, and sorted it into lots for house construction or other uses. He set about doing the physical side of the job with a will, testing his strength and stamina, and

Haast Timbers yard at Luggate, with a Bell 47 agricultural spraying helicopter parked temporarily there.

he learnt a lot about the timber trade at the same time. He also relished his spare-time pursuits.

The Old Boys' Rugby Club at Timaru welcomed the fit, rangy newcomer with West Coast experience into its senior side, and before he knew it, Tim was playing for South Canterbury in interprovincial matches. A highlight of the season was an appearance at Christchurch's renowned rugby stadium, Lancaster Park, when South Canterbury took on the formidable Canterbury team. Tim began the game as a reserve loose forward and when one of the starting forwards was injured shortly after the kick-off, Tim ran on to the field – to the delight of his parents, Uncle Peter and Aunt Thalia, who were watching from the stand. Janice turned to a stranger sitting beside her and proudly announced that that was her 'little boy' who was joining the game, and, to the embarrassment of her husband, brother and sister-in-law, who began sliding along the seat away from her, she gave the stranger an account of Tim's achievements.

By the middle of the season, however, rugby was beginning to pall for Tim. He said in a letter home he was 'brassed off with football … it's starting to tie me down'. He said he had had to forgo a wallaby shoot in the South Canterbury hill country because he was required for rugby practice with the South Canterbury team. 'It mucked a whole Sunday up,' he said. Skiing began to appeal to him more than rugby. When asked if he fancied playing for the South Island team against the North Island, he declined. It was a decision that put the skids on his rugby career.

Tim was never short of things to do. He socialised with Des Unwin's son, George, who had been at Christ's College at the same time as Tim. George's older brother, Bill, destined to become a judge, coaxed Tim into the Timaru Operatic Society, where he joined the chorus for the musical, *Show Boat*.

For his twenty-first birthday, 9 September 1959, Tim went home. His parents entertained family and friends at Geraldine Street after earlier suggesting hiring a hall at Greymouth. Tim thought a smaller party more appropriate. Small or not, the party had its boisterous moments. Someone fired a .303 rifle out of a window, and his father, who had been taking a blood-thinning drug for heart disease, suffered another heart attack not long afterwards, from which he recovered.

To the rest of the family, it seemed Arthur was grooming Tim to be his understudy in the timber industry. Towards the end of the year, he persuaded Tim to go to Hamilton, capital of the Waikato province in the North Island, to extend his experience.

In January, 1960, Tim joined Ellis & Bernand, Hamilton timber merchants, in the firm's orders department. His job was to receive orders from

Coast rep

During his time at Haupiri in 1958, Tim played rugby for the Star Rugby Football Club in Greymouth and was selected for the West Coast team. At 19, he was reckoned to be the youngest player ever to represent the region, which competed for the Seddon Shield with Buller, Nelson and Golden Bay teams. He was a loose forward of imposing size.

Tim operating the tractor he used for his manuka firewood project near Hamilton, 1960.

builders and other sources and sort them into their respective departments. Business was brisk. The company, which handled a steady supply of native timber from the King Country, was larger than Unwins. But Tim longed for southern things, especially deer-stalking. He moved into a flat in Hamilton East with three other young men, one of whom, John Chapman, had been at Christ's College with him. With mixed flatting morally frowned upon in the early 1960s and female flatmates nowhere to be seen to help with the cooking, Tim saw fit to reassure his mother, soon after settling into the flat, that the boys would not go hungry.

'We live very well,' he wrote. 'We will try and bottle some fruit ready for winter – God loves a tryer.'

At work, however, he became bored. He thought about an overseas trip and ways of earning money to pay for it. After placing an advertisement in the local newspaper, seeking weekend jobs, Tim came into contact with a farmer who wanted someone to drive a bulldozer and a truck at his quarry, about 40 kilometres from Hamilton. The farmer also wanted a hand with clearing a stand of manuka, a native tree that grew densely in the area, so he could extend his pasture.

Writing home almost as frequently as he had done at college, Tim told his parents of this new spare-time work. The manuka looked like good firewood to him. With John Chapman, his college friend, as his partner, he researched the firewood market and together they bought a tractor fitted with mudgrips for the soft, wet conditions on the farm. A tray was attached to the back of the tractor to carry the manuka stems. For transporting the chainsawn firewood to the city, they hired a 15 cwt Chevrolet truck. They put in 12-hour days at the weekends, which returned them roughly £5 profit per weekend – good money.

By the end of April, the firewood business was humming along. On 9 May, Tim wrote a letter home that stunned his parents:

'Do not send any mail to E & B as I left today … 1) The pay isn't terribly much to save on to go overseas. 2) I was a timber orderman, which is all right for a while but it does not appeal to me.' As a postscript, Tim said: 'This is nothing to be disappointed about.'

But he knew full well that they would be disappointed – even highly annoyed. They would think he was turning his back on the timber trade and a Wallis family heritage. He felt his father would take the news badly.

In the Waikato Tim continued with the firewood venture and he drove machinery at the farmer's quarry, which produced road metal.

When the lease on his East Hamilton flat ran out on 29 August, Tim signalled his return south. He would look for 'a high-paid job'. He felt sure his brother, George, could get him one.

TO BEGIN WITH, the Wallis logging operation in the Haast area was a start-stop affair. Tim's brother George started hauling logs over the Haast Pass early in 1960, utilising cutting rights in the Turnbull River area. The logs went to Colin Nolan's sawmill at Luggate near Wanaka. There was a strong market at the time for barrel staves made of kahikatea – tallow and pelts were exported in barrels. Rimu (red pine) peelers, straight and clean, were trucked to the railhead at Cromwell for Fletchers' plywood factory at Christchurch. In May 1960, the authorities told George to stop carting logs on the road, which was not officially open yet. The Coast road, between Haast and the glacier towns, was not open, either. It was years from completion. To get to the Haast area overland from Greymouth, you had to drive via the eastern side of the Southern Alps via Arthur's Pass, Porters Pass, Burkes Pass, Lindis Pass and Haast Pass. It was a long way around. Alternatively, you could fly between Hokitika and the Haast airstrip.

Tim, in a hat, and his brother George at Ross, 1960. George is driving a hired TD9 International.

Just before Christmas 1960, George landed a contract to log kahikatea in the Ross area of South Westland. He was soon joined by Tim, who was looking for a new start after the disappointment he caused his parents by bowing out of the Hamilton job. Tim felled the white pine, George hauled the logs out with a TD9 International crawler tractor. Much of the resulting timber went into the manufacture of barrel staves for the Alliance meat-processing plant at Lorneville. But the brothers' long-term prospects in lumber lay in the south, on the remote coastal duneland plains of Haast – a promising new frontier for the industry.

George and Tim were not only brothers, they were also best mates. Although different in character – George was less outgoing than Tim, and more focussed and practical – the two worked well together. When the Haast Pass road finally and officially opened towards Christmas 1960, they made plans to truck timber from the Haast area and mill it at Luggate. George had already proven the logging and transport side of the business. Tim's role would be on the marketing side, for which he had been trained at Timaru and Hamilton. They would engage a contractor to extract the logs, truck them over the Haast Pass to Luggate, and sell the timber around the Otago-Southland region – wider if necessary. Thus Haast Timbers Ltd was born. The Wallis boys struck up a deal with the mill's owner, Colin Nolan: the mill would be leased by Haast Timbers, which would pay a royalty on the lumber produced.

George oversaw the logging from a base at Snapshot Creek, inland from Haast, and Tim set up camp at Luggate as the milling and marketing manager. Tim acquired a Morris Minor van – and later an International pick-up or 'ute' – to get around his contacts in the business. There were outlets large and small to cover, including Fletchers in Dunedin,

Unwins at Timaru and small joinery factories in the Central Otago towns. Soon there was a steady stream of logs coming out to Luggate. The Haast road was narrow and one-way in places. There were creeks to ford. Across the pass itself – at an altitude of 562 metres, the lowest pass of all through the Southern Alps – beech forest crowded both sides and there were frighteningly deep drop-offs into ravines. It felt like a frontier all right. From Makarora, heading east with a load, the country changed, swiftly, almost magically, from forest green to the golden brown of the Central Otago tussock country, and from persistently wet to parched-mouth dry. The Haast Pass crossing marked one of the world's great natural boundaries as rainforest in the west gave way to a mainly treeless rangeland landscape in the east.

In March 1961, Tim wrote home: 'I can see a big future here for getting rid of a lot of our timber ... it will work out alright if we reduce our price on the awkward sizes and make a lot of profit on the popular sizes. I can see myself employing someone as an orderman within a month or so.'

In the back of his mind, something else was brewing. Driving between Luggate and Haast, he had time to survey the country. He thought a lot about deer, about how this region, brown and green, was a 'redskin' heartland. The country was moving with them and the deer plague was causing serious and extensive damage to the forest and grasslands. Something radical needed to be done to control their numbers. He had already been involved in sample consignments of venison (see box) but felt they represented only a sideshow compared to what could be achieved.

In June, 1961, the Haast Pass road closed again, this time for three months while work was carried out to replace the bridge at the dramatic Gates of Haast – a scree-lined gorge in a high-rainfall location west of the pass, where the waters of the incipient Haast River thundered over massive boulders, some the size of a cottage.

The hiatus gave Tim more time to work through his ideas about the venison potential in the vast numbers of deer. He went hunting himself when there was time to spare. It helped him think more clearly. Beside the sawmill at Luggate he set up a chiller under a willow tree. The road west reopened and Tim organised a system for the log trucks to carry out carcasses of deer shot by individual meat hunters. As the carcasses arrived at Luggate in dribs and drabs, they were hosed out, skinned, trimmed and quartered, and finally wrapped in muslin to await transport to coolstores in Dunedin.

CROSSING THE HAAST RIVER on foot for a shot at deer on the other side, you emptied your pockets first. Otherwise the river would empty them for you. On overnight visits to the Haast Timbers base, Tim often went spotlight shooting red deer when the work was over for the day. He went with Ron Hartill, who had come south from Greymouth to work for George Wallis driving the logs out. Flat land on the far side of the Haast River, opposite the Greenstone flats, was a favourite haunt. Up to their waists in tumbling glacier-fed water, they crossed the river holding their rifles high. First, though, they emptied the pockets of their shorts because they knew the current would pick their pockets clean. On the return trip, they tossed to see who would carry the rifles and who would tow the shot deer across the chilly river.

Deer hunting for venison and tails was Tim's main spare-time pursuit. On the Wanaka side of the alps he went shooting with Geoff Taylor, a friend from primary-school days in Greymouth, who had taken a contract job at the Luggate sawmill. He also went with Robert Wilson, whenever Robert travelled up from Dunedin.

There was a memorable trip with Geoff across Lake Wanaka to the mountains surrounding the Rumbling Burn and Minaret Burn, the Buchanan Peaks. Looking for stags in velvet, they slept in the tussock near the tops, at around 2,000 metres, with the summit of Mt Alta (2,339 metres) not far above them. It was not uncommon then to see substantial mobs of deer trailing across the saddles, in single file, their passage wearing deep tracks into the landscape. On the way back from the Mt Alta trip, they loaded seven deer carcasses on to Tim's four-metre-long jet-boat – five on the front of the boat and four at the back. As they passed Mou Waho (Harwich) Island on the way home, the little boat was almost swamped as a north-westerly wind, typical of the Wanaka region, built to gale force behind them. They had to manually choke the Vanguard motor to keep it running.

On a Friday evening, Robert Wilson would drive to Luggate from Dunedin in his van for a weekend shoot. Under moonlight, he and Tim would trek into the mountains around the Matukituki or Makarora Valleys, catch a couple of hours' sleep, and be up before sunrise, stalking deer at altitudes of 1,500 metres or more. If the downhill going was easy they would return to the highway or access road by about midday with their haul. The venison was sold to the butcher at Wanaka and a restaurant in Christchurch. Chinese laundries in Christchurch would take deer antlers or velvet for selling on to China. Generally the two friends earned enough to pay for the petrol and ammunition, but not a lot more.

Yet income from deer was hardly an issue as they already had paying

Chat on a bridge

In the early 1960s, Max Kershaw was the New Zealand Forest Service ranger who looked after animal control operations throughout Otago and Southland from a base at Queenstown. One day, he and government deer culler John von Tunzelman were crossing the new Pleasant Flat bridge over the Haast River on foot. A green International log truck roared towards them. The truck stopped halfway over the bridge and the passenger leaned out to have a chat. It was Tim Wallis. They had heard of Tim. For about 15 minutes, with no one else on the road, the Forest Service men and Tim talked of deer, how many there were and how the deer control programme was going. As the log truck pulled away, the two men on foot noticed an impressive pile of deer carcasses lying on top of the logs.

jobs. Tim and his mates went shooting because they loved the freedom of the mountains, the company of men they trusted, the physical challenges, the excitement and spoils of hunting – and the conversation, light-hearted or serious, that could be had on such trips. These included deep discussion about the prospects for venison recovery on a larger scale.

A sample consignment

While Tim had a firm stake in Haast Timbers Ltd, he also kept a radar turning on any initiatives involving deer. His friend, Robert Wilson, who was developing an export business out of Dunedin, phoned one day, in the spring of 1961, to ask if he would fulfil a trial order from New York for venison. How could he refuse? In the country around Haast he shot three red deer. The carcasses were placed in muslin bags to keep blowflies at bay, hung from a tree, then driven to Dunedin that evening in his Morris Minor van. Robert and Tim processed the carcasses into primary cuts and packed these in cartons, which were taken to the Tip Top ice-cream depot in the city for freezing in anticipation of shipment to New York. The order came from a New York seafood broker of Greek descent, George Bokouris. When Robert asked him if there would be a demand for New Zealand venison among New York restaurants, the broker had called for a sample.

Not long after this, Robert sought another sample. Tim and Wattie Cameron, a top deer culler, brought carcasses from the Matukituki Valley to the Wilson family's holiday home at Dublin Bay. On the dining table, they set to and produced 12 cartons of venison cuts, under the supervision of a veterinary student, Phil Boulton. The cartons were rushed to the Tip Top ice-cream depot at Cromwell, and despatched to a German distributor, Ferdinand L. Freidreich in Hamburg.

The samples had tickled up a market. George Bokouris came back with an order for five tons.

Robert Wilson and Mark Acland with three shot deer near Rainbow Valley, Mount Aspiring National Park.

In Tim's case, deer shooting was a release from the timber trade. He worked hard at winning orders, the largest being several truck loads of rimu framing and weatherboard timber for the Tourist Hotel Corporation's Wanaka Hotel. There were frustrating periods when he had to deal with either too much sawn timber from a rush of logs or not enough because the logging at Haast had slowed. At such times he would report home to Greymouth that business was 'not too bright'.

The news from home in the middle of 1961 was not good either. Tim's father had been diagnosed with throat cancer towards the end of 1960 and it had spread to his lymphatic system. On his last visit to Haast to see how the business was going, Arthur suddenly became ill and asked George to take him home. Adrian was in his M.Sc. honours year at Canterbury University at the time, and Josephine had begun a physiotherapy course in Dunedin just that year.

The family gathered at Geraldine Street, where Janice had been nursing Arthur. Grandad Blunden had died the previous year, but Arthur's illness was a new order of distress. Neither Janice nor Arthur himself had disclosed much about the illness in the previous months. Unused to openly expressing feelings and discussing relationships, the family were sorrowful and subdued. Arthur himself tried to lift their spirits. The day before he died, he told his wife: 'Well, Jan, I've got to rock bottom now and I'm going to start getting better.'

For Tim, the prospect of losing his father and mentor was extraordinarily difficult to contemplate. Aunt Betsy saw how he coped. In the few days before Arthur's death, he went into Janice's glorious garden at Geraldine Street and attacked the spring weeds, with a transistor radio blaring at his side.

An obituary in *The Press*, the Christchurch morning newspaper, which had a large West Coast circulation, said the death of Arthur Wallis marked the end of a 40-year association with timber milling on the Coast. At the time of his death, the obituary said, he was 'pioneering large-scale logging' in the Haast area through the work of his sons.

Tim returned to Luggate, feeling more on his own now, with timber still flowing through the mill and orders still coming in. He had been through several years of 'transition' after college. He was 22. It was at a significant time in his life. He could push on and develop a career in the timber business – or he could try new avenues.

While establishing the timber trade for Haast Timbers Ltd, Tim had been dabbling not only in deer meat but also in crayfish exports. The crayfish came from fishing boats operating out of Jackson Bay south of Haast, the end of the Coast Road. Working in tandem with Robert Wilson,

---

Arthur Trevor Wallis
1898–1961

Arthur Wallis died at his home in Greymouth on 11 August 1961, a month short of his sixty-third birthday. There was a memorial service for him in Greymouth then a service at the Christchurch crematorium. Janice retained his ashes when she moved to Christchurch and later to Wanaka, with the request they be buried with her.

who would nominate a price based on the New York or Los Angeles markets, Tim used to negotiate directly with the fishermen. Being relatively close to their port on the Coast, he could undercut Christchurch competitors. Nonetheless, the Haast Pass road was always a challenge, and he made sure he had a chainsaw on board his ute in case of windfalls on the road. He would return to Luggate with a load of lobsters for processing and freezing.

Meanwhile, in the interests of building a venison trade, Tim had meat safes positioned at various points along the road between Wanaka and Haast and he put the word around amongst the private venison hunters that log trucks were able to collect carcasses from these sites. The log truck drivers, working on a commission basis, would tie the carcasses on top of the load of logs and deliver them to Luggate with the lumber. The hunters were paid later, by the pound of venison processed.

The weekend shooting trips provided a good idea of deer numbers and distribution patterns. All he needed, Tim thought, was a means of bridging the gap between the open tops, where the deer could be shot, and the road transport.

WHEN THE HELICOPTER ARRIVED on a trailer, in pieces, at the Wilson family's Wanaka holiday home in April 1963, Robert Wilson wondered how it could possibly be made to fly let alone transport deer from high places. It looked like a giant Meccano construction. It was a Bell 47 D1 model, of Korean War (*Mash*) fame, and it had been hired by a trio of mad-keen venison hunters – Robert, Tim and Wattie Cameron. They wanted to test a theory: that deer could be harvested profitably and commercially by helicopter.

While Tim worked on the logistics, Robert set up the marketing side. Wattie added considerable field knowledge and experience. At 32 and a few years older than the two school mates, Wattie was already a deer-hunting legend. As a Forest Service culler, he bagged over 2,000 tails in his first season (1955), a record number for a novice deer culler. Now a private meat hunter, he knew the Matukituki country could supply scores of deer for a helicopter operation, and the region was handy to a base at Wanaka.

The three men took the plunge and hired a machine from Helicopters New Zealand in Nelson at the rate of £60 an hour for every hour flown. It arrived on a trailer, accompanied by pilot Milton Sills, a Canadian who had formerly flown helicopters in the Canadian Air Force. All the chopper pilots in New Zealand at the time had been trained overseas, including the New Zealander who managed Helicopters NZ, John Reid.

Road-end in the Matukituki Valley for the first helicopter shoot, April 1963. The shoot used a Bell 47 helicopter.
Bernard Pinney

Vehicle support for the first helicopter shoot in April 1963.

The bush pilots

In the early days of venison recovery, a squadron of fixed-wing light aircraft flown mostly by pilots acting independently, chased the trade. They used primitive airstrips hand-built on grassy river flats or, sometimes, cut out of the bush, generally about 300 metres in length. The strip builders would have picks, shovels and wheelbarrows air-dropped into their camp on mini-parachutes. Single-engined Piper Super Cubs and Cessna 180s were the most popular aircraft types. From 1959 until the mid-1960s when helicopters came on the scene, the wilderness areas of southwest New Zealand reverberated with the sound of these aircraft. Many of the remote valleys of South Westland had bush strips.

Venison was also flown from gravel river beds and beaches. Planes also operated out of the drier valleys east of the main divide, including valleys that were soon to become part of Mount Aspiring National Park. Most of the deer were shot by private hunters, formerly government cullers out to make a better living. Some of them became pilots. The bush pilots often took huge risks getting into and out of tight spots in unsuitable weather, and their loads often exceeded their aircraft's limits by outrageous amounts. To provide more cargo capacity pilots removed all non-essential gear from their aircraft – and sometimes a few items that were essential. In Fiordland, float planes carried deer carcasses out of the fiords or lakes. Some hunters wanted the skins more than the meat, with a skin worth £4 by 1961.

The southern hirers of the Bell 47 envisaged a military-style operation. They could not afford to waste flying time. A group of shooters was assembled, 11 in all, for the weekend exercise. Wattie said they should target the basins in and around McGills Creek on the Matukituki River's left bank, where the tussock country reached towards summits over 2,000 metres high. The other two partners agreed. McGills offered maximum deer for minimum flying time.

On the Friday, the shooters gathered to camp near the mouth of McGills Creek. Some of them climbed well up into the big curving valley and got above the mobs; others, including Tim, were under orders to stop the deer from entering the bush. At a pre-arranged signal, the shooters high up began driving the deer into the high basins and towards an

Team talk: Organisers of the April 1963 trial helicopter recovery of venison discuss the strategy for the shoot. From left: Milton Sills (pilot), Ivan Taylor, Robert Wilson, Wattie Cameron, Tim Wallis and John Clark.
Bernard Pinney

ambush. They were successful. Timing was everything. As the deer fell, they were gutted and piled into convenient heaps for the helicopter to carry out to the road on the other side of the river, near the Mt Aspiring Station homestead. Milt, the pilot, began flying out the carcasses from the gut heaps on Sunday morning. The carcasses were carried on racks fitted to the helicopter's skids.

At this point, there were two concerns. At the highest altitudes, the Bell 47's Franklin engine lost power and could manage only reduced loads. Then the notorious Wanaka nor'wester came hurtling out of the mountains, buffeting the machine to the point where Milton said it was becoming dangerous.

That day over 200 deer were shot. In order to minimise damage to the venison, the shooters were told to aim for the neck. About half the deer, 110, were lifted out before the gale nor'wester grounded the helicopter.

Ivan Taylor's meat-processing plant in Wanaka handled the carcasses. Fred Jackson was the butcher. The venison was despatched to Dunedin then shipped on to Hamburg, West Germany, under a contract Robert had negotiated.

Although the helicopter time had been cut short, the three partners in the venture were pleased enough with the carcass recovery rate and the efficiency of the whole operation. By the time they added up the income

The early choppers

The first helicopters in New Zealand – the United States Navy's lumbering Sikorskys – made a brief visit in support of an American expedition to the McMurdo Sound region of Antarctica, under Admiral Richard Evelyn Byrd, in 1946–47. In the 1950s, Operation Deep Freeze, the next American Antarctic effort, also brought helicopters. The first certification of helicopters in New Zealand was for machines engaged in agricultural work, including spraying and the transport of materials and farm personnel. By 1963, when Tim and his colleagues hired a Bell 47 for a venison recovery trial, there were only ten helicopters on the New Zealand civil aircraft register. Through 1963, however, the idea that helicopters could be used for more than farm work caught on. They began to be used for deer operations in both the North and South Island.

The first helicopter recovery of deer, in the mountains above the Matukituki Valley, April 1963. Robert Wilson is dragging a stag towards the hired Bell 47 for airlifting to the road-end on the valley floor. Otago Daily Times

and took account of the helicopter hire, meat processing, road transport, and the cut taken by the shooters in the form of the skins, tails and other co-products, the venture was rated a success. They had made a profit – just – and it showed that helicopters could boost venison recovery way beyond what men and land transport could achieve.

Tim reckoned there was an enterprise based on deer waiting to be launched on the back of helicopters. This was something bigger than any previous ideas of his. It had the makings of a whole industry.

Chapter 4

Deer by Air

1960s

Other transport ... Luggate Game Packers' factory ... first to train in NZ ... a Bell bought - and written-off ... 1080 threat ... the gunship era ... hooking loads ... Fiordland beckons ... a contract with the Park Board ... motherships ... winter of '68 ... Queenstown Hill crash ... Hotunui commissioned ... a second chopper wrecked ... a rescue package ... back to the front-line

BY PACKHORSE AND BUSH PLANE, motorboat and Landrover, and on the backs of swearing, sweating hunters, the deer carcasses tumbled spasmodically out of the mountains, bound for meat-processing plants that were few and far between. At times, when the weather turned bleak, a ground hunter might wonder whether the effort of venison recovery was worth sixpence a pound.

Tim Wallis, timber merchant and sometime deer hunter, of Luggate, wondered harder than most about the logistics and how they could be improved. Before the advent of helicopters, he had tried accessing the back country by jet-boat. With friend Keith Blanc, who ran the garage at Makarora, he boated up the Wilkin River. Several deer were shot as they crossed the river, and a big stag was dropped near the Kerin Forks Hut. But the boat became overloaded with just six deer on board. The men had to push it through the shallower rapids on the way home. As they tallied up the proceeds, which they split 50:50, they knew they should hang on to their day jobs. Tim thought a road around the western shores of Lake Wanaka – to Minaret Creek and perhaps beyond – would assist the extraction rate. His affinity for explosives came in handy. With the assistance of Tom Faulks and Bill Hayward, plus a bulldozer, he worked on the road for a while. On still days or in the right wind conditions you could hear the explosions from the town of Wanaka, on the opposite side of the lake, as the roadmakers blasted their way through one bluff or rocky patch after another.

The idea of an all-terrain vehicle caught Tim's imagination. Was there something that would go where no Landrover could? In Oamaru he found an ex-Army bren-gun carrier that had seen service in the North African desert during the Second World War. Soon afterwards, one Friday night, Robert Wilson arrived at Luggate from Dunedin. For Tim, there was no waiting until morning to demonstrate the find. He put the bren-gun carrier through its paces on the nearby state highway. The tracks crackled on the tarseal and a plume of sparks split the darkness. The next day he showed Robert how it could negotiate ditches. For deer work Tim trialled the bren-gun carrier in the Wilkin Valley but did not push on with using it. The McGills Creek helicopter experiment had foreshadowed the way to go. People were now talking about the 'flying Jeep'.

Following the 1963 shoot using the Bell 47, Tim organised the hiring of another helicopter from Nelson with a group of partners, including Robert Wilson and shooters Evan Waby, Max Street and Bill Hayward. The helicopter hire cost was always going to be a challenge – £60 for every hour in the air, plus the cost of fuel and maintenance. They worked out they had to get 20 deer an hour to make any money.

Tim and his aunt, Betsy Ensor, talking to a cattle musterer in the Okuru Valley during a deer-stalking trip in the 1960s.

With that target in mind, they put in horrendously long days – up at 4 a.m. and not eating dinner back at the camp until around 10 p.m. Their hunting grounds were mainly the mountains around the Matukituki and Makarora Valleys and along the western side of Lake Wanaka. In the Matukituki they lived in an old bus.

The helicopter was used to drop off shooters at likely hunting spots – usually after mobs of deer had been sighted from the air – and to lift out the carcasses, two or three at a time, to the handiest road. From there they were transported to Ivan Taylor's factory at Wanaka for processing. The chopper paid its way but Tim had a larger scheme in mind, and the hiring of helicopters was not part of it. He wanted ownership. And he wanted to fly them.

By early 1964, Tim's interest in the timber trade was truly waning. A major Auckland timber company, Carter Merchants (the forerunner of Carter Holt Harvey), which was seeking to establish itself in the South Island, had already approached the Wallises about a takeover of their South Westland operation, the timber cutting rights in particular. George and Tim were open to a deal. Tim could see a door opening on to a whole new industry that had nothing to do with logging or timber. George wanted to stay based at Haast, and his interest in trucking – especially International trucks – meant he could diversify. For a time, Tim juggled two enterprises – first, the grading, pricing and selling of timber through the Luggate mill and, second, the collection and processing of venison, the prospects for which thrilled him.

His venison enterprise grew up alongside Colin Nolan's sawmill at Luggate, a short distance from the residential area. He went into partnership with his Greymouth schoolmate and shooting buddy, Geoff Taylor, who had given up dairy farming at Inangahua on the West Coast for sawmilling work at Luggate in February 1962. In early 1963 Tim and Geoff set

Below: Tim and Geoff Taylor receiving Luggate Game Packers' first chiller.

Below right: Jim Faulks processing venison at the Luggate Game Packers factory.

up Wallis & Taylor, a partnership formed on little more than a handshake.

They started out small: processing deer carcasses under a tree by the water race at Luggate in their spare time. The venison, stored in a 100 cubic feet freezer owned by Robert Wilson's company, was trucked out to Dunedin at intervals. Robert awarded them their first contract, an export order of 50 carcasses. Despite the primitive processing facilities and part-time nature of the business, they put together 49 carcasses packed in hessian and proudly despatched the lot to Dunedin.

In 1964, they built a small factory in Church Road, Luggate, again just outside the residential area. Ron Moore, an engineer with Luggate-based Reid's Transport, was hired to manage it. In addition to deer carcasses, the factory processed West Coast crayfish, which helped sustain production and income at times when deer were scarce. The plant comprised two small rooms. One was for receiving, weighing, washing, skinning and processing the carcasses; the other housed a freezer room. There was also a tiny office.

At the time, Wallis & Taylor's main competition came from much bigger processing plants at Cromwell (Doug Jones's Game Packers NZ Ltd) and Te Anau (Evan Meredith's Fiordland Venison).

In September 1964, Jim Faulks took over as factory manager. Made redundant at a Wanaka butchery the previous month, and with a newly-purchased house and young family to support, Jim was glad to find another job, even if it was sole charge and clearly meant long hours. His boss led by example when it came to job commitment. In addition to managing the supply and marketing of venison, Tim was still selling timber, although he had plans to phase himself out of the trade.

On Christmas Day 1964, Jim got up at 4 am, laid out Santa's presents for the children, and drove to the Luggate factory. He was skinning deer by 5 am as daylight began to spread across the summer-dry Upper Clutha Valley. He knew that if he did not process the carcasses in hand the meat would go bad.

Later in the day Tim arrived at the Faulks's home with Christmas presents and Christmas cheer, knowing that Jim had gone out of his way for the sake of the business.

In mid-1965, with Geoff Taylor aiming to go back to the life of a dairy farmer (this time at Paretai near Balclutha), Tim bought out his partner. Tim was already planning his boldest moves yet. He wanted to enlarge the factory and put it on a company footing with a new name: Luggate Game Packers.

With the timber trade behind him, he would make Luggate Game Packers his primary business. First – and most significantly in terms of

Corporate beginnings

Luggate Game Packers Ltd, the company that launched Tim Wallis's business empire, was formed on 23 August 1965, with 6,000 £1 shares. As company law required more than one shareholder, Tim's brother George was allocated a parcel of shares. Tim held the majority.

Tim driving his first jet-boat, Cindy, *at Wharf Creek, Lake Wanaka.* Bernard Pinney

where deer hunting was heading and his business instincts were pointing – he would have to buy a helicopter and learn to fly it.

When there was time for recreation in the mid-sixties, Tim often chose jet-boating. He had a four-metre-long boat called *Cindy* and later a second boat, *Suzie*. When Robert Wilson acquired a jet-boat of similar size, called *Buster*, the two friends decided to introduce the boats to the sea. They launched them in the Okuru River and headed over the bar – only to find the breakers rather bigger and more boisterous than they expected. Reaching three metres in height, the waves threatened to swamp the jet-boats. Tim, who had two girlfriends with him, turned to go back over the bar. *Suzie* reared up and at times seemed to Robert to be airborne. They got safely into the estuary, but Robert's boat copped a big wave that demolished the windshield and partly filled *Buster* with water. Robert spun around to find his dog, a spaniel, swimming for his life in swirling water in the stern. They got ashore when *Buster* was tossed up on the gravel beach. They were thoroughly wet and chastened.

In another incident on the Waiatoto River, with Geoff Taylor on board *Suzie*, Tim was making his way back to the settlement when he noticed Geoff was missing. He backtracked some distance and pulled Geoff, blue with cold from the water. Then the jet-boat ran out of fuel as a result of the rescue – and they had to pole her back to the road.

LUGGATE GAME PACKERS LTD.

P.O. BOX 4 :: LUGGATE :: PHONE 594 (HAWEA FLAT)

Packers of Wild Game for Export

The original letter-head used by Luggate Game Packers Ltd.

IN SEPTEMBER 1965, a month after forming his business into a company, Tim acquired his first helicopter, an American Bell 47 G4, registered as ZK-HBB (the letters ZK identified it as a New Zealand-registered machine, and H was for helicopter). Luggate Game Packers Ltd had obtained an import licence for the American machine, purchased new from the Bell manufacturing plant at Fort Worth, Texas. At a time when the government's formidable import licensing regime made New Zealand look xenophobic, gaining a licence to import a helicopter was no mean feat. Helicopters New Zealand assembled the craft at Nelson and Tim travelled there to take delivery after test flights were carried out.

First, he had to get a licence to fly the machine. He never had the slightest doubt he would learn to fly it – and quickly. For this he turned to Helicopters New Zealand again, and its manager, John Reid, who had been a test pilot in England for some ten years and was a qualified instructor. John had returned from England four years earlier to run Helicopters New Zealand, which had been called Rudnick Helicopters till then as a result of the involvement and investment of a wealthy Californian woman, Elynor Rudnick, who was an expert in the use of helicopters for agricultural spraying. John advised Tim to train on fixed-wing planes first and get himself a private pilot's licence; the cost of teaching someone to fly a helicopter from scratch would be much too expensive and time-consuming. John recommended the Canterbury Aero Club's flying school. Tim needed no further prompting – he enrolled immediately.

Tim learnt to fly in a Piper 140 Cherokee at Christchurch. The course included 40 hours in the air. Three weeks later, with a pilot's licence in hand, he headed to Nelson for a helicopter rating (in later years, a separate licence to fly helicopters was required). John Reid was astounded by the speed at which Tim did things. He soon realised, too, that Tim was a quick learner.

After John had explained the theory of how helicopters fly and how they are controlled, the pair took to the air, with Tim in the pilot's seat on the left side of the Bell 47, a bulky presence alongside the instructor's moderate build. With his left hand on the collective and right hand on

Poisoning threat

About the time he bought his first helicopter, Tim became aware of deer poisoning operations planned for the Makarora region by the New Zealand Forest Service. At the Makarora airstrip, carrots were heaped up and about to be dropped from the air over the Siberia Valley, which runs off the Wilkin. Although these carrots were toxin-free and were merely meant to bait the deer, Tim knew that the next step would be a broad distribution of carrots laced with the 1080 poison (sodium monofluoroacetate), as had happened controversially since the late 1950s in other parts of the country to combat possums and deer. He was incensed that a government department was setting out to poison the very deer he planned to shoot. A poisoned deer was no good to a venison hunter. He got on the phone to Wellington and arranged a meeting. He went to the top. At the meeting were the Minister of Lands and Forests, Duncan MacIntyre, and the Director of Environmental Forestry, Ken Miers. Tim came straight to the point: why waste time and money poisoning deer when he had them in his sights? Why did the government give him a licence to import a helicopter that would do the job just as well? Poisoning the deer, he said, would ruin his business. Ken Miers had been a deer hunter himself in earlier years. He understood Tim's argument. The 1080 drop at Makarora was cancelled.

the cyclic Tim was soon mastering take-off, landing and level flight. The compulsory cross-country training exercise involved a flight from Nelson to Westport. When Tim requested extra hours of mountain flying experience, John directed him to practise landings on 'unprepared ground' in the mountains of the Richmond Range between Nelson and Marlborough's Wairau Valley. It was August, winter time, and these mountains were often snow capped. There were high winds to contend with as well as the cold conditions.

At the time, the helicopter pilots John employed for Helicopters New Zealand were usually North American, including some who had flown in the Second World War. Among them were an American, Sam Thrasher, and Paddy Jones, a colourful Irishman based in the United States. To John's knowledge, Tim was the second New Zealander (after Ray Wilson) to undertake and complete training as a helicopter pilot in New Zealand.

'Cross your fingers for a fine weekend,' Tim wrote to his mother, Janice, a couple of days ahead of his departure south for Wanaka, with the rating to fly helicopters secured. On the way, he planned to call at Christchurch Airport to pick her up; she had moved there following the death of Tim's father. Janice had a more than usual interest in the new acquisition. She was underwriting the bulk of it.

The helicopter cost £18,530. Tim paid a deposit of £3,000 and borrowed the rest on term loan from the Bank of New Zealand at Cromwell, using his mother as a guarantor.

Janice boarded the chopper at Christchurch. She had a map of the route ahead spread out on her knees and a four-gallon can of petrol – spare fuel – at her feet. It was a clear day, but warm enough, for the time of year, to suggest a nor'wester in the making.

They plugged on through a rising westerly that reached gale force in South Canterbury and was just as strong as they flew on into the sprawling golden-brown plains of the Mackenzie Basin. As the helicopter battled the winds, Janice was surprised to see perspiration on Tim's face but said later she was not anxious herself. Tim decided not to risk crossing the Lindis Pass area for the run into the Upper Clutha that afternoon, so put down at Killermont Station near Omarama at the southern end of the Mackenzie country, where friend Mick Thomas lived. They reached Luggate the next day, landing in a paddock by Tim's cottage.

ZK-HBB was the ninth helicopter registered in New Zealand and the first for the Wanaka region. People came from miles around to see it. Over the next few days, Tim would take friends for a spin in it.

But joyriding was not what he bought it for. By now he had worked with a number of ground shooters, and he knew their capabilities, knew

the ones who shared his zeal for harvesting deer from the hills. Among them was Gavin Overton, a venison hunter trying to earn a living on his own. They met on the Hawea-Wanaka road. Tim stopped in his International utility truck to offer this stranger a lift and they got yarning. Gavin declined a ride but sold Tim a large stag he had just shot, which was now lying in the grass by the roadside. When Gavin called at the Luggate factory next day to pick up a cheque for the carcass, he gave Tim a lesson on the finer points of skinning a deer. After that, he started selling carcasses to the Luggate factory on a regular basis and before long he was shooting for Tim. When the new Bell helicopter arrived, Gavin was among those Tim flew into the hills to make the machine earn its keep.

The tussock grasslands of the basins and ridges above the Matukituki Valley were selected as the Bell's first theatre of operation. Tim would drop off shooters when they came upon a mob then he would try to herd the quarry towards the shooters like an aerial sheep dog.

Operating one day high up in the Mill Creek catchment, on the left side of the Matukituki and about opposite the Mt Aspiring homestead area, Tim flew in to pick up some carcasses. There was plenty of snow about and when he attempted to land, the skids of the helicopter sank into a drift. The chopper's tail dipped dangerously close to the surface. The incident taught him to be more careful where snow was concerned.

Only ten days after its arrival at Luggate the helicopter was operating in the Leaping Burn area on the west side of the Matukituki below Niger Peak. Tim had Gavin Overton and Bill Hayward on either side of him. When they spotted a good mob of deer on the valley floor, about three kilometres above the Leaping Burn's confluence with the Matukituki, Tim flew in to land the Bell near the creek bed and let out the shooters. They were about 500 metres above a landform they called Hole-in-the-Rock. It was not a hole but an overhang in a tight tree-lined gorge that almost joined with the opposite cliff. From below, though, it had the appearance of a hole.

Tim brought the chopper to a 'flare', a standard manoeuvre preceding a landing, whereby the pilot reduces the forward speed of the helicopter by lifting its nose. He had selected a landing spot on the margins of the creek, away from patches of snow. He was wary, now, of such landings until he had more experience under his belt.

As he lowered the collective to plant the skids on what he thought was firm, level ground, the helicopter lurched backwards. Its tail struck a rock, which put the tail rotor out of action. Instinctively, Tim applied more power and pitch and tried to lift the machine forward. With no counter to the main rotor's torque, the helicopter heeled over and quickly thrashed itself to a standstill on the rocks. Thrown to the right, the shooters suffered extensive bruising, but they were not badly hurt. Gavin thought immediately of the risk of fire and an explosion. He was soaked in petrol from the shattered fuel tank, which, on a Bell 47, was located uncomfortably close to the engine. He swivelled around and frantically tried to disconnect the battery. There was a spark. He stopped struggling with the terminals and instead ran clear of the wreckage, urging the others to get out of it as well. There was no fire or explosion but they did have a three-kilometre walk to the Mt Aspiring Road and a ride home.

At the Luggate factory, some time later, Jim Faulks heard a vehicle pull

The wreckage of Tim's first helicopter, a Bell 47, in the Leaping Burn, Matukituki Valley. Robert Wilson (left) was among those who went up to take photos for the insurance assessment.

up. On his own and struggling to keep up with the flow of carcasses created by the Bell 47, he felt annoyed there might be another lot arriving when he had yet to clear the backlog of deer. He could process only about 25 deer a day. That was his limit.

The door opened. Tim was standing there, blood splattered over his shirt from a 10 millimetre nick in his left ear.

'Jim,' he said quietly, 'we had an accident. The helicopter's not too good.' The nick in the ear would become a permanent reminder of the Leaping Burn crash.

The Bell 47, which Tim had been operating for just a few weeks, turned out to be a total wreck. Although he had insured it, he thought he would go back to hiring helicopters for a while. Perhaps he could learn a few things from the North American pilots who were working around the country. A few machines had passed through Wanaka lately, on agricultural work.

Although not bankrupted by the loss of the Bell 47, he was in serious debt, had just had a major accident and was damned lucky to escape injury. His mother and a few friends thought he should consider quitting. He had other ideas.

EXACTLY WHEN HELICOPTERS became gunships, no one can be sure. The idea of shooting deer from the air rather than from the ground took off in 1966, when Tim Wallis stepped up his venison recovery work east of the main divide, and a Christchurch-based competitor, Graham Stewart & Co., expanded its operations on the West Coast. In March 1966, John Henham shot deer from a Bell 47 flown by Jack Askew on the West Coast while working for Graham Stewart. Reports said John Henham, a former government culler, strapped himself to a cargo stretcher bolted to a skid on the Bell 47 and fired at deer with a shotgun. That is certainly an early record of aerial shooting but was it the first time anyone had tried? Gavin Overton, working for Luggate Game Packers with French Canadian pilot Paddy Jones in the Dart Valley that year, was also one of the first shooters to kill deer from a chopper. It happened accidentally. The port door of the Hiller was wrenched off its hinges in mid-air when a pin worked loose and they had to jettison the door. When they came upon a mob further up the valley, in the vicinity of the Beans Burn, Gavin thought he would have a crack at them from the air. He shot about 50 deer that day, using a bolt-action .303. No doubt there were other shooters claiming they were among the first to down deer from the air.

At the time, it was illegal to shoot out of an aircraft. Strictly speaking,

Government culling

As commercial venison activity increased through the 1960s, the Government's own deer control programme subsided. The Department of Internal Affairs initiated culling from 1930 after it became apparent red deer numbers were exploding and causing widespread ecological damage. The culling, which involved up to 125 men in various parts of the country, peaked in the mid-fifties with culls of over 50,000 deer. When Internal Affairs conceded it lacked the resources to reduce populations to manageable levels, the New Zealand Forest Service Division of Protection Forestry was handed responsibility in 1956. That year over 90,000 deer were slaughtered, a record number. Yet a decline in the annual kill rate from then on, together with the scale of the deer menace, forced the Forest Service to look to other methods of control, notably poisoning – anathema to recreational deer-stalkers and to the concept of venison recovery by helicopter.

First time overseas

In September 1966, Tim went overseas for the first time. He flew to the United States first with a view to placing an order for Hiller helicopters. Then he travelled on to Europe and came back via Hong Kong and Bangkok. In Hong Kong, he caught up with velvet trader Bill Bong and discussed future market prospects for velvet and other deer medicinal products with him.

Hiller helicopters on board the Ranginui *and* Koutinui *in Fiordland.*

you were not even allowed to carry a firearm aboard a plane. But until the law caught up with the practice, the government ignored the anomaly. So long as the helicopter gunships did not annoy anyone, they got away with it. After all, deer were noxious animals and helicopters had the potential to make a huge impact on their numbers.

Aerial shooting became standard practice through 1966, and the routines changed to accommodate it. Instead of ferrying shooters into the field and picking up the carcasses later, venison helicopters became units involving a pilot, shooter and gutter, with a driver-cum-refueller assigned to transport the day's haul. The shooter stayed with the chopper most of the time, jumping out to strap the shot deer for the lift to a gutting location. The gutter, after about an hour's shooting, was dropped off to eviscerate the shot deer, remove head and feet and drag them into 'gut heaps' accessible to the helicopter. Gutters and shooters often had to jump several metres on to sloping, uneven ground, rolling as they hit the ground to cushion the impact. When snow conditions disguised holes and rocks, the going got really tough.

If the going was hard on the gutter physically, it was also hard on his clothing. Thick woollen shirts and swannies (Swanndri) jackets were standard, and shorts for all but the coldest days. The crews flew from daybreak to dusk, and after dark there would still be work to do – weighing the carcasses and trucking them out.

To begin with, the Luggate Game Packers crews were based anywhere between Makarora and Glenorchy. They camped at cottages and shearers' quarters and in a bus Tim bought and set up as a mobile base. Before moving into an area, Tim would seek the permission of the landowners and offer to pay royalties on every deer shot.

For several months after the Leaping Burn crash, Tim hired helicopters. But as the venison flowed through his factory and the 'books' took on a healthier look, he became confident he could build up a fleet for himself. Instead of another Texas-manufactured Bell, he opted for an American competitor, the Hiller, which was produced by a factory at Palo Alto, San Francisco. He bought two Hiller 12Es in the space of a few months. The Hiller 12E was better suited to mountain work than the Bell 47, and it was a more stable platform when it came to crew members jumping on and off the skids.

Learning from his lesson in snow with the Bell 47 in the Matukituki, Tim had 'snow shoes' fitted to the rear end of the skids to prevent the helicopter tipping backwards.

If shooting from the air was a breakthrough, so too was the advent of slinging the deer from a hook under the machine. Before the hook, carcasses were loaded on to racks on the skids or stuffed inside the machine itself. Loading the racks, a deer at a time, was a more dangerous method on a hillside than hooking a sling load. In the Matukituki area, before Tim acquired his helicopter, two hunters dragging carcasses on to the skids had died instantly when they were struck by the main rotor blades.

Hooking a load was usually the gutter's job. Four to seven deer, depending on their size, were individually tied by nylon strops about six metres long. The gutter made an incision in the lower leg, through the Achilles tendon area, with his knife and that was strong enough to support the weight of the deer.

If heaps of gutted deer were not too far from each other, the gutter might opt to ride the chain instead of getting back inside the chopper. It took nerves of steel to ride the chain, with no safety harness and only arms and legs wrapped around it. The chain-rider also had to trust the pilot not to accidentally eject the load. In a Hiller, there was a red load release button on the cyclic and a back-up manual release on the floor.

Once Tim acquired the second Hiller, he also had to employ a second pilot. He chose Russell Gutschlag. Based at Clyde, Russell had been flying fixed-wing planes on agricultural work, including spreading fertiliser from the air. He got his helicopter rating at Alexander Helicopters in Wanganui.

Best day

In one extremely long and demanding day, pilot Russell Gutschlag, shooter Peter Campbell and gutter Charles Jelley shot and recovered 248 deer from Branches Station, in the Shotover catchment. It was Russell's best one-day kill and few other crews in the industry topped it. He finished the day with snow falling.

Translational lift

Take-off with a big load – a load over the Hiller's limit of 400 kilograms – required real skill on the pilot's part. The gutter knew to position the gut heap on a knob of land or the edge of a drop-off into a gully or valley so that when the helicopter moved off with its load, it would drag the deer a short distance over the ground until it had some forward movement.

In the process of gathering this forward movement, the helicopter passed through a phase known as 'translational lift'. The principle applies to all helicopter types. With its rotor head – therefore the whirring blades of the main rotor – tipped slightly forward, the machine moves away from the turbulence created at the lift-off and into a zone of undisturbed air where it is able to build speed. When the speed reaches about 15 knots rotor efficiency increases markedly. At this point there is about a quarter more lift available than when the helicopter is at the hover – an effect that can be compared to the way a fixed-wing air-craft gains lift as airflow increases over its wings.

The Luggate pilots had to keep a close eye on fuel levels. The lower the fuel gauge, the more deer the machine could transport. Time in the air was an important factor. It de-termined when the pilot did the ferrying back to the road.

The American helicopter manufacturers were appalled to see the size of some of the loads.

Tim hovers a Hiller 12E high up in the East Branch of the Matukituki Valley as Joe Cave hooks on a load of deer. Robert Wilson

Tim and Russell would work different areas, each with his own pre-ferred shooter and gutter. Evan Waby and Gavin Overton were among Tim's earliest shooters. Sometimes they shared accommodation. Tim's crew braced themselves for his strident snoring when he stayed with them over-night. Sometimes he would sit up in his bunk, asleep but acting as if he were flying a helicopter, with his right hand moving an imaginary cyclic stick and his left where the collective ought to be.

In a way, Tim's 'sleep flying' was an expression of the intensity and adrenalin drama of the occupation itself. A pilot was on edge and compet-ing all the time – competing with himself, with other pilots in the com-pany and with the pilots of other companies, although they did not often get to compare notes.

The job required a huge level of concentration. The hardest part was to remember where the deer had fallen, given that it might be a while before the helicopter revisited each kill site.

Yet Tim had thoughts only of expansion. In 1967, he bought two more Hillers after a wrestle with the import licensing officials in Wellington. This meant two more pilots were required. Roy McIvor joined the Luggate team then Bill Black was trained. Bill had previously flown for Ritchie Air Services at Te Anau and Southern Scenic at Queenstown and was used to picking up deer in remote places in fixed-wing aircraft.

With just over 20 hours' flying experience in helicopters, Bill undertook his first job with Tim in the Greenstone Valley west of Lake Wakatipu in July 1967. Tim had shooters and gutters working in the Greenstone, and the Hillers were flying the carcasses across the lake to Mt Creighton Station, from where they were trucked out. Tim and Bill flew up the broad, curving Greenstone Valley as far as Steel Creek where there was a gut heap. Tim turned to his new pilot and said, in his usual rapid and jerky way: 'Ah, ah, Bill, you take this load out, refuel the helicopter and come straight back.' Behind the controls and on his way across the lake, Bill was horrified to see that the fuel gauge was close to empty. He got across but not without visions of a ditching in the lake as a result of the engine spluttering to a stop. Tim had calculated there was sufficient fuel, although Bill was not altogether sure whether Tim knew there was enough to get back.

Bill quickly learnt the ropes and how to get the best results out of his shooter and gutter. Pilots and crews took risks. Yet they were well rewarded for it.

An average wage in those days was around £30 a week. Shooters and

Jim Faulks and Criffel deer farm manager Les Smith inspect antler velvet from the farm. The load was taken to the Luggate factory to be graded, sorted, and packed for export.

Asian natural medicines

Bill Bong, the Hong Kong-based velvet and Oriental medicines expert, is taken for a helicopter trip by Tim.

Bill Bong, a Chinese trader from Hong Kong, helped trigger a major New Zealand export venture in deer products for the Oriental medicines market. He was the son of a Beijing medicine dealer who escaped to Hong Kong with his family during the Cultural Revolution.

He was introduced to New Zealand through Robert Wilson, who encountered the trader while investigating the Hong Kong market for velvet and other products in 1961. In February the following year, Robert sold his first collection of deer tails to Bill Bong's company, Ha Lung Hong, thus bypassing the avenues he formerly worked through, the Chinese laundries and other Chinese agents in Christchurch, whose prices were relatively low. On his first visit to New Zealand in 1963,

Bill Bong met Government ministers and argued that New Zealand should turn its feral red deer into farm deer and produce velvet. The Government probably thought he was fantasising.

By the mid-1960s Tim Wallis's Luggate business was contributing deer tails, velvet, and other body parts, including sinews and pizzles, that were keenly sought by medicine dealers.

Ha Lung Hong had access to the Taiwan market and later to the Korean market, the most lucrative, where a trader could double his money. Robert and Tim soon realised Bill Bong's margins were enormous and that he was probably making 500 percent on the New Zealand factory price. He became very wealthy and ended up owning several tower blocks on the Hong Kong skyline.

gutters, on a good week, might make over 200 quid. Some of them spent up large, buying new cars and the latest household appliances. On days when the weather was too rough to fly, they would turn to the booze. The Glenorchy pub was a favourite haunt. At Glenorchy the high-spirited Luggate pilots, shooters and gutters often had an audience for their drinking games – a group of tourists on a day trip with the lake steamer, *Earnslaw*, out of Queenstown. Beer days helped relieve the tension created by living dangerously.

LUGGATE GAME PACKERS helicopters had the 'rainshadow' country east of the main divide reasonably well covered. In anticipation of a time when deer numbers would reduce to uneconomic levels, especially if competition intensified, Tim Wallis turned his attention to the wild expanses of Fiordland National Park. Deer-stalkers' stories and Forest Service information told of deer in abundance, and there were eye-witness accounts, from fixed-wing and float-plane pilots such as Gary Cruickshank, who flew the region regularly out of Te Anau, of mobs roaming plentifully above the bushline.

Tim had to see for himself whether helicopter recovery was feasible.

Towards the end of 1966 he embarked on a trial shoot with Jim Faulks, his Luggate factory manager, and Jock Murdoch, a meat hunter and former government culler from Southland. Jock knew Fiordland well. In addition to his meat hunting, he had a shareholding in the Mossburn processing plant. Tim flew the Hiller across the central part of Fiordland between Te Anau and Breaksea Sound. The tops were 'loaded' with deer. Jim and Jock shot and gutted 40 in the vicinity of Mt Wallis (named for an eighteenth century English sea captain and South Pacific explorer) on the south side of Breaksea Sound, and Tim dropped the carcasses at Beach Harbour, inside the entrance to the fiord. A Cessna 206 float plane was organised to fly the carcasses out to Te Anau.

In the course of this exercise and in the days immediately afterwards, Tim devised an operation that would revolutionise venison recovery in Fiordland and boost his business beyond the imagining of most other operators.

Fiordland's greatest challenge, for anyone after deer, was its shockingly rugged vastness and its lack of roading. The national park covered 1.25 million hectares. It was 225 kilometres long and up to 80 kilometres wide, with 14 main fiords ranging from Milford Sound in the north to Preservation Inlet in the south. Venison helicopters working the eastern side of the region might have been able to shoot deer and evacuate the carcasses economically but as soon as they moved across to the confusing jumble of valleys and mountains on the western side, they could not cover the distances cost-effectively and without refuelling. Tim had an answer to that – a ship. He envisaged a floating base for refuelling, resupply and accommodation, a vessel large enough to keep hundreds of carcasses in cool

Wapiti

A North American elk relative of red deer, wapiti are (together with a close cousin in Russia), the world's largest round-antlered deer. In 1905, 18 wapiti were shipped from San Francisco and liberated in Fiordland, at the head of George Sound, to enhance recreational hunting. Half of them came from Washington Zoo but originated from Wyoming stock. Able to breed with red deer, the wapiti slowly lost their pure-bred status and by the 1960s there were probably few pure-bred animals remaining. Recreational hunters retained an interest in wapiti, nonetheless, and an occasional huge bull was encountered in the autumn 'roar', the mating season. The name is that of North American native peoples and means 'white rump'.

storage. Once the hold was filled, the ship could sail for Milford Sound and offload into trucks there for the journey to processing plants at Te Anau or Mossburn. Such an enterprise, involving major investment, required certainty that the deer were available, however. Tim discussed the pros and cons with Fiordland National Park staff and some of the members of the governing authority, the Park Board.

At the same time, he was negotiating with other major players in the venison industry in order to achieve a measure of cooperation that would help him secure the Fiordland venture. He promoted the idea of forming a collective of the main venison processing plants in southern New Zealand. There was strength in unity, he argued, and a better chance of everyone profiting if they worked cooperatively. If they went their separate ways, competition might kill off some of them.

In early 1966, Game Collection Ltd (GCL) was established. Its shareholder companies were Luggate Game Packers, Fiordland Venison (Te Anau), Game Packers NZ (Cromwell) and Southern Lakes (Mossburn). The Mossburn plant had started up very early in the piece – 1962.

When GCL agreed that Luggate could provide the main thrust of

Camp cooks

A shooters' camp kitchen. Bernard Pinney

The Luggate venison crews needed to eat well if they were to perform well. Tim knew it was especially important for the crews in remote locations to have a good cook. He enlisted variously the services of his mother, godmother Aunt Betsy and sister Josephine, plus a few others, including a lass from Scotland who was on a working holiday in New Zealand.

Ann Stewart, a petite, auburn-haired 23-year-old from Clydebank near Glasgow, started out cooking and housekeeping for Tim at home at Luggate, then she moved on to cook for his men in the field. Her remotest assignment was the Greenstone Valley, west of Lake Wakatipu and beyond the end of a rough, lonely road. The team she supported there was based in the shearers' quarters of a large sheep and cattle station for up to six weeks at a time. There was no electric power. Cooking was done on a coal range.

Ann was first up, at 3.30 a.m., and prepared a hearty 'binder' breakfast of porridge, toast and bacon and eggs. She also made up packed lunches for the men. A late dinner, commonly with a stew as the main dish, was the other meal of the day. Sometimes the crews went off to the Glenorchy pub and if they came home late they were given a cool reception from Ann, who later married one of the shooters, Evan Waby.

helicopter venison recovery, it allowed the other partners to focus harder on the processing and exporting aspects of their business. It also meant that the Luggate helicopters could operate in the knowledge there was a factory reasonably handy. Tim cut a deal with the GCL partners. The Luggate factory would take 50 percent of the carcasses recovered in Fiordland; the other three GCL partner plants were to take the remaining 50 percent of the carcasses and rely on fixed-wing and other operators to top up plant capacity. The deer coming in from Tim's helicopters was sold by Luggate to the partner processing plants at a negotiated price – lower than the partners paid to fixed-wing and other operators.

Fiordland was the next big frontier for GCL and Tim. Too rugged for ground shooters to make money and effectively reduce the deer numbers, the region was a headache for the deer control ambitions of the Forest Service and the Park Board. The board was concerned that the deer plague was degrading large areas of the park. Some areas of once-rich forest understorey were now denuded. Chief Ranger Harold Jacobs knew of forest 'you could ride a horse through', which was ordinarily unheard of in the jungle-like New Zealand forest unless there were hand-built tracks. The stomach contents of deer in this sort of environment contained nothing but twigs. Tussock grasslands and alpine herbfields were also suffering as a result of deer grazing.

The Park Board took the initiative and called for tenders for deer control across the whole park except for an area towards the northern end of the park reserved for wapiti deer. The board, chaired by the Invercargill-based Commissioner of Crown Lands, Joe Harty, had some wapiti enthusiasts on it, notably Jack McKenzie, a Southland representative of the New Zealand Deerstalkers' Association, who was keen to see that deer control did not threaten the wapiti population with extinction.

The board received several tenders. Most said they could target only the eastern side of the park, the areas closest to roads. The Game Collection Ltd tender stood apart from the rest. Through Tim Wallis's novel helicopter-ship-truck proposal, GCL said it had the means to shoot and recover deer right across the park. The Wallis strategy had the people, systems and hardware to do the job for the board. To be affordable, however, the operation needed access to as much of the park as possible and for as long as possible.

The Park Board agreed, and let a three-year contract, 1967–70. Tim and his new business adviser, Dunedin accountant Reid Jackson, submitted to the Park Board that three years was the minimum period required for the operation to establish itself and square off debt. There were mutterings from the unsuccessful tenderers about the monopolising of

Enter Reid Jackson

Dunedin accountant Reid Jackson became Tim's primary business adviser in 1966, after Luggate Game Packers was registered as a company. Tim was introduced to Reid by an Ashburton lawyer, Graham Sinclair, who had met George Wallis while holidaying in the south at the time George was setting up the Haast Timbers logging operation. When he realised Tim was getting accountancy advice from a Nelson firm (George worked for it after he left college), Graham said forthrightly that, being so far removed from his accountant, he might struggle to get 'properly organised'. He suggested Tim contact Reid Jackson at his Dunedin office.

It was an inspired suggestion, for Reid shared Tim's love of flying and he knew a thing or two about how to run a successful business. Reid grew up at Wright's Bush in rural Southland and worked in the local cheese factory and at harvesting cocks foot seed to earn enough money to put himself through university. He was fascinated by Tim's innovative ideas. The two men quickly developed mutual trust and respect.

Graham Sinclair also filled an important role in Luggate Game Packers' affairs by helping Tim negotiate legal hoops and licensing hurdles. When Tim applied to import new helicopters or provide services that required a licence, Graham provided guidance, and he attended all the hearings for import licences as counsel.

the park for venison recovery. Local hunters, young and keen to try their hand as 'meat hawks', were especially miffed that someone from outside Te Anau, Manapouri and Tuatapere, the fringes of the national park, should get the lion's share. They reckoned the board's decision turned Fiordland into a private farm. But Tim hardly had time to worry about the backlash. His life became more frenzied than ever.

He looked around for a suitable ship. At the little port of Kaiapoi, on the left bank of the Waimakariri River north of Christchurch, he found the laid-up coaster *Ranginui*. It looked the right size – 32 metres long, 158 tons gross. Its shallow draught, under two metres, appealed as well. The *Ranginui* had a flat-bottomed hull for negotiating bar harbours and for beaching to unload cargo at low tide. She was built for the Northern Steamship Company, of Auckland, in Glasgow in 1936. In 1957, she was acquired by the Collingwood Steamship Company for service on the Wellington-Lyttelton run, which included calls at Kaiapoi. Tim bought her for £16,500 – shortly before New Zealand's currency switched from pounds sterling to dollars in July 1967 – and she arrived at Port Chalmers for a refit towards the end of the year. By February 1968, she was ready to do business in Fiordland waters, equipped with a helicopter deck and chiller space for 600 deer carcasses.

Not one to do things by half-measures, Tim also lined up another, larger vessel, the *Hotunui* (50 metres long, 594 tons gross), which he purchased a few months later. Like the *Ranginui*, she also served the coastal trade between Auckland and Dunedin for the Northern Steamship Company. Built in Sweden in 1949, the *Hotunui* had four times the cargo capacity of the *Ranginui*.

Although the *Hotunui* beat the *Ranginui* to the Port Chalmers shipyard of Sims Engineering by about a month, the *Ranginui* had priority. The *Hotunui*'s refit, involving freezer equipment and a large helicopter deck, was going to be more extensive and expensive.

With two new Hillers and a field base at Te Anau, Tim was ready to roll out his grand plan for Fiordland deer harvesting.

The wapiti area of the national park, covering about 15 percent of the land area, stretched from Charles Sound to Poison Bay on the ocean side, and from the Doon River at the head of Middle Fiord to the Worsley River in North Fiord on the Lake Te Anau side.

CONVERTED FOR USE in Fiordland, the *Ranginui* became an aerodrome, hotel and café to Tim's pilot, Bill Black. He would be based on the ship for two to three weeks at a time as she moved around the fiords.

When an area was cleared of deer, the *Ranginui* would try somewhere else, perhaps the fiord next door. Nancy, Thompson, Doubtful, Dagg, Breaksea, Dusky, Chalky, Preservation, Long – the *Ranginui* worked from one end of Fiordland to the other, with Milford the main port of call, where she discharged her chilled cargo. There was only one other option anyway – Deep Cove, at the head of Doubtful Sound: a busy place with tunnelling for the underground Manapouri power station tailrace well under way.

In Fiordland, nature reigns powerful. The landscape is always challenging to fly around and it is certainly a struggle for anyone on foot. 'Tiger country', the crews called it. To make matters worse, moist weather systems charge in from the Tasman Sea or from Antarctic waters to the south, dropping rain by the bucketful. Gales are not uncommon. Even when anti-cyclones lie over the region, and when there ought to be little wind and clear skies, coastal scud cloud can hinder visibility. Then there are the sandflies.

Misnamed by Captain Cook' expeditions, sandflies ought to be called black flies but a sandfly by any other name will bite as ferociously. Fiordland is a stronghold and Milford Sound prime habitat. At Milford, clouds of them will swarm around people. Even moored a hundred or more metres from the land, a ship will soon attract sandflies in abundance during daylight hours. The *Ranginui* was no exception. There was always a good stock of insect repellent on board.

On mornings good for flying, Bill Black would set out early from the *Ranginui*, with shooter Errol Brown and gutter Brian King. About an hour into the shooting, the pick-up would begin and Bill would have a sharp eye on the fuel gauge as he carried the carcasses back to the ship, knowing the Hiller had only a two-hour range. On bad-weather days the teams amused themselves by fishing for groper or playing cards, and things could get tense if the rain and the cloud persisted. Generally, though, the *Ranginui* was a convivial place to be. The venison boys mixed well with the ship's crew. They ate together and enjoyed a beer together, some of which Tim 'shouted'. Fishing boats pulled up alongside reasonably often, for an exchange of crayfish for venison and a bit of a natter over a beer.

Even with only one helicopter – at that stage there was room for only one at a time on the flight deck – four good days in the air would pretty well fill the *Ranginui*, at which point she would need to make for Milford to discharge. Blackie's best tally for a day was 185, which he achieved in just over 13 hours of flying. Everyone was ready for a beer at the end of it. On an average day he would drop ten deer an hour on to the *Ranginui*. On exceptional mornings, when conditions enticed the deer on to the

Noxious Animals Act

In 1967, the Noxious Animals Act 1956 was amended. Instead of aiming for the eradication of deer, the legislation now aimed for control of deer numbers – a more realistic objective given population size and distribution. Regulations were also introduced to cover game packing and exporting, which had previously operated rather nervously in a policy vacuum. Here were businesses profiting from an animal declared noxious, an unwanted presence in national parks and on high-country farmland. The new rules legitimised their operations and provided some certainty for investment.

Jim Faulks and Tim Wallis on a deer survey in Fiordland in 1966. This was before the crash near Queenstown, which broke Tim's back and paralysed his left leg.
Jock Murdoch

slips, tussock slopes and other open areas, he and his team could deliver 20 an hour – one every three minutes.

After 50 hours' flying, the Hiller would require a mechanical inspection. For these checks Blackie flew out to Luggate, where there was a workshop and a small airstrip near the LGP factory and the Nolan sawmill. One time, after four straight days of fine weather, he had the ship filled with 550 deer and was back again at Luggate for a 50-hour check, surprising the mechanics by showing up so soon after the previous check. With constant shuttling activity of this kind, radio links were essential to keep the operation running smoothly. Tim relied on the radio to stay in touch with what his helicopters were doing and where the ship was stationed. When Blackie advised he had to come out for maintenance checks or a break, Tim or one of the other pilots would fly in to relieve him. Always rushing to keep an eye on things, Tim would sometimes drop into Milford in his Cessna 180 when the *Ranginui* was unloading to ensure all was well with his Fiordland operation.

The Milford connection required careful coordination. The *Ranginui* discharged at Deepwater Basin, the fishing-boat base at the head of Milford

Sound, where a pier had been specially built over shallow water from empty fuel drums filled with sand. A pontoon carried the carcasses from ship to pier and a tractor, custom-fitted with a long boom, swung the carcasses ashore and into trucks for the journey through the Homer Tunnel to the Game Collection Ltd processing factories at Te Anau, Mossburn or elsewhere.

By the middle of 1968 there was a new element to the Fiordland operation. Tim had bought a smaller vessel, the *Koutinui*, a 100-ton wooden barge that Blackie nicknamed *Noah's Ark*.

Lacking motors, it was towed to Fiordland by the *Ranginui* from Port Chalmers, where an accommodation section had been installed. A Gisborne company had used the *Koutinui* previously to ferry frozen meat to ships anchored in the bay off Gisborne. Now it was a floating base for ground shooters, whom Tim assigned to cover forested areas where deer could hide from helicopters. For transport between barge and shore, the shooters had dinghies, which they loaded up with carcasses in the course of a working day. The *Koutinui* was moved around the fiords as hunting strategies dictated.

Certainly, the purchase of the *Koutinui* symbolised an expansion of Tim's Fiordland business and a confidence about how it was shaping up; but it also reflected Tim's strategic thinking – if there was a way to more fully exploit the resource, why not fill the gap? The *Koutinui* was a useful adjunct in the grand scheme of things. Although he had his detractors – mostly recreational hunters who objected to the removal of deer en masse – Tim considered the Fiordland operation was going along nicely. Indeed, the deer-stalkers' complaints merely confirmed for Tim that his pilots, shooters and gutters were having a major impact on deer numbers. Also, his idea of using ships for logistical support was paying off. Cash flows were overcoming debt. He was enjoying this roll-out of an ambitious concept. When, in winter, there was less flying for deer, he could afford to pull back and focus on other ways to keep his helicopters productive. The winter of 1968, however, produced a bolt from the blue.

Although Tim was renowned for his fearless flying, no one expected him to suddenly disappear off the scene. The news he had broken his back in a crash near Queenstown – the crash that opens this account of his life – hit hard. He had had accidents before but this time it was different. Would he walk again? Or fly? Friends and associates could hardly believe that someone as physically strong and vital as Tim might be laid low for any length of time. He was born to fly – was he not? – and to behave like a whirlwind, tearing all over the place in response to some inner calling. The Queenstown crash severely dented the buoyant feeling among the

Well looked after

Tim had huge respect for the staff who looked after him at ward 13B. They were ably led by urologist Bill Utley and surgeon Bill Liddell. Although discharged from the spinal injuries unit, Tim promised to always keep in touch. In subsequent years he provided a lot of moral and financial support, especially when the unit moved to the old Burwood hospital.

The Burwood spinal unit opened in February 1979. It has developed an international reputation for advancing the treatment of spinal injuries and for its rehabilitation regimes.

Bill Black on helicopter venison recovery

'It was a bloody job. You'd be covered in deer blood from your overalls through to your singlet. But it was flying.'

Luggate Game Packers team at a time when the business was going well. When he was brought down by power lines, many people around him were shaken.

It was a consolation to the dozens of Luggate Game Packers employees, from the helicopter teams to the field base staff and truck drivers, that Tim, from his hospital bed in Christchurch, was able to stay in touch by phone and radio. He would phone or radio his colleagues at all hours, keen to demonstrate he was still in charge, although accountant Reid Jackson had taken up a lot of the day-to-day running of the show. Many of Tim's associates visited him in hospital, if only to reassure themselves he would be able to carry on with the business now that the company's fleet of four Hillers was reduced by a quarter. They generally left the hospital amazed at his high spirits and his ability to keep tabs on the many strands of the Luggate operation.

The helicopter teams responded to the crisis by working harder than ever. Among shooters who aimed to lift output was Charles Jelley, who had worked for Tim for years, first with the Haast Timbers business then as Jim Faulks' assistant in the factory. Charlie began in the field as a gutter, and he later became a shooter. Like others in the company, he wanted every day in the field to be a good day, with at least 100 deer shot, gutted and delivered to the factory.

With winter a less profitable time to be working on deer recovery in Fiordland, the *Ranginui* took time out at Bluff and Port Chalmers for maintenance over three weeks in July 1968. This released Bill Black and his crew for other work that would help the company overcome Tim's crash.

One of the jobs was on Nokomai Station, south of Lake Wakatipu, two weeks after Tim's prang. Snowfalls through June and July had stranded a lot of stock. Bill and his machine were called in for an aerial inspection of the impact, and a few days later, as Tim had done at Queenstown Hill and other properties, Bill flew stockmen into the hills to carry out 'snow raking'– creating escape paths for the sheep through the snow. Flying across the farm, Bill had seen plenty of deer. He asked station owner Frank Hore if he could shoot them. Initially, Frank said he preferred to leave the deer for his musterers to shoot because they enjoyed the recreation and the additional income. Then he relented. Deer numbers were growing on his property and they were eating his winter stock- food crop of turnips not to mention a fair bit of grass.

To keep on good terms with the musterers, Bill donated the first eight deer to them. There was no shortage. He brought in more than 300 deer in a few days, including 125 on the best day. It all helped to support the company finances.

Bill Black sitting in the wreck of his helicopter on board the Hotunui, *1968.*

The *Hotunui* had gone to Fiordland by now. Her size and manning requirements meant the helicopter teams needed to work hard to make her pay. Entering service in the middle of the harsh winter of '68 only served to make the job even harder. One drawback became apparent when the *Hotunui* arrived at Bluff to discharge her considerable cargo. In the *Hotunui*'s freezer spaces, the carcasses were welded together by ice and crew members had to use crowbars to free them.

As Fiordland thawed going into September, Tim was was discharged from hospital. It took an intensive programme of physiotherapy to get him walking again. There would be several more operations later as well. They included operations to regularise bladder function. One operation aimed to stop his toes curling – a symptom typical of spinal injury affecting the legs. Adjustments to the calliper were made as Tim became used to walking again. It was encouraging news for everyone in the company, and evidence that the Tim Wallis they knew before the crash, hadn't lost his self-belief, optimism and drive. Yet no sooner had Tim shown that he was on the mend than another blow hit the business.

On 30 September, Bill Black was in action with his shooter, Errol Brown, and gutter Brian King, who was nicknamed Blue Bottle, Blue for short. They took off in the Hiller ZK-HBM about 7.15 am. The *Hotunui* was stationed at Breaksea Sound that day. It was a grim-looking day, with gales forecast and more snow on the way. Notwithstanding the marginal conditions, Bill and his team wanted to work.

Errol was well used to Blackie's flying. He had worked with him for several years, going back to fixed-wing days of venison recovery, when Bill was flying for Ritchies and Errol and his brother Peter were meat hunters with an airstrip up the Upukerora River in the Te Anau Basin that they created out of the tussock and moss.

Before they took off from the *Hotunui* that morning, Bill attended to a problem with the gutter's door, the starboard door. Bill had become annoyed about a faulty catch, which would have to be repaired at the next maintenance check, and decided to secure it. He wired it tight. As usual, there was no door on the left side of the machine, where the shooter sat. In 40 minutes Errol shot about 10 deer before the wind got too strong for accurate shooting and safety. At this stage, Bill flew back to where he had earlier let out Blue, near Mt Richardson, a sentinel peak at the entrance to Breaksea Sound. Blue was waiting near the summit ridge, above the tree line at the top of a rocky gully. Occupying the seat by the open door, Errol offered to crawl across the pilot to the starboard seat so that Blue wouldn't have to scramble over his two mates. The helicopter approached the pick-up point. As Errol squeezed past Bill, his boot accidentally flicked the magneto to the off position. The engine died instantly.

Bill immediately lowered the collective. That removed positive pitch on the main rotor blades and induced autorotation. For a few heart-stopping moments the machine did fly and could be controlled. But there was precious little air space left and the 45-degree slope did not help.

The tail struck first. Then the main rotor and body collided with a large beech tree about 10 metres above the ground. The helicopter dropped like a rock, coming to rest 800 metres above the fiord and about three kilometres from the nearest part of the shoreline – a 'broken egg' as the boys back at the Luggate workshop would say. Pilot and crew were an awful long way from help and snow showers were in the wind.

Unbelted, Errol was thrown through the bubble on impact with the tree. With so far to fall, it was a miracle he survived. Bill was knocked unconscious for a minute or so. When he came to, Blue was on the scene, having scrambled as fast as he could over 200 metres of boulders. He had feared the worst. Bill knew he had damaged his ankle but he was more worried about his shooter. Errol was in a bad way, bleeding from the mouth, nose and ears. Most of the ribs on Errol's left side were broken. At least one rib had punctured the lung. He also had some vertebrae damage.

There had not been time to radio an emergency landing, and they were out of sight of the *Hotunui*, which was moored in Third Cove, out of sight of where they had crashed. The radio was useless now and emergency locator beacons were not standard issue then. The only way of calling for help was to reach the shoreline and try to attract the attention of a passing fishing boat or other vessel. After making his mates as comfortable as possible, Blue set out for the fiord over rough and forested, teeth-gritting terrain.

When the Hiller failed to return or make radio contact after two hours – the time its fuel would last – the *Hotunui*'s skipper initiated an aerial search. He called in a float plane from Te Anau.

Blue, meanwhile, reached the shores of Breaksea Sound. He fired three shots, waited for a short time then fired another set of three. Commercial fisherman Joe Cave had seen the float plane. That it was flying in poor weather was unusual but not alarming. Then he heard the shots. Wondering whether the shots might signal an emergency, he went to investigate.

Bill heard the shots as well but had no idea if they would trigger a rescue. It was late afternoon by now and getting very cold. There were snow showers. Bill was deeply concerned about Errol's condition. In case they had to spend the night on the mountain, he shot five kea for food.

With Blue able to describe the crash location, another Luggate helicopter, flown by Roy McIvor, was despatched immediately. Meat hunter Jock Murdoch, of Winton, was on board as well for his knowledge of the area and to lend a hand.

By the time the rescue helicopter reached the crash scene, it was just on five o'clock. The cloud was down and there was precious little daylight

Tim cleaning deer up at Makarora.

Looking down Lake Wanaka. In the mid-1960s, Tim established a road between West Wanaka to Minaret Creek for early deer recovery by ground shooting.
George Wallis

left. Unable to get close enough to Errol to evacuate him, the Hiller offloaded a stretcher. Blue and Jock eased the injured shooter on to it. The next thing, Errol was in the air, with the stretcher attached to the machine's hook by a strop. He was spinning under the Hiller. But at least he was on his way out. Lower down, the Hiller landed the stretcher on a large flat rock and Errol was repositioned on the rack of the helicopter for the rest of the trip back to Beach Harbour on the far side of the fiord. From Breaksea, the float plane took him to Te Anau. He was still conscious but thinking he probably would not have survived a night in the open, as he had lost a lot of blood.

Tim heard about the crash that evening in Christchurch. The good news, given the severity and location of the crash, was that no one had died. But there was a down side in business terms: half the Luggate fleet of four helicopters had gone in less than three months. He had to take stock, and sought the advice of Reid Jackson.

At this time Tim was recuperating at his mother's home in Beverley Street, St Albans. A patient in ward 13B for just on two months, he was discharged partly paralysed. His left leg was floppy. He had no feeling in it whatsoever. His right leg had lost some feeling as well but at least it could support him. To stand, he had to strap a steel (later titanium) calliper, extending from thigh to shoe, on to his left leg and click it straight before walking. To sit down, he had to manually 'break' the calliper behind the knee. From that time on he would walk with a stiff leg – a 'walking para-plegic', as he sometimes described himself.

Soon after Bill Black's accident Reid Jackson came to see Tim in Christchurch. Reid looked serious. He had reviewed Luggate's books. The company was in 'financial strife'.

The B word – bankruptcy – loomed larger than ever.

The business would have to change course in a number of ways, Reid said. He called it a 'rescue package'. Tim's reluctance to trim sails was balanced by his desire – as strong as it ever was – to succeed in Fiordland at least. Fiordland was probably the key to any recovery because elsewhere deer numbers were falling markedly due to the pressure from his and other firms' helicopters.

Top of the list of operational adjustments which Reid proposed in-volved the *Hotunui*. Frankly, she was unsuitable for Fiordland venison work. With several more crew members than the *Ranginui*, she was ex-pensive to run, the carcasses in the freezer hold formed a solid mass that required a crowbar to free them, and when the *Hotunui* discharged up to 2,500 carcasses at Milford, she flooded the processing plants. It was feast or famine with her. Reid, who had become Luggate's managing director in effect, persuaded Tim she should be laid up until a better use for her could be found. The *Ranginui* remained cost-effective. Her running costs, mobility and cargo capacity were reasonably in tune with venison supply-demand and the work rate of the helicopters.

The rescue package also called for the Luggate helicopters not involved in Fiordland to step up their efforts in Central Otago.

Tim took the advice stoicly. He admired and trusted his accountant. A lesser personality than Reid Jackson might not have convinced him to get rid of the *Hotunui*. In the circumstances, forsaking the *Hotunui* was not as important to Tim as getting back in charge of things, getting back to the frontline.

In October of '68, he took a flight with Bill Black from Te Anau, in a Hiller. They headed off to join a crew working in the mountains around the Windward River, which flows into Charles Sound's Gold Arm. Com-ing upon a large heap of shot deer that needed gutting, Tim told Blackie to let him out. He wanted to help with the job.

The rotor wash blew Tim over – he was still not too steady on his legs – but that did not put him off. He simply lay across the wet moss and tussock, knife in hand, and got stuck into the gutting work without hav-ing to use his legs.

Tim Wallis was back.

Chapter 5

Fiordland and *Hotunui* Heat Up

Late 1960s–1970s
Chatham Islands lobsters ... subantarctic pigs and crabs ... flying again with baling twine ... New Hebrides beef ... Hotunui *sold ... another Fiordland licence ... Alpine Helicopters Ltd ... 'Deer Wars' ... hangar fires

RETURNING SOUTH from Christchurch, a calliper keeping his left leg braced when he walked, Tim got to grips with the big decisions he had to make. He had little time to focus on his disability. Anyway, it was not high on his list of concerns, the most urgent of which was the future of the *Hotunui*. She could not continue as a venison mothership. The longer she stayed in Fiordland, the more it cost the company. An opportunity to despatch her on a short-term charter surfaced, and in January 1969 she departed for the Chatham Islands, 800 kilometres east of the mainland, to try her luck in the crayfish industry as a mother ship.

The Chatham Islands lobster boom was in full swing in 1969. Lobsters were so abundant they could even be caught by trawling as well as by the traditional and more laborious way, the setting and lifting of baited pots. A Wellington company, Capricorn Fisheries, chartered the *Hotunui* for four months in the hope of cashing in on the crayfish. The ship had blast freezer space for a medium-sized fortune in cray tails, which were fetching an alluring five shillings and sixpence a pound on the London market. Of keen interest to the media and the fishing industry at large, the *Hotunui* arrived at the fishing port of Kaingaroa on the northern coast of the main island in the first week of February, carrying two dories. Her charterers expected up to 25 boats to have their catches processed on board her.

A row flared up over the *Hotunui*'s right to process at sea – that is, do the tailing. Tailing at sea off the Chathams was illegal. Processing had to be done at factories ashore. Everywhere she went the *Hotunui* seemed fated not to fit in. By the middle of 1969, Tim had lined her up for another assignment. Again, it had nothing to do with deer.

Tim had taken an interest in the commercial potential of two species in the New Zealand subantarctic region – the giant spider crabs and wild pigs of the Auckland Islands. To investigate that potential further, Tim helped set up an exploratory visit utilising the *Hotunui*, with Colin Bell as skipper. The expedition was jointly mounted by Robert Wilson's company, Wilson Neill Ltd, which represented the exporting and marketing side, Dunedin-based Otakou Fisheries, which had the fishing capacity, and Luggate Game Packers, which had a refrigerated ship and a helicopter in support. Robert knew of the markets overseas for Alaskan king crabs and eastern Canada's snow crabs, and it led him to think that perhaps there was an export market for the Auckland Island spider crab *Jacquinotia edwardsi*, which also lived on the coast of Campbell Island, further south. The crab reportedly had a shell about 150 millimetres wide and plenty of meat on its stout legs. To Tim, the crabs represented a commodity not too different from crayfish but in a more challenging and adventurous location. Tim also wanted to investigate the wild pigs, liberated on the main Auckland Island by British explorers in the nineteenth century for the use of shipwreck survivors. The pigs were now said to be roaming all over the main island.

With government fisheries officers on board to keep an eye on the spider crab prospecting, and a Hiller dismantled and stashed in the hold, the *Hotunui* set sail for Port Ross at the northern end of the Auckland

Tim with friend Peter Wilding, a Southland farmer, and baby Toby at a favourite lobster diving spot in the entrance to Breaksea Sound. Prue Wallis

Islands group, 460 km south of Bluff. For much of the journey she punched into heavy seas created by the prevailing westerly winds of the 'albatross latitudes', the Roaring Forties and Furious Fifties, where ocean encircles the world and currents and water masses freewheel, unobstructed by land. The ship rolled fearsomely and buried her bow in the biggest of the swells. The main deck was constantly wet. Never dropping below 30 knots, the westerly winds lashed the ship and threw spume across the sea's lumpy surface. Crockery and other items hurtled out of shelving as the ship lurched. Everyone except the cook felt sick, some horribly so, others just chronically queasy. Being June and early winter, it was cold, and the limited daylight, with the days being shorter than on the mainland, seemed to accentuate that fact.

It was just as well the helicopter was lying in the hold and tied down in three main pieces – body, tail boom and main rotor head and blades. Aluminium suffers rather badly when covered in salt. A Hastings aircraft engineer, Temple Martin, was on board to supervise the reassembly of the machine at the Auckland Islands, and Bill Black was there to fly the Hiller because Tim had not yet regained his pilot's licence.

The *Hotunui* stayed about a week at the Auckland Islands. These islands are by far the largest of New Zealand's five far-flung subantarctic groups. At the Auckland Islands, volcanic mountains, often shrouded in cloud, rise to over 700 metres, and the eastern side of the 70-kilometre-long main island features a series of fiord-like inlets fringed with rata trees that flower in the new year. Snow settles in winter, although not usually for long. Five species of albatross nest at the Auckland Islands but in Port Ross the most conspicuous fauna are New Zealand sea lions and, in winter

Tim at the subantarctic Auckland Islands. The concrete plinth was built by a German expedition based at Port Ross in 1874 to observe the Transit of Venus that year.

and early spring, southern right whales. Despite the sea lions' interest in crab meat, the spider crab population at the Auckland Islands flourishes.

To sample the crustaceans, the expedition brought steel-mesh cages, similar to crayfish pots, and set them at various inshore areas. For the crabs, however, no ordinary lobster pot would do. The entrance to the trap was too small. The spider crab pots, manufactured at the Luggate aircraft workshop, had an opening about twice the size of the pots used to catch crays.

On the days when he could see the tops, Bill Black took off in the Hiller with Tim to spy out the pigs, which ranged right across the main island, from the intertidal zone where they browsed on seaweed, to the tussock tops where they attacked the chicks of white-capped albatrosses. In 150 years, the pigs had caused major ecological damage on the main island, so trapping them would have a positive effect. Yet the coastal rata forest and extensive shrubland provided them with good cover, and they could run fast when alarmed. After a few reconnaissance days – and taking everything into account, including the pigs' ability to hide, the distance from markets and the rough and cloudy weather – Tim had to conclude that a wild pork venture at the Auckland Islands would not be feasible.

Before the *Hotunui* headed home with the sampled crabs stuffed into large plastic bags, the expedition visited Enderby Island at the northern end of the group, a breeding haven for sea lions. The island was also the home of a population of short-horn cattle, first put shore there for the benefit of any nineteenth century castaways. In later years cattle were introduced as farm animals. Tim took an interest in the cattle but decided their relatively small numbers precluded any culling of them for a beef trade. Behind the sheltered beach at Sandy Bay on Enderby Island was a grass sward, home to another species, a healthy population of French blue rabbits, introduced in 1840 as food for castaways. Two of their number, a male and a female, were taken on board the *Hotunui* for the trip of their lives. They spent some time at Tim's mother's home in Christchurch before being transferred to Wanaka, where the local policeman heard about them and took them away to be destroyed. It was illegal to import animals without a permit.

As for a spider crab export trade, Tim and Robert Wilson believed they could secure a premium on the meat over the Alaskan king crabs. But the sampling showed an insufficient yield from the subantarctic crabs. Instead of giving a meat to leg weight ratio of at least 17 percent, which was the minimum for the venture to turn a profit, the samples delivered only 11 to 12 percent. Shell thickness was also an issue. The Auckland Island species had a shell two and a half times thicker than that of the Alaskan

Spider crabman

In an effort to secure a market in North America for the Auckland Island spider crabs, Tim once packed a few samples – whole crabs, unshelled and packed with ice – in his suitcase for a flight from Auckland to Los Angeles. At the Honolulu stopover en route to Los Angeles, he was called to the airline desk. Cargo handlers had noticed his suitcase leaking water. He was asked to disembark at Hawaii and travel on to Los Angeles later. Canterbury friend Mark Acland was waiting for him at Los Angeles when Tim – more distressed about an acute pain in his left leg than about the fate of the crabs – arrived. Over the next few days, with the leg pain having subsided, Tim discussed the marketing of the subantarctic crabs with American interests. In the end everyone agreed difficulties with the shell and the yield of crab meat were insurmountable. He returned home with his enthusiasm dampened, although not as dampened as his case!

Bill Black flying a Hiller in the late 1960s.

king crab, It would require a new and expensive method of extracting the meat. Robert gave the idea of a crabbing venture in the Auckland Islands the thumbs down. Tim was philosophical about this rejection. It was a challenge that hadn't worked out. At least it had introduced him to a new part of the world.

After the decision, the *Hotunui* wasn't needed for any further subantarctic voyages. She was laid up while her owners contemplated her future. The next mission would be radically different from any previous venture.

Meanwhile, Tim Wallis, owner and pilot of helicopters, had no intention of remaining laid up himself. After a few months of getting used to the calliper and building strength in his good leg, he was keen to have a crack at the controls of a Hiller. His mate, Bill Black, was only too pleased to help. He recognised, as did all the Luggate pilots, that Tim would never give up flying because of a bung leg. Anyway, it was in their interests to see the boss (who was more like a colleague) back in the air again and doing what he loved best.

Blackie believed that if Tim's right foot were tied to the right pedal, allowing him to pull as well as push it (the pulling action was equivalent to pushing the reciprocal left pedal), he could fly the machine. On the day Tim tried out the idea they were down at Oreti Beach near Invercargill. Their helicopters at that time lacked dual controls so if Tim inadvertently made the wrong move, his friend had no way of correcting it. Bill had every confidence in Tim but wanted him to be ultra careful all the same. He tied Tim's right foot to the pedal with binder twine, the kind of rope used to strap bales of hay. They agreed to go gently for a start. Tim tried lifting the machine to a hover a metre or two above the ground before putting it down again. This he accomplished several times. Then, with remarkable ease, he brought the Hiller to a hover once more, nudged it through 'transition' and away they went across the Oreti's wide expanse of sand and duneland. They were flying as good as gold. Bill saw Tim's face transform from intense concentration into a huge smile – 'a smile to beat all smiles'.

The next hurdle was to convince Civil Aviation to reissue a pilot's licence. The authority's advice to Tim was to the point: 'If you can fly, prove it.' He also needed a medical clearance and saw Bill Utley, the Christchurch spinal unit consultant, about that. He told Bill: 'I know I can fly – because I have flown.' Civil Aviation instructor Hugh Skilling, rated for helicopters as well as fixed-wing planes, took him for the test flights. Bill Utley believed that regaining a pilot's licence would be the best kind of rehabilitation possible for Tim. It would reimmerse him in the life he thrived in.

Early in January 1970, while on a yachting holiday in the Bay of Islands, Tim wrote to girlfriend Prue Hazledine, whom he had met at Mosgiel two years earlier: 'In the process of getting my licence again but Civil Aviation is awfully slow … got the modification to the rudder pedals approved.' At the time, Prue was working in New York, having left New Zealand in July 1969 for work and sightseeing overseas. Tim wrote to her frequently, usually by aerogramme. Later in January, he reported to her: 'Got my pilot's licence back last week but not the full licence yet.' He also mentioned he had bought another helicopter, bringing the number in the Luggate Game Packers fleet back up to four.

Soon Tim was back in the air working on deer recovery, exhibiting the kind of verve he became renowned for before. And had plenty to say about it. Shooters like Charlie Emmerson and Gavin Overton became used to his continuous commentary through the headphones: 'They're going that way … Let's go get 'em … can't let 'em get away …' He flew as if he were hunting, anticipating which way the deer might break, manoeuvring so the shooter had the best possible look at the quarry. During the height of the chase, his tongue would roam around the edges of his mouth and even touch the tip of his nose, which was almost as curved as a kea's beak. Russell Gutschlag once dubbed Tim a 'tongue concentrator'.

Flying after deer required the daring and skill of a fighter pilot in a war zone. It was a one-sided war, of course. As Tim used to say, the deer were not shooting back. Yet after a hectic and challenging day in the air, Tim sometimes found it hard to sleep because the adrenalin was surging through him long into the night, and because his head was always filled with ideas for how his business might develop.

LGP Management

Luggate Game Packers started out with a board of directors that comprised Reid Jackson as chairman, Tim as managing director and solicitor Graham Sinclair.

In 1969, with the business growing in leaps and bounds, Don Spary was appointed operations manager. Formerly a major in the British Army, Don had served in the Middle East, Far East, Europe and the United States. When he left the army, he came to live in New Zealand, his wife Jan's homeland. For six months, he worked for Whirlwide Helicopters, flying Hiller 12Es in support of the Manapouri power project. One of his roles at Luggate Game Packers was to supervise the company's pilots. In this, he hammered home the need for safety, warning them not to let the thrill of the chase overwhelm their responsibility to take care.

By the early 1970s, with the pace of business sometimes requiring quick decisions, an LGP board meeting might have to occur at Wanaka's airfield or a main centre airport. Often the four men would arrive from different directions – Reid Jackson in his Cessna 180 from Dunedin, Graham Sinclair in a Cessna from Ashburton, Don Spary in the company's Cessna from Queenstown – and Tim in a Cessna 182 or helicopter from 'who knows where'.

'FLYING TO SANTO TOMORROW …' Tim wrote home to his mother from Noumea, capital of New Caledonia, in the middle of June 1970. 'Business looks very promising.'

The offshore 'business' he had in mind involved exporting beef from Santo in the New Hebrides group to Noumea. Tim had gone to Noumea with friend Peter Wilding for a tropical holiday and met a French businessman, Marcel Danton, who told him of cattle surpluses in the New Hebrides. Marcel had run a coconut plantation on the island of Espiritu Santo. It was common practice for the coconut plantations there to have cattle grazing under the palms to keep the vegetation down. But the cattle had bred too well and the plantations were now overstocked.

Tim had an answer to that. With Marcel promising to help with marketing and paperwork at the New Caledonian end, he envisaged assigning the refrigerated *Hotunui* to carry beef processed on Espiritu Santo to the city of Noumea in French New Caledonia, a trip of about 700 kilometres due south. New Caledonia's tariff barriers were forbidding, but less so for imports from another French territory – and the New Hebrides were jointly administered by France and Britain.

Still at the concept stage with this project, Tim wrote excitedly to Prue in July 1970: 'Peter and I had a grand time in the Islands. I have found a utilization for the *Hotunui* over there that will require for me to be there off and on for the next few months … New Hebrides is the place and wild cattle the purpose. It's a real challenge. I will have to learn some French.'

Prue had arrived in London from New York by this time, and was working in the film industry there as a researcher of television documentaries and feature films. In a letter to her earlier in the year, Tim said he was coming to terms with his disability. 'I don't worry about it any more,' he said. 'Of course, I curse and swear occasionally but who wouldn't.'

The *Hotunui* was readied for the voyage to the tropics. In September she took on equipment for the project at Port Chalmers. It included prefabricated materials for a house to accommodate project staff at Santo; this was loaded on to a barge which the *Hotunui* would tow to Santo.

On the wharf to see the loading – a year or so into his job – was Luggate's operations manager, Don Spary, who regarded the *Hotunui* as 'an anchor around our necks'. Although it was good to see the laid-up *Hotunui* on the move again, Don had reservations about how she would perform. Of more immediate concern was the performance of the Port Chalmers wharfies. Don watched in disgust as they loaded the house lot of timber, which had been delivered to the wharf in bundles with wire strapping, board by labour-intensive board. Also bound for Santo was a jet-boat, and to further assist with transport in the islands, Tim made

arrangements to transport one of his Hiller helicopters. This was carried, disassembled, inside a DC-3 that he had purchased from the National Airways Corporation. At Santo, the Hiller's reassembly would be done by engineer/pilot Rex Dovey, who had just joined Luggate Game Packers after flying Southern Scenic aircraft out of Queenstown through the 1960s, and by Hastings aircraft engineer, Temple Martin.

Tim travelled to Santo in September to set up the operation ahead of the ship's arrival. He invited his sister, Josephine, to run the house at Santo until Christmas.

By any standards Santo is hot and humid, with summer temperatures routinely in the high twenties and sometimes over 30°C. It lies at the southeastern corner of Espiritu Santo, an oddly-shaped island 120 kilometres long and up to 60 kilometres wide. The port at Santo is sheltered by a set of smaller islands. Its main business is fishing. The flat land around the town and along the eastern side of the main island is a green sea of coconut plantations, which produce copra for export. Coffee and cocoa plantations are also found here. Dominating the landscape is a bush-clad mountain chain in the west that rises steeply from the sea to reach an altitude over 1,800 metres. Throughout the island the soil has been enriched by the volcanic activity that created the high peaks, and hibiscus, frangipani and other tropical flowers add a colourful garnish to the green backdrop – all in all, a kind of paradise.

Residents of Santo in the New Hebrides admire the newly arrived helicopter. The residents called the helicopter 'Mix-master belongum Jesus Christ.'

Into this environment the *Hotunui* sailed towards the end of October 1970, with the full heat of summer not far off. She struck trouble right away, colliding with a reef after encountering hydraulic problems that affected steerage. She was pulled clear on the next high tide.

There were problems with slaughtering the cattle as well. The cattle, half wild, would sometimes charge out of the yards and back into an adjacent paddock. Unused to handling cattle on this scale, the slaughtermen resorted to using an ancient .22 rifle. Besides the slaughter method, which he labelled 'a real Dad and Dave operation', Tim had worries about whether the intense heat around the slaughterhouse would affect the quality of the beef. In the last week of November, with killing just begun for the second shipment to Noumea, he wrote to friend Mark Acland in Canterbury: 'Gee, it's primitive here … native labour I employ to help the butchering sleep on the floor of a shed. A piece of bread and a tin of corned beef and they are set for the day. In the slaughterhouse you have to watch out, though, knives are flying left, right and centre. They love killing …' Reflecting on his mood, he told Mark he had been through 'a pretty depressing period these last few weeks … continuing problems.'

Robert Wilson flew in to check out the project and in particular to see how Marcel Danton was doing on the marketing side at Noumea. Marcel had not invested in the venture despite suggesting he would. In the event, he said he would not invest until Tim had proved the venture would work. Robert quickly formed an opinion, describing the Santo end of it as a scene straight out of a Somerset Maugham novel. Within the work force and the country's double dose of officialdom, French and British, he detected two speeds – dead slow and stop.

Bill Black came up from New Zealand at one point, intending to contribute to the business. But he went home soon afterwards, brassed off with the French way of doing things. It was not his scene.

Tim's house and headquarters at Santo. The prefabricated Lockwood house was transported to Santo on the Hotunui *and erected by Wanaka builder Bob Wallace.*

End of the *Hotunui*

Two years after Tim sold the *Hotunui* to a South Pacific tuna fishing venture, a report came in that she had been boarded by pirates in the South China Sea. They stole her valuable prawn cargo. By 1977 she was renamed the *Jado Trader* and worked in Mexican waters. In 1992, Lloyd's Shipping Register deleted the entry for the ship, then more than 40 years old, with the comment, 'Existence in doubt'.

Hotunui *leaving Port Chalmers for the New Hebrides in support of Tim's beef export venture.*

By the time the *Hotunui* had made four trips to Noumea, Tim's list of snags and complications was starting to look fatal for the business. The local slaughterhouse workers decided for themselves when they would take their holidays, and through December and January simply downed tools and departed to their villages, and sometimes other islands. There were difficulties with procrastinating officials and problems with the *Hotunui*, whose freezer gear struggled to cope with the heat. Adding to the list of woes were crew hassles and the ever-present threat of hurricanes. At one stage Tim had envisaged selling off the venture as a going concern with good long-term prospects: one French territory supplying beef to another. It was a simple enough concept. By early 1971, however, it was clear to him that would not happen.

By May, he was describing the operation as a 'mess'. When he received an offer for the *Hotunui*, he decided to cut his losses. The *Hotunui* became a mothership again, this time for a tuna fishing venture run by an American company for Italian principals: another intriguing scenario for a coastal cargo ship operating in the South Pacific Islands.

Despite the time and energy he had invested in the Santo project, Tim had kept his personal radar turning on other business opportunities. He had observed the rise in venison prices in New Zealand after a slump in the late 1960s. With his directors heaving a collective sigh, he gave his full attention once more to an industry he knew backwards.

Trimming trees

In a demonstration of the Hiller's robustness, Tim would sometimes trim the foliage and small branches of trees with the main rotor blades. He wanted to show new crew that the machine would not fall to the ground the moment it struck vegetation. Picking up deer off tussock hillsides, he would judge how close to bring the machine by letting the blade tips of the main rotor clip the tussock tops.

THROUGH ITS PARTNER status in Game Collection Ltd, Luggate Game Packers had retained the right to kill or capture red deer across the bulk of Fiordland National Park. Another three-year licence was issued by the Park Board for the period 1970 to 1973. The board's decision underscored Luggate's efficiency at locating and killing deer, and transporting them to processing plants. The company was at the forefront of innovation, and this was a mark of Tim's inventiveness.

After the Santo experience, Tim immersed himself in the challenges of his New Zealand operation. The deluge of deer carcasses coming off the Fiordland mountains posed a land transport problem: how could they more efficiently be delivered to the processing plants?

Tim had an idea. He devised an extra-long trailer that was custom-built in Te Anau and based at the company's central recovery area at Te Anau Downs Station. The freshly-shot carcasses brought out by the Jet Ranger helicopter could be hung and cooled in it, up to 100 at a time. It was towed by an International truck that could carry over 100 carcasses as well. Staff dubbed it 'Monty Python'.

On the communications side, Tim and his operations manager, Don Spary, insisted on good radio links right across the operation. There were networked radio transmitter/receivers in homes, vehicles and field bases as well as in helicopters, planes, the *Ranginui* and the main office. Luggate was one of the first companies to install emergency locator beacons in its helicopters.

Ground shooters continued to work the wet Fiordland bush in tandem with the helicopter crews and the *Ranginui*. The company had its own bullets, which were ordered in lots of 100,000 (5,000 boxes, 20 bullets in each) and supplied by the Colonial Amunition Company, of Wellington. When Alpine Helicopters Ltd was formed out of a large part of the Luggate Game Packers' assets in 1971, each bullet had an 'A' stamped on the butt end. It helped the company's arms officer, Jim Faulks, to keep track of the ammunition and limit pilfering. Ammunition was an expensive part of the operation and boxes of bullets were occasionally stolen. It was acknowledged in pub talk and elsewhere that Alpine disposed of more ammunition than the New Zealand Army.

As for rifles, the Belgian semi-automatic FN .308 became the preferred brand and calibre, the best for hitting deer from a helicopter. Swiss SIG semi-automatic rifles were also used in later years. Most shooters reckoned on using two to three rounds for every deer killed – an average as low as 1.5 shots might be possible on a good day. It tended to depend on how far you were from the quarry and whether you were aiming for the rib cage or the head/neck area, a relatively small target from a shaking platform. Generally the shooters waited until they were 50 to 100 metres from the running deer before they fired. To minimise damage to the venison cuts, Tim asked his shooters for head- or neck-shot deer.

Examples of exceptional shooting were numerous and given a fair run in the pub afterwards. Gavin Overton was at the centre of one such story. Flying with Tim and a *Time Life* magazine photographer in the Shotover area, Gavin knocked over six deer with six shots in six seconds. He pulled off this feat on the ground after the Hiller had landed not far from a mob. It happened so fast the photographer could scarcely believe it.

Working at this sort of speed had its risks. Don Spary never stopped emphasising the issue of safety in the use of firearms as well as in the way the helicopters were flown and how crews behaved around them. There were certainly enough prangs and near misses to keep the personnel reminded of the need for safety.

In a Hiller, a red button near the top of the cyclic, where the stick bulges, was pressed to release the load from the hook. There was another button in the vicinity for radio communication. A distracted pilot might mistake one for the other, and more than one load of deer was ditched accidentally

Flying on a knife edge

As Tim's shooter for several years, Charlie Emmerson knew Tim pushed the limits. But he knew Tim was competent and had enormous ability in a tight situation. Once, to instil confidence in his shooter and demonstrate that a Hiller could fly even without power to the rotor blades, Tim showed Charlie how autorotation worked. Flying over flat land and about 30 metres above it one day, Tim flicked the magneto switch. That killed the engine instantly. Tim then calmly piloted the machine to a safe landing.

There was really only one area Charlie was concerned about. Typically, Tim would tire in the afternoons if he had been working late the previous night or been involved in long ferrying flights. He was an early riser and often had to manage on little sleep.

In southern Fiordland, during a good run of weather, Charlie was shooting with Tim and bringing home a hundred or more deer a day from the tops. One afternoon, Charlie noticed Tim's eyelids sagging and his head drooping ominously. He drew out his gutting knife and held it under Tim's chin so that if his head drooped again it would strike the blade.

Tim took the hint and shortly afterwards landed the Hiller on a hill where he slept sitting in the bubble. When Charlie returned from scouting deer, Tim's face and arms were sunburnt.

Tim and Charlie Emmerson reenact the knife-under-the-chin story at the Alpine Deer Group Reunion in March 2004. Colleen Emmerson

and irretrievably. Bill Black saw Tim's helicopter jettison a sling of deer over the Pyke forest in South Westland one day. As they fell, the carcasses spread out like skydivers and crashed into the forest canopy, scattering a flock of native pigeons. Bill wondered if Tim had hit the red button instead of the radio button while discussing some serious business deal.

The venison helicopters routinely flew with the port side door off. It enabled the shooter to sit with his left leg mostly outside the door. Although he had a 180-degree view of the terrain on the left side of the machine, the shooter's firing arc was less on account of the bubble's bulge. A left-handed shooter like Errol Brown, sitting on the left side of the machine, could reach out around the bubble and fire further forward of the chopper than a right-hander could. The shooter usually wore a lap belt but would dispense with it when recovery work required him to be constantly in and out of the machine. Considering the risks the pilots took to pursue deer, and the half-in, half-out position of the shooters, it was a wonder there were not more accidents.

What did Civil Aviation have to say about the use of a helicopter with one door off, the shooter perched halfway out, and crewmen at intervals leaping out of and back into the machine? The governing authority of the airways was fairly silent – almost to the point of denial. Don Spary used to say Civil Aviation simply could not comprehend the enormity of the risk-taking. To Don it seemed that the authorities took the view that no one would be mad enough to do it.

Tim's objective as a pilot was to provide a shooting platform that was as steady as he could make it, given the terrain and weather conditions. Although he preferred his shooters to make clean neck or head kills, he believed a body shot was best if a deer was running into the bush. 'We shoot to kill' was his policy.

Fiordland was a risk-a-minute region, yet the drier rangelands and forested valleys east of the main divide also presented ever-increasing challenges as the deer became scarcer.

On the western side, Christchurch-based Graham Stewarts, with up to eight venison helicopters, had cleaned out the easier deer. When venison prices dropped around 1967–68, and the company got into financial trouble, it was taken over by the Christchurch firm, T.J. Edmonds, better known for its manufacture of baking and custard powders. Edmonds Game Consolidated Ltd rose out of the takeover and won a contract to harvest deer in the northern sector of Fiordland National Park.

Around the Haast region, Makarora and Matukituki, the big mobs of the mid-sixties had been decimated. Rival operators were competing for the remaining deer and taking risks commensurate with the scarcity.

Alpine Helicopters Ltd

Alpine is a long-standing name in the helicopter business in southern New Zealand. The company was formed in 1971 to reflect the diversifying use of the Luggate Game Packers helicopter fleet.

Helicopters had become the swift pack ponies of the mountains, adept at transporting personnel and equipment with unprecedented speed and efficiency. They supported farming and fencing operations, mineral exploration, and the installation of huts in remote places. In the fields of tourism and outdoor adventure, choppers were also coming into the picture. In 1971, Alpine Helicopters initiated heli-skiing in the Coronet Peak area and in the Harris Mountains to the north, around Vanguard Peak.

An Alpine Helicopters Bell Jet Ranger with a sling load of deer, including some velvet antlers at the top. Malcolm Wheeler

POACHING HAD BEEN GOING ON for years amongst rival helicopter operators in South Westland and the lakes region of Otago. The Graham Stewart helicopters were in the west; Luggate's choppers had the east covered. Sometimes they strayed into each other's territory. When it came to keeping helicopters from looking beyond their authorised boundaries, permits did not seem to count for much. While deer were plentiful, the antagonism was irritating but generally more a matter of pride than profit. But as deer numbers fell, the points of conflict increased – not the least with ground hunters who were also trying to make a living out of venison. Many of them hated the sight of helicopters stalking their patch.

Occasionally, when conditions were clear over the passes, a Luggate helicopter might sneak a look into the heads of various West Coast rivers – and if they were observed by a rival operator they would hear about it. There were reports of helicopters being struck by bullets.

In the 1970s, an Alpine helicopter was involved in an 'offal drop'. Pilot Bill Winefield and shooter Patrick Nolan, incensed by something, dropped deer guts over a rival operator's barbecue picnic at Mussel Point, the main airstrip for the Haast region. When they landed at the other end of the airfield, there was a skirmish with the picnic's organisers and the pair ended up in the Greymouth Magistrate's Court, where they faced a number of charges.

Although Tim, Bill Black and other pilots distanced themselves from these sorts of antics, they could understand the intensity of the feeling that caused them. Sabotage was reasonably common – sand in the oil or transmission, water in the fuel. At Tuatapere, a helicopter was tipped over. Presumably the saboteurs wanted to disable the helicopters rather than cause injury or fatality.

Manoeuvrings at a business level were also intriguing. Tim's great rival through the venison years was Rex Giles, an early processor and exporter of venison, whose North Island company, Consolidated Traders, competed in the South Island directly with Luggate Game Packers (later with Alpine Helicopters) and also with the Edmonds operation. Based in the Taupo area, where he set up one of the country's first deer farms in 1970, Rex Giles had a company called Mountain Helicopters based at Greymouth, and it operated across a large part of Westland.

Tim encountered him briefly at the Tourist Hotel Corporation Hotel at Te Anau during the height of the controversy over access to the Fiordland National Park deer. At the time Rex had a lot to say to the media about how the Park Board was being unfair to him and other operators by denying them access to the Fiordland deer. Tim and Don Spary were in the hotel dining room one evening when Rex was also having dinner. The Alpine pair arranged with hotel staff for several paging messages to be broadcast for them, alternately, to convey the idea they were extra busy and productive. They hardly needed to pull such a stunt to convince anyone of their busy lives but the competitive, prankster side of Tim's nature found it irresistible.

Nonetheless, the Fiordland venison industry was fast becoming a cauldron, and rising prices for deer meat and co-products were fuelling it. Private meat hunters and some individuals who owned helicopters ignored the licensing process of the Park Board and boldly poached along the eastern fringes of the park. The terrain was so wild and remote, and the park boundary so well protected by a series of deep glacial lakes (Te Anau, Manapouri, Monowai, Hauroko, Poteriteri) that poaching was difficult to detect.

It all came out in the pub, and in Te Anau there was only one pub – the THC Te Anau Hotel down by the lake front. When pilots, shooters and gutters from different outfits mixed in the bar, an atmosphere akin to a rough-shod frontier- town saloon bar developed. With the boozing came the threats and counter-threats, and an occasional fist fight.

Through the turmoil, Alpine did not flinch in its desire to use the

Fiordland licence as a springboard for expanding its helicopter operations in other fields and growing its venison and velvet trade.

In 1972, the company purchased a two-seater Hughes 269B helicopter, which proved too small and low-powered. In November that year, Alpine took the plunge and added a Bell jet ranger to its helicopter fleet, which numbered eight by this time. Brand new from the Bell factory in Fort Worth, Texas, and worth a whopping $128,000, the jet ranger was an all-rounder, capable of lifting 680 kg (1500 lbs, almost 70 percent more than the Hiller). It had room for four passengers.

The investment in a jet ranger was prompted by the reducing deer numbers. With Alpine choppers having to hunt further afield, it was taking much longer to load the *Ranginui* at a single anchorage. Tim and his directors envisaged the jet ranger being able to transfer shot deer from the fiords away out west directly to Te Anau or a road end east of the national park – something the Hiller could not manage safely or cost-effectively. The first of its type based in the south, the jet ranger was a fast machine, with a cruising speed of 105 knots (195 kilometres per hour) – a little less under full load – and a maximum speed without load of 130 knots (240 kilometres per hour). Also, significantly, it had a good range. Eventually these advantages, and some new regulations requiring fast processing of shot deer, meant the jet ranger replaced the *Ranginui* as a venison carrier.

Bill Black became the jet ranger's main pilot. The helicopter had a simple routine: fuel in, deer out. As a rule, the carcasses were dropped at the Waiau airfield beside the Te Anau-Manapouri road and trucked from there to a processing plant at Mossburn, Te Anau or Cromwell. The new helicopter operated flat out when the weather permitted. It was illegal to operate after dark, but whenever there was a search-and-rescue call-out, the authorities would summon Bill and the jet ranger and waive the night-flying ban.

About this time, Bill carried a pistol, a .22 magnum, on his hip – not for threatening anyone who might bear a grudge against Alpine and try to sabotage his aircraft, but in case he went down in the mountains and needed to fire shots to attract attention. It was illegal then to conceal firearms, hence he wore the pistol openly.

In February 1972, the company's aircraft workshop at Luggate was shifted to Queenstown Airport at Frankton. It was a more convenient and strategic location. For one thing, it was closer to Fiordland, the main focus of Alpine's operations. In the south, Errol Brown became the field manager with responsibility for coordinating the myriad operations going on there. His wife, Carol, operated the Alpine radio base for Fiordland from their home at Te Anau. Tim and the Luggate management never

Ranginui sold

In one of the most bizarre shipping deals of the 1970s, the *Ranginui* was sold to a group of Americans who wanted a ship to help them establish the world's smallest nation on a set of sea-washed rocks called Minerva Reef, 400 kilometres southeast of Tonga. Tonga had actually raised its flag at Minerva in 1966 after a Tongan vessel was wrecked there. But that did not deter the Ocean Life Research Foundation, of New York and London (President, Morris C. Davis) from staking a counterclaim and heralding the 'Republic of Minerva'.

At low tide the would-be colonists erected an eight-metre tower on concrete foundations, Through an ambitious programme of dredging and further concreting, they thought they could build a platform of 13 acres over which to raise the republic's flag.

The day the *Ranginui* sailed into new ownership, six .303 rifles, ammunition and a concrete mixer were loaded aboard her. Tim had provided the rifles as part of the sale price. 'A gunship for the Minerva navy' was how the media sceptically reported the developments.

Alas, for the new owners, the Tongans reasserted sovereignty over the subtropical reef and raised their flag again. The reef was destined to remain a shipping hazard.

stopped emphasising the importance of good communications. Staff safety and business efficiency both depended on a reliable radio network, and Carol provided that reliability. Her counterpart at the Wanaka head office was Nola Sims, who had diligently managed the company's office at Luggate since 1968. She had become used to Tim's ways. He would often arrive back at the office after closing time and she would find evidence of a frenetic session of paper-pushing when she arrived for work in the morning. No matter how much mess he had made, he always seemed to know where to find things. From Luggate, the office was moved to a house in Ardmore Street, Wanaka, the town's main street, and some years later it was relocated to Wanaka Airport.

Expansion in the industry was driven by soaring venison prices, which reached an unrealistic $1 a pound in the spring of 1972 (compared to 20 cents a pound four years earlier). More helicopters than ever joined the chase.

In 1973, the last year of Alpine's second licence period in Fiordland, business was hectic. A record 3,500 tonnes of venison was exported that year from all New Zealand sources, representing about 140,000 carcasses. Alpine's best annual tally – the best for any company – was 35,000 carcasses. In the New Zealand market about this time, venison was as expensive as top-shelf marine fish like snapper and blue cod. Overseas, the main markets for New Zealand venison were West Germany and the United States. The Germans valued the gamey taste of the New Zealand product.

A cartoon depiction of the involvement of the Royal New Zealand Air Force in the Fiordland deer wars.

Investor interest in the industry surged following a foot-and-mouth outbreak overseas in early 1973, which kept venison prices high for a time. There were helicopters everywhere. At one stage, there were 50 helicopters operating in the south and 17 of them were Alpine's. Some owners were paying pilots and shooters by the poundage, thereby encouraging a frenetic amount of risk-taking and pushing of the limits to get amongst the deer. Alpine stuck to its salaried basis of payment, with bonuses at the end of the year to reward exceptional effort. Generally the Alpine pilots liked the arrangement. They sometimes met with Tim over a few drinks to discuss remuneration.

But there were ongoing niggles and threats from Alpine's competitors. Newspaper correspondence columns carried letters bemoaning the Alpine 'monopoly' in Fiordland. Rival operators, Rex Giles' Mountain Helicopters in particular, lobbied the Park Board and its staff for an opportunity to get at the Fiordland deer in the next licensing round. Alpine, meanwhile, expressed nothing but confidence in its future. It acquired a second jet ranger and boosted its fleet further by taking a 50 percent shareholding (later 100 percent) in the Timaru-based helicopter firm, Whirlwide. It had sufficient capacity to be able to offer Park Board and Forest Service staff flights at no charge to various parts of the national park for management or monitoring work. Tim regarded this as a reciprocal part of the contract and important for public relations.

In November 1973, the so-called 'deer wars' hit scary new heights.

The Alpine hangar at the Waiau airfield near Te Anau was deliberately set on fire. Up to 12 gallons of aviation fuel was siphoned from another company's helicopter parked near the hangar, poured over the hangar doors and set alight. The two helicopters inside, a Bell jet ranger and a Hiller, suffered some burn damage. The blaze would probably have burnt the hangar to the ground and destroyed the helicopters had it not been reported by a courting couple shortly after midnight.

Attracting a television news crew, newspaper reporters and two detectives from Invercargill, the incident highlighted the competitive mania besetting the venison helicopter industry in Fiordland. An arson attempt on the hangar had occurred a few weeks earlier but the kerosene used then had failed to ignite properly. And eight months before that, Alpine lost a Hiller in a suspicious fire at its Luggate hangar.

There were insurance repercussions, with premiums shooting upwards the longer the strife continued. At one stage, premiums against the loss of a helicopter rose to above 30 percent of its value. One major company stopped insuring the lives of helicopter pilots 'until existing occupational troubles have been resolved'. The reponse of Tim and his board was to tough it out. They had little choice.

Don Spary, now general manager of Alpine Helicopters, told the media the Government had to stop 'pussyfooting about'. There were too many helicopters chasing venison, he said, and too many of them were not obeying the rules.

The Government sent in the Air Force. Two RNZAF Iroquois helicopters arrived at Te Anau on a law-and-order mission. Their patrols might have curbed the poaching but they did not eliminate it. The poachers simply got more cunning. Helicopters hunting illegally, if they spotted a large, thudding Iroquois in the vicinity, were known to disappear into the forest, cutting a circular swathe as they descended.

What did hit the operators and force a rethink, however, was not so much an Air Force and Police presence but the declining price of venison. From the $1-a-pound peak, it trended downwards through 1973 and by December was back to 30 cents a pound.

Another factor was the rate at which deer were being killed. Tim was aware, as were others in the business, that this all-out attack on deer would soon extinguish an economic source. Tim and his directors envisaged a time when deer would be much more valuable captured live from the wild rather than carted out as carcasses. Deer farming looked to be the future.

Chapter 6

Fentaz, Farming and a Date in Africa

Late 1960s–1970s
Live capture ... Bulldogging ... bamboo pole method ...
tranquillisers ... first farms ... stun gun ... net gun ...
the jet-engined Hughes 500 ... married in Pretoria

CAPTURING DEER LIVE FOR FARMING VENTURES had been of interest to Tim since his effort on the Criffel Range in 1968 in aid of a Lincoln College experiment. The capture methods themselves were subject to a lot of experimentation – and Tim was in the thick of it. Before the syringe dart, and sometimes in tandem with it, there was the no-holds-barred bulldogging method. Of all the methods, it had more than its share of anxious moments. One such moment occurred in the winter of 1968, shortly before Tim's Queenstown crash. Tim would remember the incident in the Doolans Creek catchment of the Nevis, east of The Remarkables, as the day shooter-cum-bulldogger Gavin Overton disappeared.

There was a lot of snow around that day. Tim and Gavin were in a Hiller and cruising through the Doolans Creek catchment when they came upon a young red deer hind scrambling over the snow. Gavin said he would try bulldogging it. Tim brought the Hiller as close as he dared and his mate hurled himself off the skid on to the deer's back. Of stocky build, Gavin wrestled with the deer momentarily then lost his grip as he plunged through the snow to the bed of a small but deeply-incised creek.

What neither he nor Tim had realised was that at the moment Gavin hit the deer, it was crossing a snow bridge. Lighter and more agile than its assailant, the hind bolted away, leaving Gavin underneath the snow and in a high-sided trench he could not easily escape from. Crouching and at times crawling, he set off downhill following the narrow cavern of the creek bed, beneath the snow, until the creek sides were less steep and he could dig his way out.

Meanwhile, Tim was perplexed. Pulling the Hiller away from the face,

Collecting breeding stock for Criffel.

he had lost sight of Gavin the moment his shooter leapt out. Now he was mystified over where his mate had gone. Thinking he might be hooked up under the machine, he landed on a flat area. There was still no sign of Gavin. A few marks in the snow on the face above provided the only clues. Tim took to the air again. Eventually Gavin reappeared – cold and rather worse for wear – about 100 metres below where he had leapt out.

Bulldogging was not for the faint-hearted. It meant throwing yourself out of a moving chopper and on to the back of a terrified beast, riding it to a standstill, tipping it over, usually by twisting neck and head, and binding its legs. But until drugs and other technology came along, it was what you did.

Tim knew there had to be a better way, and that was how he came to be catching deer on the Criffel range, as described in the opening chapter.

On that exercise he was assisted by Colin Murdoch, of the Timaru firm, Paxarms, who had developed a muscle-relaxant drug that could be injected into the deer by a dart syringe fired from a specially designed pistol. Although the method was successful, Tim was concerned about dosage levels. In his opinion, there wasn't much difference between a dose that safely immobilised an animal and one that stopped its heart and breathing.

In 1969, shooter Jim Kane and pilot Bill Black designed a different method of injecting a drug into wild deer. When the bamboo pole method was first used, they were working on Nokomai Station. The two men more or less devised the method over a beer in the Garston pub. This was after they had tried two mechanical methods – first, a spring gaff whereby two jaws snapped around the fleeing deer's neck (too hard on the deer) and second, a lasso attached to the end of a pole, with pilot and shooter acting as aerial cowboys (too difficult to execute). Eventually they settled on delivering a tranquillising drug from a syringe attached to the end of a four-metre-long bamboo pole.

It worked like this: Jim, sitting in his usual place to the left of the pilot, held the pole in one hand and gripped the machine with the other. Like a horse-mounted knight of old jousting with a lance, he leaned out when Bill positioned the chopper close enough for the deer to be stabbed with the syringe. With this method, Jim and Bill captured over 600 deer on Nokomai and various other properties.

Research and development:
Maurice Duckmanton, Tim and
John Muir at the workshop in
Beacon Point Road, Wanaka.

Another development was a specially adapted rifle that fired a syringe dart: this was more accurate than the long-barrelled pistol. Meanwhile, Tim and his colleagues looked around for drugs with wider tolerance. They consulted an Austrian veterinarian, Dr Karl Klecker, who had observed the emergence of the New Zealand deer industry and was keen to ensure Tim's company selected the most appropriate live-capture drugs. Karl knew South African wildlife managers were using a drug called Immobilon, but it ran into animal health barriers in New Zealand because of its strong morphine connections. Karl then turned to a drug that had similar properties – Fentanyl citrate. In combination with Azaperone, a sedative, it was marketed from Belgium as Fentaz. Fentaz immobilised the quarry in five to ten minutes. Its Fentanyl component is a potent narcotic capable of stopping a deer in its tracks. Once the Fentanyl wore off (its effects could be countered by a reversal drug), the sedative kept on working for several more hours while the animal was in transit to its release site.

As it turned out, Alpine Helicopters were years ahead of bureaucratic thinking. The Animal Remedies Board and Department of Health took an age to register Fentaz – three years. Through this period Tim never stopped looking for alternative methods. He researched the idea of immobilising the deer with electricity. Next stop, the 'stun gun'.

Revelling in anything to do with research and development, Tim worked with an Arizona company which was a leading-edge developer of this sort of technology – electrical immobilization. Alpine used the name stun gun instead. It involved delivering a mild electrical charge from helicopter to deer, whose muscles were rendered rigid by the current. With advice from Dave Beaty, of the Telonics company in Mesa, and Neil Edward of Canterbury University's Electrical Engineering Division, Alpine developed a system whereby two darts carrying the live wires were shot from a double-barrelled gun. The darts towed out up to 30 metres of wiring, which was wound out from a large fishing reel. If all went well, both darts would lodge in the hide of the pursued deer and it would stay rooted to the spot in a quivering spasm, its muscular control overridden by the electric impulses, while the helicopter hovered nearby attached to the deer by the two wires. Next, the shooter would jump out to tie the animal's legs with leather straps resembling dog collars. He could only manage this if the pilot, who was regulating the current, eased it off a little and allowed the deer to regain some movement in its rigid legs. But if the pilot eased off the current too much, the deer would come back to life bucking.

The stun gun demanded precision flying. It put the pilot and shooter at more risk than usual because the machine was required to work at close quarters with the quarry. At times, there might be insufficient current, leading to comical but hazardous consequences.

Pilot Doug Maxwell, who joined Tim's operation in 1973, once tried to get so close to a stag that it leapt off the hillside straight at its persecutor. The shooter fired in self defence, and suddenly they had a large stag perched on the skid, rigid with electricity, and with an antler sticking through the bubble.

As the stun gun's day passed, the company continued to catch deer with drugs but added a refinement. Radio transmitters were incorporated into the tranquillising darts. Ever on the lookout for easier and quicker ways to capture deer, Tim travelled to Arizona to check out a tiny transmitter developed there by the Telonics firm. Its principal, Dave Beaty, said there were animals in the mountains nearby that had transmitters fitted so they headed out in a helicopter to show Tim how the equipment worked. Tim was convinced.

Fitting the transmitters to the darts back home, Tim tested the refinement. The lithium batteries allowed the transmitter to send signals for up to two weeks. This beeping radio contact meant the helicopter could quickly back off after landing a dart, thereby reducing stress to the deer. While the immobilising drug was taking effect, the pilot could go away and look for more targets. Later, the beeping signal would lead the pilot back to the injected deer, even in heavy bush.

If a deer ended up immobilised but alive in the forest, a crewman would be lowered on the chain through the canopy to the forest floor,

Orphaned fawns

The first deer captured from the wild were fawns, orphaned by the venison shooters who brought them back to wives or friends who would offer to feed and care for them. Red deer fawns were born in November/December, when shooting for venison was in full swing. A novelty at first, the stream of fawns became a valuable adjunct to the live-capture industry that evolved to supply deer farming. In the Luggate/Alpine operation, George McKay, who lived near Luggate township, played a key role in raising captured fawns. Raylene Jelley, at the Criffel farm, hand-fed many fawns, and in the Te Anau area, Kay Brown, Lesley Dawson and Adrienne Reid were among the caregivers. It was not uncommon to see 50 or 60 in a paddock in the early 1970s.

where he would strap the animal, place it in a special bag with its head sticking out, and hook it on to the machine for an exit by air to a new life on a farm. Once the animal had been delivered to a support truck, the helicopter would go back to collect the crewman, who retained the little transmitter. To help the pilot find him again in an expanse of forest that looked all the same, the crewman might make himself visible by climbing a tree to its uppermost branches and reboard the machine by stepping on to the skids. The manoeuvre required skill, confidence and fearlessness in good measure.

FROM MODEST BEGINNINGS in the late 1960s, the farming of red deer, ironically a biosecurity enemy of the State for decades, took hold in many parts of the country. In southern New Zealand, deer farming became significant because of the animal's high profile in the region and because Tim Wallis and his Alpine operation were making live deer available to farmers and investors, often through public auctions.

Between 1968 and 1970, Tim's operation captured about 400 deer, many of them from the Nokomai and Nevis Valley areas, and relocated them on to a large property at West Dome near Mossburn in Southland. The West Dome project involved about 120 hectares with perimeter fencing high enough to contain the springy red deer. The runholders, the Taylor brothers, were in partnership with Southern Lakes Game Foods, a company formed by the Dunedin company, Wilson Neill, with Robert Wilson a prime instigator and director. Luggate Game Packers later obtained

a shareholding interest. Southern Lakes owned the processing plant at Mossburn and was a partner in Game Collection Ltd, which held the Fiordland National Park deer recovery licences. As the first commercial deer farm in southern New Zealand, West Dome became a model that many farmers in the region – not to mention agricultural officials – watched very closely.

A lot of traditional sheep and cattle farmers were sceptical and suspicious that anything would come of it. What if these noxious animals escaped? In earlier years, a Parliamentary Select Committee had received submissions on the concept of deer farming. Deer-stalkers, catchment authorities and the Forest Service, as well as some quarters of the farming industry, were hotly opposed.

In 1969, though, the Government made deer farming legal. That year, Luggate Game Packers purchased ten acres of land in Golf Course Road adjacent to the Wanaka Golf Course – an area of humps and hollows formed by terminal moraine debris dumped by an ancient glacier. On this block of land, earmarked today for residential development as 'Fairway Close', a few deer captured live by the Luggate helicopters were kept on an experimental basis. From this small springboard, a major New Zealand deer farm called Criffel evolved.

Elsewhere in New Zealand, some farms 'recruited' wild deer by opening gates on to neighbouring Crown land and letting them walk in. The gates were closed by hand, trip wires or time clocks. By 1974 there were 18 licensed farms, most of which were in the North Island.

The farming of red deer herds based on stock captured from the wild was the future. In a relatively short time, New Zealand would be recognised internationally for its success in introducing a wild animal into an intensive grassland farming system.

In the early years, however, deer farming was a rather uncertain enterprise. The few farmers involved were feeling their way and not at all sure that traditional sheep and beef regimes would suit deer. This new farming frontier demanded innovation and flexibility from its participants. Government agencies, including those responsible for agriculture and animal health, also had to wrestle with new circumstances and unprecedented challenges. Officialdom expressed fears of a bovine tuberculosis epidemic breaking out among the herds of farmed deer. New rules on stock movement had to be formulated.

The Agriculture Department's research station at Invermay at North Taieri, near the city of Dunedin, became involved early on. In 1973, Invermay received its first red deer from West Dome Station, including some of the animals captured by Tim's operation a few years before. Two years later a research programme utilising wapiti from Fiordland and headed by agricultural scientist Dr Ken Drew, began investigating wapiti both as a farm animal in its own right and as possible heavyweight sire over red deer.

With agreement from the Fiordland National Park Board, Tim provided Invermay with wapiti – ten cows and three bulls. Major health problems soon showed up. Within a few months all the wapiti were dead, and post-mortem diagnosis revealed a problem with unfamiliar feed and environment that produced stress and susceptibility to infection. The next group of wapiti, which Tim also supplied, again with the Park Board's approval, were run on a hill block at Invermay instead of flat paddocks. The animals thrived. The research demonstrated that supplying the wapiti with supplementary roughage such as lucerne hay all year round benefited them. It also showed that bulls in captivity would readily mate with red deer hinds – at that time still a matter of debate.

As capture methods developed and markets for venison and co-products grew, the deer farming industry began to boom. By 1979, there were 800 farms. In the next two years the number practically doubled to over 1,500.

The expansion was greatly aided by a breakthrough in capture methods – nets launched from helicopters. Tim and his Alpine colleagues were at the forefront of developing this technology.

THE FIRST NET-CAPTURE of wild deer is usually accredited to a Hawkes Bay farmer, Goodwin McNutt. He first caught deer live by bull-dogging, a method that he quickly saw was hazardous to the health of the bulldogger, who had to take his chances leaping from the skid of a heli-copter. After trying it in the Kaimanawa Range back in December 1966, Goodwin reckoned there had to be a better way.

He devised a net mounted at the front of his helicopter that could be dropped on a fleeing deer. The net was released from the cargo hook then a crewman jumped out, blindfolded the deer, strapped its legs and placed it in a bag for hooking on to the machine. Although Goodwin achieved some success with this net design, it turned out to be just a prototype.

After Tim had worked for a few years with the tranquilliser and electric-immobilisation approaches to live capture, he turned to nets as the most cost-effective way. He was convinced that it would be the best method for the deer and one of the least complicated for the operator. In the past plenty of deer did not survive the trauma of capture. Some operators re-ported losses as high as 30 percent, at which rate the cost of the operation might outweigh the revenue from it. When he added into the cost equa-tion the deaths that occurred back on the farm in the first month or two after delivery – which could be as high as 15 percent – the need to devise the surest capture methods possible was uppermost in his mind. He aimed to reduce the deer fatality rate from the capture process to around five percent.

Net guns, when properly used, were as reliable as any of the capture methods. One advantage they had was that even if a deer died while being net-captured it could be sold as venison whereas one that had been tran-quillised was no good for meat. The net guns involved hand-held and skid-mounted apparatus. With a hand-held model, the shooter was in charge, pointing the gun out the open door as the pilot brought the chop-per to the optimal distance. Its main disadvantage was its severe recoil. There were numerous stories of broken fingers and cut hands.

Real progress came with nets mounted on the skids and triggered by the pilot. In 1977, the 'Gotcha Gun' was invented by two West Coasters, Ivan Wilson and Graham Jacobs, at Reefton. It was hand-made out of shotgun barrels and iron from an old bedstead. Around the same time, Te Anau brothers Nelson and Bill Thompson built the three-barrelled Thompson Gun. In the Nelson area, the Page brothers, of Takaka, were also working on net-gun design.

When Tim saw these early models, he felt a sense of challenge and opportunity – and that he could design and produce improvements. He set up a workshop in Wanaka dedicated to doing just that.

Meanwhile, through the mid-1970s, Alpine was equipping itself with new kinds of helicopters to meet the more demanding requirements of live capture, both in terms of agility in the air and cost-effectiveness.

Hurricane Tim in the Seventies

In the 1970s, a typical day in the life of Tim Wallis, managing director of Alpine Helicopters, starts at dawn. He flies to Te Anau in his Cessna 182 to talk through an issue with the Park Board about the company's Fiordland operation. Then he flies on to Invercargill to meet the regional Commissioner of Crown Lands. By early afternoon he is back in the mountains east of the main divide, talking in person to a runholder about gaining shooting rights on his property. Then he returns to Wanaka. After a couple of hours of paperwork in his office and phone calls about fuel supplies for the 20-odd Alpine helicopters in the air that day, he drives home. There he hosts a barbecue for velvet buyers from Korea and a few colleagues. The colleagues include staff from Criffel, the deer farm, who ask if he can be down at the yards by 7 o'clock tomorrow morning. Sure, says Tim, despite having just put in a 16-hour working day.

John Muir and Tim with deer captured by a skid-mounted net gun on the slopes of the Criffel Range.

Hillers were being phased out. Hughes 300s and 500s and Bell helicopters were in. Although the piston-engined Hughes 300 was more manoeuvrable in pursuit of deer than the Hiller, its speed and load capacity were no better. A jet-engined French-built Ecureil AS 350 was imported for tourism and deer recovery but the machine that really made a difference was the Hughes 500 – both C and D models.

The Hughes 500, also jet-engined, handled being thrown around in the air in hot pursuit of deer. With a cruise speed of 224 kilometres per hour, it flew 60 percent faster than a Hiller, and it could carry a third more. It also climbed much faster than a Hiller or Hughes 300. The span of the 500's main rotor blades was a bit shorter than a Hiller's, allowing it to operate closer to the slopes. The five-bladed D model, more powerful than the C, could carry an extra crewman in the back seat.

As the import licensing red tape loosened up in the 1970s, new helicopters poured into New Zealand. Many were directed into deer recovery for venison or for farms but others, including some of Alpine's machines, diversified into tourism, air and police ambulance work, mustering of stock on high-country runs, national park maintenance, and construction or maintenance contracts in remote locations.

Although fascinated by new helicopter models and uses for them, Tim had a more compelling interest that became a mission – to perfect live-capture techniques. It took him to various parts of the world, including the United States and southern Africa. In Africa, in 1974, he discussed the use of animal tranquillisers in the capture of protected wildlife. He embarked on that trip, a 35-year-old bachelor driven by business ambitions and a sky's-the-limit approach to life, and seemingly much too busy to give up bachelorhood. At least, that was what many family members, friends and colleagues thought. On that trip, he surprised them all.

DURING AUGUST 1974, in the South African high veldt, wildlife experts were working on a project to relocate a rare species of antelope in the world-famous Kruger National Park. The antelope were trapped live then injected with an immobilising drug before they were transported. Well-read on wild animal handling techniques in various parts of the world, Tim wanted to talk to the Kruger National Park staff and their advisers about their work. He thought their techniques might be relevant to capturing deer in the New Zealand mountains. In particular, he wanted to meet Dr Tony Harthoorn, an English-born veterinarian and world authority on wild animal capture, who took a leading role in the rescue of stranded

Pilot Bill Black and Jim Kane putting deer into carry trays after capturing by the pole method.

animals at the Kariba Dam in the 1960s and the equally famous relocation of endangered white rhinoceroses in Natal. Tony used an analgesic drug called Immobilon, with doses specified according to the size of the animal. Its effect could be reversed by another drug, marketed as Revivon, which revived the animal in 90 seconds.

Whereas Tim's life continued to be driven by his multiple business interests – and the research-and-development side in particular – he found time to keep in touch with girlfriend Prue Hazledine, who was involved in the film industry in London, working as a personal assistant and researcher for film director Ken Russell. Tim had been in London three times while on business trips overseas since breaking his back in 1968, and he called on Prue each time. His business in Britain included visits to deer parks in England and Scotland. On the way there or the way home, he usually checked out helicopters in the United States. Passing through London, he sometimes stayed at Prue's flat. They holidayed in Spain once. Between these visits he kept in touch with Prue through a regular exchange of letters. He even sent her an airline ticket – 'valid anywhere, any time, so use it when it suits' – in case she wanted to come home. Resourceful, talented and sociable, Prue enjoyed her London life. Producer Sandy Howard (*A Man Called Horse*) employed her for a time, but mostly she worked for the celebrated, if controversial, film director, Ken Russell (*Women in Love, The Devils, The Boyfriend*). After meeting Ken Russell in 1972 on one of his visits to London, Tim summed him up in a subsequent letter to her. 'You have to be one step ahead of him.'

So, while planning the August 1974 Africa trip, Tim suggested to Prue that she might like to join him there. Prue agreed, saying she could take two weeks off work. After meeting Tony Harthoorn in Pretoria they headed north and booked into the Sabie River Bungalows at the edge of Kruger National Park. Tim wanted to learn how the park staff immobilised wildlife. He also had a plan that had nothing to do with catching antelopes. On the first evening, during dinner, Tim suggested it might be a good idea if they were to get married. Prue asked him if this was a proposal or a proposition. But, either way, she was of a mind to say yes. She thought it a very good idea.

At that point, with diners around them offering congratulations, Tim and Prue had their table shifted outside into the garden. Tim ordered a bottle of Dom Perignon and when they had finished it they had another one. In the course of downing the champagne in the rarified air of the high veldt they discussed the wedding and realised they both felt daunted by the prospect of arranging such an event at home. Having recently heard from Tony Harthoorn and his third wife, Lynda, about their Pretoria Town

Hall wedding, Tim decided to enlist Tony's help with setting up a similar registry wedding. Next day, Tim and Prue set off on the four-hour drive to Pretoria not knowing even whether a time had been set for the ceremony. They stopped at the first jeweller's store they saw in the main street of the South African capital and Tim bought a wedding ring. When they arrived at the university to find Tony he told them that they were the first couple on the list next morning and that he and Lynda and his children would be delighted to attend.

Tim and Prue were married on 22 August 1974. They spent the night at a motel called the Oklahoman in Pretoria before going back to Sabie River. While using the motel's swimming pool in front of other guests Tim chose not to wear the calliper and held his paralysed leg in a locked position with his hand while walking to and from the water. Prue was surprised at how self-conscious he was about the disability. It had never bothered her.

Next day the receptionist at the Sabie River Bungalows welcomed the couple back. Tim, beaming proudly, asked if the honeymoon suite might be available. It was. They could have it. Noting their names in the lodge's guest book, and reflecting the prudishness of Afrikaner society, the receptionist asked the couple in a tight-lipped manner: 'I take it you are still Mr and Mrs Wallis?'

Tim and Prue on their wedding day, outside the Pretoria registry office.

Sabie River, South Africa, where Tim proposed to Prue.

Tim's family gathered in Wanaka at Easter 1975 for a celebration and blessing of his marriage to Prue. There was a service at St Columba's Church in Wanaka followed by a gathering at the Wanaka home of Tim's mother, Janice. From left: Tim, Janice, Prue, Tim's brother, George, George's wife, Jo, and Tim's sister, Josephine.

Years after marrying Prue at Pretoria, Tim would admit in a letter to his good friend Mark Acland that when he attended full-blown wedding ceremonies of friends – with church service, reception, wedding breakfast and dancing to a live band – he felt 'sad that I had just taken Prue to a registry office'.

From the Transvaal, Tim and Prue travelled in different directions. Prue returned to London to complete her work there and give notice of her intention to return to New Zealand in October to join her husband. Tim had some urgent work back in New Zealand. He flew home a week early to tell family and friends, in particular Prue's parents, about the wedding. They were delighted by the news. On the work front, Alpine was in the midst of its third deer-recovery licence in Fiordland National Park, and with the approach of summer, venison and velvet production and live capture for farming would soon be in full swing. Moreover, Alpine's first live deer export consignment was scheduled to happen in a few weeks.

Chapter 7

Accessing Asia

1960s–70s–80s
Oriental medicines ... Bill Bong, velvet trader ... two
Korean dealers ... Luggate upgrade ... live deer to
Taiwan ... Kung See parties ... baby Toby in Seoul ...
the challenge of China ... Tim shows a leg ... deer
farmers organise

AN ELDERLY CHINESE COUPLE, market gardeners from the Kakanui area in North Otago, arrived at the Luggate Game Packers factory one day, looking to buy deer tails. Factory manager Jim Faulks welcomed them into the office. The visitors were dressed rather roughly. The woman had on an old coat and the man's clothes appeared tatty to Jim. They asked if they could see the factory's stock of deer tails. There were a few thousand in frozen storage at the time, worth about $15 each.

Jim asked them to hold on while he got in touch with the boss. He phoned Tim at home. Tim agreed to come down and soon the visitors and Tim were getting down to business.

'How are you going to pay for the tails?' Tim asked, knowing that Jim had already offered an opinion over the phone about the impecunious appearance of the visitors.

'In cash, Mr Wallis,' was the old man's response. And with that he proceeded to tip out $60,000 in notes on to a table, knowing he could get it all back with interest by exporting the tails to China or other parts of Asia.

THE STORY of Tim's life is a welter of overlapping and intersecting events and adventures, projects and technology. A true sense of its pace, intensity, variety and colour through the 1960s, seventies and eighties is best gained by observing it from above for a time then swooping in on the action, highlights and nuances – not unlike the way a helicopter hunter

The Taiwan Raw Medicine Association met with Tim, Mark Acland and Robert Wilson when the New Zealanders visited Taiwan in 1967.

surveys the prospects before zooming in on the target. From Tim's interests in live deer capture – and a marriage that took many by surprise – the story turns now to the product end of the deer industry, and particularly to deer products other than venison. The markets are in Asia, including China, where it all started.

In Chinese traditional medicine deer products abound. Velvet, the soft stage of antler growth, has been used as a medicine, in dried form, for over 2,000 years. A Chinese medicine shop may offer for sale rhinoceros horn, seal pizzle and tiger bone as well as herbal medicines such as ginseng root. But no plant or animal matches deer for versatility. Besides velvet, deer produce tails, sinews, pizzles, embryos and blood that are valued for a variety of medicinal purposes. Also, the tail hair of deer is turned into calligraphy brushes and trout flies, eye-teeth become jewellery, hard antler finds a use as light brackets, candelabras and knife handles, and deer skin is converted to leather for clothing, gloves, hats and footwear. Deer hide is much stronger than the skins provided by traditional livestock. This means that, when it is machine-thinned, it will take on a quality more like a fabric than a skin – a point not lost on the fashion industry.

But velvet is what the Oriental pharmaceuticals market has long coveted. About two-thirds of the weight of velvet antler is water and this needs to be removed before it is an acceptable medicinal product. The drying process is critical to potency and therefore market price. The traditional

Oriental way is to blanch the velvet in boiling water then hang it out to air dry for some weeks.

The blanching part of the process, akin to pressure cooking, is designed to disperse the blood evenly through the velvet. The antler blood content, colour and condition are also important factors in the potency and value of velvet as a medicine.

Processors tend to guard their methods well. Velvet can easily be too dry or not dry enough. Its preservation has much to do with the drying process. Bill Bong, the Hong Kong-based oriental medicine broker who came to New Zealand in 1962 to encourage an export trade in velvet, kept his process a secret. When Tim, Robert Wilson and Mark Acland visited him in Hong Kong in August 1967 they were warmly received by Bill Bong at his office in the heart of Hong Kong's Oriental medicine district. But they never got near enough to his velvet drying process to know how it worked precisely. Accompanied by Bill, the New Zealanders travelled to Taiwan to see first hand how the natural medicine market worked in that country and how Bill accessed it. Bill introduced his New Zealand connections to a number of medicine retailers and brokers. He also introduced them to city night life, Taiwan style: Mark Acland noted how easily Tim slotted into Asian social life. Mark attributed his acclimatisation not only to his friend's genial and attentive nature but also to his ability to treat people as equals. Tim – an expert host himself – also fully appreciated the Asian tradition of hospitality.

Bill Bong not only showed Tim the importance of hospitality in Asia; he also reiterated the view he had expressed in New Zealand: that more money could be made in the medicine market than in venison. Over the years, accessing overt and undercover medicine markets in China, Hong Kong, Korea and Taiwan, Bill made his point. Duty-free Hong Kong was the 'front door' for a trade that earned him a fortune.

Although Western media highlight the aphrodisiac properties of velvet and pizzles, deer co-products are revered in certain Asian cultures not just for their promotion of sexual vigour but also as a general tonic promoting long life. Some of these raw or natural medicines are given to children as a tonic or taken variously by adults to forestall heart disease, alleviate arthritis, reduce back or kidney pain and slow the ageing process. Users place more faith in the product's ability to prevent disease and ill health rather than in its effecting a cure. Velvet, in particular, is thought to increase blood flow and thus enhance a person's general health.

Scientists at the Invermay agricultural research centre near Dunedin have tried to identify the substances in dried velvet that might assist good health. They have produced extracts and tested them rigorously against

The velvet phenomenon

In New Zealand red deer and wapiti, the hard antler falls off in late winter (earlier in mature stags) and the new season's growth begins in September/October in anticipation of the mating season or 'roar' the following autumn. During the 'roar' the stags use their antlers in 'display mode' when competing for breeding hinds and, occasionally, in head-to-head combat.

Velvet antler is harvested towards the end of the year, some 60 to 70 days after the new antler begins to sprout and before the soft cartilaginous tissue hardens. During the most rapid period of growth the antler can increase by two centimetres (almost an inch) a day – a remarkable growth rate that continues to puzzle scientists.

In the deer industry the name, velvet, describes the whole of the antler in its soft-tissue stage, when it is warm to the touch. Massed fine hairs or velvety 'fur' surround the growing antler. Towards Christmas, the calcifying process starts and the antler hardens to become the familiar rack much sought after by deer hunters during the 'roar'. A fully-grown hard antler is indistinguishable from mammalian bone. With mating over, the hard antlers remain on the stag through the winter until cast off naturally at the base or pedicle in late winter, when the new cycle starts.

New Zealanders familiar with red deer and their close cousins might be surprised to learn that in some other species of deer, notably reindeer, antlers are grown annually by females as well as the male animals.

Velvet awaits processing at the Luggate factory.

placebos. Although there is still not a lot of empirical proof that velvet antler products provide all the medicinal benefits claimed for them, the Invermay scientists have demonstrated that velvet can stimulate the immune system. In October 1993, it was reported that people involved in the studies and taking velvet experienced an increase in white cell production. More recently, tests have shown that velvet antler extracts have a marked beneficial effect on healing wounds.

In 2003, a paper in the *International Journal of Sport Nutrition and Exercise* described an experiment centred on the University of Otago School of Physical Education in Dunedin, involving 38 young men who took velvet extract or powder over a ten-week period. Tests were conducted against placebos. Up to then, most studies had involved mice, rats and rabbits. The findings were inconsistent. However, the men taking the powder recorded a slight increase in knee strength – a finding that caused at least one Chinese medicine website to claim great things for athletic performance from velvet.

Years ago, Russian scientists extracted a drug that was given to pregnant women to assist them during and after childbirth. The day Western science proves incontrovertibly that medicines produced from velvet and other deer co-products will prolong human life and enhance wellness is the day the industry takes off in the United States and other Western countries. But the process is proving to be a long and expensive one.

In the early years, before deer farming started in New Zealand, velvet was harvested from feral deer. Velvet became a valuable sideline to the venison export trade for many high-country farmers, especially when they were told that the velvet from 200 stags was worth more than the wool from 5,000 sheep.

In the beginning New Zealand velvet was exported frozen and unprocessed, in which condition it was termed 'green'. Processing did not begin in earnest in New Zealand until 1974, when a thick-set Korean trader, K.J. Kim, set up a velvet drying operation. With the support of Robert Wilson and Wilson Neill Ltd, Kim leased space in Tim's Luggate factory and installed two large ovens.

A failed film director in his forties who was now an importer and wholesaler, Kim brought his wife and daughter to New Zealand with him. During the velvet season, which lasted several months, they would stay at a motel in Luggate. Kim's wife was never far from his side. His daughter, O.K. Kim, interpreted for K.J., who spoke very little English. An attractive young woman in her early twenties, she was known to factory staff as 'Miss Kimmy'. With the Luggate factory set up to process venison, the velvet operation was a separate exercise – and largely a secret one.

In the mid-1970s, another Korean, Jung T. Wang, better known as Johnny Wang, arrived in New Zealand to capitalise on the growing production of antler velvet from increased deer farming activity. He entered into a joint venture with the Christchurch-based Edmonds company, who were in friendly competition with Luggate and Alpine Helicopters. Johnny had emigrated to the United States in 1961 in the wake of the Korean war and had established a business in San Francisco. The Oriental medicine trade

Korean tonic

A concoction of blood from a top-quality velvet antler, mixed with whisky at a one-to-one ratio, is worth big money in Korea.

The Koreans make a custom out of drinking velvet blood, and toasting friends and family with it. A common practice is to catch the spurting blood from the first velvet harvest of the season, swallow it quickly then chase it down with a Scotch, preferably Johnnie Walker Black Label. Speed is important. You are advised not to hesitate otherwise the blood might congeal.

Sometimes the blood is collected in half-empty bottles of Scotch or gin. The alcohol preserves the concoction for up to a year.

Korean K.J. Kim and Tim with deer products at the Luggate factory.

San Francisco-based Johnny Wang grading velvet.

back home in Korea was a major part of his business. He also supplied the natural medicine markets in China. Tim and Johnny Wang would meet from time to time, and exchange news of their respective activities. Tim found his competitor, who spoke English reasonably well, a useful contact in the Oriental medicines business who freely gave advice and information.

Tim's relationship with K.J. Kim, on the other hand, was never as open. When Tim and his directors decided to upgrade the Luggate factory to produce dried velvet end-products, they were in effect competing head-to-head with Kim and his operation. Tim suggested a partnership. The Kims turned down the offer, at which point they packed up their Luggate plant and left.

About this time the Luggate Game Packers factory, run by Alpine Helicopters, was going through a metamorphosis, with co-products set to become a much larger part of the operation than venison. The factory was now managed by Murray Hamer, a trained butcher from Dunedin, who joined Luggate in 1971. When he started with the company, the factory had two or three staff and was processing 30 to 40 deer a day, most of them coming from South Westland. Co-products were just a Saturday morning task.

In the years to come, the factory would convert wholly to processing velvet and a range of co-products. Instead of air drying the velvet, as happened in some parts of the world, the velvet at Luggate was oven dried at relatively low temperatures. An important test of optimal quality was its redness. The redness of a cross-section of the velvet had to be just right, neither too light nor too dark.

Through the production at Luggate and other centres, New Zealand became the main Western country competing with Russia and China for access to the Korea natural medicines market.

Not surprisingly, Tim wanted to promote the deer business for all its worth. If deer products were so valuable in Asia, would boosting the farming of the deer themselves in countries like Taiwan and Korea not be an appropriate investment opportunity? Who better to supply the deer than Alpine?

FRESH FROM HIS MARRIAGE to Prue in South Africa (and rather amused by the wide-eyed, eyebrow-raised reaction to the wedding news among some friends and colleagues) Tim wasted no time making arrangements for another tilt at innovation in the deer industry.

Taiwan was the target, live deer the product. From his 1967 visit to Taiwan, Tim knew something about this non-Communist offshoot of

mainland China and its market in 'deer horn' and other medicinal prod-ucts derived from deer. He knew, too, that Taiwan had no deer farming to speak of. You were a rich deer farmer in Taiwan if you owned five deer. The island had native sika deer, which inhabited the forested mountains and hill country. Pigs, chickens and ducks were the commonest livestock on the small farms of crowded Taiwan, where most farms were shed-based – or under the house. The country was under martial law, ever alert to military threats from the Communist mainland. Tim figured there was a market for red deer among retired generals and other military personnel of rank in Taiwan, some of whom were setting up farms with their pensions. It was likely the generals could be persuaded to invest in deer farming for the medicinal market.

A stretch DC-8 airfreighter was chartered for a flight to Taipei, Tai-wan's capital, with 300 deer. Most of the stock were yearlings and a few of the hinds were pregnant. George McKay had reared about a third of the consignment on his Luggate property after they were captured as orphan fawns. The rest came from the hill block of Alpine's Criffel deer farm. Tim's company negotiated this consignment through a Hong Kong-based Chinese businessman, Samson H. Wong, who pre-sold the deer in lots large and small.

In the last week of November 1974, eight truck-and-trailer units transported the deer north to Christchurch and they were loaded directly on to the DC-8. It was a 14-hour flight to Taipei with a refuelling stop at Darwin.

First live deer airlift – a chartered stretch DC8 loads at Christchurch for the flight to Taiwan. Prue Wallis

'Beautiful One'

The subtropical island of Taiwan was known to college students of Tim's era as Formosa, a Portuguese name meaning 'Beautiful One'. Lying 120 km off mainland China's coast, Taiwan had been politically separate from the Communist People's Republic of China since the late 1940s. Taiwan's 20 million people, 70 percent urban, live densely around the fertile coastal plain of their largely mountainous island. In land area, Taiwan is only slightly larger than the Otago region.

Tim and Mark Acland in Taiwan in 1967.

On board were Tim and his wife, Prue (not long back from London), and the manager of Alpine's Criffel farm, Les Smith, who was assigned to look after the deer in quarantine at Taipei. Awaiting the plane's 5 a.m. arrival at Taipei was the Austrian veterinary consultant Karl Klecker, of Fentaz fame. After a three-week quarantine period the deer were despatched to their new homes a world away from Wanaka.

The Taiwan consignment paved the way for a period of live-deer exporting by Alpine through the 1970s, 1980s and into the early 1990s that sent New Zealand red deer all the way to Korea, Japan, Ireland, Australia and, in a major way, to Canada.

TIM HAD DECIDED early in his research of the Asian deer medicines industry that Korea would be the main market. Top-quality velvet was worth a fortune. A kilogram of it could fetch as much as an average Korean worker earned in a year.

Through the 1960s and 1970s, South Korea bounced back economically from its three-year war with Communist North Korea, the Democratic People's Republic. When North Korean troops crossed the border at the thirty-eighth parallel in 1950, the United States provided military support for South Korea. American defence strategists feared that the invasion, if successful, would trigger a Communist domino takeover through Southeast Asia. In the event, the forces of the North were repulsed; the border, which bisects the Korean Peninsula, remained where it was established after the Second World War.

In the wake of the war came a rapid industrialising of the South Korean economy. A lot of Koreans became wealthy as a result. The natural medicines market was one sector of the economy that boomed, and foreign traders could access it after the South Korean Government lifted tariffs on velvet and other products. Bill Bong was among the first to take advantage of this. In Korea, he could sell velvet for two to three times the price he could get in Hong Kong.

Whereas the velvet market in China was largely supplied from its own deer herds, in Korea there was very little deer farming. The deer farms that did exist were generally smallholder operations, stocked with sika deer that were typically fed grass collected by hand. Their spotted sika, native to eastern Asia, although smaller than red deer, produced bigger than expected antlers because they had been genetically selected for antler size over many generations.

Initially, Tim was interested in Korea for its velvet market. He travelled to Korea in 1973 with Peter Elworthy, a South Canterbury farmer and a long-time friend of Tim's. (Peter was a contemporary of Tim's brother, George, at Christ's College) and used to holiday with the Wallises on the

A small-holding of deer in Korea.
Prue Wallis

Above: Visiting a Korean cultural centre – Tim, Prue and Dr Karl Klecker, flanked by two guides in traditional costume.

Above right: Tim being fed at a ceremonial Kee Sung dinner party in Korea. Prue Wallis

West Coast. When Tim became involved in the venison trade, live capture and farming, Peter Elworthy kept in close touch with Tim and introduced deer on to his own farm before deer farming was properly established. Among those deer were some weaner hinds and stags caught as orphaned fawns by Tim's crews and hand-reared to weaner age. Peter flew Tiger Moths and he and Tim would sometimes fly their planes in the skies above Wanaka and in the evening discuss deals over deer at Tim's home.

Tim's trip to Korea with Peter was all about velvet. The Koreans were superb hosts, fond of entertaining visitors at elaborate dinner parties called Kee Sung, during which beautiful women would make sure the guests were served promptly and adequately with food in a multiplicity of bowls, and seemingly endless drinks. The Kee Sung parties were generally located in a small house and run by women. Only men attended.

Ceremonial drinks included one called 'Three P Wine', which turned out to be a cocktail of penis of seal, dog and deer. The guests had to drink it. There was no choice in the matter if they wanted to maintain cordiality and business prestige.

The Koreans' hospitality extended to tours of the countryside. One afternoon, after an especially long Kee Sung, Tim and Peter were taken for a drive into a magnificent mountain district. They came to a winding road. The weather was warm (in South Korea, which has a continental climate, summer temperatures reach the high twenties) and a portly Korean trader was droning on to Tim about the velvet market. Tim started to reply when all of a sudden his eyelids closed and his head tipped forward: he had fallen asleep in mid-sentence. Peter knew of Tim's reputation for taking naps in the afternoon while in the air but had never seen anything like this before. The driver pulled over so Tim could have a short sleep. After a few minutes he woke up and immediately resumed his conversation with the Korean trader as though there had never been any interruption.

Nonetheless, through force of personality and an obvious flair for business, Tim made a strong impression with his Korean hosts. Peter observed their respect for Tim. They seemed almost to worship him. The Koreans were fascinated by more than his business mind, however. They enquired about his limp and Tim would explain to them that he had broken his back in a helicopter crash. A medical academic suggested sympathetically that he might like to try a cure by acupuncture. Tim's usual response was that he was not looking for a cure. There was no cure.

Back home after this trip with Peter Elworthy, Tim and his directors wrestled with ways in which to capitalise on the Korean interest in deer horn. They knew the Korean elite classes would willingly pay high prices. The live-deer shipments, starting in the mid-1970s, represented an extension into an aspect of Alpine's business that was rapidly expanding.

Tim subsequently made a number of visits to Korea. In May 1975, when Prue was six months pregnant with Toby, their first son, she and Tim spent six weeks in Seoul and surrounding areas. Korean summers are generally hot and wet, and this one was no exception. Tim and Prue rented an apartment in Seoul.

They visited farms which had deer already or were about to acquire New Zealand deer. They entertained Korean contacts, up to about 15 at a time. In a spare room in the apartment they set up little cinema where Tim screened Super 8 film footage of his homeland, in particular the Wanaka area and Criffel deer farm. Prue made several visits to Korea with Tim, who was often flying there to do business.

The birth of Toby on 1 September 1975, a huge event in their lives, did not curb Tim's trips away, to other parts of New Zealand or overseas. Toby became a well travelled baby, visiting Korea and other parts of Asia as well as the United States. In Korea with Toby, Prue put her research expertise, developed in the London film industry, into practice while Tim went about his own work. Prue found out all she could about Oriental medicines. There was a whole faculty at Seoul University devoted to the subject, which she discussed with the dean of the faculty, a Dr No. She also researched Korean cookery and seized on a recipe for Bulgogi, a beef stew that was delicious when it incorporated venison.

Tim also took a shine to bulgogi and, back home at Wanaka, with Prue's help or on his own, he would offer it to his frequent venison and velvet visitors from Asia and elsewhere, and at times cook it at events such as a deer farmers' conference.

After a number of live deer shipments into Korea, the Korean authorities expressed some concern over the practice. Among other things, they

Populous Korea

South Korea, just two-thirds the size of New Zealand's South Island, has a population of about 45 million. Like Taiwan, South Korea is largely mountainous or hilly and most people live on the coastal plains. The capital, Seoul, embraces ten million people. Forest covers two-thirds of the country. Japan lies to the east, China, across the Yellow Sea, to the west.

Farming is widespread. There are over one and a half million farms, and they commonly raise pigs, cattle and goats. By New Zealand standards, though, they are pitifully small and unmechanised, with the average farm size under 2 hectares.

Smuggling rife

When the South Korean Government slapped an import tax on deer horn amounting to around 100 percent of its value, the trade went underground. Smugglers had a field day. Much of the product was routed through Hong Kong and smuggled into South Korea by boat.

were concerned that the vigorous-looking red deer imports from New Zealand might devalue existing sika stock. A ban was placed on imports of live deer, and no more live deer were accepted into Korea until 1992.

A LONG-STANDING home of oriental natural medicines is mainland China, famous not only for its acupuncture but also for its herbal and animal remedies. As far as deer are concerned, the Chinese have generally made more use of deer body parts for medicinal purposes than of deer meat. In North China venison was the meat of the feudal elite classes but velvet, tails, sinews and so on were widely available and their use traces back to the ancient dynasties of China.

Deer tails are purchased in dried form, sliced and added to soups. Undernourished children are fed deer-tail soups. Tails also come in tablet form. Deer sinews are popular in many parts of China, coming in powdered form and mixed into soups or stews. Pharmaceuticals made from deer pizzles are for men and more likely to be found in North China than elsewhere.

In 1981, the New Zealand deer industry investigated the markets and deer farming industry in China. The New Zealand Deer Farmers' Association organised a trip to China and sent a delegation to explore, in particular, the prospects for marketing New Zealand velvet and other products. At the time, China's leaders were pushing on with modernising the vast nation, instituting economic reforms and trying to improve the standard of living for its one billion people – a fifth of humanity. Two years earlier, in July 1979, China had re-established diplomatic ties with the United States, Japan and Western Europe after a period of political turmoil. China was opening up.

Although the Chinese were not as preoccupied with velvet as the Koreans, they still processed a reasonable amount of velvet. The delegation was led by the association's president, Bernard Pinney, a Southland farmer, and included Tim and his Canterbury farming friend Mark Acland. By plane and steam train they travelled through China. North China was where they spent most of their time. They were warmly received by a people keen to exchange ideas with farmers from another land.

Tim had his Super 8 cine camera going flat out. Not only was he delighted to be experiencing the world's most populous country and the third largest in land area after the Soviet Union and Canada; he was riveted by the prospect of seeing, first hand, the velvet processing so long kept a secret by his Asian associates, Bill Bong, K.J. Kim and Johnny Wang. As he told a conference of deer farmers back in New Zealand a few years after the trip: 'At last we had gained access to study the experts.'

Korean Bulgogi

A Korean dish that Tim sometimes prepared for his visitors was bulgogi. Here is the recipe, renamed 'Alpine Bulgogi' because venison replaces beef:

1 lb (450g) shoulder or neck venison (sinews removed)
2 level tbsp cooking soya sauce
1 level tbsp sugar
1 level tbsp sesame salt
1 tbsp sesame oil
4 medium green spring onions, chopped 2–3 cm
3 cloves of garlic finely chopped
1 tsp fresh ginger finely chopped
2 tbsp white wine
1/8 tsp black pepper

Sesame salt
Use 1 teaspoon of salt for every cup of sesame seeds.
Heat a large pan. Spread the sesame seeds on it. Do not plan to do anything else while the seeds are cooking as they burn readily. Stir constantly while they brown and pop. When they are an even dark golden brown colour, semi-pulverise them in a food processor or with a mortar and pestle. Add the salt. Mix thoroughly.

Cut the venison into thin slices across the grain. This is more easily done if the meat is half frozen. Marinate the meat in the remaining ingredients – including sesame salt – for at least 2 hours. Grill on a hot barbeque plate or frying pan.

Tim and Prue cooking Bulgogi.

The New Zealanders inspected velvet processing plants and through interpreters found out what they could. The visitors were also shown how selective breeding could be employed to improve velvet quality and output.

Tim's interest in the Chinese deer industry was matched by Chinese interest in him.

The Chinese were intrigued both by his expansive personality and his impressive size. At each place the delegation stopped, Tim would invariably attract an inquisitive group of Chinese around him. One day he was the centre of attention at a large military airbase, where the mechanics and other staff were unused to Europeans. With an interpreter's help Tim engaged them in fractured conversation. The locals were intrigued by his friendliness. They also noticed his limping gait. The mystery of his limp proved too much for one man. He bent down and pulled up the leg of Tim's trousers, revealing a steel calliper extending upwards from his shoe.

Investigating the deer co-products trade in China with a New Zealand Deer Farmers' Association delegation in June 1981. Tim is flanked by Korean Mrs Kim and her daughter, O.K. Kim. Mark Acland and New Zealand deer farmer Hans Fitzi are also in the group.

The People's Republic

Mainland China has been under Communist rule since 1949. From the late 1970s, following the death of Chairman Mao in 1976, China began throwing off its self-imposed isolation, although its borders were closed again in 1978 for a period. By the time the New Zealand deer farmers made their study visit, China was actively seeking to expand its contacts with the rest of the world. As the New Zealanders discovered, livestock farming is dominated by pigs (over 300 million), cattle (over 100 million) and sheep (110 million). Compared to these statistics, deer farming in China is small.

Tim was then required to explain what was going on.

First, he had to describe piloting a helicopter and how, after hitting wires, he broke his back in the crash. The group of locals around him thought it all a great joke. They fell about laughing. And Tim laughed with them.

Returning from China with pages of notes about velvet processing there, Tim later used the knowledge to upgrade his Luggate factory. The 1981 visit also sparked exchange visits by Chinese deer farming delegations to New Zealand and Tim hosted a number of them at Wanaka.

The New Zealand Deer Farmers' Association had a pivotal role in these sorts of exchanges and there was much discussion among its members about what, if anything, New Zealand should disclose about its deer farming to other countries. Politics played a part in the association's deliberations from the beginning.

The NZDFA was formed in Wellington in June 1975. There had been a New Zealand Meat Board field day at Invercargill two months earlier at which the idea of an association to represent deer farming interests was kicked around by Bernard Pinney, Peter Elworthy and Invermay scientist Ken Drew. The director of the Agriculture Department's Meat Division, John McNab, had thrown up a blunt challenge: he refused to deal any further with 'a bunch of strident, pushy individuals' over the issue of deer slaughtering. His concern sprang from representations made to him the year before by a number of deer farmers who wanted licences for portable slaughter facilities for farmed deer. A plant was approved on a trial basis by the officials, who subsequently decided there needed to be an expensive upgrade if portable facilities were going to be approved on a broader scale. Frankly, the director had had enough of farmers beating a path to his office in ones and twos, with all kinds of bleats about the way deer farming was developing.

At the Invercargill meeting, there was agreement that interested parties should be gathered together at Christchurch in April. Thirty people attended that meeting. Peter Elworthy was appointed interim chairman until the NZDFA was formally launched in Wellington two months later, with Peter installed as the first president, an office he held until the 1981 China visit.

The annual meetings of the association through the late 1970s, involving up to 400 delegates, were lively affairs. The delegates themselves reflected an intriguing cross-section of New Zealand society. There were West Coast possum and part-time deer hunters in black-singlets and red-band gumboots, high-country farmers in tweed jackets, smooth-talking city lawyers and investors in shiny suits. Field days and seminars were also organised by the association, and these events were attended by visitors from Asia and elsewhere on occasion.

From its inception in 1975, Tim became a member of the association's council, representing the Otago region. He was regarded as the 'velvet

Sorting sliced antler in China.
Graeme Ramshaw

The Alpine board visits the Luggate factory in the early 1990s. From left Graeme Ramshaw, Tim, Graham Sinclair, Don Spary and factory manager Murray Hamer.

king' at the time, having decided that farmed deer would provide a more reliable supply of velvet antler than deer captured randomly from the wild. Tim remained a NZDFA councillor until 1983.

The exporting of New Zealand red deer to Asia and other countries by Tim's company was an issue that caused some muttering among the association's membership. Some farmers felt he was doing a 'kiwifruit' – exporting stock to countries that would ultimately compete with New Zealand in overseas markets. The export of kiwifruit cuttings to countries like Chile in the past had led to their producers competing directly against New Zealand exporters. There was a counter to that argument, however – any overseas production would expand overseas markets and ultimately ought to benefit New Zealand producers.

Chapter 8

A Coming of Age

Late 1970s–1980s
'Stagliner' *days … * **Criffel's** *big day … * **Mararoa** *…*
Ranginui *reinstated … 'professionals' … perfecting the
net gun … the wapiti saga … elk imports from Canada*

FOLLOWING THE FIRST OF THE ASIAN live deer consignments,
Tim and his directors started thinking about moving deer around New
Zealand by air. To achieve this, the company acquired a twin-engined,
tail-wheeler Dakota DC-3, a classic post-war passenger and freight aircraft. It was soon dubbed 'Stagliner'.

The first time airline pilot John Gardiner carried deer by air from the
South Island to the North Island, it was a learning experience. A National
Airways Corporation (later Air New Zealand) Friendship captain, John
agreed to do charters for Alpine in his own time and mostly for the fun of
it. His first plane load set out from Christchurch, bound for Rotorua.
Twenty weaner stags, weighing over 100 kilograms each, were loaded into
the DC-3 freighter after being trucked there from Wanaka. Plywood partitions formed pens inside the aircraft so the deer would not charge about
and damage themselves or the plane. A soft wallboard, Pinex, was laid on
the floor to give the deer firmer footing and to soak up any urine. The
windows were blocked out to help settle them.

Whereas the stags at loading time were a touch jumpy, the unloading
at Rotorua Airport was another story. The first of them to come off the
plane missed the exit door completely and crammed into the toilet at the
rear. The crew handling them simply shut the aircraft door and went away
for a cup of tea, leaving the young stags to calm down and do the untan-
gling themselves.

At the peak of the deer airlift era in the late 1970s and early 1980s,
Alpine had two DC-3s operating. The pilots included John Gardiner,
Nigel Clark and Jim Pavitt. There were a few dozen flights to the North
Island, mainly to the Waikato through Hamilton and the Hawkes Bay

region through Napier and most of the charters involved flights out of Wanaka or Te Anau. Weaner hinds made up the bulk of the consignments, all destined for new deer farms or to supplement existing herds. At 50 to 70 kilograms each, the hinds were cost-effective to airlift while prices were high, with about 50 packing into a plane load. Trucking them north became more cost-effective later.

Most of the deer flown around the country by Alpine were raised on the company's Criffel and Mararoa deer farms from stock caught in the wild.

Criffel Deer Farm, known as Criffel Game Park at one time, had its origins in the experimental four hectares (ten acres) purchased at Wanaka's Golf Course Road in 1969 to hold deer from the wild. Within ten years, and a whole lot larger, it was arguably New Zealand's best-known deer farm.

Several properties were incorporated into the Criffel farm over the years but the key purchase of 550 hectares was made in 1972. Alpine bought the northern end of the Criffel Range, which marked the entrance to the Cardrona Valley. From the foot of the range to the summit crest, the block contained tussock, bracken and shrub country, rock outcrops and cushionfields higher up. There were natural springs on the property. It was an archetypal rangeland environment. Sold to Alpine by Hector Bell of the Criffel Run Company, it lay to the sun overlooking Lakes Wanaka and Hawea, the Upper Clutha basin and the cradling mountains – a magnificent vista. During the 1970s, two blocks of 105 hectares and 65 hectares below the rangeland country were added to the property, and a further 100 hectares of flat land was leased. At its fullest extent Criffel occupied 840 hectares and carried 4,000 head of deer. Large deer yards

Alpine's DC-3 Stagliner loading deer at Mararoa Station. The plane was used to fly deer within New Zealand. Alan Bond

were built, and the hay barn had a capacity of 5,500 bales. Les Smith managed Criffel early on, and Ray White and Bill Jelley were key members of the Criffel team in the early days.

What Criffel became renowned for in the deer industry was its deer sales. The first one in June 1977 was a sensation.

Alpine produced a brochure for the auction in which Peter Elworthy (head of the newly formed New Zealand Deer Farmers' Association), suggested that sales like the pioneering one Criffel was about to stage could provide a significant boost to the industry. In a foreword Peter said: 'The main limitation on expansion in the industry is a scarcity of animals.'

More than 1,000 farmers or their agents and would-be farmers, including city investors, attended the auction. It was held on a raw winter's day on a flat area part way up the Criffel Range. The access road was lined with four-wheel-drive vehicles, Landrovers, Landcruisers and the like. In contrast to the bitingly cold conditions, the bidding was hot. Wrightson NMA (auctioneer Lester Thorn) and the Southland Farmers company (Evan Mackie) jointly ran the auction. There were just on 400 animals in the sale from Criffel's herd of 1,500. Most of the animals on offer were weaner hinds six to seven months old. Three adult stags and 30 adult hinds were also in the mix. Prices were unreserved.

Peter Elworthy delivered an opening address after which the auction proper began. From the early bidding Nugent Dowling, of Wrightson NMA, knew that it was going to be a startling result for Criffel. Deer at such prices were 'unheard of'. The three stags fetched about $750 each, the weaner hinds about $550 and weaner stags $250. The Criffel auction of 1977 set the benchmark for the nation in terms of what deer were worth. It set another record as well – it was the first major commercial auction of deer in the world.

Tim had a smile from ear to ear. And as he did that day and at subsequent auctions, he would approach a successful bidder beaming and tell the buyer what a beautiful hind or stag he had just acquired. Buyers could see that there was more to Tim's enthusiasm for the sale and its atmosphere than simply a good profit. He really did want to enthuse with them over the animals and their potential.

The party at Luggate after the June 1977 auction was one few participants would forget. Anticipating a strong sale, Tim had ordered crayfish and oysters by the case and carton. The beer flowed well into the evening. The food and refreshments reinforced Tim's reputation as a host.

A second Criffel auction was held a year later on a cold, cloudy day. Fewer people attended – 700 this time – but prices continued their upward trend. Rising returns for velvet boosted interest. Top price: $1,200.

Yankee Zephyr

The Alpine DC-3 Stagliner, registered ZK-BEU, ended its days famously – if ignominiously. It was sunk in Lake Wakatipu as a key prop in a feature film called *Race for the Yankee Zephyr*. Directed by David Hemmings, the film told the story of a dramatic search, by competing interests, for a Second World War aircraft named the Yankee Zephyr, which crashed into a lake carrying $50 million in wartime treasure. Tim and his directors decided to let the old plane be scuttled as its engine and fuselage had reached their use-by date. ZK-BEU was sunk head first, tail up in Lake Wakatipu near the peninsula where the Queenstown Gardens are located.

First auction sale at Criffel Deer Farm, June 1977.

Alpine claimed its Criffel red deer were top producers largely because their bloodlines harked back to the original nineteenth century 'Otago Herd', whose origins lay in the Highlands of Scotland. A lot of animals were captured live from the West Wanaka, Makarora, Hunter and Wilkin areas – a region renowned internationally for the stature and antler quality of its red deer in the past. The Criffel stags also became known throughout the industry for their quiet behaviour.

When deer from Criffel turned up at auctions in other parts of the country, they often had stellar value. At a Hawkes Bay sale in late 1979, in-calf red deer hinds from Criffel topped the sale at $3,650 each, an extraordinary price. It would prove to be a peak.

ALTHOUGH TIM WALLIS was not the first to go deer farming in New Zealand, by the late 1970s he was reputed to be the largest deer farmer in the country – some said, the world. Criffel, which grew incrementally, could not by itself support this claim. What made the difference was Mararoa.

Four times the size of the Criffel farm, Mararoa Station in the Te Anau Basin was purchased by Alpine in October 1976 from Chris Stevens. Tim had earlier flown over the country east of Lake Te Anau in a helicopter, assessing the lie of the land with associates, including Peter Elworthy. He undertook one reconnaissance in snow showers. Near Lumsden in western Southland, unsure of the way to one large property, he landed the helicopter and scraped the snow off a road sign to find out the direction.

The Mararoa purchase was a complex deal, involving Graham Sinclair's legal expertise, but in typical Wallis fashion it was signed and sealed in just a couple of days. The property's 3,500 hectares spread across river flats, shrubby hill country, copper tussock grassland, swampy areas and patches of beech forest. Native vegetation covered about two-thirds of the property. The Mararoa River, draining the Mavora Lakes, ran by the farm, and the mountain backdrop reached heights of about 1,200 metres. At the time of the purchase, Mararoa was running sheep and cattle, a total of about 8,000 stock units. But to Tim and his directors, Mararoa looked like prime deer country. And they had the air power to make it so. Deer captured live from the wild were transferred to Mararoa in their thousands.

Mararoa was strategic. It lay near the edge of Fiordland National Park's deer resource. It was a lot closer than Criffel to the main theatre of operation and just a few minutes' flying east of the town of Te Anau, where the newly captured deer were quarantined on a 30 hectare area. George Reid was appointed manager at Mararoa and with his wife, Adrienne, ran the place for 18 years.

Farm subsidies were still Government policy then and highly supportive of farm expansion. Alpine also took advantage of a Rural Bank Land

Brochure for the first Criffel deer sale.

Young deer in velvet at Criffel.
Bernard Pinney

Development and Livestock Incentive Scheme to treble Maraoa's carrying capacity – the number of stock units that could be profitably run – over a seven-year period. This equated to 8,000 breeding ewes, 400 Hereford cattle and a base herd of 1,000 deer. Deer numbers were often much higher. At their peak, the Mararoa and Criffel herds comprised 7,000 deer, including 3,600 breeding hinds, running on 3,000 hectares. It was estimated that, thanks to the Criffel auctions and other sales as well as the Stagliner distribution of stock into the North Island, half the country's farmed deer originated from these two properties.

Another reason for acquiring Mararoa was to test a theory. Tim was certain that deer fresh from the wild would do much better – for feed and habitat requirements – on hill country than on flat paddocks. Invermay research had shown this to be the case, after its early failure with a consignment of wapiti from Fiordland.

THE YEAR MARAROA became an Alpine asset, the company bought back the coaster *Ranginui* – for about half the original price. With the farcical 'Republic of Minerva' gunship period behind her, the *Ranginui* was reassigned to her old haunts in Fiordland, although not everyone in the company thought her return to the Alpine fold was wise. Reid Jackson

Aerial view of Mararoa, with the homestead prominent.

and others would come to dub her the 'Alpine Sinking Fund' because of the cost of keeping her afloat. She did have a certain charm and character, nonetheless, and Tim envisaged her in the twin roles of venison recovery and live capture.

The year 1976 was also a turning point for Alpine's Fiordland National Park operations. A new licensing period to operate in the park was negotiated. There was frenetic pressure on the Park Board from other operators to have the park opened up to competition. Around this time the *Southland Times* newspaper printed numerous letters to the editor, mainly from independent operators, who attempted to blacken Alpine's name in the hope the board would change its stance on licensing. The New Zealand Deerstalkers' Association hit back in Alpine's defence, with its Gore and District Branch president claiming in a letter to the editor that Alpine had done well in the Wapiti Area to cull out red deer and hybrids that were reducing the quality of wapiti and thus the trophy prospects.

In coming to a decision, the Park Board acknowledged advice from its staff that political pressure was also mounting and that, politically, a monopoly on public land could not be justified. The upshot was a block system, allocated by ballot and rotated on a monthly basis. Alpine was allocated a small block in which to operate exclusively. Tim was disappointed in the decision but not bitter. His relationship with board members and staff remained cordial, and the park staff realised that over the years they had had a good deal from Alpine. The company had provided many helicopter trips at low cost or no cost.

Tim at sea aboard the Ranginui.

From the start of the 1976 licence period, the deer were caught in a pincer movement – shooting and live capture. With the population already reduced by Tim's operations and by poaching in earlier years, deer numbers in the more accessible eastern areas in particular fell dramatically under this new multiple-operator assault. There were 24 helicopters in the air at the start of the new regime. Wally Sander, the national park's chief ranger at the time, saw shot-deer rates fall in some blocks from 60 or 70 deer a day to just three or four. By the end of 1977 some operators were pulling out, unable to make ends meet.

The wild venison days were all but over. Live capture was the way to make the helicopters pay in this region. And Tim was primed.

He had recruited and trained pilots who had a skill base second to none in the industry. They considered themselves the professionals when it came to live capture. They were.

And the company expected each of them to pay his way in deer captured. Among the pilots of this era were Doug Maxwell, who joined Alpine in 1973, and Richard ('Hannibal') Hayes, whom Tim recruited from Milton in 1975. Doug spent a month in the North Island with Tim and became Alpine's test pilot for net-gun development in the late 1970s. Richard had been flying a leased Hiller on agriculture work and when he fielded the phone call from Tim at his Milton home he could hardly believe his luck. Here was a legend in the helicopter industry phoning him, a 23-year-old, with a job offer, sight unseen. Richard did think, however, that Tim had probably done some homework on him and checked his credentials with sources in the industry. As for the lease on the Hiller, Tim said that would be no bother. He would take it over.

Tim had a highly experienced team of pilots to draw on. They included Bill Black, Jim Kane (who had become a pilot after a distinguished career shooting from helicopters), Dick Deaker, Alan Duncan, Alan Bond and Doug Maxwell to name a few. Working under Tim, they needed to be innovative. Because their boss was. His interest in devising new technology for catching deer live bordered on obsession.

The two-barrelled net gun was a reasonable tool but if it was not fired exactly right it could bring down the helicopter. Doug Maxwell was among those who knew there had to be a better system. There was. It was a simple formula: Four barrels better than two. Better than three barrels as well which was the Thompson brothers' design.

At Tim's urging, Alpine set up a dedicated research-and-development arm. A workshop was built below Tim's home at 241 Beacon Point Road, to where he and Prue moved from Matai Road towards the end of 1979, five years after their marriage. By this stage they had three sons.

In December 1979, Dave Conmee, a development engineer who previously worked for a munitions company, was recruited by Tim to take charge of an R&D workshop that would, among other things, refine the net method of capturing deer. The workshop had a novel setting. It was built into the slope below the Wallis house, with its wide frontage facing Lake Wanaka. A rectangle dug out of the slope, the workshop had a roof that was grassed over. A casual observer might describe it as an underground facility, a bunker camouflaged and ready for some sort of covert operation. This was serious business.

Pioneer pilots – from left, Russell Gutschlag, Bill Black and Roy McIvor. The first three pilots engaged by Luggate Game Packers meet again at the company reunion in 1993.

Criffel deer farm sale arena and yards; Criffel sign.

Tim realised that unless he perfected a net gun to increase live capture, he could say goodbye to a business based on feral deer. Deer were scarcer than ever and not worth the helicopter time shooting. They were much more valuable alive than dead.

Dave Conmee set up the workshop. About a third of it was filled with mechanical/electrical tools and equipment, including gear for welding aluminium. It doubled as a hangar for one Hughes 500 helicopter, with an office built into the ceiling, a suspended mezzanine. One or two cars could also be parked in it.

Dave was no stranger to the live capture of wild animals – in his case for zoological purposes – as he had worked on projects overseas in the early 1960s that utilised syringe-firing rifles. He and Tim travelled around the country assessing the state of the art. Then they worked on improvements and refinements – on net shape, size and weight, and different methods of propelling it. They gave a lot of thought to the shape – triangular or rectangular. They tried nets for different habitats and conditions, even a net for use in areas partly covered by bush.

John Muir, an electrician and sometime deer-stalker, joined the R&D team in 1981 after working on the installation of a swimming pool for Tim to exercise in, and a spa at the Wallises' Beacon Point Road home.

There were lots of trials in the hills and on the grass slope in front of the workshop. The guns were loaded with .308 blanks. Tim was not concerned about secrecy and patents; he just wanted the gear developed and deployed. Even when overseas on business trips, he would feed back his ideas by phone or fax. It was a race to create tools of increasing sophistication before the feral deer resource diminished too much.

The most advanced net gun was skid-mounted. It had four barrels, with the barrel length and angle carefully chosen for optimum range. The nets themselves, prepacked and stowed aboard the helicopter, a dozen or more at a time, were designed to be easily reloaded into the gun's housing.

With skid-mounted apparatus, the pilots fired the net guns instead of the shooter. It required the shooter to have a canny regard for how deer run when pursued. The pilot's thumb pressed a button to fire the net out. To Doug Maxwell it was more exciting than anything he had experienced so far in his flying career. Most of the pilots felt this way. Doug took things a step further, equipping his chopper with a second gun. The conventional model faced forward. Doug had a second gun mounted on the front leg of the skid directly below the pilot's seat, which in a Hughes was on the left side. He found it gave him greater shooting options.

Pilot Richard Hayes with captured hybrid stag with heavy antler.

If he and his crewman came upon a mob of deer and netted one, Doug would let his crewman out to tie up the animal and prepare it for airlift to the road end. While that was happening, and with the forward net gun reloaded, he would fly off to try for another deer from the same mob with two guns at his disposal. It was the ultimate challenge for a pilot: alone in the machine, man against beast.

The peak years for live capture were 1979 and 1980. Alpine deployed some eight Hughes 500 helicopters to net deer, and a Bell Jet Ranger to fly fuel in – and the captured deer out.

It was a lucrative time. The market was paying over $3,000 for a top-quality hind – a staggering increase on prices paid just three years earlier, around the $250 mark. In a 12-month period, Alpine captured over 7,000 deer. That was reckoned to be about half the national tally for the same period.

Not surprisingly, some of Alpine's pilots were attracted to the idea of going into the live-capture business on their own accounts. Jim Kane and Richard Hayes departed – Richard after five rewarding years working for Tim – and Doug Maxwell went out on his own in 1981. With no hard feelings, Tim helped Doug set up. He sold him a Hughes 500. Tim assisted other pilots this way as well. Sometimes, with no more than a handshake to settle it, he would ask them to keep out of certain operational areas.

Tim had a not-so-secret weapon up his sleeve. It was called *Ranginui*. The ship provided Alpine with a staging post in the remotest parts of Fiordland. When the economics of shooting deer were overtaken by the live-capture imperative, Tim knew it was time to convert the *Ranginui* from a venison-recovery vessel to one that could handle live animals. For a start, the helicopter deck was extended to take two machines at once. Below, refrigerated spaces became areas for holding live deer safely and humanely until they could be transported to a farm. To shift live deer from the helipads to the pens below deck, Alpine installed a hydraulic lift.

Although the Jet Ranger was an effective way to carry trussed-up deer from wilderness to farm, the *Ranginui* gave the Alpine helicopters another option if logistics did not suit the Jet Ranger operation or if the weather was bad. Typically through these years, the ship would be based in Dusky Sound, which skipper Frank Finnegan reckoned had the best mooring sites of any fiord. Besides, the fishing was good there as well. As a rule, the ship and helicopter crews loved the lifestyle. Where else would they find such a stunning environment to work in? An Australian, Frank had served on merchant ships in the Pacific Islands and transported cattle live to Hong Kong. He became the *Ranginui*'s last and longest-serving captain (eight years) after a number of others, including Bas Hollows, Colin Sinclair, Hugh (Foss) Elder and Dave Comer, had served in the role.

NOTHING STIRS THE BLOOD of deer hunters in Fiordland more vigorously than the thought of a wapiti bull at the autumn 'bugle' carrying a mighty rack of antlers. Introduced into the region from North America in 1905 by the New Zealand Government, wapiti were the ultimate trophy of recreational hunters for many decades. Crossbreeding with red deer, however, produced hybrid animals that tended to be smaller and of less quality than the original stock. Tim had observed that the wapiti component in Fiordland deer lessened in proportion to distance from the breed's original release site around George Sound. Overpopulation, which led to reduced feed, also compromised the size of wapiti and wapiti-red hybrids. Some deerstalkers thought helicopter shooting that targeted red deer and hybrids in the Park Board's designated Wapiti Area was about the only way to increase wapiti quality. It was still possible to identify the wapiti strain in the field. Wapiti typically had a body lighter in colour than that of a red deer, and their head, neck and legs were darker, grading from dark brown to black.

An approved number of these animals were captured to enhance the genetics of farm stock at Criffel and elsewhere. In 1978, Alpine caught a group in the Catseye Bay area, between George and Bligh Sounds, for transfer to Invermay Agricultural Research Station after a period acclimatising to fences at Mararoa Station.

Wapiti Society

In 1976, about 40 wapiti enthusiasts met on Jack Pullar's Southland property to establish the New Zealand Wapiti Society, whose aims were generally to advance the interests of the breed.

Tim was elected to chair the society and Winton veterinarian Mike Bringans became the secretary. Members appreciated Tim's straightforward way of dealing with society business and with the challenges of promoting the wapiti name. At the time, many deer farmers were unaware of the advantages of crossbreeding with a wapiti bull for venison production and velvet.

A few years after the society's formation, the membership was asked to vote in a referendum about whether the society should affiliate with the New Zealand Deer Farmers' Association. At the next annual meeting, Tim called on the secretary to announce the result. Mike Bringans declared the referendum lost. Those opposed to affiliating outnumbered the ayes about three to one. Tim, who had been convinced of the need to affiliate, was shocked and he said to the meeting that the result was 'not what we want'. He was not used to being defeated. He wondered, out loud, how the outcome might be changed. From the front row of the audience, a voice said wryly: 'I think you'll find that democracy has spoken, Mr Chairman.' It was Peter Elworthy. Tim had to accept the decision.

Wapiti bulls on Criffel.

The recreational hunting sector continued to advocate for wapiti's survival in the wild. In 1981, the Fiordland National Park Board and New
Zealand Forest Service set out to form the nucleus of a recreational hunting herd of wapiti. At the frontline of this operation was a consortium of
helicopter pilots, most of whom had once worked for Tim and Alpine.
They included Richard Hayes, Jim Kane and Dick Deaker. Their mission
was to capture 300 wapiti and 200 hybrids over a two-year period and set
them up to breed behind fences. The concept was that their progeny would
restock the park's Wapiti Area. The Crown Wapiti Herd concept fizzled
out in the late 1980s, however, with the Government deciding, to howls
from the deer-stalkers, that rather than go back to the park the herd should
simply see out its days on a Landcorp farm near Manapouri.

Meanwhile, a New Zealand Deerstalkers' Association survey some years
earlier came up with a figure for the wapiti population – 1,375 animals. It
was a tally many deer-stalkers thought wildly overestimated the resource.

Amidst all this wrestling over how to sustain the Fiordland wapiti,
Tim Wallis had a plan. As the venison side of his business declined in the
mid-1970s and the live capture side grew to fill the vacuum, he saw a vital
role for wapiti on farms. If the Fiordland ones were in doubt because of
crossbreeding with reds, why not go back to the source?

In the late 1970s, Alpine, in conjunction with Wilson Neill Ltd, applied to import a shipment of wapiti from their homelands. It was a historic moment. No deer had been imported into New Zealand for almost
70 years, since 1910. Would the Government agree?

It spoke volumes for the maturity of the New Zealand deer farming
industry and the confidence the Government farming and animal health
agencies had in the industry that, after much deliberation, the application
was approved. Strict quarantine conditions had to be adhered to. The
import signalled the deer industry had come of age.

Tim wanted the Canadian elk for Criffel. He wanted Criffel to be a
showcase wapiti stud farm. Twenty-one elk, a mixture of bulls and cows
from various game parks and zoos in Canada, were assembled for the
flight to New Zealand. On arrival in 1981, three years after the application to import them was lodged, the elk were placed in quarantine on
Somes Island in Wellington Harbour, with Wanaka veterinarian Gilbert
van Reenen appointed by Alpine to supervise their quarantining. After
two months they were transported to Wanaka and released on to Criffel's
hill block. In 1982, the two-year-old bulls among the imports were mated
with some New Zealand wapiti cows.

Sharing the same aircraft with the Criffel animals were 21 wapiti from
Elk Island National Park in Alberta – a gift from the Canadian Govern-

Imported Canadian elk surround Tim's vehicle at Criffel Deer Farm.

ment to the Invermay deer research unit near Dunedin. The gift caused a stir back in Canada. Opponents of the exporting of elk from a national park took out a court order, claiming the animals going to Invermay were ear-marked for commercial use in New Zealand and that 'the people's' wapiti should not be treated this way. No Elk Island animals were ever sold by Invermay nor were they ever intended to be for sale. They were used in evaluation studies to measure performance against red deer and in cross-breeding studies with reds. In years to come Tim's company would finance post-doctoral studies at Invermay of value to the industry as a whole.

The imported Criffel elk, meanwhile, went on to become famous in New Zealand deer circles. They were huge animals. One bull, Blue 116, imported as a two-year-old, grew to be over 500 kg in three years. In 1984–85 he produced antler velvet of 11.9 kg that took top honours in the national velvet competition.

The 1981 Canadian elk shipment paved the way for red deer imports to boost the genetic base of farmed deer in New Zealand. Criffel im-ported animals from Warnham Park and Sweden. By the mid-1980s deer shipments had arrived from countries such as Yugoslavia, Hungary, Ru-mania and Germany to supplement farm stock in various parts of New Zealand. Overall, the red deer imports gave New Zealand deer farming a stronger genetic resource.

Breeds other than red deer and wapiti arrived in the 1980s as well. Criffel imported 18 rare Chinese Père David deer *Elaphurus davidianus* in 1984 from the Duke of Bedford's estate at Woburn, England. Another small herd was established at Invermay where scientists were able to produce a few hybrids of red hinds using Père David semen. A further group went to the Auckland region. The breed was named after Father Armand David, a French missionary in China, who, in 1865, was the first Westerner to report their existence. The ancient breed was almost lost to extinction in 1917 but by the mid-'eighties the world population was believed to be about 2,000.

Of all deer, wapiti are regarded as the most majestic. Although some red deer farmers, especially stud farmers, thought otherwise, Alpine claimed the progeny of the imported elk and New Zealand wapiti had the potential to produce up to 300 percent more velvet by weight than red deer. Some deer farmers thought the wapiti too dangerous to handle. Alpine pronounced those fears 'entirely unfounded'. The bulls were very quiet up to velvetting, it said, pointing out that Chinese deer farmers, on the whole smaller than their New Zealand counterparts, handled their malu deer (similar to elk) with ease.

The tame behaviour of the Criffel elk was emphasised in published photographs of them investigating vehicles, poking heads through windows and open doors, and grazing in the Criffel paddocks in close proximity to children. More often than not, the children in the picture were those of Tim and Prue. Their family was expanding apace. Tim acquired the experience of being a father at the same time as he grew used to the business of farming deer and capturing them live from the wild.

Chapter 9

Winging It

1980s
Four sons under five ... bighorn sheep rescue ...
helicopters galore ... tax shocks ... The Helicopter
Line emerges ... Mararoa sold ... BNZ comes calling ...
sharemarket crash ... **Ranginui** *entertainment ...*
incident at Cast-off Point ... live trapping ... Reid
Jackson's death

FOUR SONS were born to Prue and Tim Wallis in the five years from 1975 to 1980 – Toby, Jonathan, Matthew and Nicholas. Before Toby went to school he had three brothers at home. Toby (September 1975) and Jonathan (November 1976) were born 14 months apart and Matthew came along in January 1979, the month after Prue and Tim moved from Matai Road to Beacon Point Road. Nick was born in June 1980. In their preschool years all four went to the Wanaka Playcentre for a few hours a day, and they all attended Wanaka Primary School.

A kind of Cinderella to Queenstown, Wanaka was not the outdoor adventure centre, year-round playground and tourist resort that it is to-day. Compared to Queenstown, Wanaka had a quiet backwater feel to it in the late 1970s. And for all its physical appeal and potential, the town had little cultural stimulation for a mother of four preschoolers used to the pizazz of London not so long before. But her involvement in the boys' activities provided new friends and interests for her.

To assist with looking after the boys and the housework, Prue engaged 17-year-old Shirl Flynn, the daughter of a duck-shooting mate of Tim's, former Southland policeman Jack Flynn. Shirl worked for just on seven years as a nanny and home help, first at Matai Road, where there were two toddlers, and later at the new house at Beacon Point Road, where Matt and Nick joined the family. Shirl loved working with the boys and they loved her, and she would sometimes be in charge of them, with a helper of her own, when Prue joined Tim on a trip.

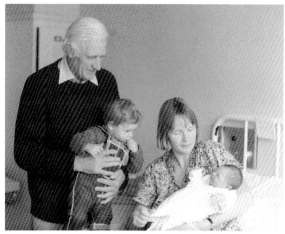

Above: Three generations. Tim's mother, Janice, visits Prue and new-born Toby in the Queen Mary Maternity Centre at Dunedin.

Above right: Prue's father, Jock Hazledine, holding one-year-old Toby, visits Prue and new-born Jonathan in the Queen Mary Maternity Centre at Dunedin in 1976.

Tim's business had grown steadily larger and more complex through the mid to late 1970s. He travelled frequently. Somehow he had to fit fatherhood into his business imperatives, but it wasn't always an easy fit. Occasionally, Prue and the boys joined him on a trip. The first time all four sons went overseas with their parents was to the United States, where they visited Disneyland and Sea World in California in conjunction with a business visit Tim made to the Telonics firm in Arizona. Notwithstanding the delight he felt at the arrival of each son, Tim pursued his business life and the development of Alpine with vigour, and before he knew it, the babies became toddlers then fair-haired little boys.

Like his father before him, Tim involved the boys in his business life when and where he could. Sometimes he took the older ones with him in his Hughes 500, registered HOT, on net-capture operations. Sometimes one or two boys turned up at a board meeting or they would fly with him in his Cessna 210 to business meetings in other centres and deer farmers' conferences, sitting on his aluminium briefcase so they could see out the windows and wearing headphones much too big for them. Back home at Beacon Point Road Tim taught them in turn how to handle an air rifle then a bolt-action .22 rifle, with which they would shoot rabbits in the wide open grassy spaces behind the house where today residential housing is adding to Wanaka's sprawl. Tim taught the boys two basic rules – 'Always break your gun' (in the case of a break-action air rifle), and 'Never keep a bullet in the breach'.

At about the age of ten each of the sons in turn went to boarding school at Waihi Preparatory in South Canterbury where they spent three years (Toby had four years at Waihi) before going on to Christ's College in Christchurch – the third generation of Wallises to go there and the fifth generation to attend the college on the Blunden side of the family. Years before, with no secondary school established at the time at Wanaka, Prue had enrolled the four of them at Otago Boys' High School in Dunedin (a rival of Christ's on the rugby field and a boarding school as well). She felt that the individual personalities and educational needs of a child ought to be taken into account in any decision on secondary education and that it was wrong to automatically assume the boys would go to Christ's. Tim thought enrolling the boys at Otago Boys as a back-up was reasonable. Prue knew the Otago enrolment would raise hackles in the Wallis family, though. Tim's mother, Janice ('Granny' to the boys and friends of the family as well), was most put out about the prospect of Tim Wallis's boys not going to Christ's.

In the end, however, Christ's won the day. Following tradition, the boys joined School House where they saw their father's name listed in bold letters (for prefect and sporting honours) on the hallowed walls of the library. From 1952 Dad also appeared in the annual School House photographs displayed on the stairs, and one day his name was discovered carved on a brick just below the fire escape on the back wall of School House, two storeys up. One of the boys' teachers, Zane Dalzell, also taught their father. Zane was a house tutor, aged 25, at the time Tim started at college. Up to three Wallis boys attended Christ's at one time, and occasionally one or other was mistakenly called 'Tim' by Mr Dalzell.

Apart from the extended Christmas break, school holidays were three weeks long in the 1980s, with the school year broken into three terms. Holidays meant Mum's cooking, camping, *Ranginui* – and work. Tim and Prue were determined to teach the boys self-reliance and the value of

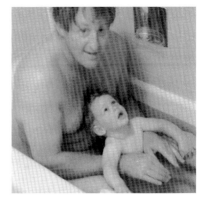

Tim and baby Toby take a bath.
Prue Wallis

The Wallis and Jackson families at Matthew Wallis's christening in 1979. Standing, from left: Reid Jackson, daughter Nicola, Prue holding Matthew, Tim, Rachael and Diana Jackson, and Reid's wife, Pat. Toby and Jonathan are seated.

money, recognising they were more privileged than many of their generation. They never got an allowance. Before any fun was had aboard the *Ranginui* they had to earn pocket money, and Tim made them phone the Criffel farm manager to see if there were jobs going and negotiate an hourly rate. Grubbing thistles was a common holiday job.

When the boys weren't working, the family went camping, and not just around the traditional Dublin Bay and Stevensons Arm sites near Wanaka with old family friends – the Wilsons and the Burdons. They also flew to wilder places like the Hunter Valley. On the undulating gravel margins of the Hunter River, setting up a tent-fly camp, Tim would invariably ask a boy to steady him while he cut manuka or beech poles with a chainsaw – one hand on the boy, one wielding the chainsaw. With the poles he built a scaffold for the tent fly. For company, the boys might be joined on these adventures by the Wilson children – Ben, Angus and Annabel. They took part in deer stalking in the Hunter Valley and hunting wild pigs on Mt Burke near Wanaka. Flocks of Canada geese, numerous on the river flats of the Hunter, were also targeted. In his Hughes 500, Tim had the measure of the geese, chasing one down till it slowed and flattened itself on the river bed, where Tim could pin its neck with the skid of his helicopter while Toby or someone else jumped out and wrung the large bird's neck.

The boys soon realised that their dad overcame the disadvantages of what he called a 'busted leg' the moment he climbed into a helicopter. The helicopter gave him super-human mobility. Because the boys never knew their father without a braced leg, Tim's disability was nothing unusual to them. They never heard him complain of the disability, although

The Wallis house at Beacon Point Road, Wanaka, in the early 1980s. Today the foreground is covered in houses.

they knew that whenever Dad had an active day or perhaps consumed a few too many glasses of red wine in the evening, his face would mirror the onset of severe pain in his left leg.

There were times when Tim became aware that one or more of his sons had done something wrong. At such times his body language and tone of voice would express his displeasure. 'I'm very disappointed … ' he would say. The expression constituted an effective telling off.

What the sons also knew was that their father had business in faraway places – and the films and photographs he came back with showed adventures out of this world. New Mexico was an example.

When Tim took part in a rescue mission in the colourful desert valleys and mountainlands of New Mexico, home of the endangered desert bighorn sheep, third son Matthew was ten months old, and Prue just pregnant with Nick.

While planning a trip to the United States in1979 to pick up a new Hughes 500 D helicopter Tim learned of the concerns of the New Mexico Department of Game & Fish about the future of a small population of bighorn sheep living in the state's San Andres Mountains. In the previous 12 months a scabies outbreak had wiped out all but 70 of the area's 250 bighorn sheep, famous in America for their huge curved horns, male head-

Above: Good shot: Toby Wallis with his first air gun. Toby used an eye-patch to enhance his aim.

Above right: Tim taking part in a tug-of-war event at a Wanaka Primary School gala day.

Trout for tea: Nick and Matthew Wallis with their catch, and Digger.

butting and ledge-to-ledge leaping. Weighing up to 150 kilograms, they live in the mountains and rocky hill country down the western side of North America, from British Columbia to Mexico. Since European settlement, their numbers have declined markedly.

The parasitic scabies mite thinned the sheep's coat, which is more like coarse hair than wool, to such an extent, infected animals died of the winter cold. The New Mexico wildlife managers turned to a New Zealander named Tim Wallis, who was introduced to them through Phoenix electronics company Telonics, which had developed radio transmitters for his red deer capture work.

In November 1979, with winter fast approaching, Tim and his shooter, Colin Yeates, spent ten days on the bighorn sheep round-up. It took place in a rocky area not far from the White Sands National Monument and the United States Defence Department's White Sands Missile Range. There was intense media interest in the operation, with newspaper and magazine reporters and a television crew or two turning up at the base camp to cover the story. The netted animals were treated for scabies and kept in quarantine until the wildlife staff judged the epidemic was over. Altogether, 47 animals were captured in the San Andres Mountains.

Soon afterwards, near Silver City in Arizona, Tim and Colin caught a number of Mexican elk. The wildlife authorities there were mystified by the loss of elk fawns and called in the New Zealanders. Having professed an interest in importing the Canadian subspecies into New Zealand, Tim was happy to offer his services. A number of Mexican elk females were captured by net, after which radio transmitters were attached to them so the authorities could carry out a study that might reveal why the fawns were dying.

Following these projects Tim left for Los Angeles with the Hughes 500 to catch a commercial flight home. Not allowing for time-zone changes, and with daylight hours reduced by the winter season, he underestimated how long the flight would take in daylight and was well short of the airport by dusk. At one stage, he relied on the lights of a freeway and a map of the greater Los Angeles area to keep him on track to the airport. He flew at low altitude, below detection by radar, aware that he did not have permission to fly at night. At the airport, before rushing off to catch the 12-hour flight to Auckland, he instructed staff to pack up the new helicopter and make arrangements to ship it to New Zealand. From this episode, a story developed that Tim had triggered a security alert with his low flying. He heard nothing from the authorities, however. They might have had a job keeping tabs on him.

By now, helicopters were big business for Alpine, especially after Tim's company bought into two major helicopter firms – Whirlwide and Wisharts. The first acquisition was in 1973, when Alpine bought 51 percent of Timaru-based Whirlwide, which was managed by Graham Gosney, a friend of Reid Jackson's from university days. Alpine later owned 100 percent of the company and began expanding its work beyond the traditional agricultural spraying, fencing and the like into live-deer recovery and tourism. The Aoraki/Mt Cook area was a focus for the latter. In 1978, the Hamilton-based Wisharts came into the picture. With Graham Gosney taking over as managing director, Wisharts expanded into tourism and other commercial areas.

Although separate companies, Alpine, Whirlwide and Wisharts worked closely together when they needed to, sharing helicopters and staff as projects and locations required. A key project requiring helicopter support (up to six Hughes 500s at a time, with one on standby) was oil and gas exploration on rural land in Taranaki in the 1980s. The contract was with the consortium, Petrocorp (Reid Jackson was on the board of Petrocorp), which also later explored for hydrocarbons off the North Otago coast and in Western Southland.

Don Spary, Alpine's general manager, who had worked for Whirlwide before joining Tim's company, ran the day-to-day management of Alpine and supported the operations of its sister companies with the zest and snappiness of a professional soldier, which he had once been. He needed to be on his toes to manage the Alpine empire, whose helicopter fleet was expanding impressively.

With import licences easier to obtain, it purchased 14 Bell Jet Rangers from American and Canadian sources to cope with developments in tourism and other commercial fields.

Citation

After the desert bighorn sheep rescue project, the New Mexico Department of Game & Fish presented Tim with a Certificate of Appreciation, acknowledging his 'assistance and dedication' and noting that 'he helped save a rare and beautiful wildlife population from extinction'.

Magazine cover about bighorn sheep rescue.

Tim and Robert Wilson with their sons after a successful fishing and shooting expedition in the Hunter Valley. The boys are, from left, Angus Wilson, Jonathan Wallis, Toby Wallis and Ben Wilson. They are holding Canada geese and, in Robert's case, a large trout.

Southern lakes tourism, centred on Queenstown and Te Anau, was starting to boom. Tim's helicopters were also spreading their wings in other ways. They became involved in work as different as movie-making, heliskiing and oil exploration.

Helicopters remained an integral part of the deer industry. But in the early 1980s, the industry encountered some glitches.

IN 1980, THE FIRST OF THREE tax shocks hit the New Zealand deer industry. The Muldoon Government revised the standard values upwards, which radically diminished tax advantages to farmers. A low standard value meant farm owners could achieve a 'book loss', a deferment of tax liability. Along with a slump in velvet prices, live deer prices declined. The New Zealand Deer Farmers' Association lobbied the politicians and the Inland Revenue Department, complaining of a blow below the belt. Later in the year, the Government relented and restored the standard values to previous levels. Deer prices recovered. So did confidence in the industry. Deer-farming syndicates sprang up everywhere. Applications for deer farm licences reached 70 a month.

In 1982, income tax changes heralded a jolt that was more long term. They restricted farm investment write-down to $10,000. Investment in the industry slowed. Tim described it as 'a blow to free enterprise'. The industry took a third, more severe hit in December, 1985. The Minister of Finance was no longer Robert Muldoon, but Roger Douglas: and the Labour Party, with David Lange as Prime Minister, had taken over the Government benches in parliament from National. Sweeping economic and financial reforms included another round of tax changes for all forms of farming, including deer. Standard values were cancelled. This time the changes were unlikely to be overturned. Roger Douglas was on a mission of reform, characterised by the philosophy of 'user pays'. He would not be distracted. This time the tax changes really hurt. Deer values declined by as much as two-thirds. At the same time, the Labour Government re-forms dismantled farm subsidies, reducing farmer spending in such ac-tivities as the spreading of fertiliser by helicopter. Land values fell in sym-pathy with these reforms. For Alpine, the tax package and the demolition of farm subsidies for work that involved aerial support were doubly hard to swallow.

Alpine and Tim faced some hard realities. Tim could see that in the short-term at least the deer industry would move from an expansionary phase to a holding pattern – or worse. With farmers discouraged and unsure of how the industry would emerge from the reforms, including the cancellation of government subsidies, the demand for feral deer would inevitably decline. Alpine had 14 helicopters involved in live recovery at the end of 1985. In a matter of months it reduced its fleet of these ma-chines to just two.

Alpine's Board of Directors, led by Reid Jackson, who was by now a director or board chairman on many leading New Zealand companies, reviewed its activities, which were declining on a number of fronts, and contemplated its options for future growth. Reid had some blunt advice. The company's deer focus had to change. Tourism was the future. In the interests of raising capital for the necessary investment in tourism, Alpine would need to restructure. It would have to go to the public with a share float.

In April 1986, just four months after Roger Douglas's fiscal reforms, a prospectus was issued for a bold new company, The Helicopter Line, which was formed from a merging of the commercial and tourism arms of Al-pine, Whirlwide and Wishharts. The Alpine Deer Group (formerly Al-pine Helicopters) retained the Luggate factory, the deer farms and a small fleet of helicopters for deer work. The Helicopter Line, or THL as it be-came familiarly known, also acquired a 54 percent interest in the Treble

Venison consortium

As farmed deer became available for slaughter and added to the flow of wild venison, a consortium of industry stakeholders planned the upgrade of the original Mossburn processing plant. Alpine/ Luggate Game Packers, Wilson Neill, Wrightson NMA and Southland Farmers Cooperative Association formed Southern Lakes Venison Packers Ltd to develop the Mossburn facility. The plant was re-equipped to produce a new range of venison products and to lift production. Already one of New Zealand's leading deer slaughter-houses, Mossburn became a state-of-the-art facility. Tim was on its board of directors.

Queenstown Scenic Helicopter

Above: The start of Treble Cone
Skifield: Tourism Minister Warren
Cooper makes a ceremonial scrape
with a digger, watched by, from
left, Tony Hill, Peter Thompson,
Tim and Don Spary. Prue Wallis

*Above right: A postcard promoting
Alpine Helicopters' sightseeing
trips out of Queenstown. The
Hiller is flying over Deer Park
Heights, with Queenstown in the
background.*

April 11, 1986   National Business Review

NBR INVESTMENT REVIEW

Helicopter Line set for take off

by Mike Wilson

National Business Review *coverage
of the THL float.*

Cone skifield, its buildings, ski lifts and other facilities (in 1987, THL
would acquire the remaining 46 percent shareholding). Alpine had invested in Treble Cone, which overlooked the Matukituki Valley near
Wanaka, in a bid to diversify out of deer and into a part of the tourism
sector that would make good use of the company's helicopter fleet. THL,
said the prospectus, would become New Zealand's largest helicopter company. It had 42 helicopters worth over $11 million and carrying 60,000
tourists a year. Total assets amounted to about $15 million. The public
share float amounted to eight million 40-cent par-value shares, available
at the issue price of 50 cents.

But would the public buy the concept? In the event, with the
sharemarket booming at the time, the issue was well subscribed and The
Helicopter Line was launched with a flourish in May 1986. Tim was the
single largest shareholder, with 14 million shares. Besides Tim, the new
board comprised the old firm of Reid Jackson, Graham Sinclair and Don
Spary and Whirlwide's managing director, Graham Gosney, who became
the managing director of THL. When Reid died in January 1987, his
partner Murray Valentine became the chairman of the THL board. Murray's
father, Jim Valentine, had been a partner of Reid Jackson's in W.E.C. Reid
McInnes and Co (subsequently Deloitte). Murray took responsibility for
THL's financial needs, and Alpine's books were the responsibility of Graeme
Ramshaw, who was part of the Jackson Valentine partnership in 1985.

Alpine Deer Group, meanwhile, with Tim firmly in charge, still operated the Luggate plant, where venison and co-products processing had
been phased out in favour of a focus on velvet. Alpine still owned two
large deer farms in the form of Criffel and Mararoa.

When Roger Douglas sent the deer industry reeling with his tax changes,
creditors with a stake in deer farming became nervous. The Bank of New
Zealand contacted Tim, Alpine's governing director. His company, having
invested heavily in helicopters, farms and plant in recent years, had some

large loans with the BNZ. Bank representatives wanted to talk finance with him and perhaps look around his operations.

Three BNZ executives arrived from Wellington. Tim received them warmly. Expert at keeping on the front foot in matters of this kind, he outlined the plan for the day. Accompanied by one of his staff, Peter Hamer, Tim said he would take them on a helicopter tour of his beloved Aspiring country. Then they would return for lunch and inspect the Criffel and Mararoa farms in the afternoon, again by helicopter. Okay? The bankers agreed. This was decidedly better than warming a seat in a Wellington tower block.

A brother of Murray Hamer, the Luggate factory manager, Peter was an all-rounder in Tim's scheme of things, able to turn his hand to shooting, driving or farm work. Not long after joining Alpine, Peter had asked Tim why he was always rushing. Back came the reply: 'Can't afford to stop, Peter. I owe too much money.'

With the bankers and Peter on board and belted up in his Hughes 500, Tim headed the chopper up the Matukituki Valley towards Mt Aspiring. This was certainly a world away from Wellington. And it quickly became thrilling. At the Leaping Burn confluence of the main Matukituki Valley, Tim turned left out of the broad and braided bed of the Matukituki

'I love NZ' tramped out on the slopes of Treble Cone skifield. Tim's Hughes 500 HOT transported the signwriter.

River and put the 500 into a climb. They were soon looking at the 'hole in the rock', near where Tim had crashed his first helicopter in 1965. Curiosity on the faces of the bankers turned to incredulity as Tim guided the machine under the overhang in the Leaping Burn's gorge. He heaved the machine one way then the other. In the back of the 500, Peter saw the pallor growing in the bankers' faces. One started to vomit.

Undeterred by his visitors' discomfort, Tim flew on to the Bonar and Volta Glaciers and around the carved faces of Mt Aspiring, New Zealand's 'Matterhorn'. West of Aspiring the glacial ice plunged deeply into the wild and forbidding headwaters of West Coast rivers. Tim skimmed across the glaciers and cleared the ridges with little air to spare. On board the helicopter stomachs churned.

By the time Tim returned to Wanaka, the bankers had had enough sightseeing. They ate a light lunch rather slowly, and when Tim said they had better be getting on with inspecting Criffel and Mararoa by air, the BNZ fellows looked at their watches and declared a need to get on back to Dunedin Airport to catch a flight home. Tim thought that the head office bankers had come to vet his personal integrity and probably were less interested in checking out his business operations. He had set out to demonstrate his enthusiasm for helicopters, tourism and deer farming and put on an optimistic face. As far as he was concerned, the 'audit' visit by the bank was behind him.

Nonetheless, the launch of THL took him into challenging new business territory and a new way of operating. For one thing, he had to face up to a significant shift in direction, with deer not the main driving force. The changes hit him at a personal level as well. He had to explain to chief pilot Bill Black and others who had worked for him for up to 20 years that THL was different from Alpine Helicopters. The business was diversifying. The management structure was changing. There were going to be staffing changes and downsizing. He was no longer the boss.

To Tim, this loss of corporate power was of little moment compared to the loss of intimacy in the organisation. His colleagues and employees were friends to the point of being family. In the months preceding the reorganisation, when he realised things would never been the same again, Tim brought his despondency home. Once, after visiting Bill Black at Te Anau to explain the new reality, he was tear-stricken and slumped in his leather chair in the study, shaking with emotion.

The summer of 1985–86, the lead-up to the transformation of his business, was a difficult time for Tim. Although few people around him were aware of it, summer triggered periods of mild depression in Tim. Commonly, people feel down in the dark and cold of winter and more

Colin Yeates

A few years after the New Mexico wildlife work, Colin Yeates died of head injuries in a helicopter crash in the Crooked Arm area of Doubtful Sound, aged 37. He was working with pilot Stuart Feaver on live deer recovery in violent winds when the accident occurred. Friends described Colin as a big man with a heart of gold. He was Tim's shooter for several years.

Colin Yeates with a red deer stag captured in Mount Aspiring National Park in the course of filming the Wild Kingdom *documentaries for an American television channel in 1982.*

upbeat in the summer. This seasonal low-mood bias was around the other way for Tim. In the winter months he would feel highly energised, on top of the world and at the height of his innovative powers; in summer he would experience gloomy periods, which by and large he managed to disguise.

Prue became aware of Tim's seasonal mood swings early on in the marriage, although there had been one or two clues before then. In a letter to her in London at the end of the 1972 summer, Tim wrote: '…Have been in a lazy mood in the last few weeks. It happens every now and again. Don't seem to have the enthusiasm that keeps me fired up. One's brain just seems to switch off … I think part of it is that competition is pretty brisk these days.'

The 1985 tax hits and moves to transform the company heightened his summer melancholy that year. For both Prue and Tim, it became an issue too serious to overlook. Mood swings put pressure on a marriage and Prue persuaded Tim to seek help. He began taking the prescribed anti-depressant drug, Mianserin. It worked well for Tim until Civil Aviation announced the drug was on the banned list for pilots and that he would need to find alternative medication. Mild forms of depression are not a bar to flying, and it is recognised that pilots subject to mild depression are often better off with acceptable treatment than without it.

Tim was soon back in the air and facing the challenges at the board

Tim's family hosted a Chinese
oriental medicine group led by
Madam Wu in Fiordland in the
1980s. The visitors took a fishing
trip in the jet-boat, Big Bertha.

table. In 1987, the Alpine board decided to sell Mararoa Station, lock,
stock and barrel. The deal was worked out on board the *Ranginui* with
representatives of Wrightson NMA and its offshoot, Challenge Deer. There
was nothing like a break aboard the *Ranginui* in a remote part of Fiordland
region to get some business clarity. Fiordland and Mararoa Station were
closely linked. Mararoa's impressive stocks of deer originally hailed from
Fiordland.

TIM AND PRUE LIKED NOTHING better than to entertain visitors
aboard the *Ranginui* in Fiordland. The *Ranginui* provided a unique adventure in an other-world setting, as far away from a built environment as
was possible in New Zealand. Alpine's helicopters, followed by those with
the THL livery, flew a well-used route to the *Ranginui* with visitors from
overseas and other parts of New Zealand. Numerous Asian groups associated with the oriental medicine trade spent time aboard her. The National
Government's Minister of Energy and National Development, Bill Birch,
visited the *Ranginui* in his role as a director of the State-owned oil and gas
development company, Petrocorp, whose chairman was Reid Jackson.
    Sometimes the visitors were from inland North America or Africa or
China who had next to no experience of the sea. A Zimbabwean wildlife
expert, with whom Tim had been communicating over live capture techniques, arrived at Wanaka one day to look at Alpine's use of nets and traps
for catching deer. He was barely over the jetlag experienced on the long
flight from Africa before Tim had him in a helicopter and away to the

Ranginui. The route Tim took that day was one he often treated guests to. The route tracked across the Doubtful Sound area to Breaksea Sound. The highlight was a place Tim called Campbell's Kingdom, an offshoot of Doubtful Sound. A steep mountain valley about ten kilometres long and studded with lakes, Campbell's Kingdom opened on to the fiord at a tight, tortuous gorge, tight enough to make any passengers unused to flying in this kind of terrain pop-eyed and breathless. Their hearts were often in their mouths. Tim delighted in showing it off to visitors. As the valley plunged towards its climax at Doubtful Sound's Malaspina Reach, the canyon curved one way then the other to form a gigantic S through the landscape. Below the helicopter, the river foamed over its boulder bed, stringing together a series of lakes large and small, jewels in a necklace. Often there would be deer in the open, grazing the flats around the larger lakes with the bush comfortably close by.

The Zimbabwean, who came from a brown landscape a long way inland on a big dry continent, was suitably impressed by this extraordinary green and granite-grey canyon country by the sea. After exiting from Campbell's Kingdom, Tim lifted the Hughes 500 out of Malaspina Reach and across a waterfall generator called Lake Browne, perched high on the southern side of the fiord. From there the route was down into Vancouver Arm at the head of Breaksea Sound. In a short time the *Ranginui* hove into view at her mooring near the John Islands. In this main part of Breaksea and from somewhere near the tops of the ranges, the vessel always appeared as a small, insignificant rock, hardly a source of rollicking hospitality. But when Tim roared his customary 'RAAANGINUUUI!' the passengers knew something special was in prospect.

It was Tim's custom to treat *Ranginui* visitors to a meal of crayfish fresh from the sea. For this visit with the Zimbabwean, he decided to take the helicopter rather than the jet-boat called *Big Bertha.* He knew a good spot. He had two passengers – the Zimbabwean and a Dunedin employee of Tim's, Steve Dyet. They headed for Breaksea Island, which lies at the entrance to the fiord, about 60 kilometres from the *Ranginui*'s mooring.

Before Tim's overseas visitor knew it, the helicopter was easing down on to a flattish rock on the ocean side of the island. Waves were starting to splash against the rock as Tim, with a wet suit on, disappeared into the water to look for lobsters. By the time he reappeared carrying a small bag stuffed with crayfish, water was sloshing over the skids of the helicopter. The Zimbabwean was pale with worry. He had already asked Steve whether Steve could fly a helicopter and learnt that if Tim did not come back, they would be stranded on a tide-washed rock. Tim did come back. He also realised the helicopter was at risk of swamping by a rogue wave. Steve and the visitor helped Tim, dripping wet, into the pilot's seat, and they quickly departed for the ship where a warming plunge in the spa pool awaited them. Next, as promised, came a magnificent lobster feast.

Live crayfish, which Tim called 'beetles', figured strongly in the commercial life of the *Ranginui* in the late 1980s, after the formation of The Helicopter Line. Steve Dyet ran the venture, whose aim was to establish an export trade in live crays to Asia, chiefly to Japan. Key to the operation at the *Ranginui* end of things were three red Para pools covered by blue tarpaulins. They sprouted on the top deck, serving as holding tanks for the crayfish. There was room now for just one helicopter, which transported the wriggling crays to a complex of pools and tanks set up at Te Anau. All this was happening as the net-captured live deer business wound down. THL entered into the venture with Wilson Neill and Otakou Fisheries – the same partners as Tim had engaged for the subantarctic spider crab venture.

Like the Auckland Islands spider saga, the Fiordland live crayfish venture was experimental. It involved buying in catches from local commercial vessels working lobster pots along the Fiordland coast.

Tim assisted in marketing the lobsters, as he had done with the spider crabs. Accompanied by Steve, he visited Japan, and did the rounds of the lobster trade in Tokyo and Osaka. An old hand at relating to Asians, Tim was a hit with his Japanese counterparts. They – just as the Chinese had been – were impressed not only by his business instincts and flying prowess but also with how he managed to succeed at both with his limp. The Japanese were as interested as the Chinese and other peoples in his disability, and especially how he managed to be successful in business and in aviation despite it.

The *Ranginui*-based live cray export business ran into difficulties, however. These included opposition from Fiordland crayfishing interests, and a quirky train of events that affected the Japanese market.

At the heart of the difficulties in the Japanese market were the colours of the crayfish – red shell and white flesh. Red is a symbol for joy in Japan; white is the royal colour. Unfortunately for the export venture, the Emperor of Japan was ill, and the Japanese people shunned white products and joyous red ones as well. Cherries and red apples also suffered in the Japanese market through this period.

The *Ranginui* had seen various forms of primary produce come and go – shot deer, live deer and now live crayfish. What outlived them all was her capacity for entertainment. A steady stream of guests, family members and friends enjoyed *Ranginui* hospitality. The Wallis boys often marked their birthdays at the *Ranginui*. They were growing up fast, and the

First Arm crash

One Easter, Tim and Prue invited their friends Mark and Jo Acland, their boys and the Fitzgerald family, Beau, Anne and their son, Gerald, to holiday aboard the *Ranginui*. An English lad, Angus McDonald, was also in the party. It was about 4.30 in the afternoon by the time all were on board. Although a storm was brewing, Tim had set his sights on a traditional first-night dinner of fresh crayfish.

With five passengers in the helicopter, Tim flew off to a favourite diving spot. By the time they had rounded up enough lobsters, the cloud had descended, the wind had increased to near gale force and in the murky conditions darkness was falling prematurely.

As they entered First Arm, first turn right after Bauza Island heading in from the ocean, massive gusts of wind were sending water spouts into the air. The *Ranginui* was at the head of the high-sided inlet. Her lights showed up through the storm.

As a precaution, Tim decided to ferry his passengers to the *Ranginui* in two loads and remove the door beside him so he could better see the flight deck while landing. For a staging point he chose a beach not far from the ship. Just as he approached it, a water spout with almost tornado-like power smashed into the helicopter, enveloping it in spray and knocking out the tail rotor. The machine began to spin. Tim had no choice but to put it down as fast as he could. Although, fortunately, the beach was handy, the Hughes became unstable and tipped. Its main rotor was thrashed to bits. All on board were injured. Beau Fitzgerald and Angus were knocked out temporarily.

Mark Acland, who had a cut on the head and a sore foot, was ready to swim over to the *Ranginui* when he heard the ship's dinghy approaching through the dark. Prue and Jo, unable to hear any sounds from the helicopter above the roar of wind, had seen its strobe lights go out and raised the alarm.

A Te Anau doctor, Trevor Walker, who was flown in by Bill Black, attended to the wounded in the lounge area, which resembled a small hospital ward. Two of the injured flew out for treatment at Kew Hospital. The helicopter was a write-off.

Ranginui aided and abetted the process, introducing them at an early age to diving, fishing, swimming, boating, hunting, exploring, and waterskiing behind the seven-metre jet-boat, *Big Bertha*, which doubled as a dive boat.

On warm days, with or without swimming togs or wetsuits, the boys, their school mates and the not-so-young as well, delighted in leaping off the flight deck into the cool deep waters of the fiord. Many of the family's guests, spurred on by the intrepid atmosphere aboard the *Ranginui*, were challenged to try things they never thought they would ever get to do.

Each day started with someone – often Tim – getting up early and starting the generator. It was an alarm clock that had a comforting ring to it. If they were aboard, the boys would get dressed and help make breakfast, and even sometimes bring their mother breakfast in bed.

In the school holidays, the family would fly together in Tim's Hughes 500. There would be four youngsters jammed into the front seats with Tim on the left, and Mum and a lot of gear stashed in the back. On these trips, Tim would fly his regular route to Breaksea. If the cloud was low on Wilmot Pass, Tim would buzz the tourist buses grinding to the top of the pass, startling the unsuspecting driver. In the Bell jet ranger, Bill Black used to keep in radio contact with Tim, and would be ready to race the Breaksea-Doubtful area if they did not report a safe arrival at the *Ranginui*.

Tim enjoying a day out with his Hughes 500 off Bauza Island, Doubtful Sound.

Tim taught all the boys to scuba dive. This was an environment in which he could fully enjoy their company unlike in the bush, where he rarely ventured beyond the margins with the boys. In the bush, showing them deer trails, prints and browse signs, he needed a boy on either side of him to maintain balance; in the Fiordland waters, with only one flipper, he seemed to the boys to be as swift and agile as a dolphin or a fur seal. They had trouble keeping up with him. Their father had taught them to dive for paua or crayfish from the age of six or seven. They also dived to explore an extraordinary underwater world that included 'forests' of tree-shaped black coral colonies clinging to the sheer rock faces. At the end of a day's diving, Tim insisted the boys wash the salt water off their gear. Eventually, all the boys gained their scuba diving certificates.

Besides diving, boating was high on the list of favourite activities for the boys during the *Ranginui* holidays at Dusky Sound and finally Breaksea Sound. The Wallis boys were rarely without similar-age company on holidays. The Wilson and Acland families often joined them, as did friends from school.

Putting about in a four-metre aluminium dinghy with a feeble Seagull outboard motor was not something Tim could readily participate in but he enjoyed organising the boys on fishing expeditions. Two boys might set out in the morning, and the other two in the afternoon, and at the end of the day Tim would count the catches to see which pair had more success. The family dinghy acquired a challenging character when someone fired a bullet through it. From then on, whether the boys went fishing in the dinghy or used it to get ashore to go hunting, they had to make sure the hole was corked.

There were a few dramatic moments. The youngest Wallis boy, Nick, was 13 years old the day that Tim took him, his brother Matt, then 15, and two of their friends, to the *Ranginui* in his Hughes 500 D. With their diving gear on board, Tim thought he would give them the opportunity to dive at an unfamiliar place – the entrance to Dagg Sound. He landed at a beach on the north side, near the entrance, which broadens out to be two kilometres wide. Nick teamed up with Robert Lamplough, the son of English friends, and Matt entered the water with his friend, Sam Savill. Tim, generally a starter for an afternoon nap, nodded off at the beach.

He awoke to an alarming situation. The tide had turned. It was sweeping out the entrance and had carried the two pairs of divers with it.

Swimming as hard as they could, Nick and Robert only just managed to reach rocks at the foot of the cliff near the northern promontory, a hook of land ominously called Cast-off Point. They scrambled ashore in a surging sea. Robert had to ditch his buoyancy compensator device (BCD), tanks and weight belt. Still in their wet suits, the boys carefully made their way to the top of the cliff, where Tim could safely pick them up.

When Matt and Sam surfaced they found themselves outside the entrance to the fiord, caught in the rip and unable to make headway against it. The westerly swell steepened as the tide met it head on. Tim could see they were in trouble and gunned the Hughes into life. Seeing the other two were back on land, he brought the helicopter to a hover alongside Matt and Sam. There was only one way to help them. He moved towards them, keeping the skid so low to the water they could grab a hold of it. He had to watch the swell at the same time, and move the helicopter up and down to match its rhythm, and so avoid a tail-rotor strike. Slowly he pulled Matt and Sam to the shore.

Afterwards, with all four boys safe, Tim flew out to search for a bright yellow patch marking the presence of the ditched BCD. When they found it, Matt leaned out and plucked the gear aboard.

There was not much discussion about the incident after their arrival at the *Ranginui*. Tim was fairly tight-lipped about it. All he would say was: 'It's amazing what you can do when you have to.' The boys all knew it was an awesome feat of flying. Tim's helicopter had 'short' skids fitted. Some pilots preferred them for deer recovery work and in Tim's case the short skid legs enabled him to get into and out of the machine more easily. But short skids also meant he had less leeway when it came to hovering within

'No more boats!'

In the 1980s, Tim travelled to the North Island to invest in more shipping. He bought a car ferry and a game fishing vessel. The Alpine directors, concerned that the new vessels might be surplus to requirements, decided they should be sold. It was politely suggested to Tim that he cease playing with boats for a while, even in the bath!

Air race

In March 1987, Tim Wallis and Tom Middleton, an expert pilot, entered the Singapore-Christchurch air race in the company's Cessna Centurion 210 turbo-prop aircraft. Tom was The Helicopter Line's corporate pilot; Tim, for this race, was his co-pilot. The race, marking the jubilee of Christchurch International Airport, involved about 30 aircraft, representing many different types, from around the world. With programmed stops at Bali, Darwin and Brisbane, the race covered a distance of just on 4,800 nautical miles. At an average speed of 160 knots, the Cessna Centurion completed the trip in less than 30 hours to take third place and $3,000 in prize money. Tragically, Tom was killed in the year 2000 when a Pitts Special he was piloting crashed on the Luggate side of Wanaka Airport. An English passenger also died in the crash.

Tim with the Cessna 210 used for the 1987 Singapore-Christchurch air race.

centimetres of a lumpy sea. Less clearance not only for the airframe but also for the tail rotor.

The Dagg Sound dive incident joined a growing list of 'Don't tell Mum' stories (even if Prue sooner or later became aware of the detail) – and everyone got on with enjoying the hospitality of the *Ranginui*.

Given the level of outdoor activity, the food on board *Ranginui* was always hearty. Hearty and full of character. Hunters on board could turn on a meal of fresh venison in a few hours, and passing fishing boats would hand over crayfish and other seafood – ideal for Tim's shipboard speciality, a seafood chowder. To the fish and shellfish, he added chopped onions and spring onions, and with a flour and milk paste, he made the chowder thick enough to stand a spoon in.

Tim always knew where to catch crayfish. The day a group of eight recreational divers from Canterbury came on board the *Ranginui*, at Tim's invitation, the ship was in Doubtful Sound. Tim readied *Big Bertha*. John Muir was on the ship at the time and joined the group. They set out for Bauza Island, which dominates the entrance of the fiord, dividing it into two navigable channels. *Big Bertha* arrived at a spot beside the island that Tim had selected. Two at a time, the visitors dived with their scuba gear and they returned to the surface well pleased with their catches, comprising mostly four to six lobsters.

'Okay, John,' Tim said. 'It's our turn.' With Tim leading and powered only by the flipper on his right leg, he descended to about 15 metres. Here Tim signalled to John a sudden change in direction. Holding a similar depth, he led John a couple of hundred metres away from *Big Bertha* until they reached a crevice that John realised his boss must have known about. In it, the lobsters were lined up 'like Watties cans on a supermarket shelf'. When they got back to the boat, their catch bags were bulging. The Cantabrians were goggle-eyed.

IN JANUARY, 1987, Reid Jackson, one of the *Ranginui's* most popular visitors, and a pillar of support for Tim's business interests, succumbed to cancer. He had been treated for the disease in his mid-thirties and in the middle of 1986 the disease reappeared, more invasively this time. His death at the age of 52 was a blow to the business world – Reid was a director of major companies such as Petrocorp, Renouf Corporation, R. and W. Hellaby, Winstones and Alliance Textiles as well as The Helicopter Line. It was also a massive personal blow to Tim. Reid was at once a stabilising influence on Tim and an enabling force. Tim put many a business proposition to Reid and respected the opinion he got back. The two were very close friends.

Reid Jackson

In Reid's Mornington home, there was a room for Tim at the top of the stairs which he often used. Reid was both a close friend of Tim's and his most trusted business adviser.

Both men were achievement-driven. They worked tremendously long hours. They shared a love of flying and they built up a unique business that took them around New Zealand, to the New Hebrides, Hong Kong and other exotic places.

The *Otago Daily Times* described Reid as 'arguably the most influential businessman in southern New Zealand'. To acknowledge his involvement in aviation, there was a fly-by over St Paul's Cathedral, Dunedin, where the funeral was held, involving an unusual collection of planes – a

Tiger Moth, Harvard and Cessna 185. Reid had flown all these aircraft
types.

Now, without his business confidant of 20 years, Tim knew he might
have to wing it with his ideas. In the business hurly-burly of the late 1980s,
he was certainly not short of them.

THE MONTH AFTER ALPINE sold Mararoa, and ten months after
the loss of Reid Jackson, the bottom fell out of the sharemarket. The
October 1987 crash, triggered by collapses on Wall Street and other major international stock exchanges, caused widespread mayhem in the New
Zealand business world. Many businesses went under. Of the 100-odd
New Zealand companies formed in the previous 12 months, only five
survived. THL was one of them. Its share price, however, fell below issue
price, bottoming out around 30 cents. Across the board, shares declined
in value by tens of millions of dollars.

There was collective belt-tightening throughout the business world,
and Christmas 1987 was gloomy for countless families around New Zealand. Alpine had already begun downsizing on its deer work. Letters
advising of the company's circumstances and the need to retrench were
sent to a number of employees, many of whom were like extended family
to Tim. His research and development assistant, John Muir, was among
those laid off. John and his wife, Di, had been close to Tim and Prue and
occasionally minded the boys while their parents were out of town.

Tim was about as shocked by the staff redundancies as were the affected staff members. Having worked hard to build the expertise, he was
now seeing elements of it frittered away. Still, there was a good chance
Alpine would bounce back and reemploy them in some form. Mararoa
Station sold for several million dollars more than the property might have
yielded a few months later.

Within a year of the sharemarket crash, The Helicopter Line embarked
on acquiring assets in the tourism sector. Auckland-based Maui
Campervans was the first. It was the country's largest campervan business
at the time. Maui's Chris Alpe joined the THL board of directors as a
consequence. Newmans' large campervan fleet and the popular Auckland
tourist venture, Kelly Tarlton's Underwater World, were acquired in 1990.
Investment in Fiordland tourism came next. In 1992, THL bought a 50
percent interest in Te Anau's lake-front Travelodge, which incorporated
the Milford Track Guided Walk business and the hotel at Milford. THL
also bought into the Red Boats operation at Milford Sound.

The company entered the coach tour business as well, purchasing fleets of coaches in New Zealand and Fiji. In 1995, the fabled Hermitage hotel at Mt Cook village and the Waitomo Caves, Waitomo Hotel and a hotel in Rotorua were added to the investment portfolio. By 1997, THL's expanding empire had reached into the Australian and South African travel industry. Acquisitions overseas included a South African motor homes business. There were, by now, several hundred employees in the group. In about ten years the group had expanded ten-fold. Tim regularly appeared on the *National Business Review* 'Rich List'.

Through the late 1980s and into the 1990s, as THL raised its stake and profile in the New Zealand tourism industry, Tim continued with his deer work. As a THL director and major shareholder, he was closely involved in the tourism investment decisions but his commitment to the deer industry did not waver. He was convinced the deer industry would continue to develop despite the Roger Douglas fiscal blows. If anything, the Douglas interventions would allow the industry to find a more honest footing. As farming writer David Yerex commented, '… it was the beginning of deer farming's growth on the basis of market returns, not tax credits.'

Tim's focus on netting deer from helicopters had switched by now to an entirely new concept – live trapping. Although deer farmers were becoming more self-sufficient, there remained a market for captured feral deer, especially red deer from Fiordland that embodied wapiti bloodlines.

Riding the strop under Tim's helicopter with a captured deer at the world deer farming congress at Mt Hutt in 1993.

Tim's R&D staff experimented with designs for a self-activating pop-up trap that would work in remote locations, even in dense bush. It was a case of trial and error – and many hours spent at the drawing board. A few ideas were not pursued. One involved the use of a rocket to activate the trap. Set off by a deer (or other animal) entering the trap, the rocket hurtled down a 50 metre-long wire, hoisting the sides of the trap with its momentum. The method was tested on the grassy slope below the R&D workshop in Beacon Point Road but was soon rejected on the basis that it might scare the living daylights out of trampers or possibly injure them.

Traps with cloth and netting sides were designed. Models with four poles were standard, with weights suspended at the tops of the poles. When an animal set off the trap by way of a trip wire or solenoid, the weights dropped and the cloth or netting slid up tracks on the poles in one to two seconds, enclosing the animal.

In October 1986, with the permission of the authorities and following trials at Beacon Point Road, Criffel and elsewhere, the first of the pop-up traps were deployed in Fiordland National Park. Each trap transmitted a radio signal that helped the helicopter or fixed-wing aircraft with a receiver locate it in the expanses of forest. Wanaka pilot Rusty Knight, who started out as a shooter with Jim Kane in the heyday of *Ranginui* deer

Donation to research

At a deer sale in June 1985, Tim announced he would donate the value of the highest-priced animal to a deer research group whose name would be drawn out of a hat. An 18-month female wapiti, which had some Canadian elk breeding, fetched $17,500 at the sale, providing a windfall for the fledgling Ruakura research group in the Waikato.

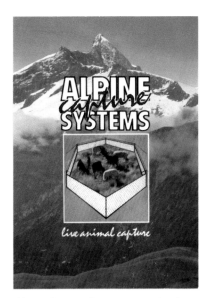

Alpine Capture Systems promotional booklet.

work, played a leading role in this phase of live deer recovery. During 1987 and 1988, Rusty helped set up traps in Fiordland between Doubtful Sound and the southern Waitutu coast. Most of them were located in the bush. Some traps captured more than one animal at once. Tim's dream, ultimately, was to equip the traps with NASA satellite communications technology whereby, at the triggering of each trap, a signal was despatched to his Wanaka base via satellite. However, the government tax changes and consequent decline in investment by deer farmers depressed the market, which in turn affected the economics of the trapping operation. It was put on hold.

Keen to capitalise on all the R&D effort, Tim's company went into partnership with the Ministry of Agriculture at Invermay through the auspices of MAF Deer to develop and produce traps for marketing overseas. They were branded 'Alpine Capture Systems', and sales were made to countries as diverse as Japan, Spain, Hawaii and the United Arab Emirates. In Japan, the traps were used to catch and relocate deer straying on to rice fields. In Spain, native sheep were the target, and in the UAE native antelope were caught and transferred to new areas in the hope they would establish new populations. This technique replaced previous 'Hatari'-style noose and vehicle operations, and hundreds of animals were successfully relocated.

The traps project was an example of the way Tim approached innovation. If he thought any new venture was a winner, his enthusiasm knew no bounds. In June 1990, the traps were demonstrated at the Second International Wildlife Conference in Edmonton, Canada, and at one stage

Net trap demonstration day at Lillburn Valley, western Southland.

in the conference they 'captured' about 50 delegates, some of whom had previously declared the technology would never work!

Back home, meanwhile, with the traps scattered about Fiordland falling into disuse, deer farming bravely kept its chin up in the face of marketing and financial pressures. It looked to new ideas in farming practice to survive. The first World Deer Farming Congress was held in Christchurch in 1993, with field visits for the delegates to farms in the Canterbury high country. Tim, a keynote speaker, described the history and evolution of deer farming in New Zealand and the development of the velvet antler trade. Tim organised a full afternoon's flying display that traced the history of deer recovery and capture systems over the previous 25 years. The congress reinforced New Zealand's reputation as a leader in pastoral deer farming and Tim's reputation as a pioneer.

Actually, the industry's first international conference had been held in Dunedin ten years earlier, in 1983. Deer biology was the theme, and how it linked to production. Invermay's Ken Drew played a leading role in organising this conference, at which a visiting professor, Roger Short of Monash University, Melbourne, hailed the world's newest 'domesticated animal'. He told the audience: 'Today New Zealand unquestionably leads the world in the development of intensive husbandry systems for farming deer and as a result of your efforts you can truthfully claim to have created a new domesticated animal.'

New chairman

In the wake of Reid Jackson's death, Murray Valentine became chairman of the THL Board of Directors. WR Jackson and Company became WR Jackson, Valentine and Co., with Murray Valentine taking over this firm.

Chapter 10

Into Canada

Late 1980s–1990s
A new frontier ... Coldstream Deer Group ... red deer
airlifted to Canada ... disease scare ... Orr Lake Elk ...
elk genetics to the world

IN 1988, WITH THE DOMESTICATION of red deer firmly established
in New Zealand, Tim and his business colleagues created a new frontier
for red deer farming a hemisphere away from its New Zealand roots. The
country they chose was Canada. As was his practice and his passion, Tim
had done a lot of homework on Canada before deciding to pursue a commercial venture there. Behind him was his experience of exporting red
deer from New Zealand to South Korea and Taiwan and his familiarity
with deer farming in those countries. In Korea and other parts of Asia,
deer were mostly hand-fed; in Canada, they were put out to graze, although during Canada's harsh continental winters, supplementary feeding of farmed deer was necessary. Culturally, Canada was easier to operate
in. Like New Zealand, it was a member of the Commonwealth and many
New Zealanders felt a greater affinity to Canadians than to Americans.
When it came to red tape, Canada was less entangled than neighbouring
United States. Nonetheless, Tim thought there might be commercial prospects in the future in America, using Canada – the province of Ontario in
particular – as a staging point.

In the early 1980s, in the course of importing Canadian elk into New
Zealand, Tim had been impressed with the Ontario environment, the
climate, topography and the quality of the pastures. He thought red deer
would thrive there. Moreover, Ontario's provincial government seemed to
be reasonably relaxed about the prospect of red deer farming, which Tim
felt Canada was ripe for, based on the two major products: venison and
velvet. Thus the Coldstream Deer Group was born. It was set up by Alpine and Canadian interests on a 50:50 basis. Initially, the Canadian partners were Todd Grignon, an Ontario mink farmer, and his friend, Henry

*Opposite: The New Zealand red
deer airlifted to Canada were
quarantined at this farm in
Ontario.* Mike Bringans

Regelink. Todd's uncle, Norman Bradley, who owned a cable television company, became the principal Canadian investor. Alpine engaged the services of Southland veterinarian Mike Bringans, a Massey University graduate who had a practice at Winton and an elk farm there based on imports from North America that arrived after the Criffel imports.

From a farming point of view, red deer offered Canadian farmers an efficient means of entering the North American venison market. Red deer cost less to supplementary feed than the larger elk. In terms of price, New Zealand red deer competed well with the local elk and the introduced fallow deer, even after shipping and quarantine costs were taken into account. A New Zealand hind might fetch up to $NZ3,750 in Canada at the time.

The first consignment, 307 all up, was despatched to Todd Grignon's mink farm in Ontario in October 1988 for on-selling. It comprised a mixture of hinds and stags, and a large number of yearlings. The deer were shedding their southern winter coats at the time and in the new home, the further loss of insulating hair was of concern to their handlers there. But they adapted well to the onset of winter in Canada. Within three weeks of their arrival they were romping in snow in temperatures down to minus 15 degrees Celsius. Only one died.

In a land of beef and wheat farming, there were few deer farms. Most deer farmers ran elk or the smaller European fallow deer. The latter were introduced into British Columbia by New Zealanders with fallow deer farming experience about the same time as Tim was introducing farmers out east to red deer.

Red deer were practically unknown until the Alpine shipments turned up. The second consignment, in March 1989, was followed by four more that year. A stretch DC-8 airfreighter was used for the initial airlifts; an American Boeing 747, with capacity for up to 1,000 yearlings, was engaged for later ones. The planes unloaded the deer at Hamilton Airport near Toronto, the capital of Ontario..

In charge of assembling this exodus of deer was Simon Bartlett, who joined Tim's company in November 1988 and later became the Criffel manager. A former fencing contractor, Simon had managed the Wilson Neill deer park at Mossburn and before that a large red deer farm at Mount Hutt. He toured New Zealand to source and buy deer for the Alpine shipments to Canada.

At Wanaka, exclusive handling facilities – shelters, feeding areas and exercise yards – were set up to prepare the animals for their long journey and to comply with New Zealand and Canadian animal-health and other protocols. Some of the deer were prepared for the journey at North Island

Canada farming

Deer farming is a small player in Canadian farming. In 1990, half of the huge country's 280,000 farms ran livestock and half grew crops, mostly wheat. Beef, dairy, pigs and poultry made up the bulk of the livestock, with cattle ranches predominant.

Big Curve Acres in Ontario where the red deer went for breeding if not sold in quarantine. Mike Bringans

quarantine locations. Although Alpine staff, including Raylene Jelley, had raised hundreds of fawns captured in the wild over the years, the Canada operation involved larger herds, as many as 1,400 at one time, and more red tape. It was a concentrated exercise, involving new methods of feeding and handling.

To keep the deer in top condition, a high-protein feed meal based on lucerne, barley and milk powder was developed. In the interests of hygiene, the animals ran around on a floor of sand. They grew used to the presence of human handlers. By the time they were ready for airlifting to Canada they were a lot quieter than if they had been run in paddocks.

About this time, Tim and Prue and their four sons moved from Beacon Point Road to the Criffel property at Mount Barker Road. They lived in the existing cottage at the foot of the range until a new house was built on a bench about 100 metres above the flat land. The view from the new place was prodigious. A 180-degree sweep took in the country dearest to Tim's heart. Out left were Mt Aspiring, Roy's Peak and the Matukituki Valley, with glimpses of Lake Wanaka and the Minaret Peaks beyond the water. Ahead lay the mountains around Dublin Bay, scene of many an adventurous schoolboy holiday, and across to the right, Lake Hawea, the Hunter Valley and the mountains bounding the lake. In 1989 Tim and Prue moved into their elegant new stone-clad home on the lower slopes of the Criffel Range. They called it Benfiddich, meaning Mountain of Deer.

The deer exports to Canada were driven by sales arranged through the Coldstream Deer Group. The biggest deal involved 600 deer, which were sold to a cable television associate of the group's Canadian partners, Bill Stanley, who was based in New Brunswick. Moving the deer from one province (Ontario) to another (New Brunswick) required the negotiation of stringent animal-health protocols, a job that fell to Mike Bringans. In another significant deal, 200 deer were despatched to Wisconsin in the United States following their quarantine period in Canada and the issuing of a clean bill of health that made them Canadian 'citizens'.

The deer trucked over the border to Wisconsin, in December 1989, were bought by Norb Berg, who had helped establish a billion-dollar business in data processing and now wanted to go farming. They were the first New Zealand red deer shipment to arrive in America. It was a cold welcome, with snow lying thickly on the ground and temperatures as low as minus 14° Celsius. Also on the farm was an elk herd, which the farmer intended cross-breeding with the reds.

In anticipation of the arrival of the live deer shipments from New Zealand, Coldstream ran investment seminars to promote sales from its base at Cold Water near the town of Barrie, about 90 minutes' drive north

Orr Lake Elk farm in Ontario.
Mike Bringans

of Toronto. Coldstream promised anyone purchasing the New Zealand deer back-up in terms of deer 'ranching' techniques and ongoing advice.

By March 1990, Alpine had flown about 3,500 deer to Canada. Then the Canadian authorities suspended the trade. They were concerned about the possibility of bovine tuberculosis arriving with the New Zealand deer and infecting local stock, despite the precautions taken at the New Zealand end, and despite the quarantining on arrival in Canada. Word had spread among recreational deer hunters in Canada that the country was receiving an influx of red deer from a country with a bovine TB problem. The hunters, numbering 100,000 in Ontario alone, became agitated and vocal about the threat of disease being imported. They took their case to the authorities. The door for red deer imports closed for a time.

AS ONE DOOR closed, another opened. Orr Lake Elk proved to be a door that opened to the world. In partnership with Mike Bringans, Tim had been discussing for some time the establishment of an elk stud farm in a suitable environment. His Canada connection with Tim began when Tim offered him a job overseeing the quarantine requirements of Alpine's first shipment of red deer to Canada. Mike also provided Canadian farmers acquiring New Zealand deer with advice on animal health and breeding issues.

In early 1990, winter time, he and Mike set up Orr Lake Elk on 120 acres in an attractive area of Ontario. The property was owned by Mike and his wife Dianne, and leased to the partnership. The low hills and gentle slopes, running down to a lake a little smaller than Queenstown's

Tim feeding out.

Lake Hayes, were covered in lush pasture and patches of forest. The aim of the operation was to produce the finest possible elk for velvet and trophy-antler markets as well as top-line herd sires and genetics in the form of semen and embryos.

Imports of New Zealand red deer continued for some time that year. But, finally, a tiny nematode parasite, known commonly as a tissue worm and to scientists as *Elaphostrongylus cervi*, put an end to the shipments, which were already under a suspected TB cloud. Larvae suspiciously like those of the parasite *E. cervi* – but never proven definitely to be so – showed up in the faeces of two animals in a shipment of 230 New Zealand deer. As far as the Canadian authorities were concerned, the mere hint of a problem parasite was enough to shut down the importing.

Shipping the 230 deer back to New Zealand was reckoned to be too expensive an option. After six months' wrangling with scientists and bureaucrats, Alpine sadly ordered the shipment destroyed and forfeited revenue from sales that might have reached over $CAD700,000.

The banning of the shipments into Canada proved fatal to the Coldstream joint venture. Investor Norman Bradley had already pulled out of the venture over the concerns about New Zealand deer carrying diseases such as tuberculosis. After months of wrangling with the authorities over the deer import ban – and following the defection of the tall, moustachioed Todd Grignon to a competing operation – the New Zealanders threw their energy into Orr Lake Elk.

Tim was not one to look back with regret. He had set up in Canada in order to succeed. As he told *The Deer Farmer* magazine in 1990: 'I am doing this because I have 30 years' experience in deer capture, farming, transport, export and import … I am doing what I enjoy doing.' And in

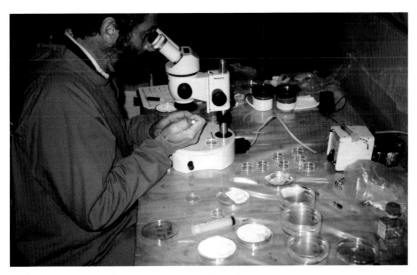

Mike Bringans he had an expert and loyal partner.

Orr Lake Elk acquired its breeding stock from Manitoba after selling some New Zealand hybrids. The partnership's aim was to breed stud elk that would boost velvet production, supply prize animals for Canada's trophy hunting business, and provide stud animals to farmers who wanted to upgrade their stock.

In light of their experience of managing wapiti back home, the New Zealanders began producing elk of impressive size and velvet yield. Orr Lake grew steadily. It had as many as 700 bulls and cows at one time. Mike's expertise in deer genetics was a significant factor in the success of

Guest judge

When the North American Elk Breeders' Association decided to stage its first velvet competition in 1989, Tim Wallis was invited to participate as guest judge. Tim became a regular name on the guest list at deer farming conventions in Canada, and he was often invited to speak about his experiences.

A refreshment break at an elk auction at Orr Lake Elk. Tim is flanked by Norbert Berg and the Wallis sons, Toby, Jonathan and Matt. Mike Bringans

'Hurricane Tim', an outstanding elk bull, at Tutira. Mari Hill Harpur

the business, which turned to supplying elk semen and embryos to farmers in many parts of Canada and the United States.

Orr Lake expanded through the purchase of a farm in Horseshoe Valley to run more elk and target world-class red deer genetics development. Embryos were imported directly from Warnham and Woburn deer parks in England and from several New Zealand breeders. Soon, Orr Lake's genetics services were being sought in many parts of the world. Elk semen was exported to New Zealand, Australia, Korea and Hawaii. Semen from one bull earned $1 million in a year for Orr Lake. Embryo transplants were also delivered by Mike, who is an embryo transplant specialist, and a team of veterinarians employed by Orr Lake, some of whom saw business opportunities for themselves and set up in competition. Orr Lake Elk carried out work in Britain, Spain, Poland, Hungary, Croatia, Mexico, South Africa, Chile, China and Russia.

Of all the countries they worked in, Russia loomed large. Its breed of elk produced the highest velvet yield of all. Tim had a master plan. It involved upgrading the Orr Lake herd with genetic material from Russia. He could imagine the Russian elk being willing partners in such a scheme. But what of the Russian farmers, politicians and bureaucrats?

What of the Iron Curtain?

Another day in the life of 'Hurricane Tim'

A summer's day, 1993. At 5 a.m., Tim Wallis, international businessman, flies into Auckland from Canada and the United States – a 12-hour flight from Los Angeles, business class. Feeling well rested, as he usually does after these long flights, he has a breakfast meeting with executives of Auckland-based Maui Campervans, one of The Helicopter Line group of companies.

Then he boards an Air New Zealand flight to Christchurch, where he picks up the Cessna Centurion 210 he left there on his way overseas. He flies the Cessna to Glentanner Station, a developing tourist attraction in the Tasman River Valley near Mt Cook, to attend the opening of the new THL helicopter base and office. Then it is on to Wanaka in the Cessna, where he has an early afternoon appointment with Korean oriental medicine dealers, who are interested in his company's deer-antler and other products.

By late afternoon he is in the air again, bound for Queenstown. This time he is accompanied by the director of the New Zealand Fighter Pilots' Museum at Wanaka, Ian Brodie. They plan to farewell friends who have been visiting from a war museum at Duxford, England. By 6.30 p.m., the Cessna Centurion is back at Wanaka Airport, and Tim Wallis is in his office at the airport, unloading his briefcase, checking faxes and generally catching up with his business affairs after several weeks' absence. He will be home for tea shortly.

Luggate Game Packers/Alpine Helicopter deer recovery pilots, shooters, gutters and other staff, with Tim and Don Spary (centre, front row) at the company reunion in 1993.

Chapter 11

Russian Machinations

1990s
A Canadian warning ... first ideas about Russia ...
perestroika ... a joint venture called Altyn Kerl ...
velvet trading ... deer farming attempted ... rafting
the Kartun River ... Russian mafia ... supermarket
development out east ... strategic withdrawal ...
coping with pain

'THE AMBASSADOR WILL SEE YOU NOW.' In the company of his New Zealand partner in Canada, Mike Bringans, and two Canadian deer industry associates, Tim Wallis is shown into the Moscow office of the Canadian Ambassador to Russia.

The Ambassador is a woman. After welcoming the visitors, she delivers some formal and sobering advice. She tells the four men that, although the business climate is changing in Russia, they ought not to expect to make a lot of money out of any investment here. Foreign capital has the habit of 'draining away'. If a foreigner in business can walk out in a few years' time without losing a bundle, he ought to count himself fortunate. There are many pitfalls. Banditry is rife, thieving endemic.

The Ambassador's visitors notice that she keeps the spare wheel from a car, presumably her car, in the office. On her desk is a set of windshield wipers and the car's shiny badge of manufacture. A precaution against theft, she says.

TIM HAD BEEN THINKING about doing business in Russia for a long time. In December 1971, in a letter to Prue, who was working in London at that stage, Tim revealed an interest in an exploratory visit to check on how the Russians farmed their elk and sold the velvet to China.

Four months later he reported to Prue on the 'negative results' regarding a visit. He said he had been advised by people who had experience of

Russia that it would be a 'mission impossible' (a term that had particular resonance around that time because of a television drama of the same name). The Soviet Embassy in Wellington were 'little better than useless', he told Prue. Still, he had not given up hope entirely. He asked Prue if she could enquire in London about a particular region of the Soviet Union – Gorni Altai in southern Siberia.

Through his knowledge of the oriental medicine market, he knew that this isolated region was a main supplier of velvet to the Chinese and Korean markets. He knew Gorni Altai was the centre of deer farming in Russia and that the deer in the region's mountains and downland areas produced velvet of phenomenal size and quality. Iron Curtain and Cold War regardless, he just had to see the place for himself. The more he was dissuaded, the keener he felt about making the acquaintance of these legendary Russian elk for himself.

In the event, Russia came to him first. In February 1989, with planning for a series of live deer exports to Canada in full swing, a delegation from the Gorni Altai region arrived in New Zealand at the invitation of Sovenz, the trading arm of the New Zealand Dairy Board in Russia. Sovenz managing director Bruce Gaffikin brought the Gorni Altai politicians and agribusiness delegates to Criffel to meet New Zealand's most prominent deer farmer. Tim was delighted to host them at Criffel and show them how his red deer, wapiti and imported elk were managed for venison and velvet. A visit to the *Ranginui* went down well. Recognising hospitality as warmly embracing as their own, the Russians insisted on a reciprocal visit.

Two months later, Bruce Gaffikin put together a small delegation from the New Zealand deer industry to explore issues of mutual interest in

Russia. Bruce, at the age of 35, probably knew more about doing business in the Soviet Union than any New Zealander. His first visit was in 1977 as an assistant to trade consultant Joe Walding, formerly the Minister of Overseas Trade in Norman Kirk's Labour Government. Bruce had run Sovenz since its inception in 1987. The Dairy Board set up Sovenz to trade its products into the USSR and raise its profile in that potentially huge market. With the trade between the two countries heavily in New Zealand's favour, Sovenz not only sold New Zealand butter and milk powder to the USSR but also purchased Russian products such as tractors, Lada cars, fertiliser and vodka for sale in New Zealand. In the Soviet Union it had investments in meatworks, cheese factories and in fish processing plants on Soviet trawlers. Bruce had connections all over Russia.

For the delegation to Gorni Altai, Bruce had no hesitation in selecting Tim. Also on that visit were the current political leaders of New Zealand's deer industry – the president of the New Zealand Deer Farmers' Assocation, James Guild, and the chairman of the Game Industry Board of New Zealand, Tom Williams. They flew into Moscow, checked into the lofty

1,000-room Ukraine Hotel, which overlooked many of the landmarks of the city, then flew on to Siberia to be welcomed at the Gorni Altai capital by a song-and-dance troupe in long red cloaks and fur busbies. In their songs, including a performance of throat singing, the troupe expressed a mixture of Mongolian and Eastern European traditions that reflected the geographical crossroads occupied by the Altai people. At the toast afterwards, everyone drank a special 45 percent proof liqueur made from deer velvet.

The New Zealanders were among the first foreigners to tour Gorni Altai. This most inland region of the Soviet Union, about the size of Otago and Southland, comprised mountainlands, downlands and flatter areas. Agriculture was the main employer and economic driver in the region. Tim likened the region's mountain country, interspersed with valley floors and lower slopes cleared for pasture, to the mountainlands at home. In spring, the time of their visit, the pastures were lush and sprinkled with wild flowers, promising a good hay and silage harvest.

Gorni Altai's mountains ran up to the border of China and Mongolia. Not far from where the deer were farmed, at altitudes well above those of New Zealand's highest mountains, you could stand in the snow of three countries. The region had a population estimated at 200,000, about 40,000 of whom lived in the main town, Gorno Altaysk. To get there from Moscow, the men flew for about four hours to the Siberian capital of Novosibirsk or to Barnaul, a smaller city about 200 kilometres south of there. From there they were driven at breakneck speed over seriously rough roads with their hearts in their mouths – for three or four hours – to get to the centre of the region.

Feeding out hay in Siberia.

Here, in a continental climate of extremes, deer were farmed on rangelands and valleys that carried a mixture of forest and alpine meadow. Temperatures range from minus 30ºC – sometimes colder – in the winter to intense summer heat reaching over 30ºC. The region experiences warm weather for only about three months a year, and mid-summer daylight lasts till about 11 p.m. at this latitude (52 degrees north, equivalent in the southern hemisphere to the latitude of subantarctic Campbell Island).

The farms, collectives under Communism, ran mainly cattle, deer, horses, camels and yaks. For administrative purposes the farms were grouped, and each group was under the control of a farm director. One group had more than 100 farm units. The deer paddocks tended to be huge, and typically, the deer were mustered on horseback and herded into yards in the velvet season.

Tim had his eyes wide open during the visit – and the video camera rolling. Touring a forbidden land was exciting in itself … mandatory vodka parties, saunas, salami and fried potatoes, scantily-stocked grocery shelves, fast driving over rough roads, the simple grimness of life in the villages where there was commonly no reticulated water supply or sanitation, and on the collective farms, the reliance on wood for heating and cooking. But to see the Siberian deer *Cervus elaphus sibericus* and the massive velvet they produced was a revelation. There was a record of one animal producing an incredible 27 kg. The Siberian elk were known as maral deer. Back in geological time, when sea levels were a lot lower, ancestral elk from Europe had ventured a long way east and crossed a land bridge to North America, hence the presence today in Canada and the United States of elk that are closely related to the Siberian deer. To Tim, the maral deer looked similar to the Canadian elk. The only distinguishing feature was the hair on the maral elk velvet antler, which was darker. Over 50,000 deer were farmed in the Altai region.

The New Zealand delegation's arrival in a formerly closed area of the Soviet Union in April 1989 was a symbol of an economically liberalising process the Russians called perestroika – literally, restructuring – which was mooted in 1985. The remoter regions of the Union of Soviet Socialist Republics were starting to feel perestroika only the year before the New Zealanders arrived in Gorni Altai.

The Kiwi pioneers here were bounced from farm to farm, feast to feast. They got through up to five feasts a day. It seemed incredible to them how there could be so much food available in the midst of conspicuous poverty. At each stop there was a customary bout of vodka toasting. It was critical to the visitors' business prospects. It verified the visitors' good intentions and cemented the contact. Locals believed that if a visitor harboured any bad intentions, these would be revealed under the influence of vodka. The New Zealanders soon understood why the average life expectancy for men in Russia was under 60. Often the food and drink made the delegation late for the next appointment, which was somewhere a long way off, down a bumpy road. Towards the day's end, according to Bruce, the Kiwis were often 'pretty bloody ragged'.

As Bruce had predicted, Tim won over his hosts. Socially, he was in his element. He could match the alcohol-hardened locals at vodka drinking –

They breed 'em tough

What Tim saw of the Gorni Altai elk during the 1989 delegation's visit convinced him they were probably the world's hardiest breed. They had to be tough to survive the prolonged winter, with temperatures extending below minus 30°C, and the method of velvet harvest. As a rule, the elk were herded into a wooden crush by a team of men, and firmly tied before one of the men sawed off the velvet antler without any sedating of the animal or pain relief. A powder containing camphor was rubbed on to the bleeding stubs to ward off flies.

The winter feed area of an Altai farm, with the elk mustered off the snow-bound hills.

as could Bruce, who was also of imposing size and had the stamina for it – and his ebullient personality shone through. His limp added to his magnetism because usually Russians regarded a disability of this kind as an impediment to success in sectors like agriculture. To the locals, Tim was a big man, made of special stuff.

The farms the delegation visited were huge, but by New Zealand standards they were low-tech, low-productivity operations. What stood out was the size of the workforce. The larger ones employed three or four thousand people; yet to the Kiwi eye the methods for harvesting and processing velvet were all strange and somewhat crude, despite the 150-odd year history of elk farming in Russia. Among the members of the delegation, ideas differed about the reasons for the phenomenal velvet production. Tim thought the velvet was robust because the bulls could not survive in the conditions without being robust themselves. Not only did they have to withstand harsh, prolonged winters (temperatures went below minus 30° Celsius), but velvet harvest involved no sedation or pain relief. The deer were placed in a wooden crush, with legs dangling, and the antlers were sawn off by a team of men. Camphor was rubbed on to the bleeding stubs to ward off flies.

One particularly important farm the New Zealanders visited was Karagai, home of the Popov clan. Karagai ran about 2,000 bulls, making

Getting ready for a deer muster on horseback at the Karagai farm. Peter Popov is riding the white horse.

it one of the largest velvet-producing farms in Russia. It produced eight tonnes or so of velvet a year, about a quarter of the country's dried velvet exports. Its boundary ran for 110 kilometres. The mountainlands of the Karagai collective were only 20 kilometres from the border of Kazakhstan, a region that sprawled southwest towards the Caspian Sea. The head of the clan, Peter Popov senior, who was in his eighties, was introduced to Tim. It was a 'very special moment' in Bruce's view – a meeting between the leading figures of the Russian and New Zealand deer industries. Tim got on well with the old man from the outset, which was fortunate for he knew that to get the measure of Russian deer and their extraordinary velvet output, and to have any hope of accessing their genetics, he had to get on side with the movers and shakers.

From this preliminary visit Tim felt the business opportunities here perhaps more than he could put his finger on them. He felt them in the warmth of the welcome and in the rapport he seemed to be able to develop with the locals, many of whom had Mongolian ethnicity or were part-Mongolian.

Through Bruce Gaffikin's knowledge of the way Russia worked and through his own research and observations, Tim could see that perestroika and a companion reforming principle known as glasnost ('openness') would allow Alpine to establish a base in Gorni Altai. He was not too concerned about criticism at home of the delegation's visit as it sprang from a perception that the Russians were potential competitors. Tim's view was that the trade in deer products was global and New Zealand could only stand to benefit from the Russian experience of it.

But to establish a venture in Russia, timing was everything. Mikhail

Gorbachev had just assumed supreme power in the Soviet Union. Appointed president in 1988, he had been a member of the Politburo since 1980 and a champion of perestroika. Revolutionary in its vision, perestroika set out to dismantle the decades-old Communist system of centralised economic power. Now regions were encouraged to take control of their own economic affairs.

Tim Wallis and his colleagues watched perestroika roll back the Iron Curtain and penetrate into regions as remote as Gorni Altai – and they rolled with it.

A JOINT VENTURE between Tim and Bruce Gaffikin was formed in 1991, with the blessing of the region's leadership. Under the name, Altyn Kerl, meaning Golden Mountain, the Russian joint venture became the springboard for a number of business initiatives. Bruce organised imports of consumer goods such as cosmetics and foodstuffs. Tim focussed on the velvet trade. Using Alpine's contacts in Hong Kong, he was confident he could lift the revenue the collective farms received from their velvet production.

Tim also wanted to establish a deer farm in the region, a place where he could focus on breeding for velvet. He asked his friends from Mount Somers Station in Canterbury, Mark and Jo Acland, to help him select a New Zealand farmer to manage such a farm. The Aclands interviewed and recommended a West Coast farmer, Robin Biddulph, and his wife Noelene, who managed a Government (Lands and Survey Department) farm near Westport.

Tim talking to curious Russian children after arriving at their farm village in the Altai region in a Mil 6 helicopter.

In April 1991, Tim organised a New Zealand group to visit the Gorni Altai region and assess the farming prospects. It included Graeme Ramshaw from the Alpine Deer Group, Mike Bringans, who came over from Canada, Mark Acland and Robin Biddulph. An interpreter from Sovenz, Svetlana Grebenkina, joined them. She was a 22-year-old from Barnaul who had majored in English at university. Her first encounter with Tim was when he emerged from a helicopter with video camera whirring and children rushing towards him for a closer look at the foreigner wielding a camera. Other key staff who worked for Tim were Manuel, a driver and logistics man, who had a Russian mother and a Mexican-American father, and an Armenian man called Armin, who had a brotherly relationship with Manuel. Both also worked for Sovenz.

Getting around the Altai region was a challenge. For longer journeys between farms, Tim used helicopters operated by the government. Heading out to inspect one remote deer farm, they chartered a 16-seat Mil8 helicopter. It cost the visitors a case of Australian Fosters beer. Tim got to fly the helicopter that day. These large helicopters were operated by the government but the Kiwi charterers knew the trip would run more smoothly if the crew received a sweetener, typically imported beer.

The year 1991 was pivotal in a number of ways. First, the feasibility study by the delegation came to the conclusion that, yes, they would be able to set up a deer farm. A Russian counterpart manager would be assigned to work with Robin at a place called Kiska, two hours' drive west of Gorno Altaysk. At Kiska, Alpine planned to establish fences, yards and worker accommodation on a failed former collective farm. A 99-year lease was negotiated with the support of the regional government. Tim had struck up a cordial working relationship with the region's president, Valeri Chaptinov, and its top administrator, Vladimir Petrov, who had the status of a state premier.

Second, on behalf of Altyn Kerl, Tim began selling Gorni Altai velvet into Korea, via Hong Kong, on a commission basis. Altyn Kerl would take five percent of the revenue to offset trading and other costs. This initial season generated five tonnes of product, which earned about $US5.4 million. The top dry-weight velvet fetched $US1,200 a kilogram.

Although a good deal of the revenue was appropriated by the farm directors personally, Bruce and Tim envisaged the new wealth would assist the development of the region's resources, including minerals (gold and marble in particular), timber and tourism. In the honeymoon period of Altyn Kerl, and with perestroika gradually extending business horizons, the two New Zealanders came to be regarded locally as saints of commerce. They certainly had the respect of the region's political leaders, who at one point proposed to display bronze busts of the two men in the town centre, and name streets after them.

But dark forces in Moscow were lining up to oppose the New Zealanders. Through the Sovenz operation, Bruce had an ongoing relationship with the Moscow-based government agency, Prodintorg, whose role under the old regime was to control imports into the USSR. Prodintorg's senior people, including the head of the agency, Alexander Krivenko, were graduates of a foreign trade academy and considered themselves a cut above other officials: they were permitted to associate with foreigners and indulge themselves in Western commodities, foods and fashion. They were also greedy. Over the years, and to one side of its core business, Prodintorg's dairy and meat division had developed a high-value export trade – Russian elk velvet, especially that of Gorni Altai. The main beneficiaries of this trade were the men who ran the agency. They had total power over the velvet producers, who received a mere fraction of the revenue.

About a year and a half before the advent of Altyn Kerl, Alexander Krivenko explained to Bruce one day that the decentralising of the Soviet economy was stirring up producer expectations in the regions. He asked Bruce to offer Gorni Altai some Sovenz-style infrastructure that might 'pacify' them. Once in that region Bruce appreciated the value of the elk velvet. He thought the impressive tradition of deer farming in Siberia might be of interest in New Zealand – hence the visit of a Russian delegation to New Zealand.

When Tim opened up velvet export channels for the Gorni Altai producers through Altyn Kerl – bypassing Moscow – the Prodintorg powerhouse and Krivenko in particular moved smartly to shut down the initiative. Clearly, Krivenko had underestimated the New Zealanders' expertise and nerve. He summoned Bruce to a lunch meeting in a restaurant in central Moscow. Bruce, aware of an ominous tone, took along two New

A high-altitude toast: New Zealanders Mark Acland, Mike Bringans and Tim visit the snow-bound border of Siberia, Mongo-lia and China, a helicopter flight from the Gorni Altai region.

Zealand associates. When he saw no one else in the restaurant, except for a small orchestra that was launching into a rendition of the well-known tune, 'Moscow Lights', he knew the discussions would be serious.

A stern-faced Krivenko asked Bruce if he had any American dollars. Bruce produced a $10 note, which Krivenko took over to the leader of the orchestra. The musicians promptly packed up and left. Krivenko, fury in his face, came straight to the point: the New Zealanders would stop the export of Gorni Altai velvet immediately. If they did not, he would order the cancellation of all dairy and meat imports from New Zealand (worth more than $US100 million a year at the time). Krivenko's rage was backed up by expletives in English, including a phrase commonly heard in Russian business circles … 'I'll fuck you over …' Bruce, trying to keep a cool head, asked for a month to work something out. He realised he could hardly face a bigger 'flashpoint' in his career.

Bruce contacted the Gorni Altai political bosses, Chaptinov and Petrov, and they came to Moscow for a high-level meeting. The fact they were accommodated at Stalin's old dacha or holiday home spoke volumes for Moscow's respect for them. The regional president and his premier went off for talks with Krivenko that Bruce was not party to, and they emerged with a deal satisfactory to them. It showed on their faces. From then on, Bruce suspected that Altyn Kerl would struggle to make headway in Gorni Altai, although he knew Tim well enough to realise his partner in the joint venture wouldn't give up just yet.

The year, 1991, was also momentous in Russian history. President Gorbachev, on a reforming mission, faced intense pressure from Communist hard-liners. He also had to deal on the one hand with die-hard

Bruce Gaffikin on the phone under a portrait of Lenin.

nationalists who wanted the old USSR to remain, and on the other, with secessionists who sought independence for their republics. In August, the tensions boiled over. Hard-line Communists staged a coup. Gorbachev was put under house arrest. The coup lasted only three days, the time it took the reformers to wrest back control and restore Gorbachev to power.

The writing was on the wall for Communist Party domination of the USSR, the world's largest country. Gorbachev suspended party activities and put reformers in charge of the military and the KGB police. Latvia, Estonia and Lithuania were the first republics to gain independence. By the end of 1991, the USSR ceased to exist. The world was astonished by the events.

Meanwhile, undeterred by the geopolitical crisis unfolding during the year – and more likely to regard it as a moment of opportunity – Tim pushed on with securing a stake in the deer industry in Gorni Altai, both through the joint venture, Altyn Kerl, and through Alpine's ambitions to set up a farm. He also wanted to show Prue and the boys something of the magnificence and mystique of Russia, in particular a region of southern Siberia formerly forbidden to outsiders. The two oldest sons, Toby, approaching his 16th birthday, and 14-year-old Jonathan, were students at Christ's College. Third son Matthew and the youngest, Nick, who had just turned 11, were still boarding at Waihi Prepatory School in South Canterbury.

The family set out from a wintry New Zealand at the start of the August school holidays, knowing there was political tension building in Moscow.

WHEN THE FAMILY ARRIVED IN THE SIBERIAN CAPITAL, Novosibirsk, they received a phone call from Bruce Gaffikin, who told them that the recent political tension had reached crisis point and that all domestic flights had been cancelled. Civil war was on the cards. So in place of the scheduled commercial flight to the Altai region, Tim chartered a Mil 17 helicopter for the last leg of the family's long trip from New Zealand. And he sweetened the arrangement with the helicopter crew by providing a case of Fosters beer and several cartons of Marlboro cigarettes.

To the boys, life in the Altai region seemed to be behind the times. Shops, vehicles and roads had a 1960s appearance. They were quickly made aware they were guests of the regional government, and Tim expected them to behave accordingly, especially at the banquets. When seated at the table, he would give them looks that said, 'You will eat this food – and you will enjoy it!'

Prue and the boys went horse-trekking at Karagai.

The boys each kept a record of their travels. Recalling the trip in an article in the Waihi school newsletter after getting home, Matthew wrote: 'We met up with Dad's farming partners … For lunch we had sheep intestine with grass still in it and blood sausage which was like rubber!'

At the Karagai farm the Wallises went trekking on horseback through colourful meadows of wild flowers and along trails darkened by conifer forests. The horses were unshod, and the bits in their mouths were fashioned from nails. Toby's horse bolted. Toby, a video camera in one hand and reins in the other, tried valiantly to control it but he was thrown off and it took half an hour to catch the horse. The trek through the afternoon took Prue and the boys to a magical hill-country setting where several hundred elk cows with calves grazed the forest-girt meadows in dappled sunshine. From the herd came a cacophony of squeaky calls and bawling – cow and calf conversation, strange to the visitors' ears. Later they gathered alpine berries and pine nuts under the guidance of the sons of farm workers, and they acquired the distinctive fur hats of the region.

To amuse the family while he conducted business, Tim arranged a

*The Wallis boys watch a Mil 8
leave after unloading at the
Kartun River for the rafting trip.*

four-night rafting adventure on the Kartun River. Prue and the boys flew
by helicopter to the upstream starting point without any idea of what to
expect. They suspected that Tim had no idea either. In the Altai region,
no one offered white-water rafting for visitors as a matter of course. Adventure tourism was a foreign concept.

Three guides, who were dairy factory workers, had been coopted for
the journey, with Svetlana tagging along in the role of interpreter. At the
starting point, two large deflated rubber pontoons were laid out on the
river bank. To pump them up, the guides took a flexible length of hose,
slipped one end over the exhaust pipe of a Lada van and the other into the
pontoon opening, and revved the Lada's engine like mad. Once the two
pontoons were inflated, freshly-cut birch poles were strapped to their sides
to link them, and a rectangular piece of cargo netting was slung between
the poles to carry the visitors' gear and food for camping. Home-made
paddles were loaded to assist steerage, everyone donned crude rubber wet
suits and off they went.

Like most rivers in this region, the Kartun was swift. Through the
gorges, it bucked and frothed with snow melt – a challenging Grade 3 in
places. They saw no people until the last day. At nights they set up a camp
on the river bank and ate boiled beef, cucumbers, tomatoes, cheese and
bread, which grew more crumbly by the day. At one camp site, the guides
built a sauna. A fire was lit under a pile of rocks until the rocks were too
hot to touch. With the fire doused and embers scraped away, a tent fly was
thrown over the rocks to form a cubicle held up by birch poles, water was
splashed on the rocks and, presto, the visitors had a steaming bathhouse
to enjoy, standing up. Tim arrived on the last day, choppering to a rendezvous

point and bringing with him Manuel, Armin and a pig that broke the boredom of the diet.

Trying to fit all this overseas travel into a three-week school holiday, the family was soon on the move again, bound for Moscow from Barnaul. But the coup against Gorbachev was under way, and suddenly flights into and out of Barnaul all but ceased. To the rescue came the negotiating skills of Manual and Armin, who managed to get them a flight to Moscow.

Once the Wallises had checked into their Moscow hotel, Tim needed to send a fax, which he wrote out by hand. Late at night Prue took it down to the hotel's reception where she discovered merriment coming from behind the front desk.

'Sorry to break up the party,' she said to the concierge, who emerged, beaming, with a glass in hand.

'No more party,' he said. He meant the Russian Communist Party.

The next day was even more revealing and concerning. The family visited Red Square, where tanks had charged at a crowd, killing several people. There were flower posies on the kerbside, and barricades of scrap metal surrounding the Russian Parliament buildings. The Kremlin's stone walls were pocked by tank cannon fire. Nonetheless, the violence had been shortlived, and people were now going about their business more or less as normal. The Wallises believed that as they were not part of it – and merely passing through – they would remain beyond the reach of any further disturbances. So they carried on exploring Moscow.

Of special interest to the boys was a big red M that signalled a McDonalds. They could hardly miss it. There was a queue that encircled the block where the takeaway hamburger shop was located. Toby was delegated to stand in the queue. Two Mormon missionaries told the New Zealanders they regularly had breakfast, lunch and dinner there.

Clutching Russian Special Forces (Commando) jackets that Manuel presented them with, the Wallises left Moscow for home via London and Canada. They flew home on Tim's birthday, 9 September, on a British Airways plane, celebrating with the biggest gin and tonics Prue had ever seen.

IN RUSSIA AND ELSEWHERE, Tim often used a shiny aluminium briefcase to form a table across his knees so he could pen a memo or fax. Sometimes he drafted important business contracts this way. A trademark accessory of his, the briefcase could tell a story or two. On a trip to the *Ranginui* one day, it worked loose from the side rack of his Hughes helicopter and crashed on to a snow slope in the mountains backing the Shotover catchment, sliding 300 to 400 metres before coming to rest. Tim put the chopper into a corkscrew dive to keep track of the briefcase's tobogganing fall and son Nick hauled it in as the Hughes hovered close to the snow.

At Karagai, on a warm summer's day in the middle of 1992, he sat inside a giant Mil helicopter, with the slightly battered briefcase on his lap, and penned an agreement he hoped Peter Popov would find accept-

New yards at the Kiska farm, featuring the traditional post-and-rail fences.

able. Wearing glasses for this close work but perching them on his nose so he could see over them to discuss some points with Svetlana, he wrote down what he wanted from Karagai – 100 maral cows, if possible a mixture of yearlings and two-year-olds. A short time earlier he had been picnicking with Peter Popov junior, son of the formidable father of the Russian deer industry, in a paddock knee-deep in pasture, chewing on a grass flowerhead and chatting about the deer industry. Peter had already indicated no two-year-olds were available from Karagai but Tim thought he would put the order in writing anyway, backed up with an offer to pay a really good price in American dollars, cash on the table. Alpine's Kiska farm needed stock from somewhere, and Karagai had the best.

Although there were farmer reservations about what the New Zealanders were going to do at Kiska, Tim remained on good terms with the region's political leaders and felt that, despite Moscow's block on velvet exporting, there might still be a chance of getting a deer farm going. To help him in these ambitions, Robin Biddulph and his wife, Noeline, a registered nurse, arrived in Gorno Altaysk in January 1993, the depths of winter, with snow lying about. But getting a farm going at Kiska quickly became difficult. Robin constantly hit bureaucratic brick walls.

By April, his and Alpine Deer Group's attempts to set up the first foreign company in the Altai region still had not met with success. There were only two solicitors in town who could help them. But Tim, back in Gorni Altai to check on progress, was determined that only after the Kiska elk farm company was registered would deer fencing work begin. Meantime, wheeled and crawler tractors, trucks, a post-hole driver and a hay-baler had been ordered.

Another setback came to Tim's notice on that visit. The Popov stock that he hoped to purchase had been allocated to other farms, apparently under direction from officials. The official line was that Kiska had missed out because it was not set up yet.

Stung by this development, Tim requested a meeting with the President Chaptinov and Premier Petrov. He put Kiska's case as firmly as he could. 'There's no point,' he told the two top men in a meeting recorded on video, 'our putting one post in the ground unless we get the same rights of access to stock as any farmer in the Altai … we're prepared to invest in the region and show what we can do.' At Kiska, the New Zealanders would try to improve on the average fawning rate in Altai of 40 percent. Tim said he knew it was difficult to compare the Altai fawning rate against rates in other countries, but for the record, in Canada his operations expected a 90 percent fawning.

He confided to Robin that although the Altai farming community might

Politician's son in Wanaka

As a sign of his friendship towards Gorni Altai and his commitment towards its development, Tim sponsored Andrei Chaptinov, son of the region's Vice-President, on a visit to New Zealand to further his education. He studied at Mt Aspiring College in Wanaka, worked at Criffel part time, and went on to do a course at the University of Otago in Dunedin. His parents told Tim they had heard he was 'living like a Czar' in New Zealand compared to the standard of living available to him as a student in the Altai region.

be suspicious of the Kiska project, he did not believe they were truly or immovably against the New Zealand attempt to farm the local deer.

By June 1993 the company had achieved registration. Fencing work began on Kiska's hillside pasture. Robin had a local counterpart to help him, Victor Kravetz, whom the New Zealander at first regarded as a go-getter and well-respected in the community. He would later think less of him. At the local village, unemployment was running at 50 percent, no doubt reflecting the demise of the collective farm in the district.

In early 1994, Robin returned to Kiska after a Christmas break in New Zealand. He returned to a mess. He found equipment had been stolen, including fence posts and the crawler tractor's tracks. Robin suspected an 'inside job' – the gear had been stolen by some of the local men he employed. When he asked why local people would steal from the very project they relied on for work, he was told: 'We can't help it. We steal to survive.' The Biddulphs were regarded by local people as rich and resourceful – 'goldmines', as Robin put it. They were often asked if they could provide television sets, stereos, clothes, even jet-boats.

Dishonesty was not confined to the poor. The velvet trade often involved stolen product, and the revenue from velvet sales did not always end up reinvested in the farms for the benefit of their workers. True, perestroika had removed the grasping hand of Moscow in the velvet trade. But misappropriation of the proceeds still occurred. One farm director took off on an extended cruise ship holiday in the Mediterranean with his family.

Theft was incidental, however, compared to the obstacles facing Tim and Robin when it came to setting up a stud elk farm and initiating a breeding programme that would produce genetic material. Tim's dream – the thing that kept him in Gorni Altai when other investors would have given up long ago – was to secure semen and embryos (fertilised eggs) from the best animals at Kiska, and export this genetic material to Canada and hopefully other countries.

By and large, he had the politicians on his side. But he could not win the support where it counted – at the farm director and farm manager level. The farm managers and directors and many of their staff consistently opposed the idea of exporting genetic material. In trying to win them over Tim consumed cognac and vodka from brimming mugs. There was one session by a river where Tim, Mike Bringans and Victor Kravetz started drinking cognac with the farm's senior people. They got through five bottles of cognac. At one point, Tim waded into the cold river water with his video camera and recorded the scene on the river bank, with people sprawled around asleep or in a drunken stupor.

Desperate to acquire stock for velvet production and genetics work, Tim and Robin looked outside the Altai region and at last found some animals – 35 maral deer. They were earmarked for transfer to Kiska but they never got there.

In 1994, Tim changed tack. He decided to leave dysfunctional Kiska to its own devices and form a relationship with another farm community, Proletarka, about an hour's drive from Gorno Altysk towards the mountains. Tim attracted the interest of a group of Americans, and one of them, Patrick Cooper, took over managing the operation, which involved new fencing and other developments. Robin and Noeline Biddulph pulled out and went back to their farm in New Zealand.

In terms of genetics work, however, Proletarka was no more successful for the New Zealanders than Kiska, Karagai or any other farm where they had tried to establish a platform for the export of Russian elk genetics.

One incident sums up the New Zealanders' frustration. In 1994, Mike Bringans arrived from Canada with microscopes and other equipment destined for a scheduled embryo 'flushing' exercise involving the purchased deer. Mike was well aware that although the authorities in Moscow had agreed to a protocol, it had yet to be signed by the regional government. With the farm directors hotly opposed to the politicians signing any approvals, he knew it would be very difficult to obtain the necessary permits. At Novosibirsk Airport, his luggage was impounded after an X-ray search revealed microscopes in it. Through Svetlana, the New Zealander argued strenuously for the equipment to be released. He needed it immediately as the elk cows had to be flushed in the next day or two. Timing was critical; the window of opportunity very small. Mike arrived on a Thursday. The authorities said he could uplift the gear on Monday. That was too late.

Although by this time Tim had brought in American investors in an effort to succeed with the genetics work, he could see the odds stacking up against him and his chances of pulling off a genetics coup.

TIM'S OPTIMISM THAT HE could succeed in the deer business in Russia, despite the knock-backs he was experiencing at Kiska, spilled over into a new venture altogether. He and Bruce Gaffikin launched the NewTrade in partnership in June 1993. NewTrade took over the non-dairy business of Sovenz, the New Zealand Dairy Board subsidiary, in the new-look Soviet Union. Yet looming over the Dairy Board's dealings in Russia was a $200 million debt the Soviet Union had amassed through a shipment of New Zealand dairy products in 1991.

'Embryos'

The genetics work envisaged with the Russian deer relied on advanced reproductive technology rather than genetic engineering. Minute 'embryos' – fertilised eggs, six days old – are considered more valuable genetic material than semen because diseases can be washed off eggs. In the 'flushing' process, the embryos are recovered surgically.

NewTrade sold goods as diverse as cosmetics from Japan, woollen knit-wear from New Zealand (half a million dollars' worth) and coffee-bean roasting equipment from Italy. The roasters were sold into Riga, capital of the newly-independent Baltic state of Latvia, north of Poland on the western side of the old USSR. Latvians are addicted to coffee.

The company's largest project was a supermarket in Khabarovsk, a city of over one million people 650 km north of the port of Vladivostok on the Russian eastern seaboard. It was one of the more accessible parts of the old USSR, with flights two times a week from Japan. Bruce knew Khabarovsk well, having been involved in numerous dairy deals there in the past. He believed a supermarket there would flourish as perestroika pumped up a demand for consumer goods.

Sadly for NewTrade the supermarket development collapsed before it could really get going properly, and certainly before it could show a profit. The project was hammered for a number of reasons, including corrup-tion, Russian mafia involvement and inflation. Inflation was the biggest jolt. Almost overnight the Russian rouble collapsed. The bank NewTrade had been dealing with suddenly disappeared. Many Western investors took flight. In Bruce's view, the devaluation of the rouble set the country back ten years. The New Zealand clothing was diverted to Latvia. NewTrade suffered losses on the supermarket project of over $NZ1 million.

There were other worries. Tim knew of the existence of white-collar gang-like elements in Russian society, collectively called the mafia (but not connected to the Sicilian mafia). They operated in the business world, feeding off transactions they could influence through notorious techniques such as extortion, protection rackets, graft and nepotism. As perestroika moved business opportunities away from centralised official control, the mafia expanded with the changes. In some cases, mafia cells were formed around 'old boy' networks or sporting clubs; others were created by offi-cials who knew how to navigate the old trading systems and who quickly adjusted to the deregulated arena. It was as if they had grown organically to fill a vacuum created by perestroika. Mafia leaders were often respected names in the business and industrial world.

In the few years Tim had been visiting Russia, the mafia appeared to be growing stronger – and more ruthless. People at the edge of Tim's busi-ness circle were turning up dead. Two business acquaintances were shot when their car was fired on by mafia assassins with semi-automatic rifles. In another incident the victim was the son of Tim's Kiska farm manager, Victor Kravetz. The young man's body was recovered from the Kartun River. Some of his clothes were on the river bank. He had regularly driven Altai primary produce, including butter, cheese and honey, to Moscow

and back-loaded his truck with consumer goods that he traded at home. The New Zealanders never worked out precisely what motivated the killing but the assumption was that he owed money or had been straying into territory under mafia control and jealously guarded. Then, in what appeared to the New Zealanders to be another politically motivated death, President Chaptinov died in suspicious circumstances.

Left: Tim's Russian assistants, Manuel (above) and Armin, posing with a huge velvet antler.

Above right: Tim buying a Russian helmet at a central Moscow street market.

Tim had faith in Manuel and Armin to keep him safe. They worked well together. Manuel, especially, was quick-witted and resourceful, and adept at handling authority figures. He knew how to use Fosters beer and European cigarettes to secure a favour, especially with the helicopter pilots, who were salaried but not averse to taking a bribe. On his visits to Russia Tim always bought a supply for Manuel to distribute. Manuel was also somewhat enigmatic. It was said he kept a semi-automatic pistol handy. Adding to the air of mystery was his parachuting ability, possibly learnt in the Russian military.

(On the helicopter flight that carried the family to the rafting launch point on the Kartun River, Manuel had leapt out with his parachute on, to make arrangements for Tim to meet the people at a remote farm).

Notwithstanding Manuel's skill and influence, Tim faced immense challenges. On the one hand, interference in Kiska and Altyn Kerl projects by mafia operatives was ever threatening; on the other, Tim still had to convince the farming community to accept his ambitions. In addition to his wanting to export elk genetics he hoped to import Canadian elk semen or embryos that would improve the local elk stock in certain ways. He had made headway at the political level but was losing ground on the farms. Apparently, hard-line farming interests were threatening to kill any official who signed documents permitting the New Zealanders to export semen or embryos. And Bruce Gaffikin, who had important sources in Russia, told Tim that one of the farm directors had said point blank that

no elk genetics material would ever be allowed out of the country. Nyet, nyet, nyet! The locals believed that sharing such a resource would be tantamount to losing it.

In the early 1990s, Tim visited Gorni Altai four or five times a year, and he always felt warmly welcomed. But in terms of establishing an elk farm – one that would be trying radical things in the field of genetics – the Canadian Ambassador's advice seemed all too prophetic. Kiska still had no deer, although Alpine now owned about 250 animals, which were being looked after at Proletarka.

If having to suffer the machinations of the Russian business world were not enough, Tim also had to deal with physical pain. His paralysed left leg caused him acute pain at times, particularly after he had done a lot of walking and travelling. Tim was not one to travel light and he insisted on carrying his luggage. After days on the road, his metal calliper sometimes rubbed the skin raw. A couple of times he called on his friend, Mike Bringans, to dress the wound. At other times he was in so much leg pain he would have to inject himself with pain-killing pethidine, and lie down for some hours.

When, in 1994, there was more frustration with officialdom and genetics protocols, Tim decided enough was enough. Besides the bureaucratic issues, he was worried that an employee – or even a New Zealander – might be the next target of the mafia. There was now evidence of mafia pressure and control across much of the deer farming scene and in the velvet trade. Would they turn on him? Would he be next?

In the circumstances, Tim decided that pushing on with the Proletarka project was not worth the struggle. Alpine Deer Group executive director Graeme Ramshaw, who visited Gorni Altai several times from his office in Dunedin, concluded that the business environment was simply 'too hard'.

Tim made his moves discreetly – yet summarily: abandoning the Altyn Kerl velvet trading business, 250 maral deer (for which they made arrangements for ongoing management), and the leased farm at Proletarka, whose assets included deer fencing and yards, two vehicles, two houses (one, near the Kartun River, was dubbed the Kiwi Lodge) and an array of plant, machinery and veterinary gear.

To Tim, pulling the plug on the Russian deer work was painful. He loathed wasting time and resources. At the same time he was 'counting blessings' on the home front. These included his family, his New Zealand business involvement and an expanding new line of interest – vintage warplanes. Asked by a New Zealand television documentary maker in Russia what he hoped to get out of his business operations in the country, Tim replied: 'To make a profit you'd be dreaming. But what we've learnt has been immensely valuable.'

Just before the Gorni Altai withdrawal occurred, Tim's long-standing friend in deer farming, Peter Elworthy, paid a visit to Russia. Sir Peter, knighted in 1988 for his services to New Zealand agriculture, was fascinated to see Russia turning her back on autocratic Communism in favour of a free-enterprise state. He observed also the flourishing black market in goods, especially agricultural products, the frugal living conditions in the villages, where owning a car was considered a luxury, and the impact of an inflation rate running at 1.5 percent a week and out of control.

Sir Peter was impressed by the sacrifice of the Altai people in the Second World War. He noted that of the 42,000 soldiers from the region drafted into the Russian military, 27,000 had been killed. He also noted Tim's fascination with Russian aircraft from that war, the chunky Polikarpov fighters in particular, which were being restored for Tim at an aviation factory in Novosibirsk, the Siberian capital and Russia's third-largest city after Moscow and St Petersburg.

At one point in his tour, Sir Peter joined Tim on a visit to the aviation factory to see the planes. The New Zealanders and their hosts sat down to a lunch of salads, soup, beef and potatoes, accompanied by numerous vodka toasts that grew more convivial with each toast.

Although Tim was thwarted in his dream to export Russian elk genetics, he looked set to export Russian heritage of an entirely different kind – warbirds.

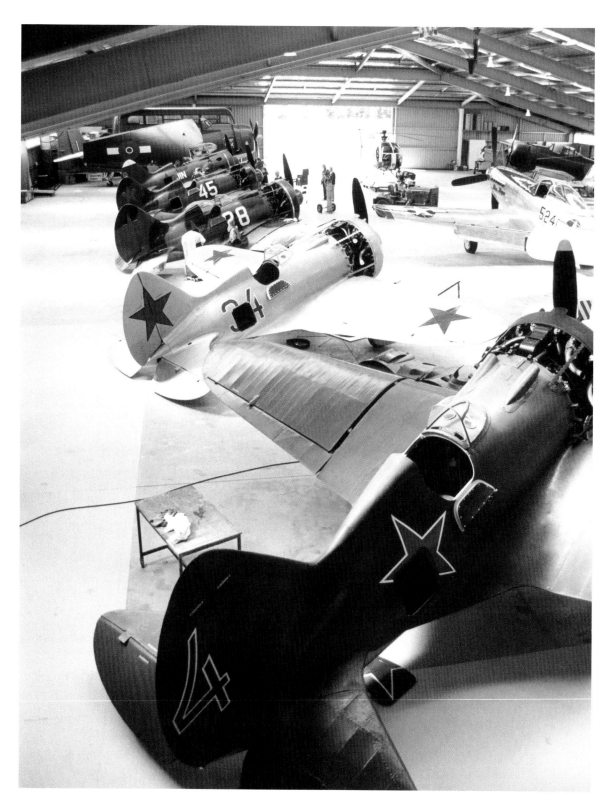

Chapter 12

Warbirds

Late 1980s–1990s

Creating Russian aviation history ... stolen money belt ... first Warbirds show ... starved of fuel at Waipukurau ... father-and-son team ... NZ Fighter Pilots' Museum ... stuntman ... knighthood ... VE Day show ... a roar over Burwood ... the sinking of the Ranginui ... a cold night ... Minaret Station

BACK IN 1991, when Alpine Deer Group's chief engineer Ray Mulqueen was despatched to Moscow to oversee the shipment of three Russian transport planes to New Zealand, he knew there might be bureaucratic hold-ups and that it might take some days to arrange. Tim had already paid $US12,000 for the three Antonov AN-2 biplanes, without actually sighting them. After ten days, Ray was no closer to being shown Tim's purchase. He phoned his boss back in New Zealand. Soon the conversation became unusually terse. It followed along these lines:

Tim: 'What do you mean you haven't seen the three AN-2's yet? What have you been doing?'

Ray: 'Your agents here haven't shown them to me, and I don't think we will ever see them.'

Tim: 'Don't be ridiculous. I've paid for them, and all the spare engines etcetera.'

Ray: 'Prove it! Have you got a contract, serial numbers and registration numbers?'

There was a long silence at Tim's end.

Ray: 'I think you've been screwed, Tim.'

The three Antonovs were never found. Ray came back empty-handed – the end of an expensive episode.

Still, he and Tim were working on more promising leads in Russia, involving aircraft that Tim was tremendously excited about. They were stubby Russian fighter aircraft called Polikarpovs, hundreds of which

Opposite: Five Polikarpovs inside the Alpine Fighter Collection hangar at Wanaka.

formed part of the Soviet defences against Hitler's forces in the Second World War. The Chinese Air Force also flew them against the Japanese in the Far East. Hundreds of them were lost in the Second World War. A few still lay where they had crashed in forlorn areas of Russia. To Tim, the concept of recovering and restoring some of these wrecks was a challenge totally different to the export of Russian elk genetics but probably more realisable. Probably.

Knowing that German planes also crash-landed on Russian soil in the war, Tim wanted to acquire wrecked Messerschmitt ME-109 or Focke-Wulf 190 fighters which were highly valued by collectors of vintage war-planes around the world. When the German planes proved elusive he switched focus to the Polikarpovs. Ray and he put out feelers and soon they were inspecting wrecks in the tundra.

A key contact in the search for these planes and their subsequent resto-ration was aviation researcher Boris Osietinski, who at that point was one of Tim's contacts in Moscow. With Boris, Tim went on visits to the Murmansk area of Russia, 1,500 kilometres north of Moscow. There, in the land of the midnight sun near the border with Finland, they came across a number of wrecks, for which Tim paid cash. Contracts were hand-written, usually drawn up in a hotel room.

Ray Mulqueen, who visited Russia seven times in four years in the 1990s, also visited Polikarpov wreck sites, one of which was in a forested area where he was taken by five Russian men, one of whom carried a rifle. The further they walked into the forest, the more nervous Ray became about the guy behind him with the rifle. He had heard of Westerners on business in Russia disappearing. At last he asked why the group needed to be armed. 'Oh, the rifle – that's in case of bears,' he was told. After that he stuck close to the armed escort.

By May 1993, Tim and Ray had decided on restoring six Polikarpov I-16s and three I-153s (the latter being a biplane). A factory where they could be restored had already been identified. It was in the Siberian capital of Novosibirsk, a four-hour flight from Moscow.

The Soviet Aeronautical Research Institute (Sibnia), which ran the factory, entered into an agreement with Alpine to undertake the work. There was a better chance of success doing this sort of work in a regional centre rather than in Moscow, where there might be competition with other Western warbird collectors. In Moscow they were more likely to encounter what Tim termed 'Russian trickiness and double-dealing'. Other factors in favour of the Siberian location were that aircraft engineers who had worked on Polikarpovs were still living in the region, and the relevant aircraft drawings and plans were discovered lurking in dusty drawers.

Tim struck up a cordial working relationship with the head of Sibnia, Professor Alexei Serioznov, who pointed out in halting English and through interpreters that they would be breaking new ground with the project. The institute had never before restored a 60-year-old Polikarpov fighter, let alone nine of them and two different models. The project required some retooling in the factory, said the professor, and a lot of labour – probably as many as 200 men. They would be using local birch timber and resins for the wooden framework.

Tim and Ray soon saw that the project was employing more workers than it would have in the Western world. To Ray, a job that took a day in, say, the United States, looked like taking four or five days in Russia. The Kiwi Polikarpov project represented a kind of State social welfare scheme,

Tim with Professor Alexei Serioznov, head of the Soviet Aeronautical Research Institute in Novosibirsk, 1993. Alpine Fighter Collection

Engine tests prior to the maiden flight of Tim's first Polikarpov I-16. Alpine Fighter Collection

keeping some families above the breadline. Tim had no qualms about that – because if it served to enhance his credentials and goodwill, it might mean he could jump to the head of the queue for any worthy WWII German fighters discovered in Russia.

In the event, the Polikarpov restoration work was anything but cheap and timely. There were excessive delays and cost overruns that often doubled, trebled and even quadrupled the quotations. At times Tim had the option of walking away from it all or digging deeper and carrying on. He always pushed on, dogged to the end.

In early 1995, as if to appease his client for the cost blow-outs and delays in delivering planes, Professor Serioznov took Tim on an adventure to an area north of Novosibirsk that had riverboat access only. Interpreters Manuel and Armin came along. On disembarking they checked into a guest lodge. Tim noticed they were being observed by a young fellow, probably in his mid-20s, but thought it nothing unusual. As a foreigner, he often attracted attention. On this trip, though, with payments due to be made on the Polikarpov and Gorni Altai farm projects, he carried a money belt bulging with American cash. The visitors checked into their own rooms, and when the professor invited Tim to take a sauna, Tim put the money belt in his briefcase and hid the latter under his bed.

He returned an hour later to find the briefcase still there but the money belt gone. Also missing was his toilet bag. The professor and interpreters were on the case immediately, and within a few hours KGB-type police arrived from the Siberian capital. Tim told them about the young man who had been following them on arrival.

Tim, accompanied by Manuel, inspects wartime aircraft wrecks in the disputed Kuril Islands between Japan and Russia's Kamchatka Peninsula. Alpine Fighter Collection

Two days later, the police reported they had found the thief and all the money except for $US3,000, a fraction of what he had been carrying. It transpired the guest house receptionist was the girlfriend of the thief. She had lent him a spare key to Tim's room. Before Tim had emerged from the sauna the robber had disappeared into the village and lined himself up to take the next available boat out of town. But he had not covered his tracks sufficiently well to avoid detection by the police. The robber was brought back to the village to face a makeshift court hearing at the guest lodge, with the local policeman presiding and Tim sitting with his video camera by his side surreptitiously filming the whole remarkable event. The robber received an eight-year jail sentence. Tim wrote off the $3,000 in the hope it went to worthy causes in the village and got back to the Polikarpov restoration.

Later in 1995, Tim and Ray were back in Siberia for the first flight by a restored Polikarpov. One of the I-16s was readied for a test flight in an airfield out in the countryside, three years after work started on its restoration. Tim was the first vintage aircraft collector in the world to own a flyable Polikarpov. It was a significant moment.

TV3 documentary-maker Melanie Reid and a camera and sound crew from the New Zealand channel were on hand to record the event. Tim had already decided he could not fly the Russian planes. He told the documentary team the Polikarpovs were 'too twitchy an aircraft for me'.

Towards sunset, the I-16's 1,000-horsepower Shvetsov 9-cylinder radial engine crackled into life. Nothing happened for a while then the pilot taxied the old fighter towards the airstrip, swerving one way then the other across the grass in order to see the way ahead, which was obscured by the engine canopy during taxiing. Poised for take-off, the plane picked up speed, with its engine roaring in a clackety, stuttering way characteristic of the Polikarpov type … then the pilot aborted the take-off. There were oil temperature problems.

Above left: Tim and Alpine Deer Group board chairman Don Spary visit the memorial to famous Russian scientist S.A. Chaplygin at the Soviet Aeronautical Research Institute in Novosibirsk. Alpine Fighter Collection

Above: Tim and Russian aviation historian Michail Maslov meet a former Russian Polikarpov fighter pilot in Novosibirsk. Alpine Fighter Collection

The first Polikarpov I-153 biplane takes shape in Novosibirsk. Alpine Fighter Collection

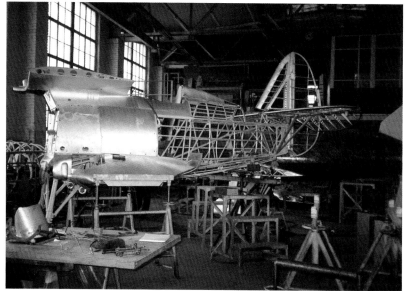

Tim Wallis, Peter Elworthy and Graeme Ramshaw in front of the Soviet Aeronautical Research Institute in Novosibirsk. Ray Mulqueen

The maiden flight of the restored I-16 would not happen for a couple of days. But after the first one became airborne, the others followed at steady intervals over a four-year period.

As each plane was restored and tested, it was transported by rail from Siberia to Vladivostok then shipped on to Wanaka via Hong Kong. All nine aircraft were unloaded from wooden crates at the Alpine Fighter Collection's hangar at Wanaka Airport, with one being sold soon afterwards to American interests based in Seattle.

TEN YEARS EARLIER the idea of an exhibition of vintage warplanes, run by private enterprise, had such novelty the Civil Aviation Authority offered no prescription for the way the airshow should be conducted. At least, that is how it appeared to the organisers, Tim and his brother, George. Until the mid-1980s, airshows for military aircraft were the domain of the Royal New Zealand Air Force and they featured their North American Harvards and a sole ex-RNZAF Mustang owned by a Canterbury farmer. Skyhawks and Aeromacchi trainers were introduced later.

Tim seized on the concept of a vintage fighter airshow of international interest after purchasing a P-51D Mustang from the United States in 1984. Ray Mulqueen was contracted to go to America to locate a Mustang and, in consultation with Tim, arrange for its purchase. Ray came upon a P-51D in the state of Indiana, where it was in the hands of a warbird enthusiast and pilot, John Dilley. Ray supervised its disassembly and crating for shipment to New Zealand. Ray had first worked for Tim in 1982 on Tim's corporate aircraft, the Mitsubishi MU2, nicknamed the 'rice rocket'.

The Mustang contract was something completely different. He assembled the aircraft with RNZAF help at Wigram and the former owner, John Dilley, who had travelled to New Zealand with the plane, had it in the air just in time for the Wings and Wheels pageant staged by the Royal New Zealand Air Force at Wigram in January 1985.

Curious about the arrival of the Mustang, the Christchurch newspaper, *The Press*, asked Tim why he had acquired it. Tim's response: 'I bought it for its historic value. It's a shame there are not more of these planes around.' He recalled Wigram-based Mustangs flying full throttle and at a fairly low level over Christchurch city in the 1950s, while he was at College. Tim was at the 1985 Wigram show, hugely proud of his new possession. At the same time, he was thinking of grander things.

Through 1987, from his Alpine office at Wanaka Airport, he worked on plans for a flying display and kindred attractions that he figured would appeal to the public. He contacted the Auckland-based New Zealand Warbirds Association, which agreed to contribute a number of fighters to the display. 'Warbirds On Parade' had a nice ring to it. That would be the show's brand name. Wanaka Airport sold itself as the venue, and as for timing, Tim thought January, when Wanaka's population swelled with holidaymakers, would ensure a crowd. To look after the numerous tasks involved in an airshow, Tim turned to the Wanaka and District Lions Club, whose members were renowned for pitching in to help with community projects.

The Polikarpov types

Polikarpovs, named after their Russian designer, were produced in monoplane (I-16) form and also as a biplane (I-153). Despite the monoplane's more modern appearance, it was actually designed and manufactured first, in 1933. The I-153 biplane appeared in the late 1930s.

The I-16s were just six metres long, with a wingspan less than nine metres – a span about four metres less than that of, say, a Hawker Hurricane. It could fly at up to 323 miles per hour (516 kilometres per hour). It performed barrel rolls and loops so fast it was freaky. All in all, the Polikarpov I-16 was a swift, squat package.

Tim, Prue and the boys with John Dilley, the Mustang's previous owner.

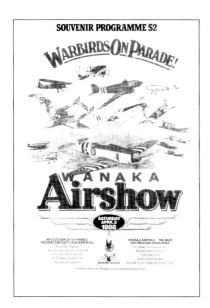

Programme cover from the inaugural 1988 airshow, Warbirds On Parade.

Everything was gelling well except for a date. Prue suggested Easter – a four-day long weekend – rather than New Year. Although the Easter timing would conflict with the traditional family holiday in Fiordland based at the *Ranginui*, if Warbirds were to become biennial, it would still mean a *Ranginui* holiday every second year instead of annually. The Lions Club agreed. There would be more benefit to the Wanaka community if the show could be held at Easter – and probably more members around to help.

At Easter 1988, the Wanaka Warbirds phenomenon was launched. In addition to the flying stars of the show there were displays of vintage vehicles and agricultural machinery (George Wallis was an avid collector of tractors in particular), all of which helped create a country fair atmosphere. Wanaka Airport was much less developed then. It was a quiet corner of the aviation world, embedded in sheep country, with the only permanent residents the Alpine Deer Group, with its head office and attached hangar, and Aspiring Air with its base buildings nearby. Tim and his team put in tremendously long hours to get the show ready. Would anyone turn up? They did – in uplifting numbers. Warbirds on Parade attracted an estimated 14,000 visitors, who were enthralled by the displays from a 1953 Hawker Sea Fury, one of the fastest piston-engined fighters ever produced, and a de Havilland Venom jet fighter, owned by Warbirds Association president Trevor Bland, a retired Royal New Zealand Air Force fighter pilot. Tim's Mustang was there, and the RNZAF turned up with its Red Checkers aerobatic team, a Strikemaster, Iroquois helicopter and Friendship transport plane. To the delight of the crowd, the Warbirds Association's 'Roaring Forties' team flew formation aerobatics with its multi-coloured Harvards.

Many different aircraft types brought in warbird enthusiasts, from individuals arriving in their Cessna 180s to a warbirds syndicate's North

The Warbirds Over Wanaka organising committee, from left, Gavin Johnston, Tim and his brother, George. Ian Brodie

Prue and Tim celebrate, Russian style, the arrival of one of the first Polikarpov I-16s in 1996. With them are Alpine Fighter Collection engineers, from left Malcolm Brown, Greg Parker and Ray Mulqueen.

Island-based DC3 and an Air New Zealand Fokker Friendship, whose seats sold out in a week, suggesting strong public support from beyond the Otago region. All these planes parked out of the way of the stars of the show but nonetheless added to a buzzing sense of anticipation.

Tim had always envisaged benefits for the local community from the event, and this was reinforced when the $41,000 proceeds were divided between the Wanaka Swimming Pool project and the next Warbirds. A debriefing at the Edgewater Resort in Wanaka decided to make the show a biennial Easter event: in future it would be called Warbirds Over Wanaka, a snappier, more identifiable and perhaps more marketable brand name. Its acronym certainly packed a punch.

Fired up by the support for the inaugural show, the electrifying aerobatic displays and the elegance and growl of powerful piston-engined planes hurtling through the air, Tim could not resist another taste of Warbirds before the scheduled 1990 rendezvous. At Easter 1989, several Warbirds Association members assembled at Wanaka with their vintage aircraft for a relaxing weekend's flying and a taste of Tim's hospitality. Warbirds collecting was clearly on the rise in New Zealand. Tim himself was not about to stop at a Mustang. The arrival of a Supermarine Spitfire at his Wanaka hangar in a crate, on New Year's Eve 1988, said as much, and Ray Mulqueen, who had just joined the Alpine staff, set about reassembling it with a burgeoning engineering team.

The P-51D Mustang had been sold in October 1988 to an Auckland syndicate, opening the way for Tim to invest in the Spitfire, an aircraft type he had long coveted. The Spitfire, from Mark 1 to Mark 21, epitomised Britain's Second World War effort, the Battle of Britain and the

Prue and four-year-old Nick Wallis in the first Mustang, 1984.

An impressive line-up: four I-16 Polikarpovs over the mountains around Wanaka. Phil Makanna, 1998

aerial campaigns over Europe. Over 20,000 were built but only 50 or so are airworthy now. More than any WWII fighter type, the Spitfire had a heroic image. Tim acquired his first Spitfire, a Mk XVI registered TB863 with the squadron code of FU P, from England. Built in 1944, it had been flown by the Royal Australian Air Force (453 Squadron) towards the end of the war. It had minor roles subsequently in the films *Reach for the Sky* (1955) and *Battle of Britain* (1967). The former portrayed the life and feats of wartime flying ace Douglas Bader, who flew with tin legs and had numerous crashes.

Tim, once described by a television documentary as New Zealand's Douglas Bader, had to get a rating to fly the Spitfire. He achieved this at Whenuapai Airport, Auckland, with the help of English Spitfire collector Stephen Grey, from whom he had bought TB863, and New Zealand airline and warbirds pilot Keith Skilling. Keith was the son of instructor Hugh Skilling, and had known Tim a long time. He flew with the 'Roaring Forties' aerobatic team at the first Wanaka airshow.

Armed with his rating, Tim resolved to make the most of it. First stop on the flight south in January 1989 was Ardmore Airport, South Auckland, where the Spitfire participated in an airshow the same weekend.

Hours later Tim was in the air again, heading for Rotorua and Gisborne to put the Spitfire through its paces at those two provincial cities. Next call, Masterton.

Well short of Masterton, however, he suddenly realised the Spitfire was suffering fuel starvation. He had misjudged the Spitfire's consumption and overlooked the requirement to manually select fuel transfer en route prior to exhausting the main tank (there were three fuel tanks fitted to this Mk XVI).

He coaxed the misfiring plane in the direction of the aerodrome at Waipukurau but during final approach the Spitfire suffered total engine failure. Six hundred people attending a music festival near the aerodrome saw the whole thing. Tim force-landed in an adjacent paddock and may have come out of it with an undamaged aircraft but for a railway embankment. To avoid it, Tim had to put the plane down in rough ground, which resulted in the undercarriage collapsing and the propeller ripping into the pasture. Its blades were wrecked. The Spitfire was considerably damaged.

It was embarrassing. Tim freely admitted his error to a *Hawkes Bay Herald-Tribune* reporter. He now owned one damaged Supermarine Spitfire. It took nearly a year to get it in the air again.

Tim's business associates could read the signs. From his own resources, not the least an increase in the value of his shares in The Helicopter Line, Tim was expanding a new frontier – in this case, vintage warplanes – and they knew he would not let up until he had exhausted the potential on three fronts. The first was his desire to build a personal collection. The second was to let the planes fly and inspire the public to contemplate the magnificent contribution made by New Zealand's fighter pilots to overseas wars. As for the third, could Warbirds Over Wanaka become an institution? Alpine Deer Group had its hands full trying to start up business ventures in Canada and Russia, run the Criffel deer farm and develop

Oshkosh

Tim's links with airshows go back a long way. In August 1972 he attended a fly-in run by the American Experimental Aircraft Association at Oshkosh, Wisconsin. Here he gained ideas for how airshows were organised. Also, he met members of the American Wheelchair Pilots' Association at the show, and told them how, despite his disability, he was flying 600 hours a year – 400 hours in helicopters, 200 hours in his adapted Cessna 182.

Below left: Forced landing at Waipukurau, January 1989.

Below: Cartoonist Tom Scott's view of the Waipukurau forced landing. Tom Scott

YOU GOTTA HAND IT TO HIM – A ONE-LEGGED DEER FARMER FROM WANAKA HAS MANAGED TO DO WHAT THE COMBINED MIGHT OF THE 3RD REICH COULDN'T – HE DOWNED THIS SPITFIRE...

its oriental medicine markets. It realised nothing could deflect Tim from what looked liked a full-blown obsession.

The second airshow in 1990 tested the public's appetite for vintage warplanes at a time when Anzac Day commemorations were encountering unprecedented popularity. Till the 1990s, Anzac Day, April 25, was simply a day off work and study to most people. Through the 1990s, it generated an extraordinary aura, as if New Zealanders at large had suddenly decided to embrace it as a national day more significant than Waitangi Day, February 6. In their thousands, New Zealanders turned up at Gallipoli, the infamous Turkish battlefield, to take part in a moving dawn ceremony. Around New Zealand, similar ceremonies attracted massive support on the day.

When it comes to big-picture ideas, Tim has an uncanny sense of timing. So it was that through the 1990s Warbirds Over Wanaka ran a parallel course with surging public interest in war history.

Visitor numbers doubled to 28,000 for the Easter 1990 airshow. In part, this was due to more detailed organisation and promotion, with Tim, brother George, and Wanaka and District Lions Club president Gavin Johnston forming an organising committee that took some of the load off Tim. Gavin had worked on the 1988 show as a Lions Club volunteer, and, having now sold his motel business in Wanaka, he agreed to join the committee. Expert at tapping shoulders, Tim put the idea to Gavin ('I have a proposition for you, Gavin') outside the Wanaka Town Hall on Anzac Day, 1989.

At the 1990 show, Tim's Spitfire was a sensational sight sweeping over Wanaka Airport and looping effortlessly high in the sky. You had to follow the commentator's instructions on where to look to catch its fly-past at full throttle. In swift level flight it seemed to purr rather than growl. It was a sound bound to dig deep into the soul of any warbird enthusiast. Backing up the aerial excitement were the ground displays, including, as the poster for the show said, 'New Zealand's biggest display of World War II Military Aircraft and Military Vehicles'. Vintage tractors and traction engines were also on show. Easter Sunday was the country fair day, with the warplanes parked for inspection.

For the next Warbirds Over Wanaka, Easter 1992, the organising committee members knew they had to introduce new acts to sustain crowd numbers. Enter the Messerschmitt ME-109. Having served in the Spanish Air Force at one time, it was brought in from England, and billed to engage in a dogfight with Alpine's Spitfire. People poured through the gates to see the show – 50,000 over two days.

A father-and-son team, Ray and Mark Hanna, from The Old Flying

Ray Hanna flying the Mk XVI FUP and Mark Hanna flying the Mk XIV. John Dibbs

Machine Company at Duxford, England, flying the Spitfire and ME-109 respectively, amazed the spectators with bouts of tail-chasing and aerobatics. Takapuna-born Ray Hanna, an ex-RAF pilot and leader of the famous Red Arrows display team, met Tim when Tim acquired the Spitfire FUP in England. At the 1992 show, Mark also flew a Curtiss P-40K Kittyhawk that Tim had added to the Alpine Fighter Collection. It was a type used extensively in the Pacific sector of the Second World War, with the RNZAF operating almost 300 of them.

Tim had been keen to display fighters used by the RNZAF in the Pacific. The 1992 show debuted two of them – the Kittyhawk and a Vought Corsair, with its characteristic gull wing design. He had an even greater ambition – to own and display warplanes from all nations engaged in World War II. And if he could not own them, he would certainly try, through Warbirds Over Wanaka, to display them.

Easter 1993, the airshow's year off, ought to have been a *Ranginui* holiday for the Wallis family; instead, it was given over to the official opening of a warbirds dream of Tim's – the New Zealand Fighter Pilots' Museum, built alongside the Alpine Deer Group premises at Wanaka Airport. Addressing 300 guests at the opening, Tim said the museum, a couple of years in the making, would be a memorial to the air and ground

Supermarine Spitfire Mk XVI

Tim Wallis flying his Spitfire Mk XVI at the Warbirds Over Wanaka 1994 airshow.
Phil Makanna

Length: 31 ft 4 in • **Height:** 12 ft 7 in • **Wingspan:** 32 ft 7 in • **Gross weight:** 8,700 lb • **Maximum speed:** 416 mph • **Range:** 712 miles • **Power:** by 1 Rolls Royce Merlin 1,670 hp, 12 cylinder engine • **Weaponry:** 2 x 20 mm cannons, 2 x 1/2 in Browning machine guns, 1 x 500 lb bomb, 2 x 250 lb bombs

crews of two world wars. 'It does not seek to glorify war,' he said. In the programme for the weekend, 10-11 April 1993, guests were told: 'The aim of the museum is to collect, preserve and display information and memorabilia relating to those who flew fighter aircraft in our defence during the First and Second World Wars'.

A decorated Spitfire pilot, Retired Group Captain Colin Gray, of 485 Squadron, unveiled the museum plaque and officially opened the Alpine Fighter Collection in the hangar across the field. The new AFC hangar had expansion of the collection in firm view: it was large and as Tim cast about the world looking for aircraft to acquire, the engineering challenges grew more complex. The two facilities were set up to complement each other. Among the renowned wartime pilots who attended the opening ceremony was Wing Commander Johnny Checketts.

Of the 5,000 New Zealand pilots who served in World War II, some 70 percent were with the Royal Air Force in Europe. Among them was an uncle of Tim's, Neil Blunden, his mother's younger brother. Neil had joined the RNZAF at the outbreak of war, aged 24. He became a bomber pilot with the Royal Air Force and participated in a raid on the feared German battleship *Tirpitz* in a Norwegian fiord. There were four raids altogether on the *Tirpitz* in the spring of 1942, and 13 aircraft from the RAF Bomber Command were downed, with the loss of 60 lives. Neil was among those who died.

In 1992, the year before the opening of the Fighter Pilots' Museum at Wanaka, Ian Brodie was engaged by Alpine to help with its set-up. He became its curator. Formerly on Air New Zealand's Christchurch staff, Ian was a computer specialist with photography and writing skills – and an encyclopaedic knowledge of Tolkein's *Lord of the Rings*. Vintage aircraft were an abiding interest of his. He had attended the Wanaka airshows from the outset. To Ian, the museum was always going to be a 'movable data base', with some planes owned, some on loan, some coming, some going – and most of them flyable. Between the airshows, the museum and its displays did much to foster support for the biennial event.

For Warbirds Over Wanaka 1994, the gull-winged Corsair and a new-comer, a Japanese Mitsubishi Zero replica, were the star performers. Underlining the organisers' interest in innovation, the show's poster listed no fewer than 11 aircraft types new to the WOW. They included the

Bullet-proof skins

In World War II, tanned deer skins were wrapped around the fuel tanks of some Royal Air Force fighter planes, in six layers stretched four ways, to stop fuel leaking from bullet holes. Although a tank might be holed in battle, the deer skin was self-sealing through its special properties and the lamination technique. The price of deer skins soared as a result.

Tim invited a number of WWII fighter pilots to the museum opening in 1993. Back row, from left: Ian Brodie (NZFPM curator), Des Scott, Johnnie Houlton, Jamie Jameson, Johnny Checketts, John Patterson. Front row, from left: Tim, Johnnie Johnson and Jim Sheddan. Mike Provost

torpedo-carrying Grumman Avenger, a Catalina flying boat and something that made Tim's heart race just a little bit faster – a Spitfire Mk XIV. It had been purchased for the Alpine Fighter Collection in March after a rebuild and restoration job in England at Stephen Grey's Flying Legends base.

The Corsair and Zero were featured on the poster in a dogfight over a tropical Pacific island. When Tim combined his longstanding interest in pyrotechnics with Pacific war naval history, the result was a kind of re-enactment of the sinking of the Imperial Japanese Navy battleship *Yamato*. A canvas profile of the battleship, 65 metres long, was bombed and strafed time and again by the Corsair, Kittyhawk and Avenger. Huge orange fire-balls, wrapped in black smoke, erupted over the battleship effigy until finally it sank from the sight of the long line of spectators on the other side of the runway.

Tim wanted these airshows to contain stunts, capers and special acts of one kind or another. He has always loved stunts blending skill and technology, and the idea of staging them for a large crowd was irresistible. The 1994 show's oddities included a race involving a John Britten motorcycle, a helicopter and a Pitts Special biplane. The motorcycle astonished the

Museum interior. Ian Brodie

crowd with its acceleration and speed, winning easily. And for the first time in New Zealand, a helicopter towed a glider to a launch point high above the airfield.

WOW programmes have invariably included helicopters performing aerobatically to their limits, with spinning dives, crazy angles, and graceful pirouettes down the runway with rotor tips sometimes just a metre off the seal. Helicopters were sometimes called on to demonstrate their lifting capacity – to drop things like a car or caravan from a height calculated to smash them to bits. Tim liked to be in the thick of these displays.

Warbirds also gave vent to Tim's sense of humour and intrigue. He needed accomplices. Graeme McLeary, part of the Warbirds commentary team from 1990, was among them. Tim concocted a scenario that required a serious input from Graeme. It involved telling the crowd a Stealth bomber was on its way to Wanaka. Graeme conducted a fake radio dialogue with the bomber's pilot, an American voice. Just as the mysterious and still invisible aircraft was about to appear over the airshow, the pyrotechnics crew detonated an enormous explosion around a tank on the other side of the runway from the crowd. The tank disintegrated, and, naturally enough, the Stealth bomber also disappeared off the airwaves, mission accomplished. For months afterwards, people who believed they had missed seeing the bomber's pass wrote asking for photographs of it.

Reunions are part and parcel of warbirds shows, and WOW, which by now had developed an international reputation for excellence in its displays and for being a consistent crowd-pleaser, provided the platform for groups such as the fighter pilots of World War II to get together. At the 1994 show, acknowledging the fiftieth anniversary of the D-Day landings

Woodbourne prang

In November 1992, Tim set out from Wanaka in his Spitfire Mk XVI to perform at Air Expo '92 at Auckland. On a refuelling stop at the Air Force base at Woodbourne, near Blenheim, he approached the grass runway in a crosswind. Just as the wheels met the grass the plane was caught by a powerful gust of wind. The plane slewed on the wet grass and skidded towards a sealed taxiway. The left undercarriage leg collapsed when the wheel met the tarseal. This tipped the left wing, which was damaged as it hit the sealed surface. As the aircraft accident report noted, Tim had 120 hours flying experience with the Mk XVI (and total flying time, in all aircraft types, of 11,221 hours).

The NZ Fighter Pilots' Museum trustees, from left: Graham Sinclair, Don Spary, Graeme Ramshaw, Tim, retired Air Commodore Graeme Goldmith and Jules Tapper. Ian Brodie

in France, Tim's committee invited a number of celebrated World War II fighter pilots to attend, including Air Vice Marshall 'Johnnie' Johnson, the RAF's leading ace, who downed 38 enemy aircraft. Also in the group was Mo McAuliffe, who had flown Tim's Spitfire, FUP, in early 1945 as a member of the Royal Australian Air Force's 453 Squadron.

The 1994 show outstripped its predecessors for innovation and complexity. For the first time, the flying displays were spread over two days – Saturday and Sunday. The new format set a pattern for future shows. But just when things looked to be on the up and up for Warbirds Over Wanaka, tragedy struck.

On the Saturday of the 1994 show, a brilliantly fine day, with everyone enjoying the spectacle, a Chipmunk displaying its aerobatic capabilities crashed on a section of the grass runway opposite the crowd, killing its pilot, Ian Reynolds. Ian had been attempting a manoeuvre involving a roll but left himself insufficient room. On the point of completing it, the aircraft smashed into the ground. The pilot was killed by the impact.

Some time after the removal of the wreckage, the programme of displays resumed. Tim fronted up to the media to defend the organisers' decision to carry on. He was clearly shaken by the death of a pilot, and he grew more emotional when a reporter later suggested the organisers might be accused of callousness by continuing the show.

'Motorists don't stop travelling if they come on a fatal crash ... We've tried to be respectful.' With a tremble in his voice, and tears welling, he continued: 'There's a bloody lot of work goes into it [the airshow]. We've lost a mate. We don't often share our emotions ... I've been through it in the deer days, having to go and see wives and children. It's not easy.'

A tree that was planted outside the Alpine Deer Group office the day before was dedicated to the memory of Ian Reynolds subsequently, and a bronze memorial plaque installed at its foot.

Later in 1994, Tim got to fly the Mk XIV Spitfire, which carried the registration ZK-XIV, for the first time. He compared the plane to 'a wild gypsy woman'. The Mark 16 was rather more sedate. He remembered what Ray Hanna had told him about the type: 'It could be a beast.'

IN MAY 1994, Tim became Sir Tim. The visionary son of the West Coast and Wanaka regions flew to Wellington for the investiture conducted by the Governor-General, Dame Catherine Tizard, at Government House. Naturally, Tim wanted all his family present for the knighthood ceremony. Prue had flown to Wellington earlier in the week. Accompanied by his four sons, aged 13 to 18, Tim set out from Wanaka the day before the investiture in his Cessna 210, the single-engined turbo-charged speedster he had flown in the 1987 Singapore-Christchurch air race. Winds approaching storm force were forecast for Cook Strait. Nearing the top of the South Island, they heard that Wellington Airport was closed to all flights. The control tower advised Tim to divert to Nelson or the airport at Paraparaumu on the Kapiti Coast north of Wellington. Neither option appealed to him. He had a dinner engagement in Wellington that evening. He pressed on.

Retired Wing Commander Johnny Checketts (left), Tim and Tim's uncle, Peter Blunden, enjoying the 2002 airshow. Phil Makanna

Now the plane was bucking and bouncing across the strait, with the sea, not far beneath the plane, a fury of enormous, breaking waves. The boys were not unused to rough weather but this was something else. Toby, the oldest boy and already in training to be a pilot, was in the co-pilot's seat, helping his father work the controls to try to keep the plane steady on its course. His brothers, growing concerned but not airsick, tightened their seat belts and held on. Tim told the air traffic controller he had to land at Wellington. He told the control tower he was low on fuel so they would allow him to land. The boys could hear the conversation because Tim still preferred to use a microphone and speaker rather than a modern radio headset. They came in fast to counter the gale and the gusts, with no flaps applied. The Cessna touched down at about 90 knots instead of the usual 50 to 55 knots. This wasn't the only drama associated with his knighthood.

The nomination was supported by the New Zealand Deer Farmers'

Association and Sir Peter Elworthy in particular. It acknowledged Tim's inspirational and pivotal contribution to deer farming and deer research, his pioneering role in deer-recovery aviation, his founding of the Warbirds Over Wanaka phenomenon, his support for the Burwood Spinal Injuries Unit, his patronage of numerous community organisations, and his contribution to New Zealand exporting and the economy generally. Besides the Deer Farmers' Association, several organisations put their names to the nomination – the New Zealand Warbirds Association, New Zealand Rural Trust, Electricity Distribution Reform Unit and Canterbury Health Board. The nomination described Tim as 'a world-famous New Zealander who pioneered the helicopter recovery of wild deer in New Zealand and the evolution of deer to a domesticated farmed animal.' His achievements were listed up to 1991, when the nomination was finalised and lodged with the New Zealand Government. Months passed. What unfolded was a sequence of misunderstandings that produced a contretemps that made news around New Zealand and overseas.

In November 1992, around the time of his Spitfire Mk XVI prang at Woodbourne, Tim received a 'personal and confidential' letter from the

A cold night out

When Tim and his second son, Jonathan, flew out of Wanaka for Dunedin in the winter of 1995 to attend a reunion of Christ's College old boys, the last thing they expected was to be stranded on a remote mountain in their helicopter. They left after lunch in Tim's Hughes 500. Approaching the Lammermoor Range, they encountered a snow storm. In whiteout conditions, Tim had no choice but to land. He had seen the high-voltage transmission lines tracking across the southern edge of the Great Moss Swamp Area, now the Loganburn reservoir, so he had a good idea the terrain would soon fall away towards the Strath Taieri. If they could get to lower country perhaps the snow would clear. To provide something visible to steer by in the whiteout, Tim instructed 18-year-old Jonathan to walk ahead through the snow. But after a short time of stumbling through the snow-covered tussock, Jonathan decided it was much too cold and difficult and he climbed back on board.

With snow piling up around the skids, the two waited. Tim used his cellphone to call helicopter operator Doug Maxwell at Alexandra and check on the conditions there. Doug said Alexandra had clear weather but that Tim should not take any risks in the whiteout. By 5 o'clock,

it was getting dark. It was also getting very cold. Several times Tim fired up the helicopter and turned on the machine's heater. A grimly cold darkness enveloped the machine.

Tim phoned Prue at home. She already knew they had not turned up at Dunedin and was getting concerned. 'We're okay,' Tim said. 'We've landed by a hut. There's some food here and we've got a fire going.'

All the food they had was in a survival pack – some barley sugar sweets and a bar of chocolate that had turned powdery with age. Aluminium-foil survival bags were useful, however, especially for Tim, who had poor circulation in his leg. They spent a near-sleepless night bitterly cold and cramped, with Tim occupying the front seats and Jonathan in the back. It was a long way from the warmth of an old boys' reunion.

In the morning, they could see a hint of blue sky through the blowing snow. Jonathan cleaned out snow from the air intake with his bare hands, a painfully cold task. The engine fired, Tim lifted the chopper straight up and with an abruptness that seemed surreal, they emerged into sunshine. Tim said: 'What a beautiful day.' He said little more. They backtracked for home, where Prue had two hot baths ready for them. She was not fooled by the hut story, the food and the fire.

Governor-General, Dame Catherine, acknowledging that his name had been submitted to the Queen for the honour of Knight Bachelor. He could 'gratefully accept' the honour or 'respectfully decline' it. Would he please indicate which. Tim at first thought he would accept but had second thoughts. He was concerned that the honour might change his relationship with colleagues and friends. People might be less inclined to phone him up, not knowing whether he was the formal 'Sir Tim' now or down-to-earth 'Tim'. Sir Peter Elworthy signed his letters, 'Sir Peter'. Tim felt unnerved by the thought of a more formal relationship with his associates. Moreover, his Woodbourne prang had been very upsetting and embarrassing and he was not really in the mood to take on a knighthood. He decided to decline the honour.

When word of Tim's decision reached Sir Peter, he phoned Tim straight away in a bid to get him to change his mind. Mark Acland, another of Tim's Canterbury farmer friends, also pleaded with Tim to accept the honour. In addition to the phone calls, Peter and Mark visited Tim in person. Tim was told he had to accept the knighthood because it would be an honour for all of the deer industry and for everyone associated with Warbirds, and to turn it down cast a shadow over their value to him.

Tim was persuaded. He informed Wellington of his change of mind. When the 1993 New Year's Honours were announced, however, Tim's name was missing from the list issued from Wellington. But it did appear, under the Kt (Knights Bachelor) heading, in the full Commonwealth honours list issued from London and published by the *London Times* and *The Telegraph*. He was named as one of three new New Zealand knights.

Contacted by the *Otago Daily Times* in the United States, where he was on business at the time, Tim was laconic in his response: 'There was obviously a mistake'. But whose mistake – Wellington's or London's? New Zealand officials, at risk of making matters worse, said that he had been shortlisted but not included in the confirmed list. Tim's indecision no doubt sowed the seeds of confusion in officialdom. At the British end of the confusion, the blame was laid at the door of Her Majesty's Stationery Office, and British Government sources said his name should have been deleted after he declined the honour. Apparently they did not know of his change of mind.

The story of the 'knight who wasn't' gained widespread media attention around New Zealand. It was also carried in Britain and a few other Commonwealth countries. The fuss died down, and the following November Tim received another letter from Dame Catherine asking if he would accept the honour of Knight Bachelor. He signalled back his acceptance. A fortnight later, the Governor-General wrote again to confirm the honour had been awarded, and this was duly announced in the 1994 New Year's Honours. Among others on the list that year was the celebrated author Barry Crump, then living at Waikanae, who said with characteristic dry humour his OBE 'might be good to hang on a Swanndri'.

Tim was equally relaxed about the knighthood. To the *Otago Daily Times* he commented: 'Everybody will still call me Tim. My mother will still call me Timothy. I don't think the "Sir" bit will get used very often.' At the time, however, his waggish sons went around describing themselves as the 'sirloins'. Tim was keen to pay tribute to associates such as the late Reid Jackson who had helped him implement his ideas. In the end, he said, his successes were 'a team thing'.

The knighthood may not have changed his business operations but it did increase his public commitments. There were now many more requests to attend functions, open facilities, act as a patron and make speeches.

His Warbirds involvement also intensified. During October 1994, there was a fighter pilots' reunion at Wanaka, centred on the museum dedicated to their war efforts. More reunions were staged in early 1995 in the lead-up to a VE Day airshow in May that year, marking the fiftieth anniversary of the end of World War II. The Wanaka Warbirds 'rest' year provided an opportunity for Tim and the Alpine Fighter Collection to put on a commemorative airshow at Wigram. Three thousand war veterans were invited. With Tim overseas for a few weeks in the months preceding the event, it fell to Prue to do much of the organising and, with admission free to the veterans, to coordinate sponsorships. The Returned Services Association was responsible for the guest list. Prue's responsibilities included the catering. Twelve thousand savouries were ordered and 6,000 club sand-wiches. The Alpine planes were put through their paces for the appreciative veterans; and the hundreds, if not thousands, of onlookers who crowded the streets surrounding Wigram air base.

Tim delighted in displaying his Spitfire. But not everyone appreciated it. In December 1990, he decided to put on a display specifically for the spinal unit patients at Burwood. It was his way of showing that someone with partial paralysis could fly an aircraft as challenging as a Spitfire, and that, as the American John Wooden had famously said, no one should let what they cannot do interfere with what they can do. He advised the Burwood office he was coming over in the Mk XVI and would they care to tell patients and staff to be out on the lawns. For about five minutes he performed aerobatics over the Burwood area and adjacent suburbs in the northeast of Christchurch – loops, barrel rolls, the works.

The display went down well with the patients but a North Beach resident rang the authorities to complain of the noise and 'dangerous' manoeuvres. A charge against Tim was heard in the District Court in Christchurch. It was dismissed. The judge said he had 'no reason at all to enter a conviction'. There was no point, he said, in imposing a penalty.

ON MAY 6 1995, the day before the Wigram airshow that marked the fiftieth anniversary of VE Day, Tim received some shocking news. His beloved *Ranginui* had sunk at her mooring in Breaksea Sound. It was hard to believe. One day she was afloat and waiting for her next group of adventure-seekers, the next she had given up her place in the sun and was resting at the bottom of the fiord, under 60 metres of water.

Flying over Breaksea in the late afternoon, chopper pilot Richard Hayes, an employee of Tim's in the 1970s and now a helicopter operator in his own right, had noticed that the *Ranginui* appeared to be settling and acquiring a list. Richard radioed his concern to Bill Black at Te Anau. Bill rounded up former skipper Frank Finnegan and a fireman from Te Anau, and they were quickly on the scene with a pump. By this time it was dark. The *Ranginui*, at her mooring opposite the John Islands, was certainly taking on water. Under torchlight the men found it was rushing into the engine room. The engines were flooded, which meant they couldn't start up the pumps. And the list was increasing alarmingly. Dishes were starting to crash out of kitchen cupboards. Bill worried he might lose his chopper. There was nothing they could do but abandon ship. He radioed Richard, who was on his moored barge further down the fiord, and Richard asked if he could do anything to help. Bill suggested they go by boat and rescue the jet-boat *Big Bertha*, which was tied alongside, and a Stabicraft off the stern. Richard and a colleague set out and just managed to liberate the two boats before their mothership sank.

The first person to alight on the *Ranginui* from a helicopter, Bill Black, also became the last person to leave her. Bill was no stranger to dramatic rescues, having hooked out about 100 helicopter wrecks since 1968 and answered some 300 search-and-rescue or ambulance call-outs. But when it came to rescuing the *Ranginui* that night, he was helpless to intervene. The ship of a thousand laughs and pranks, and a thousand more moments of drama and bonhomie, sank 45 minutes after he flew off her helipad, around 7.30 p.m.

The *New Zealand Marine News* reported later the sinking was 'probably due to cumulative leakage of the hull due to old age'. Tim was not so sure. He wondered if someone had inadvertently switched off the bilge pump. Whatever the cause, the sinking of the *Ranginui* was almost like losing a family member. For almost half of her 60-odd years, she had been in the Alpine family.

A week later Tim flew a team of professional divers to the site to check for fuel leaks, salvage what they could and assess whether the ship herself could be refloated. They decided the depth of water and the damage to her hull would prevent a successful refloating. But the one item Tim and Prue and the boys really wanted to recover was the *Ranginui*'s visitor book, filled with names of guests going back to 1980. On Tim's directions the divers were able to retrieve it. At the surface it was immersed in fresh water immediately and reached Wanaka wrapped in a cold wet towel.

Prue took advice from a conservator of books at the National Library in Wellington about how to treat the visitor book. First, she placed an absorbent paper between each page. Then with the book standing up and fanned out, she placed it in front of a cold air fan. It blew non-stop for nine days before the book was dry. Remarkably, after 10 days at the bottom of a fiord, the *Ranginui* visitor book was brought back almost to its original condition, with most of the entries legible.

THROUGH THE WINTER of 1995, Tim was disconsolate about the loss of his ship. He needed a distraction: and in the spring of that year, he acquired one – a high-country sheep and cattle station called Minaret overlooking Lake Wanaka. The property took in the Minaret Burn and Estuary Burn catchments, the jagged Minaret Peaks, which are as high as the Remarkables at just over 2,200 metres, and 20 kilometres of shoreline on the west side of Lake Wanaka. There is farmland to the north (Mt Albert

Tim decompressing at 10 metres after diving on the Ranginui *at the bottom of Breaksea Sound.*

Station) and the south (West Wanaka Station) but to the west, only a mountain wilderness in the form of Mount Aspiring National Park. No road reaches Minaret Station. Access is by boat across the lake or by air. The station comprises 19,753 hectares (48,811 acres) of pastoral lease-hold land. Only about 20 percent of the land, the 'front country', the foothills bordering the lake, is 'improved' – that is, oversown with intro-duced pasture grasses, top-dressed with fertiliser and fenced for livestock. The bulk of the property remains in 'native' condition, predominantly tussock grassland and shrubland. The mountain tops are the preserve of snow and ice in winter and spring; in the warmer months the exposed rocky terrain provides habitat for only the hardiest alpine plants.

It was a dream of Tim's to own a property bordering the Southern Alps. Although Criffel and Mararoa properties had impressive mountain settings, they could not match the rugged remoteness of Minaret. Minaret was underutilised when his company purchased it. From Tim's viewpoint, that was all the better; it gave him a fairly clean slate to work from. Holding a few ideas himself about its future potential, he decided to test them against the views of a select group of colleagues and contacts. Tim revelled in the cut-and-thrust of the debate that surrounded new projects. It was second nature to him, although some of his associates thought he canvassed the ideas of others mainly to find support for his own. The Minaret focus group was assembled at the Edgewater Resort at Wanaka in June 1995 while negotiations were proceeding over the purchase of the station. All sorts of ideas surfaced in the 'think-tank' and also next day during a visit to the station by boat and a picnic on the lake shore. By and large, they reinforced Tim's own vision, which was to develop a deer farm on the lower country and reserve the wild backblocks for trophy hunting with rifle or bow. He envisaged the quarry being red deer stags as magnificent as the hunters encountered in this sort of country 100 years earlier, plus chamois, which also ran wild here, and perhaps even another, larger introduced animal of the alpine zone, tahr. Throw in some trout fishing as well in the vigorous mountain rivers, 100 percent pure, the epitome of New Zealand's clean, green image. Plus helicopters ready to facilitate access.

For 30 years Tim had envisaged such an opportunity. In a letter to his mother in Christchurch in 1965, when he was setting up Luggate Game Packers, he wrote: 'I am looking at starting a Game Reserve at Wanaka for the Tourist Hotel to show its visitors. All I want of course is some natural country ...'

By the mid-1990s, his involvement in Canada with Mike and Dianne Bringans was showing up the potential to breed trophy elk, and he saw how this could benefit a Minaret hunt camp attracting well-off North Americans who fancied an adventure in the mountainous wilds Down Under. As for developing Minaret's farming, Tim had already thought of transport. Stored at Criffel was an odd-ball collection of craft – a large flat-bottomed barge and three pusher tugs, which he acquired in 1994 from the Clyde Dam hydro-electric project, thinking they would come in handy some day.

When it came to boats, Tim could never resist a deal, notwithstanding the warnings of his directors years earlier not to dabble.

Chapter 13

The Last Crash

Mid-1990s
Hectic years ... World Scout Jamboree aerobatics ...
a practice flight with Brian Hore ... upside down
in a paddock ... intensive care ... 3,000 messages ...
homecoming ... 1996 Warbirds ... back at the office
and in the air ... the 'Tim Wallis factor' ...
a Millbrook concert

THE YEARS 1992 to 1995 were hectic for Tim. Life was more up and down than usual for a number of reasons. These were the frustrations in the Russian deer industry, the laborious Polikarpov restoration work, a series of deals going on over vintage warplanes, the evolving Warbirds phenomenon, the sinking of the *Ranginui*, Tim's acquisition of Minaret Station, and his mixed success in Canada and in business interests at home. Yet The Helicopter Line, in which Tim was then a major shareholder, had shaken off the sharemarket woes of the late 1980s and it quickly became a New Zealand tourism leader in the early 1990s, with a dynamic, diversified portfolio of investments, starting with the acquisition of Maui Campervans in 1988.

THL's asset base, including tourist hotels at Mt Cook, Te Anau and Rotorua, large coach tour companies, Milford Sound's Red Boats and the Waitomo Caves, had grown from $15 million to $230 million in under ten years. The motor fleet alone – 1,000 campervans, 800 rental cars and 90 coaches – was moving hundreds of thousands of overseas visitors around New Zealand every year. Caught up in a surging sharemarket, THL's share price hit a peak of $5.80 in 1994. This prompted the *National Business Review* to trumpet THL's prospects: watch THL's share price, it could go as high as $9.

There was a lot going on, therefore, of direct interest to Tim within New Zealand let alone elsewhere in the world. By and large, he thrived on the busyness but there were private moments when, under the stress of all these competing interests, he became unusually argumentative and seemingly less self-assured. By mid-1995, he was getting a strong message from his Alpine Deer Group directors: slow down on the vintage warplane projects. Together with the Minaret purchase, these warplane deals were in danger of overcommitting the company financially. The restoration of just one old fighter could cost one or two million dollars.

Through 1995, THL's share price began to slide. It rebounded to $5.30 in May 1995, but then the downward trend set in again. Although Tim had sold large parcels of shares to pay for fighter aircraft, it was of major concern to him that the share price was trending steeply downwards.

On 1 December, with its shares selling at $3.85, almost $2 below the 1994 peak, The Helicopter Line released a statement to the media about repositioning its assets to 'insulate itself from weather-dependent activities'. *Otago Daily Times* business editor Dene Mackenzie reported that THL's tourist hotel acquisitions would help it get through times when adverse weather conditions bedevilled skifield revenue and helicopter charter work. But a looming Asian economic crisis was something THL could do little to counter. Many of THL's customers were from Asian countries like Korea, Taiwan and Japan. Inbound package tours involving those nationalities were declining, and they were set to disappear almost entirely as the Asian economies headed into recession.

Towards the end of 1995, the THL directors had some vigorous debates about the cyclical nature of the tourist industry and about the best ways of smoothing troubled commercial waters during the downturns. THL had just received Deloitte's Best Corporate Strategy award. But not even that news could correct the slide in the company's share price. Managing director Graham Gosney noted wryly in the *Otago Daily Times* business pages that 'sometimes company strategy is not well understood by shareholders and analysts'.

On 23 December, the stock market's last trading day before Christmas, THL shares were being offered at $3.06 – a 20 percent erosion in value in just six months. It left Tim with a sick feeling. In December 1995, Don Spary took over as chairman of the Alpine Deer Group board of directors. But he had a word of caution for Tim. He definitely wanted Tim to curb his spending.

Tim looked flushed and preoccupied before and during Christmas 1995. Some Christmases in the past were similarly 'down' times for Tim. Over Christmas 1995, he became ill. He vomited on Christmas Eve. Prue put it down to pressure of work and perhaps financial worries. She thought he might have been reacting to some business or financial scare, although she was unable to identify it.

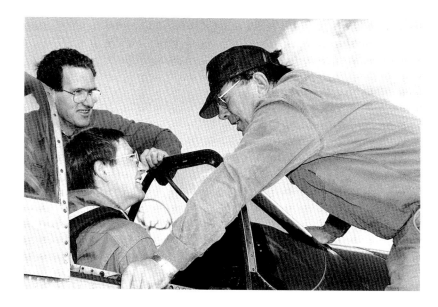

SEVERAL HUNDRED SCOUTS from around New Zealand and from a range of Asian and Pacific nations were attending an international jamboree near Lake Manapouri over the Christmas-New Year period. Their tents were spread out over a large area of the Manapouri airfield, and on New Year's Day they were treated to an enthralling helicopter rescue demonstration. Te Anau-based Richard Hayes showed off the capabilities of his French-built six-passenger Squirrel helicopter. Although the scouts could see the adjacent Kepler Mountains of Fiordland National Park, dark clouds pushed along by a westerly airstream were scudding through the area, bringing passing showers. Rainbows flared as sunbeams burst through the cloud cover. Richard Hayes knew what was next on the programme after his performance in the Squirrel but few of the assembled scouts would have had any idea that Sir Tim Wallis, pioneer deer-recovery aviator and fighter plane enthusiast, was about to arrive in a Spitfire.

It was early evening when the Spitfire Mk XVI made a dramatic entry in the skies over the jamboree site. The scouts heard the Spitfire FUP before they saw it. Tim, a friend of the scouting movement and glad to respond to a request for an aerobatic display, came dashing though a hole in the clouds, diving low over the camp and banking away into a large loop. It was the opening manoeuvre of a display that extended into a Cuban 8, which involved a backward twist and turn. He then made several passes doing barrel rolls, and several more swoops over the camp at high speed, around 500 kilometres per hour. Necks were getting sore by the time Tim turned the Spitfire north for his return to Wanaka. Towards dusk he was back over Lake Wanaka and he put the Spitfire into a display over the campsite at Mt Burke Station on the shores of Stevensons Arm, where family and friends were holidaying.

The next day, 2 January 1996, a Tuesday, Tim was up early as was his custom. He had a date with pilot Brian Hore in the skies over Wanaka that morning. Brian co-owned with Tim's Alpine company a North American P-51D Mustang, acquired in 1993, and Tim had invited him to practice formation flying for the next Warbirds show, due to be staged over Easter, the first week of April. The show was billed as 'The ultimate non-stop action airshow!' and the line-up for it included a very rare ME-109, the Alpine Fighter Collection's newly-arrived Russian Yak-3M, and AFC's two Supermarine Spitfires, the Mk XVI FUP and the Mk XIV. On 2 January, Tim chose to fly the Mark 14, having thrilled the scouts at Manapouri the day before in the Mark 16. Although he had clocked up 210 hours' flying time in Spitfires by then, he had just five and a half hours' experience aloft in the Mark 14 type. He had flown the Mark 14 a total of seven times. His most recent flight was in May 1995, eight months earlier, at Wigram.

For the scout camp flight, Tim had hoped Brian could join him in the Mustang, which was nicknamed Miss Torque, but the northern Southland farmer was unable to make it. Brian Hore farms 38,000-hectare Nokomai Station, where Bill Black and Jim Kane developed the bamboo pole method of capturing red deer live in the late 1960s. At that time, Brian's father, Frank, ran the huge high country property. Brian's links with Tim, therefore, began in the 1960s and he would sometimes join the Wallises for an adventurous holiday in Fiordland based on the *Ranginui*. In the early 1990s, following the first two Warbirds shows, Brian decided he wanted to fly World War II fighter aircraft. He trained in a North American Harvard based at Wanaka Airport.

When Tim asked Brian if he could form a twosome with him in the air over Wanaka on 2 January 1996, Brian was able to say, yes, he could make it. Because it was holiday time, he said he would probably invite a few friends to the airport to watch the display. To one friend, Anthony Young, of Mossburn, he promised a flight in the Mustang. Tim's decision to fly the Spitfire ZK-XIV surprised Brian, mainly because he knew Tim's experience of the Mark 14 was limited. He wondered if Tim had chosen the Mark 14 because it would better match the Mustang's speed (both its cruise speed of 325 miles per hour/520 kilometres per hour and its maximum speed, 505 miles per hour/808 kilometres per hour, eclipsed the Mark 16's capabilities). The Mustang was considered the finest fighter produced by the Americans during the war.

Tim sitting in the cockpit of his Mk XIV Spitfire. Ian Brodie

Brian and his friends were at the airport by 10 a.m. It was a fine day for a spin. Tim, held up, had phoned ahead to Ian Brodie, director of the Fighter Pilots' Museum, with a request for the Mark 14 to be wheeled out of the museum and made ready for a flight. Brian had seen a small pool of oil under the Mark 16, and he figured it might require inspection by engineers from the Alpine Fighter Collection before it flew again.

With the Mustang pretty well ready for take-off, Tim arrived at the airport and began some pre-flight checks on the Mark 14. He fired up the Griffon engine but shut it down when he discovered a problem with the aircraft's radio. He advised Brian he would have to get someone to look at it. 'I might have to give the flight a miss,' he told Brian, who decided to take off with his passenger anyway. He headed off over the town of Wanaka and on up the lake.

Back at the airport, Biplane Adventures founder Grant Bisset noticed that Tim had shut down the Spitfire's engine and went over to see if there was a problem he could help with. Grant and Tim were partners in Biplane Adventures, which offered visitors and vintage aircraft enthusiasts flights in a de Havilland Tiger Moth, P-51D Mustang Dominie or Pitts Special. Grant could see the radio had come loose in its cradle. When he tightened it back into place, it worked again. Tim gave Brian a call to say he was under way and about to take off in the Mark 14. Brian advised he would be stationed over the lake, well clear of the take-off path.

Tim donned his flying helmet, a Second World War leather type with fitted earphones, made himself secure in the pilot's four-point harness and taxied the Mark 14 to the runway. Not only was he aware his friend had been in the air for a while and was cruising around waiting for him; Tim was also aware there were visitors to his museum who were standing outside to see this special event – a vintage fighter taking off. Tim gunned the powerful Griffon engine and the plane accelerated swiftly. About halfway along the runway, the Spitfire began yawing to the right.

Too late, Tim knew what was wrong: he had failed to manually preset the rudder trim fully left. In a hurry to get airborne, distracted by the glitch with the plane's radio, and with a hundred and one business things to think about at the end of a fitful year, Tim had overlooked the rudder trim setting in the pre-flight checks. In a Mark 14, a full-left trim is critical. In the Mark 16, which he had flown the previous day, such a setting was not required. The two Spitfire types differed in their engines types. The Mark 14's Griffon engine was 600-hp more powerful and its propeller turned in the opposite direction (to the left). During the Second World War there had been several crashes arising from uncontrolled swing on take-off.

As the Mark 14 slewed to the right, and in the few seconds he knew he had available to him to correct the veering and bring the plane under control, Tim tried frantically to counter the torque effect of the roaring Griffon engine and its 'opposite-sign' five-blade propeller. Having been coached on the Mark 14's right-yaw eccentricity, he knew what was going on. All he needed was space to the right of the runway to correct his mistake. Intersecting the space, however, was the airport boundary fence, a regular sheep-farm fence, waist high on a man. He came upon it too soon. The Spitfire's tail-wheel snagged the top two wires. Tim felt a jerk and the aircraft's nose lifted. Instinctively, with take-off power maintained, he tried to fly the plane clear of the obstruction.

The aircraft stalled. Falling to its right, it struck the ground 130 metres from the fence in a flat paddock grazed by sheep – part of an old river terrace occupied by the airport complex and farmland.

On contact with the ground, the right wing snapped off at its base. The plane continued rolling to the right, with the wooden propeller blades tearing at the soil and sheering off on impact. Canopy and windscreen splintered and collapsed as the plane, practically upside down, ploughed on for about 40 metres. The propellers, before disintegrating, gouged a trench up to half a metre deep over a length of about sixty metres.

Wreckage of the Spitfire Mk XIV, with the propeller gouge mark in the foreground and left wing in the air.

'Very seldom does an aircraft let
you down. You usually let the aircraft down.'

*Tim interviewed on a TVNZ
Country Calendar documentary,
1987.*

The wrecked plane came to rest 170 metres from the breach in the
fence, with wire still entangled in the tail-wheel assembly. At the bottom
of the wreck, still in the cockpit, Tim lay unconscious and unmoving. He
had fearful head injuries.

'Watch the Mark 14,' Spitfire authority Ray Hanna had warned, 'it
can be a beast.'

'Plan your flight carefully,' pilot/instructor Stephen Grey advised, 'and
always leave time for yourself.'

AT THE FIGHTER PILOTS' MUSEUM, Ian Brodie was busy organising a busload of about 40 Australian visitors when Tim took off in the
Mark 14. Recognising that his visitors were much more interested in a
vintage warplane in action than in a whole collection of them resting
silently inside the building, he opened the door so the visitors could get a
good look at the Spitfire taking off. The next thing he heard was a shrill
cry, 'He's crashed!'

Ian was out of the museum like a shot, leaving staff there to summon
emergency services. Among the first on the crash scene, together with Ian,
were the principals of two air charter and tourist ventures based at Wanaka
Airport, Grant Bisset, of Biplane Adventures, and Barrie McHaffie, Aspiring Air's managing director, whose four sons, aged from 13 to 26, were
doing odd jobs at the airport. Twenty-three-year-old Jeff McHaffie had
been mowing lawns as a holiday job when he saw the Spitfire veer away
and crash as if it were a model aircraft out of control. He began running
towards the wreckage, yelling at his brother, Scott, to bring a fire extinguisher.

Grant had seen Tim lift off and knew he was in trouble. He appeared
to be flying slowly at a reduced power setting, to try to minimise the yaw.
Grant thought he would abort the take-off and put the Spitfire back on
the ground – and Tim might have had he not encountered the fence.
Grant saw the nose pitch up and the aircraft become inverted and dive
into the ground. He considered the accident unsurvivable.

Wearing his Nomex flying suit at the time, Grant ran to his Toyota
Hi-Ace van and headed for the torn gap in the fence. As he caught up
with Jeff he passed out his mobile phone and asked him to phone 111 and
call for fire and ambulance services. Grant drove on through the broken
wires of the fence into the sheep paddock but was stopped short of the
wreckage, with his wheels spinning, as the van pulled the wires taut. He
ran the rest of the way. Grant could see Tim trapped in the cockpit and
still in his harness. He looked in a very bad way, with his head severely
mauled. There was no movement. Then he heard a gurgle from Tim.

The demolished canopy and cockpit of Tim's Spitfire Mk XIV.

Those who arrived first on the scene of the wreckage found the ground around it awash with aviation fuel, which had spilled from ruptured tanks forward of the cockpit. Fuel was still hosing out. Engine oil was also spewing out and smoking as it contacted hot metal. What were the chances of the whole thing exploding and going up in flames? The engine had stopped but it was making crackling and ticking noises as it cooled. One of the Spitfire's wheels was still spinning. Ian Brodie did not know how anyone could survive such a crash. With an AFFF-type foam fire extinguisher he began spraying everything in sight – the wreckage and the surrounding ground – as a precaution against an explosion and fire. The foam would reduce the risk of a vapour explosion. He and Grant realised the wreck was a potential bomb.

Keen to get to the pilot, Jeff McHaffie checked out the starboard side first but found no way to reach him. He heard a gurgled gasp for breath. He then tried the port side. His father, on the scene by now, peered into the smashed cockpit area, saw a small movement and heard another gasp. They had to do something – and smartly. More people arrived on the scene, including Tim's 20-year-old son, Toby, who was flying for Biplane Adventures at the time and in the process of getting his commercial helicopter licence.

To extricate Tim, the plane had to be turned. Everyone pitched in to lift the left wing until it was more or less upright. With the plane balancing on the stub of the amputated right wing, it pointed skywards. It looked shockingly like a headstone from a distance.

Now they were able to remove Tim from the wreckage. To safety? Was he still alive? His head and face, the left side in particular, were gruesomely lacerated. While his father and brothers supported Tim, thinking his neck might be broken, Jeff released Tim's safety harness and parachute straps. Together they pulled Tim out, no mean feat given Tim's weight and bulk and the cockpit's mangled condition. He was carried about 25 metres from the wreckage. Terry, another McHaffie son, cradled Tim's head. His breathing was irregular, little more than shallow gasps. Barrie cleared Tim's mouth and throat of a mixture of soil, blood and regurgitated stomach contents and this restored his breathing to something like normal. Then Tim was placed in the 'recovery' position recommended for unconscious crash victims.

Ian Brodie's next thoughts were for Prue. Someone had to go and tell her. He knew the family had been camping and he hoped she was back at Benfiddich. He drove down Mt Barker Road from the airport with the gravel and dust flying.

Meanwhile, Brian Hore, awaiting Tim's arrival in the skies over Wanaka, was wondering why he had not had a call from Tim. Brian had tried several times to raise Tim on the radio. Thinking his friend might have had more radio problems, he headed the Mustang back towards the airport. When he swooped low over the strip, he was appalled to see the Spitfire in a crumpled heap in the paddock beside the runway, with its left wing pointing up, its right wing gone, and people coming to the aid of the pilot. Was he still alive?

At Benfiddich, Prue was in the kitchen when Ian burst in, calling out for her. He told her Tim had had an accident. Thinking he might have crashed during aerobatics practice, she asked: 'Did he fall out of the sky?' No, the accident had happened at take-off. 'Is he alive?' asked Prue. Ian was non-committal. The best he could say was that Tim was unconscious. 'He'll be all right then,' said Prue.

In Wanaka, the Wallis family doctor, Dennis Pezaro, rushed to the airport on getting an emergency phone call. He arrived about 15 minutes after the crash. At her Dublin Downs home near Wanaka, Robert Wilson's wife, Prue, received an alarming call from the Alpine office at the airport. She learnt there had been a serious crash in the Spitfire, involving Tim. Alpine staff knew the two Prues were close friends and that Prue Wallis might need her friend's support. She left for the airport immediately.

Tim's sons, who were at various locations, were advised of his crash as soon as possible. Toby was the first son on the scene, and Nick arrived about the same time as his mother, 25 minutes after the crash. Nick, the youngest at 15 and still at Christ's College, had planned a visit to Minaret Station that day with some friends, and his father had said he would fly them over. He saw his father stretched out on the paddock but he did not recognise him. His face was too disfigured. But Nick could hear a familiar kind of coughing. It sounded like his dad.

Matthew was driving back from a holiday with friends in Canterbury. It was his 17th birthday the next day. By the time Matthew reached the airport, Tim had been flown to Dunedin in an Aspiring Air Britten-Norman Islander and admitted to the intensive care unit at Dunedin Public Hospital, with those attending him reckoning it was touch and go whether he would make it to Dunedin alive. The second son, Jonathan, was out of the country. He was visiting friends in England before starting a degree course in agriculture at Lincoln University that year. Prue phoned Jonathan later in the day, having arranged a flight home for him. She said Tim had been involved in another Spitfire crash. He had 'a bang on his head'.

IN CASES WHERE patients are unconscious, medical specialists make an assessment based on an internationally-recognised measurement known as the Glasgow Coma Scale. The victim is scored across three parameters (eye opening, communication, motor activity), with level one being the lowest in each category. Tim's tally over the three categories, out of a possible of 15, was three – the lowest possible score. Level three on the Glasgow Coma Scale usually signifies little chance of survival – at best, a persistent vegetative state. The top end of the scale indicates a fully conscious state.

Tim arrived at the hospital still unconscious and with terrible head wounds from being dragged along the ground in a cockpit mostly upside down. The left side of his face had been stripped backwards – 'degloved' is the medical term – with skin and flesh from forward of his left ear now sitting behind the ear. He had fractures to his left eye orbit and cheek, and severe left-frontal lobe damage. That night he was operated on for over six hours. But the big question in Prue's mind – in everyone's – was whether the crash had damaged Tim's brain, and if so, to what extent? CT scans showed moderate frontal-lobe contusions consistent with a deceleration injury. Swelling and raised intracranial pressure in the hours and days after a crash are what often kill brain-injured people. These effects can be counteracted by keeping the patient in a state of deep anaesthesia and by hyper-oxygenating him/her to maintain a healthy blood flow. In Tim's case, it was a matter of buying time and hoping for the best, as intensive-care nurse Michael Lucas explained to Prue and the boys. Michael, who had five years' experience in intensive care, was on duty the day after Tim was admitted and at each subsequent shift in the unit he was assigned to Tim. He became Tim's primary nurse.

Within a couple of days some hospital consultants were preparing the family for the worst: in their opinion there was no more than a ten percent chance Tim would regain consciousness – even open his eyes – let alone get back to anything like a normal life. Prue had another view. Tim would get better – much better than anyone in the hospital expected. After all, he was only 57.

She and one or more of the boys were constantly by Tim's side. In intensive care, ventilated and under dialysis because of renal failure, he was festooned by a forest of lines, wires and tubes, including a trache-otomy tube to secure an airway, and surrounded by monitoring equip-ment. Michael Lucas was bombarded with questions from the Wallis boys about how to interact with Tim and what to expect. They knew from the outset that it was okay to talk to Tim as normal, and imagine he was listening. They learnt that hearing was often the first sense to reactivate in an unconscious person and that this might show up subtly and without any obvious indication from Tim through slight jumps in his monitored heart rate or blood pressure. The nurses kept up a one-way conversation with him as they took care of dressings, suctioning, washing or changing his body position, and Prue and the boys read to him, massaged him and held up photographs in front of his unseeing eyes.

After two and a half weeks, the decision was made to transfer Tim from intensive care to Ward 6A, a neurosurgical ward, which was higher up in the main hospital block. He had survived the initial trauma and, although basically still asleep, he was beginning to respond to stimuli.

To challenge Tim's sense of hearing the Wallises introduced taped sounds that were a strong part of Tim's life, including a Spitfire's engine noise and a mobile phone dialling. Alpine Deer Group executive director Graeme Ramshaw came in from his Upper Stuart Street office to give Tim updates on business affairs. Other Dunedin associates of Tim's rang in for a one-way chat, and at those times Prue or one of the boys would hold the phone close to Tim's ear. From Wanaka came the family pet, Digger, Tim's (formerly Nick's) little Jack Russell dog, who loved nothing better than to climb into the cockpit of a vintage warplane. Digger met his master again when Tim was wheeled out into the fresh air and summer sunshine one day at the hospital, still attached to a ventilator. It was a special moment for the boys. Here was their father in the fresh air again, with his beloved Digger. Perhaps Tim really might be able to return home soon to the things he loved.

But Tim also needed spells without movement or anyone talking to him, and there were many long hours when his family and close associates sat quietly at his side. From the time of his arrival at the hospital there were meetings at least once a week to review his progress and treatment, and to plan the next steps. These meetings involved consultants such as Albert Erasmus, David Bowie and Mace Ramsay, senior nurse Michael Lucas, Wanaka general practitioner Dennis Pezaro, Prue and, when they were available, the Wallis boys.

Senior medical staff, although encouraged by the first tentative signs of recovery, were not predicting when Tim might fully emerge from the coma. Head injury, they said, was a devilishly difficult and fickle thing. No one could say how far the recovery would progress.

Prue, meanwhile, had firm ideas of where and how Tim might be cared for and rehabilitated and she was forthright in arguing them. She wanted Tim transferred to home care – back at Wanaka – even if he were still comatose. She was convinced that at home he would have the best possible chance of recovery. In this view, she took encouragement from a long-standing friend of Tim's, Professor Alan Clarke, director of the Burwood Spinal Unit in Christchurch. Alan himself had become a paraplegic in 1991 after falling off the roof at home and breaking his back. Tim had raced to his bedside then, coming straight from the airport after a flight from Russia and waking other patients in the process of explaining to Alan that, paraplegic or not, Alan just had to keep flying. So it was that, five years on, Alan Clarke arrived in a wheelchair at Dunedin Hospital expressly to talk to Prue and the boys about rehabilitation techniques, in which he had a strong professional interest. Rehabilitation, Alan said, was not so much a medical process as a learning process, and he insisted, 'as soon as it's safe to take him home, take him home.'

Alan sent Prue a copy of a technical paper published in an American nursing journal on the rehabilitation of the victims of brain injury. It was the beginning of a journey of discovery for Prue. A brain injury could affect movement, any of the senses, and the victim's intelligence, behaviour and personality. Prue explored deeply into the world of coma, brain injury and rehabilitation. Medical staff emphasised the importance of her role as Tim's advocate. But she knew she had to go one bold step further in order to achieve home care at an early stage: she had to think and behave like Tim; she had to be like him – audacious, courageous, firm to the point of being bloody-minded.

Professor Alan Clarke, of Christchurch, and his wife Jane visiting Tim at the Alpine Fighter Collection hangar at Wanaka. They are pictured with a Polikarpov I-16.

A public outpouring

The crash made headline news not only in the *Otago Daily Times* but also in many other metropolitan and provincial newspapers around New Zealand, and on radio and television bulletins. News of the crash and Sir Tim's critical condition also spread around world, to countries such as Britain, the United States, Russia, Japan and Germany, and updates on Tim's condition were reported in the succeeding weeks. The hospital was deluged by bunches of flowers and 'Get well' cards. Letters arrived by the sackful.

An enormous card was sent from the international Scout camp at Te Anau, where Tim had entertained with an aerobatics display the day before the crash. The card contained over 700 signatures, leaving no room, as the Scout leaders complained, for the writing of personal messages. Another large-format card arrived from North America with over 200 signatures underneath a message addressed to Tim, 'We know *you* don't mind these plane crashes, but *we* are stressing out over it!'

The flowers were banned from the intensive care unit in case pollen clogged the ventilators or otherwise affected patients' breathing. Instead, they were dispersed around the hospital's various wards. Well-wishers included children and adults who had never met Tim but clearly held him to be a southern legend. Most staff had never seen anything like this level of public outpouring of sympathy and concern before. Typically the cards contained prayerful messages. After Tim had arrived in Ward 6A, Prue started to collate the cards and letters into plastic clear-files. She thought he would want to reply to each one. When a ward nurse saw her processing the swags of mail, she asked Prue what she was doing. Prue said she was getting the cards and letters sorted for Tim to work on replies when he recovered. Without pausing to consider a more tactful reply, the nurse implied that would probably be a lost cause. She interrupted herself mid-sentence, awfully embarrassed.

Rescue services in action at Wanaka Airport on Tuesday where Sir Tim Wallis crashed his MkX1V Spitfire just after take-off. Sir Tim was seriously injured in the accident.

Photo: Karen Howard

Inquiry complete at air crash site

AIR accident investigator David Graham yesterday concluded his examination of the wreckage of the Spitfire in which Wanaka airman Sir Tim Wallis crashed on Tuesday, sustaining serious injuries.

Sir Tim is in Dunedin Hospital in the intensive care unit. He was flown there after the crash, just before noon.

Mr Graham's examination of the air crash site will be aided by statements from eyewitnesses, still being taken by the Wanaka police.

Sir Tim was to fly the MkX1V Spitfire at an informal air display of Alpine Fighter Collection planes at Wanaka Airport this weekend but Warbirds over Wanaka general manager Gavin Johnston said no decision had been made on whether the display would still go ahead.

"Even if the fighter collection does not fly, the planes will still be on the ground for people to look at," Mr Johnston said.

He confirmed the Warbirds over Wanaka air show, planned for Easter weekend in April, would still go ahead.

Emergency services from Wanaka, Luggate and Hawea rushed to the crash scene on Tuesday.

By JACKIE BURGESS

Wanaka doctor Dennis Pezaro, who also attended the accident, said the plane crashed just after take-off from the Wanaka Airport.

"The plane apparently rolled slightly and crashed upside down.

"Witnesses rolled the plane partially over to get Sir Tim out of the cockpit because of the amount of fuel around," Dr Pezaro said.

Sir Tim was flown to Dunedin Hospital with serious injuries and his wife, Lady Pru Wallis, also flew to Dunedin to be with her 58-year-old husband.

Sir Tim was knighted two years ago for his services to the aviation and deer industries.

The founder of the internationally-famous Warbirds over Wanaka airshow, which takes place every two years, Sir Tim also established the renowned Alpine Fighter Collection based at Wanaka Airport.

A Dunedin Hospital spokesman said late yesterday Sir Tim was still in a serious condition and in intensive care.

Family hopes for 'slow but steady' recovery

Sir Tim's condition serious

By Dave Cannan

Sir Tim Wallis is still on the seriously-ill list at Dunedin Hospital and is likely to remain in the intensive care unit for some time, according to his wife, Lady Wallis.

In a statement yesterday Lady Wallis said her husband was in a "serious condition". Doctors were keeping him under heavy sedation.

"He has a serious head injury and we don't expect any significant change in his condition for several days," she said.

Sir Tim (57) was flown to Dunedin Hospital on Tuesday after the Mk14 Spitfire he was piloting crashed at Wanaka.

An investigation into the accident will take up to four weeks to complete.

Sir Tim's popularity has resulted in hundreds of messages of support, according to Lady Wallis.

But while she and her sons were "very grateful" for the interest in Sir Tim's condition, Lady Wallis asked that the family's wish for privacy be observed.

"We would appreciate people understanding that his condition is serious and that we will not allow any intrusion into what we hope will be a slow but steady recovery," she said.

Healthcare Otago communications manager David Swindells said people were welcome to send faxed messages to Sir Tim on 03 474 7719 or by mail, c/o Dunedin Hospital, 201 Great King St.

Sir Tim Wallis

Foto: Purbold AP

Dog big hit at air show

By Dave Smith

Wanaka. – Sir Tim Wallis' dog Digger proved a hit with the nearly 2000 people who turned out for the Alpine Fighter Collection display on Saturday night and almost stole the show.

In the absence of its owner, who is in Dunedin Hospital seriously injured after a crash last week, Digger, a Jack Russell terrier, raced along the runway each time one of the historic planes passed overhead.

Sir Tim crashed his Mk14 Spitfire last week and is in a serious but stable condition in hospital.

Obviously taking its duties seriously, Digger scampered this way and that along the grass adjacent to the tarseal, but only when the Mk18 Spitfire or P-51 Mustang roared

above the field.

Also flying during the display was a Fox Moth once owned by King George VI, a Chipmunk, a Harvard and a Tiger Moth.

Alpine collection general manager Gavin Johnston said the display had proved very successful on a balmy summer's night.

During the day commercial operators displayed their activities and products to a steady stream of people who also wandered around the static fighter planes and through the New Zealand Fighter Pilots museum.

At the end of the day's activities Digger was observed escorting the fighter planes back to the hangar, making sure the day was completed to Sir Tim's satisfaction.

5mal abgestürzt, und alles überlebt

Wellington. – Er ist ein leidenschaftlicher Flieger, bisweilen aber vom Pech verfolgt. Immerhin aber hat Tim Wallis (57) stets Glück im Unglück: Schon fünf Abstürze hat der Neuseeländer mit Schrammen und ein paar Knochenbrüchen überlebt.

Jahrelang flog Tim mit seinem Hubschrauber Gäste zur Rotwildjagd. Dabei machte er zweimal Bruch – zum Glück ohne Passagiere. Zweimal stürzte er ab, weil er bei Kunstflug-Shows mitmachte, und überstand auch dies so halbwegs. Jetzt liegt Tim Wallis wieder mit Knochenbrüchen im Krankenhaus. Er war mit einem britischen Oldtimer-Flugzeug, einer der zwölf noch existierenden „MK 14 Spitfire", kurz nach dem Start auf eine Viehweide gekracht.

Newspaper cuttings of crash.

Only determination of that order would succeed in breaking the usual model; in cases as serious as Tim's a long spell in a hospital rehabilitation unit was invariably prescribed.

WHAT WOULD TIM have thought about being in a hospital ward for months on end – an outdoors man, occupying a room smaller than a prison cell and breathing recycled air? It was an environment alien to Tim's experience and natural inclinations. If he were to shake off the coma and start talking, Prue knew what he would say straight off: 'Get me out of here!' He needed the hospital equipment and treatment regime through the critical first few weeks, no question. But could intensive nursing care not be replicated at home? Neurological consultant Albert Erasmus argued for at least another three weeks of hospital care before reviewing the home-care option. He had seen others with comparable brain injuries who had had poor outcomes. But he did acknowledge Tim was 'lightening up'. The idea of an early transfer home struck the consultant as ironic. Usually he had to urge and encourage families supporting a brain-injured person to take on home care. Rarely did he have to argue the other way.

Prue, with a resolve Tim would have been proud of, and with encouragement from her sons, set about planning and organising a home-care regime. She wanted it to happen as soon as possible. She described her role through the metaphor of a ladder. She would provide the rungs that would allow him to climb back up to the world of the living.

A meeting of medical personnel and Prue at the end of Tim's first three weeks in hospital discussed the steps necessary for setting up home-based care. Dennis Pezaro said a multi-disciplinary nursing team would be established on a 'waiting basis'. ACC had to be approached about Tim's gaining a Complex Personal Injury (CPI) classification, which would help fund the home care. CPI was a relatively new concept. It had been introduced by Government regulation in 1994 to facilitate home care for severely injured accident victims on the basis that, in high-dependency cases, it was cheaper for the Government to support home care than it was to provide hospital care. A bed night in intensive care cost about $1,500 and the cost per night of a patient in the neurological ward was in the vicinity of $400.

A CPI assessment was applied for in Tim's case. Hospital staff said the paperwork, reports and cost estimates would probably take some time. So would the acquisition of a bed. Tim required an adjustable bed that could bend and be lifted up and down, and delivery of such a bed usually took weeks. Being disabled already, Tim would also need a wheelchair with special features. Recommendations on wheelchair design came from Christchurch disability specialist Allan Bean, whose professional association with Tim spanned more than 30 years. Allan also gave advice on how to manage Tim's bladder and bowel functions.

Prue focussed on selecting someone who could assemble a team for Tim's rehabilitation at home and the kind of equipment required to replicate a hospital setting. She had no doubt who that person could be: Michael Lucas. Through his nursing skills, his confident personality and his rapport with Prue and the boys, Michael had been a pillar of support for the family from the outset. He was 37, with a wife and two young sons, one of whom was a baby. Going to live in Wanaka for long periods would be challenging enough let alone having to lead and coordinate the rehabilitation at home of a man who was, at this point, essentially unconscious.

With Michael, Prue was persuasive – as persuasive as Tim would have been in the situation. Michael accepted the challenge, although he admitted to feeling daunted. There were few precedents to follow and hardly anything in the medical literature about caring for someone at home who was brain-injured and likely to be still comatose. Over the past few weeks the strength of the Wallis family had impressed him, and that was important because brain-injured people, in his view, recovered the best when their support network was strong. There was little time for worrying about the unknown. Michael set about sourcing equipment as well as coordinating the interviewing and selection of staff. Jobs were advertised in daily newspapers. In addition to nursing skills, the home-care team had to include disciplines such as physiotherapy, massage, occupational therapy, speech therapy and neuropsychology. It was the view of the hospital's consultants that even if Tim recovered to the point of talking and walking, he would still have significant cognitive problems to overcome. Dunedin neuropsychologist Barry Longmore was assigned to Tim's case.

ACC agreed to pay Michael and the team but Tim's company, Alpine Deer Group, kicked in funds from the start and topped up Michael's remuneration. Michael was granted three months' leave without pay from the hospital. He would end up working at the Wallis home for 15 months. Applicants wishing to join the nursing team were interviewed by Michael, and some were flown in by Alpine Deer Group from other parts of the country.

Equipment began rolling up at Benfiddich, the Wallis home off Mt Barker Road at the foot of the Criffel Range near Wanaka. It included an adjustable bed (at $17,000 the most expensive item), a hoist to help get Tim into and out of bed, intravenous equipment, oxygen bottles, a shower table, a portable suction device with pump, and a generator in case of power failure. Michael negotiated the equipment purchases 'on appro' (payment on customer's approval after a trial run), knowing that ACC would not pay for equipment already purchased.

At the end of Tim's seventh week in hospital, Prue was sitting with Tim in Ward 6A, opening mail. Tim had been bathed and was lying back in a Lazyboy chair, eyes closed. The mail included a handful of photos showing new fencing at Minaret Station.

Without expecting a reply, Prue said: 'Tim, would you like to see some photos from Minaret?'

But there was a reply. With eyes still closed, Tim mumbled a few words. They sounded like: 'See … Minaret photos.' Prue turned to the cleaner who happened to be in the room and asked her to get the charge nurse.

Dr Erasmus was called. He sat close to Tim and said, 'I hear you're waking up.'

'This is Dr Erasmus,' said Prue. 'The boys call him Dr Razzmatazz.'

Slowly, Tim extended a hand. In a slurry voice he said: 'How do you do … Razzmatazz.'

The consultant laughed heartily. He said he had often had patients wake up angry, confused and violent but none had ever shaken hands with him coming out of a coma.

That evening Tim said, "Hello, Prue.' He also named the boys. Anything he said, no matter how mumbled, was music to the ears of his family. These first words after the crash intensified plans for his return home. By now, Tim could move an arm or squeeze a hand. Before long, when a son came into the ward, greeting him with a cheery, 'Hello, Dad', Tim would raise an arm with his eyes closed, and feel around the boy's face as he lent over his father. Tim also reached out this way to his brother, George.

Just as the crash made front-page news, Tim's homecoming was also a major news event, attracting widespread newspaper reporting. On 26 February, 55 days after being admitted to Dunedin Public Hospital, Tim went home, semi-conscious and utterly dependent. He was unable to sit or swallow. He could not speak or see clearly and he had no memory of what he said, even if it had to do with feeling sore somewhere an hour or two earlier. He could turn his head from side to side, and extend a hand. He slept for about 20 hours a day. Nursing care was provided around the clock, with four nurses engaged full-time on shifts and three part-time. To provide accommodation for the nurses the games room at Benfiddich was modified.

Michael Lucas, who settled into Benfiddich's cottage below the family home with his wife, Sally, and their two young sons, knew there was no way of predicting how much improvement Tim would make, if any. Prue

Sharon Mackie (left) and physiotherapist Lyn Weedon helping Tim to walk.
Prue Wallis

and the boys were counting on his will to fight back. They were sure that the Benfiddich experience would aid his rehabilitation – the fresh air and vivid light of the Upper Clutha Valley, the uplifting mountain-lake vistas, the weathered schist tors and rosehip bushes, the autumn mating calls of male elk, red deer and fallow deer – and, not least, the proximity to his office at Wanaka Airport. Inside the house were the mementoes of a life lived at a cracking pace, including framed photographs, artwork and treasures from exotic places. Then there was his collection of ornamental turtles in ceramic, metal, wood and plastic forms, which lived near the wooden front door. Over the years friends had presented Tim with them in honour of his indestructibility. Those who knew how many crashes he had survived – few were able to keep count – called him 'Turtle'. He had a very hard shell. The term was first used at school by rugby team mates who were impressed by his hard back, especially at scrum time or in a ruck.

Although a chief concern of Wanaka GP Dennis Pezaro's was that Tim would get an infection at home that would be a serious challenge to his weakened immune system, Tim in fact returned to Wanaka with a bug acquired from the hospital – MRSA, Methicillin-Resistant Staphylococcus Aureus, a bacterium that was an ongoing problem for hospitals and rest homes as it attacked people with weakened immune systems. To prevent the bug from spreading, family members took precautions when they were in Tim's room, although Michael was forever having to remind them.

Recruited for her nursing skills and her experience of working with stroke victims while private nursing in London, 26-year-old Sharon Mackie, originally from Waimate, was part of the nursing team from the outset and was on duty for Tim's first night at home. He had to be turned every two hours. As in hospital, he had a gastrostomy tube fitted for feeding and a catheter bag to drain his bladder. Oxygen was delivered through a mask. In the daytime, Tim had only brief moments awake, generally for not more than five minutes at a time in the first week or two.

There were occasional communication problems. A few days after Tim was transferred home, Michael asked Prue to come and help him work out what Tim was saying. He seemed to be obsessed about a washing machine overflowing. It turned out Tim was asking: 'What are the chances of getting my licence back?' There was much to be done before anyone could answer one way or the other.

Physiotherapy and massage routines were introduced into the afternoons. It was important to keep Tim's limbs moving and to build muscular power. Wanaka-based physio Lyn Weedon knew she was entering unknown territory with Tim. She knew that brain-injured patients were sometimes prone to violence and inappropriate behaviour but Tim was never violent

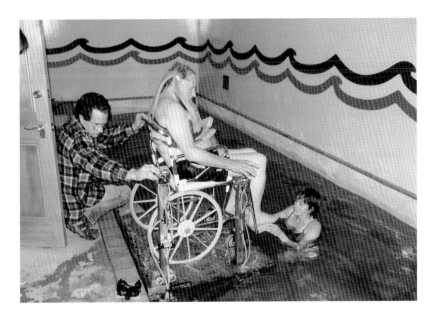

or disagreeable. Like a student hungry to learn, he accepted Lyn's directions implicitly. As the days rolled into weeks, Prue and the boys watched for anti-social behaviour typical of the brain-injured, much of which they had been warned about – anger, frustration and physical and verbal aggression. These, the literature said, were often signposts on the way to recovery and not necessarily negative omens. The family members knew to keep the dialogue and any requests simple, one deliberate thing at a time. Moreover, family and staff realised their mission was to rehabilitate a man who already had a disability and only one good leg.

Family members, friends and business associates of Tim's needed to be briefed on what to expect and how to relate to Tim. For most of them, this was going to be a strange experience. Michael gave plenty of advice. He went down to Tim's office at Wanaka Airport and spoke to the Alpine Deer Group and Alpine Fighter Collection staff in the hangar. From the start of his 15 months at Benfiddich, Michael realised the enormous extent of Tim's social and business contacts and how these would have to be carefully managed. At times he needed to limit access to Tim – or at least try to limit it – in the best interests of his recovery. He also had to deal with the family's expectations. The family wanted Tim out and about as soon as possible as if he were the Tim of old. Occupational therapist Mariann Fairbairn was engaged early on to devise strategies for Tim and his caregivers that would maximise his functional independence. The strategies called for a good deal of commitment.

On the nursing side, from her work in England, Sharon Mackie was used to balancing medical needs with family expectations but each case was different. In Tim's case she soon realised the balancing of stimulation and exercise with a regime of rest was going to be difficult to achieve. Here was a man who seemingly had nine lives and a family who were used to his relentless pace and his numerous passions.

Tim's first outing in a car came in the second week of March, less than two weeks after he arrived home. He was driven about two kilometres along Mt Barker Road to his brother George's home to celebrate George's birthday. He was floppy and could hardly speak but managed a garbled 'Happy Birthday, George.'

Easter – and the 1996 Warbirds Over Wanaka – was looming. Would Tim be alert enough to appreciate it? Prue became firmer with him. On 4 April, the day before Good Friday, with many of the vintage warplanes already at the airport and preparing for the airshow, she told him that his friends and supporters expected a lot more of Tim Wallis than he was delivering. He had never flinched at any hurdle in his life, so why was he baulking at accepting what he had to do to recover? Later that day, he became more fully awake than at any time since the crash. It was the breakthrough Prue longed to see.

On the eve of the '96 Warbirds, some of the show's stalwarts flew over Benfiddich, waggling wings in salute. Tim was wheeled out on to the lawn in front of the house in his bed to watch the fly-past. He watched with only one good eye. He had limited sight remaining in his left eye after the left side of his face was mauled in the crash. But he could hear the planes roar overhead. It was the kind of stimulation Prue had dreamed of creating for him.

Tim turned up to watch some of the airshow itself from a small marquee on the terrace above the airfield, a natural grandstand. He attended both days of the show in a wheelchair nick-named Big Blue. It was the kind tetraplegics used, providing support for his upper body, head and neck. He saw the rare German ME-109 fighter go through its paces and a Yak-3M in grey-green livery emblazoned with Russian red stars, a new purchase for the Alpine collection. Tim's Mk XVI Spitfire, FUP, was flown by his friend, Ray Hanna, reminding many in the crowd that Tim might still be flying if he had chosen to practice in the Mark 16 three months earlier instead of the Mark 14.

After a few hours at the show Tim became fatigued yet didn't recognise how tired he was becoming and protested about being taken home. Having wanted so much to give a speech, he recorded a few words on a tape that was played later to the show's organisers and pilots. Those who had not encountered Tim since the crash were taken aback by his poor command of spoken language. Some were unable to understand what he was saying.

Formation flying by the Spitfire Mk XVI, Yak-3 and P-51 D Mustang. Ian Brodie

He spoke like someone severely affected by a stroke. Unaware he was speaking poorly, Tim had to be taught to enunciate with precision, a skill that can take a brain-injured person months if not years to achieve.

But Prue knew things were on the mend. On Easter Monday he sat up unaided and unsupported for a good length of time. It was a significant moment. His family and medical team wondered whether the airshow had provided the incentive for him to really stretch into rehabilitation. Matt and Nick had come home from Christ's College for the airshow (Matt was head of School House and a prefect) and for the second school term they attended Mount Aspiring College so they could be near their father.

Mark Hanna in the cockpit of the Me-109, with engineer Roger Sheppard (left) and Ray Hanna.
Phil Makanna

Later in April, Tim went back to Dunedin Hospital for a week-long assessment in the neuro ward. There were inevitable comparisons between hospital and home care. Prue felt that her husband regressed in hospital. The regenerating spark and interest levels he had shown at home were less obvious and he appeared passive. Prue thought he was going into decline in the hospital. She wanted him back home as soon as possible.

With Tim back at Benfiddich, the physiotherapy programme with Lyn Weedon and occupational therapy with Mariann Fairbairn advanced Tim's rehabilitation, especially the more awake, aware and active he became. His reputed 'will to fight' was becoming more apparent. As Prue commented to friends and family, she had a husband who had endured a disability for 28 years – and who had done so without complaint.

From the outset of rehabilitation, Tim demonstrated that he would be giving his all to every task the therapists set. He had to go right back to basics and to learn from scratch. Learning to write again took weeks to master as Tim's eyesight and motor skills were severely impaired.

For a start, he needed guidance on how to use a pen. Many hours were spent at 'visual tracking', which involved work with patterns and colours. Mariann, who had worked with brain-injured people before, investigated his pre-crash traits and habits because she understood some of them might be useful as springboards for his physical and cognitive rehabilitation. She delved into archival records. His film and photographic collection became memory-jogging; his pre-crash motivation and social strengths were utilised to try to improve his speech and memory. Mariann found technical drawings of Tim's in the archives, referring to projects like the deer traps and net guns. This enabled her to identify Tim's visual memory strengths, which she built into his therapy exercises.

Tim started exercising in the swimming pool at home. It was something he remembered doing and something he was certain he could do again. Alpine's aircraft engineers rigged up a hydraulic platform so he could be lowered into the pool sitting in his shower chair.

He was impatient with the precautions the nursing staff took – then devastated when he could not stay stable in the water and had to be supported. It was clear there would be many weeks of exercising before he would be able to swim as before, with his good foot fitted with a flipper. Progress was painstaking.

A task Prue assisted him with, aimed at exercising mind and memory, involved replying to the cards and letters that had poured in while he was in hospital and which continued to arrive in number as he emerged from the coma.

Everyone close to Tim wondered whether his personality had survived the brain injury. As Lyn Weedon observed, it was not possible to retrain personality; it had to find its own way back. Tim lost his characteristic smile during the time in hospital – the 'lost' three months, about which he could remember little – but back at Benfiddich it was returning. Prue could see his sense of humour resurfacing as well. When Graeme Ramshaw arrived one day from Dunedin to brief Tim on Alpine Deer Group business, Graeme came through the door with a cheery, 'Hi, Tim. How're you doing?' Without missing a beat Tim said: 'Rough enough.' Prue hoped, too, Tim's generous nature would return. With these endearing features of his personality in place, the fear that Tim might be a stranger to his family and friends – a highly-dependent stranger – would dissipate.

Increasingly, key staff spent time with him. Criffel farm manager Simon Bartlett came to discuss farm operations and, like many of Tim's associates, had to learn new ways of communicating with Tim. Compared to the Tim of old, he appeared damaged and feeble, and his associates wondered just how far down the rehabilitation path he would – or could – travel. But to the medical specialists, something special was unfolding. His recovery was already exceeding expectations and it looked as if it would continue for some time yet. They were starting to talk of it as 'the Tim Wallis factor'.

The weather cut up rough at Bells Hut, Minaret Station, when Tim made one of his first flights into the mountains following his Spitfire crash. The day started out fine enough for a barbecue for Tim's rehabilitation and medical team, but suddenly turned to rain. Prue Wallis

Goals were set. They included basic things like sitting, standing, walking and talking clearly. Beyond these were occupational and recreational targets – office work, helicopter and fixed-wing flight with or without a try at dual control, a visit to Minaret Station, diving in Fiordland, a trip to Canada. Of prime importance, though, was establishing and maintaining a daily routine. Routine and good planning set a secure platform for anyone with a brain injury, in Tim's case an injury severe enough to have damaged wiring. Some connections were broken, some were loose. What he needed for the recovery to continue was a daily routine that avoided sudden changes or the introduction of new or unplanned activities. Visits from family members and close friends had to be scheduled. Adequate rest is required to balance an active routine, and is no less important. Tim, in common with most brain-injured people undergoing rehabilitation, had little idea when fatigue was setting in.

As soon as he was well enough to be driven on a regular basis, he was taken to the Alpine office and helped into his chair, cushioned with a dark-brown sheepskin, at his large wooden desk. His office was festooned with mementoes and paraphernalia – miniature fighter aircraft and other model planes suspended from the ceiling, deer skins on the floor, antlers on the wall, a Russian pilot's helmet with the letters CCCP and a red hammer and sickle imprinted on it, Russian fur hats, framed certificates and awards, a chart of Breaksea Sound, dramatic helicopter photography, and various ornamental turtles. He lasted little more than 15 or 20 minutes at a time initially. But it was a start, with all the paraphernalia no doubt triggering memories and reactivating cognitive areas.

The office visits incorporated physio and massage sessions as well as paperwork. Office administrator Nola Sims, who had worked with Tim since late 1968 and had grown used to a whirlwind for a boss, found the new circumstances challenging and hard to come to terms with. Before the crash, Tim would be here, there and everywhere, with meetings arranged at airport Koru Lounges and offices or airfields in many parts of the country. Now he was usually either at home or at the office. At times Nola struggled to make out what Tim was saying, but she thought his speech would improve with therapy.

As the weeks rolled by, she noted his increasing interest in the old days. Before long, he was remembering things that she herself had forgotten, concerning people or incidents from distant venison and deer-recovery operations.

His long-term memory might have been coming back fast but his physical recovery was a slower process. It was a top moment when he managed to walk to the main entrance of his home from the living-room, using a frame. With the physiotherapist, nurses and his sons egging him on and guiding his legs when they looked unresponsive, Tim steered the frame slowly towards the door. Face screwed up with concentration, he was hellbent on getting there. At other times he used the standing frame to write letters or read things. One of the handgrips on the frame was the handle of a helicopter cyclic, complete with buttons to push.

Tim was back in the air before the winter of 1996 was over. At Wanaka Airport, he got into his old Hughes 500, HOT, with the aid of his hoist, modified for helicopter use, and Toby flew him to Minaret Station. His nurses were rather concerned at how the flight might affect him. Later, Tim flew with Queenstown-based helicopter pilot Denis Egerton in a dual-control training situation. They took off from Wanaka Airport, flew to Benfiddich and hovered close to the lawn before returning to the aiport. The flights, which Prue and the boys supported, were milestones in his rehabilitation.

Tim approached the morning swims fiercely determined, knowing that his ability in the pool would decide whether he could go diving in Fiordland again. The heated indoor pool at Benfiddich was not one for lounging about in with a whisky or gin-and-tonic in hand; it was strictly for exercise, 11 metres long and 2 metres wide. By September he was able to complete 20 lengths a morning on his stomach with the aid of a snorkel.

Power of attorney

Tim's head injury invoked a power-of-attorney arrangement that Tim himself had put in place in 1989. It saw Alpine Deer Group directors Don Spary, Graham Sinclair and Graeme Ramshaw assume control and management of Tim's assets and finances. Tim (60 percent), his sons (33 percent) and a family trust (7 percent) still retain full ownership of the company. Decision-making on investment and divestment is the responsibility of the directors, and their decisions are overseen by the attorneys acting for Tim's personal interests.

On 1 October 1996, The Helicopter Line became Tourism Holdings Ltd, which cleverly enabled the acronym THL to be retained. In mid-November at THL's annual general meeting at Queenstown, Tim retired as a director of the company, just over ten years after he became a member of the board. He attended the meeting, one of his first public appearances after the Spitfire crash. The directors appointed him to the position of Company Founder in recognition of his seminal role in its establishment. The company's annual report that year said Tim had been nominated for the position and it paid tribute to him as a pioneer of deer farming and live deer capture. 'His appreciation of the helicopter saw him develop the craft for commercial and tourism use,' the report said. 'The name Tim Wallis has irrevocably been written into the aviation and deer industry in New Zealand.'

His left arm was weak and he had no use at all of his left leg, paralysed in 1968. But he managed as he had before the crash, propelled by his good right leg with a flipper on it.

The promised Fiordland trip took place in November. The family chartered the vessel *Cindy Hardy* for a visit to Breaksea Sound that featured a picnic crowned by a feed of fresh crayfish. On the day, Tim's dry-suit, which he had tried out in a Christchurch diving shop's demonstration pool, had too many pockets of air inside it and they prevented Tim from gaining negative buoyancy in the water – the trapped air stopped him from sinking. Would he do better in a wetsuit? That was a question he asked his nurses, who realised by now that his penchant for exploring a way around a challenge was starting to express itself again. The nurses were constantly having to negotiate with him over activities that used to be second nature but were now frustratingly difficult.

He kept talking about a diving opportunity. Wary of what water pressure might do to his recovering brain, the nurses persuaded Tim to seek specialist medical advice. He turned to Mike Davis, a consultant at Christchurch Hospital who dealt with diving injuries. Mike was adamant – Tim should not try any sort of diving, at least not in the meantime. It might put at risk the progress he had made to date. Tim reluctantly took the advice.

That decision did not, however, keep him out of the sea. He headed for a holiday in Fiji at the Vatulele Island Resort off the west coast of Fiji's main island. With him were Prue, the boys and nurse Sharon Mackie. The family had thought they would do without a nurse but at Christchurch, on the way to Fiji, Tim fell out of bed, struck his head on a bedside table and had to have several stitches put in the wound. Prue thought better of travelling without medical assistance. In haste, Sharon was equipped with travel documents and bookings for the flight to Fiji and the resort. Tim took to the tepid waters soon after arrival. He was borne across the beach and into the sea like a Fijian chief of high rank, on a chair supported by two poles, with a son at each of the four ends. He wore a mask and snorkel and he had a bathing cap protecting the cut on his head. But the experience was not as comfortable as he imagined it might be and the swim lasted just 20 minutes.

His progress, nonetheless, continued to make an impression in the press. The November 1996 edition of *North and South* magazine carried the story of his crash and rehabilitation. On the cover was a picture of him sitting on the lower wing of his Fox Moth biplane at Wanaka Airport. The story was titled, 'Never Say Die'. Writer Cate Brett said Tim had beaten the odds again, a reference to a story she wrote for the same maga-

Nurse Sharon Mackie and the four Wallis boys take Tim snorkelling at the Vatulele Island Resort in Fiji. Prue Wallis

zine two years earlier that outlined Tim's knack of surviving adversities in the air, the business world, and in life generally.

'The slurred speech and sometimes laboured replies can lead the un-prepared to assume Tim is not fully comprehending,' wrote Cate Brett. 'After a short time in his company I quickly realised that was a mistake.' In the article, Tim assessed his situation this way: 'Yes, I'm damaged. But I'm not buggered.'

The *North and South* cover story pointed out that a hospital intensive-care unit treated all accident victims the same and it did not matter whether the patient was a boy racer who had pranged his Ford Cortina on a drunken Friday evening or a millionaire knight who had upended his Spitfire on the way to practice formation flying. But when it came to arranging and resourcing home care, were there any dispensations or special favours for Tim because of who he was? The magazine cited his wealth at $42 mil-lion, based on the latest *National Business Review* Rich List assessment. Prue welcomed the *North and South* enquiry because she was adamant ACC had made no concessions at all and accorded Tim nothing more than would be provided to anyone else with his degree of injury. Moreo-ver, she wanted Tim's home care – and her initiation of it – to be an example to other families choosing to rehabilitate a loved one with a head injury themselves.

Tim's ACC case manager, Judy Hamilton, who was based in the cor-poration's Alexandra office, told *North and South* the level of support the Wallis family had received from ACC was no different from that available

Back in his element

In the spring of 1996, Tim's son, Toby, flew a group that included his father to Martin's Bay, a remote and roadless West Coast location near the northern edge of Fiordland. When it comes to outdoor adventure, Martin's Bay takes some beating. Few people ever experience its wildness, its fishing or its hunting opportunities. Sir Peter Elworthy was in the party, and Michael Lucas was also there to look after Tim. They took off from Glenorchy, heading west, with the weather murky to the point of being closed-in and snow falling on the tops. Michael had some concerns about the safety of flying in such conditions. And when Toby asked his father to confirm directions, Michael grew even more anxious. Tim was back in his element, though, and demonstrated this by pointing out pathfinding landmarks to Toby. They arrived safe and sound, and were soon enjoying the natural delights of Martin's Bay, not the least a feed of whitebait.

Tim leaving for Martins Bay, 1997. Michael Lucas is on the left. Prue Wallis

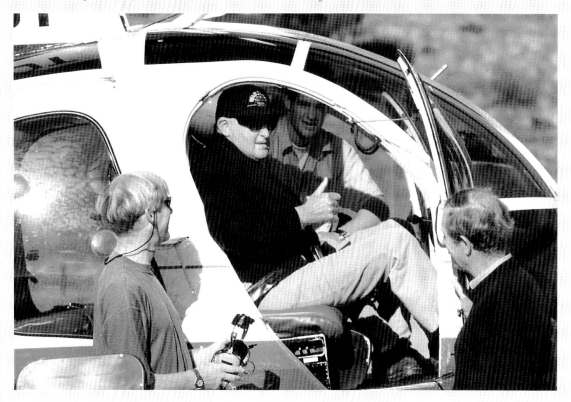

to anyone with an injury similar to Tim's. 'I am aware there are people saying Tim is getting more than anybody else would be entitled to, but that's simply not true.'

The magazine's investigation turned up cases where rehabilitation treatment had been delayed by hold-ups in assessment reports, and it pointed out that such delays could affect a patient's prospects for rehabilitation and recovery. 'In a very real sense, rehabilitation delayed is rehabilitation denied,' Cate Brett wrote. She also concluded that the most effective re-

habilitation is driven and controlled by the injured person and his or her family and supporters, and the more quickly it is put in place, the more effective it is likely to be.

Tim certainly had a lot going for him – his own determination and that of his advocates, Prue in particular, and the financial backing of his company, Alpine Deer Group, to top up the ACC contributions to home care and equipment. Of all the factors working in his favour, the 'Prue Wallis factor' was pre-eminent. She got him home early; she made sure the recommended treatment was delivered. At the time, Prue was perceived by many people as being extraordinarily brave to take on the care of a brain-injured husband at home. She refuted the 'brave' label, declaring she was simply doing what she knew she had to do.

By September, when he was interviewed by Cate Brett, Tim had formed a view of how the brain injury had affected his life and his relationships. It had been a blessing of sorts. 'This accident has brought me to heel. It has taught me to appreciate my wife and my sons and my friends. I have always loved them but now I am telling them I love them. I want my sons to know how important they are to me.'

And the boys had reciprocal thoughts and feelings. Matthew, back at Christ's College after a term at Mount Aspiring College in Wanaka, spoke for all four sons when he said it was a joy to have their father at home instead of always being away on business trips. When he was able to, Tim would travel to Christchurch and other places to observe Matt and Nick participating in rugby and rowing fixtures. That meant a lot to them.

The summer after his crash Tim went to the Millbrook Resort near Arrowtown for an open-air concert by American country music legend Kenny Rogers. Tim had missed out on a similar concert involving New Zealand opera star Kiri Te Kanawa the previous summer. A fan of country music, he was determined to make the Kenny Rogers show and at Millbrook he joined a crowd of thousands. For company he had a Southland friend and fellow deer farmer, Jack Hazlett, of Winton, a legend himself as a long-serving Southland rugby representative and an All Black prop forward in the 1960s.

A *Southland Times* reporter spotted Tim in the crowd and, knowing of his rehabilitation after a near-death experience, asked him about his goal for the coming year, 1997. Back came the reply: 'To be as independent as possible.'

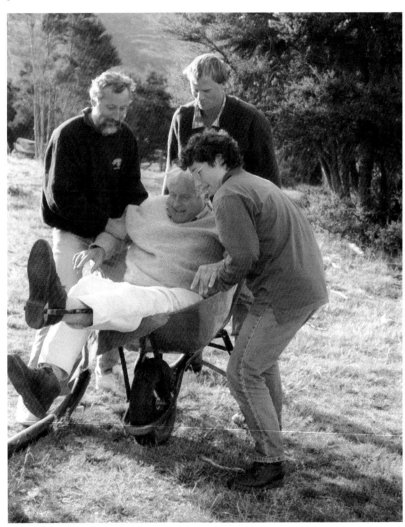

Mike Bringans (left), Sharon Mackie and Mark Faulks help Tim into the helicopter at Minaret Station. Mike Bringans collection

Chapter 14

Shades of Hurricane Tim

Late 1990s–2005
Flying to Christchurch ... office therapy ... speech breakthrough in Canada ... Ontario trophy hunting venture ... a Hurricane for Tim ... Burwood centre opens ... Warbirds for new ... millennium ... a new museum ... life today ... Twenty-first century ideas ... next generation

THROUGH 1997, with his strength and stamina building gradually, Tim flew to Christchurch a number of times for appointments with disability specialists. Mostly he flew in his company's Cessna 210, with Grant Bisset as pilot. Grant and Tim had jointly owned Wanaka-based Biplane Adventures since 1994, when Tim added a de Havilland Dominie biplane to the business. He acquired the biplane from the Mandeville vintage aircraft centre near Gore in Southland. Grant welcomed his new partner, and he especially enjoyed their 'board meetings', which typically lasted just a few minutes because both men were practical, knew what had to be done and got on with it.

The Spitfire crash changed everything. Grant knew it would be a long time, if ever, before Tim could contribute again to the business, which had started in 1992 with a Pitts Special and a leased Tiger Moth. But he was glad to help Tim get to and from Christchurch for the hospital appointments and, as a flying instructor, was able to accommodate Tim's request to get back to flying a fixed-wing aircraft. The first such flight in the Cessna 210 to Christchurch struck weather so rough Grant flew the Cessna at low levels practically all the way. To nurse Sharon Mackie, who worried about their heads hitting the ceiling in the turbulence and especially Tim's head getting knocked about, it seemed they were flying at 'pylon height' most of the way. On a subsequent flight, with conditions smooth, Grant offered Tim the controls, and Tim was in command the whole way with Grant alongside. He landed the plane at Christchurch –

but Grant was concerned that Tim had not seen a Mount Cook commercial aircraft in the vicinity of the airport at the time. He thought then that poor vision in Tim's left eye would probably prevent him from regaining his pilot's licence. Still, Grant agreed with Prue – Tim would benefit from as many familiar experiences as he could handle, and what was more familiar to Tim than flying? Potentially, the experience might work wonders for Tim's cognitive rehabilitation.

Tim is virtually blind in his left eye as a result of the massive damage to the left side of his face, and vision in his right eye is about ten percent reduced because of retina bruising. There is a small blank spot in his right-eye vision. Eye specialists have suggested it will be permanent. But of more concern to him, his family and nursing staff in 1997 was his speech. He had made some progress with speech therapy, but 12 months after the accident he was still slurring words. When he became tired he was even harder to understand.

Many friends and associates of his who were in touch with him reasonably frequently before the crash eschewed his company altogether, presumably because they had misgivings about how to handle a conversation. Some people regard a brain-injured friend as not the friend of old. But for every friend or associate of Tim's who shied away, there were others in his social network who went out of their way to keep in touch. If anything, his network expanded. For example, even his Dunedin barber, Errol Sharp, would drive up to Wanaka to give Tim a haircut and enjoy a break at the lakeside town at the same time.

The Alpine staff at Wanaka Airport had the most to do with him on a daily basis. When Annie Trengrove transferred from the Fighter Pilots' Museum to the Alpine Deer Group office to become Tim's personal assistant, she had to become acquainted with rehabilitation strategies. She remembered Tim before the crash as always on the move, whether as a kind of Pied Piper guiding visitors through the museum … or flying in fresh crayfish and paua from Fiordland for a directors' meeting … or dictating a letter while piloting his Hughes 500 somewhere in southern New Zealand. In the new PA role alongside Nola Sims, who continued to manage the office, Annie formed part of a team who were closely involved in Tim's rehabilitation

To coincide with his return to the office, occupational therapist Mariann Fairbairn, who was based in Wanaka, developed strategies for staff to follow. It was a strange and stressful time for everyone. In the first few months the staff had to relate to a boss who was inclined to simply sit and stare vacantly until they directed him to a task. His diary was a focal point. When he arrived at the office, he had to peruse the diary and, with the

Alpine staff, 1997. From left:
Grant Bisset, Stan Vowles,
Malcolm Brown (behind) Sharon
Mackie (behind), Tim Wallis, Lyn
Brenssell, Peter Brenssell, Kevin
Harris, Doug James, Greg Parker
(behind), Annie Trengrove,
Johnathon Skogstad (behind),
Ewan Fallow. Prue Wallis

advice of Annie and whichever nurse was on duty, decide on the things that had to be done that day and in what order. Mariann emphasised how important it was to structure and organise Tim's time. At first, he needed to be reminded even to pick up a pen if the task was a letter. From being barely able to use a pen properly, Tim worked hard and methodically on his handwriting skills, which in time even showed improvement on his writing before the crash.

Once he had mastered writing, he was guided into replying to the great stack of get-well cards and letters. He would allocate one to two hours a day to this work. Again, his face would screw up with concentration. Annie had cue cards and other aids to prompt Tim on what to write. He was encouraged to question himself on what he was writing. Had he covered the essentials: who, what, when, where, why and how? Typically, a brain-injured person can be slow to process challenging statements, conceptual questions and so on. Tim would sometimes take 20 minutes to come back with a response. Mariann equipped him with phrases such as 'Can I sit on that a while?' or 'Can you put that in writing?' as a means of handling perplexing questions. Repetition – of written and spoken word – can be another symptom of brain injury, and in fact, Tim would draft similar letters to the same recipient a few days or weeks apart – although often this was simply accepted as a mark of his innate enthusiasm and renowned persistence.

His staff also always had to remind him to drink. Dehydration was a real risk; if his fluid intake was too low, he risked the onset of severe leg pain.

For Tim and his rehabilitation, one of the big events of 1997 was a reunion of former staff of the Luggate-Alpine business network. It turned into a weekend gathering of about 200 former staff – pilots, shooters, gutters, drivers, field hands, farm and factory employees, and office staff, with Nola Sims taking a pivotal role on the organising committee. The Alpine hangar was taken over for the drinks evening and sit-down dinner, and display boards containing photographs and newspaper clippings encircled the venue. Tim's mates flocked in to pay tribute to their former boss. Although extremely tiring for Tim, the reunion noticeably stimulated his mind and memory.

Through 1997, Tim attended planning meetings to do with the next airshow – the 1998 Warbirds Over Wanaka. Gavin Johnston was still managing the airshow but Tim was able to contribute ideas and make contact with some of the key participants. The theme for the show – 'Red Stars Rising', starring Alpine's Polikarpov I-16 fighters – triggered a flood of memories for Tim. It was the culmination of years of restoration effort in Russia and New Zealand, driven by his ambition to do something in the vintage fighter arena that no one had done before. Some of the planes had been recovered from the tundra as wrecks. In all, Alpine were able to

The Luggate Game Packers/Alpine company reunion of 1997.
Wanaka Tourist Craft

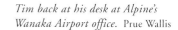
put five I-16s into the air at once at the 1998 show. No one had seen five I-16s flying in formation in over 50 years, not even in Russia. Their simple design – some would say sparse, with no trim or flaps – impressed the big crowd at Wanaka, numbering 85,000 for the two days. The crowd went away with the distinctive roar and crackle of the stubby fighter's 1000 hp radial engines ringing in their ears. Russian music and dancing added atmosphere to the show's theme, and a group of Russian engineers and staff involved in the restoration of the Polikarpovs in Siberia travelled around the world to witness the event. Warbirds Over Wanaka was definitely on the world stage.

The 1998 show's special guest was a distinguished American aviator, Brigadier-General Charles (Chuck) Yeager, best remembered for being the first person to exceed the speed of sound, the sound barrier. An aerobatics highlight was the display by Australian champion Nigel Arnot in his Sukhoi Su-31. Among the first appearances at the show was that of a Curtiss P-40E Kittyhawk nicknamed the Wairarapa Wildcat, the only airworthy example out of almost 300 of these aircraft operated by the Royal New Zealand Air Force in the Second World War.

Warbirds '98 took a lot out of Tim. Two years and three months after his Spitfire crash, he still became tired by too much stimulation and activity. But the event also engaged him once more in the business of organising these airshows, and he revelled in the avalanche of letters and phone calls that they generated.

As a rule, Tim would become too exhausted by around lunch time to function properly, and after lunch he would require a nap. A room off the old hangar behind the Alpine Deer Group office area was set aside as

Russian dancer Masha Volobueva helped create a Russian atmosphere at the 1998 airshow. Geoff Sloan

The Cessna 210 in formation
with the Yak-3 at the 1998
airshow. Mike Provost

Tim's 'flat', where he could stretch out on a single bed, surrounded by
files, films and photographs recording his past achievements. When he
had rested sufficiently he would bang on the wall with his hand to let the
office staff know he was ready to get up and back into some work.

The nursing staff, reduced by now to two with Sharon Mackie in charge,
watched his progress but knew that improvements were more likely to be
subtle than substantial. Some days Tim would be alert and, in Sharon's
view, 'spot on'; other days he would be slow to comprehend. Given the
physical and cognitive frustrations he faced, she was amazed at how little
he complained. Tim hardly ever became angry with anything or anybody.

Down at the office, his tasks swung between letters, phone calls and
therapy, although in essence all of it had 'rehab' value. Without power of
attorney he was unable to make decisions as in the past. But he attended
meetings of the Alpine board of directors in an advisory role and participated in discussions. As part of the rehabilitation, whenever he repeated
himself, spoke indistinctly or drifted off the subject, he would be 'buzzed'.
A special pen vibrated in his pocket. Annie, the nurses, or Graeme
Ramshaw, Alpine's executive director, operated the buzzer.

Tim's injury and incapacitation saw Graeme take on an increased responsibility and workload. Having joined the Alpine team in 1986, he
was familiar with all aspects of the business. The business portfolio com-

prised Criffel Deer Farm, Minaret Station, the Canadian projects, Warbirds Over Wanaka, the Alpine Fighter Collection and Fighter Pilots' Museum, and the Luggate factory, springboard for the whole works. There were new things going on in all these areas. Canada was at the forefront of change.

THE YEAR TIM CRASHED the Spitfire Mk XIV the Canadian deer industry – and Alpine's interests in it – took a dive, too. The discovery of Chronic Wasting Disease in one herd of Canadian farmed elk in 1996 sent ripples through the industry. In Mike Bringans' view the outbreak was overstated by the media. He knew that the disease, nicknamed Mad Elk Disease, had been found in Colorado in mule deer and a few wild elk at least as far back as the 1960s. In so far as it attacked a deer's brain, Canadian CWD was compared with Britain's Mad Cow Disease. But its transmission to humans had not been proved. It was unlikely to be a threat to humans; hunters had been eating venison out of the affected areas for many years.

Orr Lake Elk, a joint venture between Mike and Tim's company, had been doing brisk business in stud animals and genetics services. Yet with CWD putting a brake on Canadian velvet, stud animal sales and genetics, and with a prohibition against the imports of New Zealand red deer into Canada as a result of another animal health issue, the Orr Lake partners contemplated alternative options with deer.

By 1999, the concept of a trophy hunting experience based in neigh-

Top trophy Manitoban elk in a clearing at Laurentian Wildlife Estate. Jonathan Wallis

bouring Québec was mooted. It became a new frontier for the Alpine-Bringans partnership and Tim contributed to its development. The Laurentian Plateau mountains, located on the great Canadian Shield that makes up the eastern half of the country, are an outstanding feature of Canada's geography. In autumn, the forests cast red and yellow hues across the landscape. Yet this is a land of lakes. Canada's 9.9 million square kilo-metres contain more lakes and inland waters than any country on earth.

Into this striking land, a group of New Zealanders brought their concept of hunting. They called it the Laurentian Wildlife Estate. It was

Guides and clients at Laurentian Wildlife Estate. Jonathan Wallis

located in rolling hill country 20 minutes' drive from the popular skifield and resort town of Mont Tremblant, 90 minutes from both the St Lawrence Seaway and the city of Montreal. With trophy hunting legal in the Province of Québec, the New Zealanders encountered few bureaucratic hurdles. Laurentian was billed as 'A Sportman's Paradise'. It was a relatively high-priced one, with lodge accommodation offering fine food and wine and ensuite comfort. Laurentian pitched its advertising to appeal to hunters from the United States who were mostly used to hunting white-tailed deer. They came with rifle and bow, and a fishing rod for the rainbow and brook trout on the property.

The hunt camp opened in the year 2000, with 310 hectares (750 acres) of hardwood bush and grassy clearings available to the hunters. The place was stocked with large Manitoban and Rocky Mountain elk, and red deer stags. American hunters used to white-tailed deer hunting could hardly believe the size of the Canadian animals. Younger bulls were not harvested. A guide accompanied each client and a trophy animal was virtually guaranteed – 'no harvest, no pay' was LWE's policy. The guide took a video camera to provide a video record of the hunt for each client.

In 2000, before the inaugural season opened in August, Tim travelled to Canada with nurses Sharon Mackie and Nicky Olds. They were based at Orr Lake for about seven weeks, during which time Tim was updated

Laurentian Wildlife Estate.
Jonathan Wallis

on the Orr Lake operation and the new Laurentian hunting venture, which Tim's second-son Jonathan was going to develop and manage. At the same time, Prue had further rehabilitation in mind for Tim. She thought he might benefit from attending an intensive course in speech therapy in Toronto that she had found out about.

The speech course, run by Joy Gilbert, spanned six weeks and specialised in improving the speech of people with brain injuries. Tim went back to Orr Lake at weekends – an hour's drive from Toronto, Canada's largest city. The tuition was all positive, except for the tambourine tapping, which he and Prue hated. Tim gained a lot from the course. For the first time he was among people he couldn't understand, and it made him focus harder on improving his own speech. Back in Wanaka, friends and colleagues all remarked on how much improvement he had made.

The millennium year was also notable for Warbirds Over Wanaka 2000. Easter was late that year – the last week of April. The show's regular fans expected something special, and they received it in the form of the debut of the Alpine Fighter Collection's newest acquisition, Hawker Hurricane P3351. Of a classic British fighter type, it had been delivered to Wanaka from Air New Zealand's Christchurch workshop by Keith Skilling.

Tim had always wanted to own a Hurricane. He heard about this one in 1992 after the remains of it were shipped to England for restoration. P3351 was wrecked in the Siberian tundra near Murmansk, close to the Arctic Circle, during war service. Bullets holes in the radiator and air cooler suggested the cause of its downing. It had been produced by the Hawker factory in England in 1940, one of over 14,000 built up to 1944. It is said that the Hurricane accounted for more enemy aircraft during the Battle of Britain (July–October 1940) than all other British air and ground defences combined. In 1942, P3351 was seconded to the Russian air force and was probably assigned to protect Russian convoys travelling in the

Below: P3351 in Russia following recovery.

Below right: Pilot Keith Skilling and Tim are delighted by the arrival of restored Hawker Hurricane P3351 at Wanaka.
Ian Brodie

Murmansk region. No records exist of its combat history but it was believed to have crashed in the winter of 1943.

In August 1993, almost exactly 50 years later, Tim acquired the wreck of the Murmansk Hurricane, which became the first restoration job for a new English firm, Hawker Restorations Ltd. The Hurricane P3351 flew again, 57 years after crashing, in January 2000, and was of huge interest at the Warbirds show that year. Two New Zealand pilots flew the plane during her days on war service based in England. Both men, William (Dusty) Miller and Ness Polson, were born in Invercargill. Dusty Miller retired to Wanaka in 1978 and was on hand for the arrival of the aircraft from Christchurch – a reunion that made television news and was featured in the print media.

The Hurricane's strong billing for the 2000 show attracted a record crowd, estimated at 110,000 for the three days – a practice day followed by two days of displays. The sight of a Hurricane flying in formation with its more famous cousin, the Spitfire, was a highlight of the show. Tim had recovered well enough to be able tour around the airport precinct for a considerable time seated in an army Jeep, and the wide smile on his face at the sight of the Hurricane dashing past was a touching moment for his friends and followers. His appreciation of these old planes and their mod-

A Warbird special moment: Tim's Hurricane and Spitfire flying in the skies above Wanaka.
Ian Brodie

ern pilots clearly was as strong as ever.

Three Polikarpov I-153s of the Alpine collection joined five I-16s for the show and flew in a formation of eight that will probably never be repeated (since 2000 several of these planes have been exported to vintage aircraft collectors in the United States and Spain). Another main attraction at the millennium show was an 82-year-old Bleriot XI, rebuilt in the early 1990s and imported from Sweden for the show. A Bleriot was the first aircraft to cross of the English Channel, in the year 1909.

Although the millennium year was notable for the Warbirds show, it ended in tragedy for Tim and everyone in the Alpine company and the aviation world at large, when pilot Tom Middleton was killed in a Pitts Special at Wanaka Airport. Tom had taken the highly manoeuvrable biplane for an aerobatics flight with an English client when the aircraft crashed near the airport, killing both men. Tim was deeply shocked to lose a friend as close and as gifted as Tom.

Over the years, Tim had lost a number of friends and colleagues in air crashes, and he himself had been in more crashes than he cared to remember. There were 15 significant ones, including the back-breaking 1968 crash and the near-death experience in 1996, plus a few minor mishaps. Yet no one had died while he was at the controls. Among the helicopter operators working deer in the dare-devil sixties and seventies, the Luggate-Alpine operation had a remarkably good safety record, given the size of its fleet, the extent of its range and the ruggedness of its territory. The venison industry and the live deer recovery sector at large, however, notched up an appalling number of crashes involving fatality or serious injury. By 1986, 201 crashes had been recorded, half of them listed as serious. Seventeen pilots and 25 crew members died in helicopter mishaps through the main years of the aerial venison and live-deer recovery era.

Visits to Burwood always reminded Tim of the toll from such chopper crashes. He went there not only for medical consultations but also to lend support for the continued good work of the Burwood Spinal Unit. He was an advisory trustee for the New Zealand Spinal Trust, which was headed by his friend, Alan Clarke. In October 2001, thanks to fundraising by the trust, Burwood gained a new facility – the Allan Bean Centre, whose name honours the work of Allan, a senior consultant in spinal injury. It was essentially a learning centre for the use of patients, former patients, Spinal Unit staff and researchers. The centre had a large library and rows of computers. A research room bore Tim's name – acknowledgement of his donation of more than $100,000 to Burwood for research and development at the spinal unit. On the wall outside were photographs of Tim flying Second World War fighter aircraft.

In the main corridor of the new centre is a plaque, presented by Tim, bearing the encouraging words of American John Wooden. Tim carried a spinal injury from the Hiller crash near Queenstown in 1968 and a brain injury from the wreck of the Spitfire in 1996, and he knew the chances of his putting on a Spitfire aerobatics display again for the Burwood patients were slim. Yet he had no intention of letting the second – and more seriously disabling – crash of his life knock his appetite for innovation or his desire to live life as fully as he could. Canada was one outlet for his creativity.

TO SUPPORT TROPHY hunting on the Laurentian Wildlife Estate in Québec the Alpine-Wallis-Bringans partnership purchased a 300-hectare farm 20 minutes' drive from the Laurentian hunt camp in 2003, specifically to breed elk of trophy quality. A New Zealander from the East Coast of the North Island who owned it previously called the property Tutira, a Maori name. Seemingly, the name was introduced to Canada in honour of a well-known New Zealand sheep farm of the same name in Hawke's Bay, south of the East Coast region. In 1882, Scottish-born Herbert Guthrie-Smith, a naturalist, philosopher and author as well as a farmer, took over the New Zealand Tutira. Guthrie-Smith wrote the classic book *Tutira: the Story of a New Zealand Sheep Station*, published in 1921. Elk, not sheep, were the focus of the Canadian Tutira, where Tim and Mike Bringans planned to run up to 500 elk and 100 red deer. Mike had had

Ace pilots

Per capita, New Zealand had more ace fighter pilots in the two world wars than any other country – a total of 94. Ace status is based on the downing of five or more enemy aircraft.

Tim with son Jonathan at Laurentian.

spectacular results at Orr Lake, raising bulls with outstanding antlers in half the normal time. In 2004, the partnership moved to Québec from its Orr Lake base. Laurentian, under Jonathan Wallis's management and with inputs from his brother, Matthew, achieved its aim of 65 hunters a season in the second year, 2001. The Sars epidemic, however, which affected Toronto and its visitor industry, reduced the American interest in visiting Canada in 2002 and 2003.

Back home, Warbirds Over Wanaka 2002 kept Tim with plenty to do. His speech and writing were much improved, and he was keen to contribute to the Warbirds organisation. He still needed crutches to walk, and he got around very slowly, but there had been some progress with his general physical fitness. His improvement in six years had been miraculous. In reality, though, Tim's determination is largely responsible for his journey back from helplessness. It has been a hard slog.

For Warbirds 2002, conditions were cool, with snow dusting the surrounding mountain tops over Easter. The show continued to enjoy massive public support, with an attendance of 85,000 estimated for the two display days. The star acts included a United States Navy Grumman Wildcat, which featured in the Pearl Harbour battle of the Second World War, and a Sea Fury from the Korean War era.

The Alpine Fighter Collection based at Wanaka Airport contributed strongly to the 2002 show, although its stock of planes had been reduced following the sale of a couple of Polikarpovs to American interests. The Alpine collection peaked about the time of the millennium show, when there were 20 aircraft in the hangar and 14 planes performing in that show. The Alpine collection had aircraft, airworthy or undergoing restoration, from five countries – United States, Britain, Russia, Japan and Germany. Ray Mulqueen continued in the role of chief engineer, juggling restoration jobs with the maintenance of airworthy planes of many kinds, and doing well to meet what he considered were impossible deadlines at times. He had become used to Tim's sudden requests and short-notice deadlines. Each airshow brought its own unique set of challenges.

The tenth anniversary of the New Zealand Fighter Pilots' Museum in 2003, across the road from the Alpine Fighter Collection, precipitated plans for not only a new museum but also a reconfiguring of the museum and the fighter collection so they could get together under one roof. The two units were umbilically tied – the fighter collection providing the engineering back-up for the planes on display at the museum, and the museum providing a profile-raising window on the public's interest in vintage warplanes. Both were important to maintaining interest in the biennial airshows. The fighter collection was also open to the public, although visitors were kept at arms length from the planes being stored – or restored – there.

In 2004, the New Zealand Fighter Pilots' Charitable Foundation, set up in 1995 with five trustees, announced the redevelopment of the museum at the fighter collection hangar building. As a result of a land swap with the Wanaka Airport authorities, the Alpine group had room to enlarge the AFC building, which it said would be extended to accommodate the museum.

Towards the end of 2004, Prime Minister Helen Clark, who held the portfolio of Arts, Culture and Heritage, visited Wanaka to discuss the project. The plans called for a remodelling and extension of the AFC building over two levels at a cost of about $10 million. The trustees sought the Prime Minister's assistance with fundraising. Although she admitted to the media at the time that 'heritage tourism is big', the Prime Minister would not be drawn on how much money, if any, the Government would invest in the project. Don Spary, the foundation's chairman, announced that the new facility would integrate the museum and fighter collection and there would be new features such as a memorial wall to salute the efforts of the New Zealand fighter pilots, as well as interactive displays that would give visitors a virtual experience of flying a vintage warplane.

Tim has been involved in developing the concept for the new museum – and this is but one of several ventures he has given much thought to in recent years. To be able to pursue ideas, interact with people and travel about the country and overseas in the way he does, Tim needs to work hard.

TIM'S DAY BEGINS EARLY, as it always has. He can wake as early as 4 a.m. For the next couple of hours, between bouts of dozing, he will be thinking about the day ahead. By 7 a.m. he is up and ready for a swim in the indoor pool at Benfiddich. With the nurse on duty that day assisting him, he manoeuvres his wheelchair on to a hoist that lowers him into the pool. He has a flipper on his right foot, a sock on his powerless left, and a snorkel and mask that allow him to swim face-down. The sock prevents his left foot rubbing on the floor of the pool. He will do 30 or 40 lengths of the 11-metre pool. He counts the lengths himself. A light at each end of the pool tells him when a turn is coming up. As a way of measuring how far he swims, nursing staff began plotting his distances on a map of Lake Wanaka after the 1996 Spitfire crash. He completed a full circuit of the lake's shoreline some years back.

Out of the pool, he showers, shaves and gets dressed – during which he needs help only with his calliper and shoes. His suprapubic catheter is reconnected, his calliper refitted. Breakfast is next. His standard breakfast is a large bowl of cereals, fresh fruit and yoghurt, washed down with a cranberry fruit drink. He must watch his sugar intake and calories. Tim was diagnosed a Type 2 diabetic some time after the 1996 crash. Diabetes of his kind may develop with age. Although he is not insulin dependent, he has to be careful about what he eats. He follows a glycemic-low diet. There is little in the way of potatoes or bread in his standard diet. Still broad in the upper body, Tim weighs in now at about 100 kilograms – some 20 kilograms less than his peak.

Breakfast over, he walks slowly to his car in the garage. For support he uses two elbow crutches. The nurse on duty will drive him down the winding drive to the fallow deer paddocks then on through an avenue of redwood trees to Mt Barker Road. It takes a little over five minutes to reach Wanaka Airport from there.

Ever courteous, he greets staff, and once at his desk, checks his diary with Annie Trengrove and his nurse. Although Tim is freshest in the morning, they will be keen to see he is rested enough to undertake the day's tasks and appointments. There is usually mail to read, including email messages that Annie retrieves for him. He replies to correspondence promptly, by fax, post or phone. His memory for telephone numbers is still exceptional. He will dial long strings of numbers from memory to reach frequently-called overseas associates, for example, Mike Bringans in Canada.

Friends and associates often call at the Alpine office to see Tim. The presence of the Fighter Pilots' Museum and Alpine Fighter Collection in buildings adjacent to his office produces some of the traffic. Alpine executive director Graeme Ramshaw, who is based in Dunedin, visits the Wanaka office most weeks, for several days at a time, and will confer with Tim over business matters. From time to time there will be a meeting of the board of directors, and Tim will contribute to the discussion.

By 4 p.m., Tim may be heading off to a workout at Proactive Gym in Wanaka after a post-lunch nap. This happens a couple of times a week. His personal trainer at the gym, Jon Turnbull, supervises exercises designed to enhance muscle tone and balance. The equipment Tim works with includes weights and a Swiss ball. Whether he goes to the gym or not, he likes to arrive home by about 5.30 p.m.

His evening routine is much like anyone else's. He'll watch television news, read the daily newpaper and dine with family or friends. That said, hardly a month goes by when he is not travelling somewhere for a night or two – to other parts of New Zealand or perhaps to Australia. Stewart

Tim salmon fishing in Canada in 2004.

Island is a favourite destination. A launch trip to uninhabited Port Pegasus on the island's spectacular southeast coast is a special treat. He usually flies to Canada in the New Zealand winter to inspect progress with his Quebec projects and discuss trends and initiatives with his business partner, Mike Bringans.

At times, Prue travels with him; otherwise, he is accompanied by a nurse (in 2005, Suzanne Mannering or Sara Churchill). Prue has never let Tim's ongoing rehabilitation slip from her sights. Even some 10 years after the Spitfire crash at Wanaka she is open to new insights into brain injury that might benefit Tim. She remains his staunchest advocate – and she manages their modern home, Benfiddich, with energetic efficiency. Nonetheless, despite her focus on Tim and maintaining their home, Prue has time to develop interests of her own, particularly in the arts sector. They include assisting with the organisation of a new biennial arts event at Wanaka: The Festival of Colour. She is also a trustee of the New Zealand National Parks and Conservation Foundation, which raises funds for natural heritage protection in New Zealand, and the Aspiring Arts and Culture Trust.

The Wallis sons are equally busy. In 2004, they were all living in Otago for the first time in many years, doing things their father could relate to with a passion. Two sons, Toby and Nick, were in the helicopter industry and the other two, Jonathan and Matthew, were developing Minaret Station and its trophy-hunting potential. The youngest brother, Nick, returned from Australia, where he had been training as a helicopter engineer, to take up work in that field with a Queenstown-based firm. Toby continued to develop Alpine Helicopters from its Wanaka base. From his own resources and without any financial assistance from his parents, he bought Tim's Hughes 500, HOT, and subsequently, in partnership, a Squirrel. Jonathan, with an agricultural degree from Lincoln University, became stock manager at Minaret Station, then succeeded Mark Faulks in the role of station manager in April 2005. Jonathan formerly managed and developed the Laurentian Wildlife Estate in Canada. Matthew, with a degree in commerce from the University of Otago, has provided the marketing expertise for Minaret Outfitters, a hunting and fishing adventure business associated with the farm and co-owned with Jonathan. Matthew has advertised the hunting and fishing opportunity in North America and Europe, tempting clients with images of magnificent trophy stags and splendid brown and rainbow trout from the Minaret property's rushing rivers, the fish being a catch-and-release proposition. The means of transport are tempting on their own – helicopter, jet-boat, bush plane, four-wheel-drive. Matthew is as also contributing to the business side of Alpine and its Luggate Game Packers offshoot.

Tim is delighted to have his sons 'back home'. Not only that, he closely identifies with their kind of work. Jonathan's marriage to Annabel Hutchinson – a marquee wedding at Benfiddich in January 2004 – gave Tim a feeling of family consolidation. Jonathan and Annabel, whose family farmed in the high country above the Rakaia Gorge in Canterbury, have settled into an elegant new farmhouse on Minaret Station that doubles as a base for hosting clients of Minaret Outfitters.

The Wallis sons continue to carve out vocations for themselves and develop their expertise and business interests in the go-getting Wallis tradition. Yet it does not necessarily follow that their father is happy to ride along on his past achievements and simply hand down fatherly advice to the

Relaxing in tussock grassland at Minaret Station with Annabel, Jonathan and Toby.

next generation. Not a bit. Tim has his own ideas and agenda to pursue.

But it is not like the old days. He no longer has decision-making power in the boardroom. Far from being the dynamo he once was, he gets around very slowly with the aid of crutches or wheelchair, and he has a nurse on duty through the day. He works slowly, methodically. Anyone used to the Tim Wallis before 1996 will recognise the changes. Some might say he is too focussed on project ideas relevant to the 1980s and early 1990s and not sufficiently cognisant of current realities. At times he may repeat himself in conversation or in the letters he sends out. When he is tired his speech becomes more laboured and he may stray off the topic. Nonetheless, he interacts with associates and visitors more or less as he once did, with a genuine interest in what they are about, with courtesy and charm and a sense of humour. His social skills remain largely intact – an impressive achievement given the seriousness of his injury.

As his rehabilitation progressed, there were questions about whether his seasonal low-mood syndrome would return and interfere with the rehabilitation strategies. It did not, certainly not strongly enough to be noticed.

Today, Tim's life is as about as hectic as he can manage within physical and fatigue limits. In 2005, he travelled widely in New Zealand, attending weddings, conferences, sporting fixtures and other events. He also went to Greymouth to catch up with his childhood roots. Then there were a couple of overseas trips in his crowded diary. They included something out of the ordinary. Mid-year, he and Prue had three weeks in Mongolia in the company of friends, and from there they went to England.

Overarching all this movement is a deep-felt desire of Tim's to keep developmental ideas rolling. The brain injury may have curbed his ability to drive home the more viable of his schemes and visions but in no way has it suppressed his enthusiasm for them. He regularly expounds his ideas on tourist development, including better access to the West Coast and Fiordland; nature conservation involving increased efforts to control stoats and other predators of indigenous birds and kiwi in particular; a native timber supply through the sustainable and careful harvesting of mature trees from selected indigenous West Coast forests utilising heavy-lift helicopters; and a possum fur, pelt and pet-food trade through commercialising possums. He was discussing a possum harvest scheme (large-scale processing and export of fur products, pelts and carcasses for pet food manufacture) with Sir Peter Elworthy at the time of Sir Peter's sudden death. Sir Peter died in Wanaka the morning after attending Jonathan and Annabel's wedding. Tim felt the loss of his long-standing friend and business associate very deeply, and he continues to advocate the possum harvest scheme they were planning together. Having been a strident opponent of the use of 1080 poison for the control of deer in the 1960s, Tim is just as opposed to using 1080 for widespread possum control when other means are available.

Of all the new ventures Tim holds a torch for, none burns more deeply inside him than the relaunching of a large-scale wild-venison recovery operation. In the southern mountains of New Zealand red deer are again becoming a major problem for ecosystem health. Fiordland is a region of particular concern. Deer are reaching pest proportions in Fiordland because commercial exploitation has been of limited extent or at a standstill for some years, and recreational hunters by themselves are not able to curb the growth in numbers. The 1080 poison issue, which incensed Tim back in mid-1960s, reared its head again when the food industry got wind of 1080 poison operations against possums. There was speculation the wild venison might be affected. The reduction in helicopter shooting of deer has led to annual population increases of something like 20 percent, which means a doubling of the population every four years. Such growth rates will inevitably lead to food shortages, starvation and a slowing of the population growth till some sort of balance, called 'carrying capacity', is reached. By then, however, the deer will be a plague upon the landscape, just as they were before the 1960s.

Tim's answer is to hit them hard again using helicopters and the venison industry. Where helicopter shooting is restricted by forest cover, he believes good numbers of deer can be trapped and carried out by helicopter. Some assistance from the Government might be required to launch

Sir Peter and Lady Fiona Elworthy with Tim at Jonathan's wedding in January, 2004.

*Tim's 2003 trip to Port Pegasus,
Stewart Island. Mark Acland is in
the dinghy with Tim.* Prue Wallis

the operation. Tim envisages an ongoing export market for wild venison, especially in China when the proposed free-trade agreement between New Zealand and China kicks in. He points out that in the heyday of New Zealand venison exports, 150,000 carcasses a year left the country – and similar numbers could be achieved again. In consultation with his Wanaka-based friend Robert Wilson, he has been working on the idea of limited processing of the carcasses in New Zealand. His idea is that the carcasses could simply be processed into quarters, giving New Zealand processing factories a rapid turnover and leaving the Chinese themselves to further process the venison into cuts of their liking. But as with any venture of this kind – on the scale Tim contemplates – there are economic viability hurdles to overcome.

As a schoolboy Tim expressed concerns about the multiple threats facing indigenous wildlife. Now, having helped convert one of those threats, red deer, from intractable pest to farmed asset, he feels a personal obligation to do what he can to curb their numbers again for the good of New Zealand's natural heritage – not to mention the economy.

Tim freely admits he has disabilities – but all that does is increase his determination to be creative, perhaps be an entrepreneur again, and to live the philosophy he has spent decades teaching by example. Tim Wallis: Can Do. It is as simple as that.

Tim flying in the Southern Alps in 1994. Phil Makanna

Chapter 15

Tim's Way

Then till now
Peeling spuds in Fiordland ... 'a real Kiwi joker' ...
skirting a southerly front ... a high-altitude Hiller ...
Christmas shopping by chopper ... barbecue host ...
'Persistence' ... a persuasive, energetic charm ...
following dreams

ONE FINE DAY in a remote part of Fiordland in the 1970s, several venison chopper pilots, shooters and gutters, up since dawn shooting the tops, were gathered on the deck of their mothership, waiting for lunch. They looked like aircrews taking a break between sorties in some exotic war setting. The spoils of their war that day were in the ship's hold – 100 red-deer carcasses. Tim Wallis, the boss, was among the group, and they filled in time before the midday dinner swapping stories about how the flying had gone so far. The ship's cook was peeling potatoes for the meal, and at one point he walked to the side of the ship to heave the peelings overboard. Distracted by something, he selected the wrong container and threw the spuds themselves into the deep, dark water. The helicopter crews erupted in laughter as the potatoes sank. Tim laughed with them. But when the cook went inside to prepare more potatoes, Tim slipped away from the group. They found out later he disappeared to give the cook a hand peeling a new lot of spuds.

That Tim would sympathise with someone who had made a bit of a fool of himself – to the point of pitching in on a menial task – hardly fits with the image of Tim Wallis, aviator and entrepreneur, boss of a large helicopter business and a leading light in the New Zealand deer industry. But it does offer an insight into Tim's character and approach to life. Mostly he is portrayed as a dynamic, determined, self-made Southerner who likes nothing better than to be pushing boundaries and creating new opportunities. All this rings true. But there other sides to Tim.

His father encouraged him to be a leader. At the same time, advised

Tim and his siblings, celebrating George's 70th birthday on the West Coast. From left, Adrian, George, and Josephine.

Arthur Wallis, he should never lose touch with the people around him. If they were employees, the way to command respect was to show them you could do the work, that you were a practical fellow and prepared to mix it with them. Tim rarely made an example of any staff member who had stuffed up somehow. He was not a blaming sort of boss. Although the people who worked for him knew that, few took advantage of it. On the contrary, they generally demonstrated an intense loyalty towards Tim and what he was trying to achieve, and this loyalty tended to strengthen whenever the odds mounted against a business initiative or direction.

His capacity for work is awesome. Tim developed a '24/7' reputation – seemingly capable of working round the clock seven days a week. His early morning phone calls, however irritating to those at the receiving end, demonstrated when he was at his most creative – before breakfast. Tim's right-hand man in Te Anau, Errol Brown, fielded a good deal of the ideas that poured out of Tim in the 'seventies and 'eighties – so many, says Errol, 'that he'll never know how much money I've saved him by not carrying them all out!' To Errol, Tim demonstrated a Mastermind kind of intelligence, and energy to burn. Evan Waby, an associate from the 1960s, reckoned that even when Tim's body was asleep his brain simply had to be scoping new ideas.

Even when he was flying – the kind of flying he called 'aerial truck driving' – he was thinking. Back in phone range, he would pursue a new line of thought with associates.

When the phone system acquired services such as redialling or call waiting, Tim would utilise those services to the maximum, and it was a common experience for the recipients of calls from Tim who had been engaged on another call to have him stammering on the other end when he got through because his mind had dived off in other directions and he had forgotten what he was phoning about. On those sorts of days, he might have a dozen calls in mind at any one time.

In his hey-day Tim could hardly contain himself when he was seized with an idea. And even now he goes out of his way to research and scope ideas, initially by phone and later in person if he needs to check out a site or some technology. Invariably he wants to know now. Some associates regard him as a 'big-picture' man happy to leave details to others.

To pilot Richard Hayes and many others, Tim lived to create new projects, and the journey leading to their fruition was the reward, not necessarily the end product or the financial return. The thrill of the chase is everything. His enterprising spirit has rubbed off on others, not the least on the pilots who headed off into businesses of their own and became innovative in their own right.

In 1992, the *National Business Review* cited Tim in its Rich List (suggesting his equity in his business empire was worth $30 million), and the news-magazine described him as 'the real stuff of rural legend … a real Kiwi joker. Step aside Barry Crump.'

Crump himself, who popularised the New Zealand backblocks in his books and lifestyle, reckoned Tim was a good keen man. 'I don't know a single backcountry bloke who doesn't respect Tim Wallis. He's way out in front. You can't not like him … no scandals, no pretensions. I reckon we could use a few more Wallises.' The late Barry Crump also summed up Tim as 'a bloke who's hard to get to know' mainly because he was forever on the move – 'always just arriving or just leaving, always busy'. To Luggate factory manager Murray Hamer, spending a day with Tim could seem like a week's activity.

To Tim, business and busyness – mental and physical – have been inseparable. His mind would race ahead, urging his body to follow. In the hurly-burly of the venison days and the live recovery era that followed, Tim was well known for asking a question and before he got an answer, leaping ahead to another topic. Yet his colleagues knew that he would be taking in what they said even if he appeared to be in another frame of mind or in some far-away mental space. More often than not he would regurgitate what they had said when they least expected it.

Before the 1996 crash limited his mobility and his capacity to take on new projects Tim was constantly on the move. Mostly, his associates adapted to his whirlwind lifestyle. It was usually a case of getting on with their work, and anyway, they knew their boss vested a fair amount of trust in them. When it came to a young family, though, a father who was al-

ways on the move could be unsettling. Tim's trips away and his long days in the air took their toll on Prue's patience at times – a young mother with four young sons. When Tim's Makarora mate, Keith Blanc, turned up at the family home one day, asking to see Tim, she replied that she was not sure of his whereabouts that day, indeed most days she found it hard to keep track of his movements. But she had a photograph of him inside the house if he would like to see it!

Prue knew that he flew at the edge of safety at times and that he was fearless. But she reassured herself that his real interest was to carry out a task or get somewhere and that he did not deliberately set out to scare anyone, or show off, or take risks needlessly.

When it came to weather, though, Tim was certainly fearless. There are numerous stories of his flying in awful conditions. Like the time in 1984 when he was heading for Fiordland and a job aboard the *Ranginui* with John Muir. He flew a Hughes 500 into a southerly storm that had snow and high winds associated with it, and they pressed on past Queenstown when many pilots would have called it quits. By the time they arrived at Te Anau snow was caking up on the helicopter. Tim sought refuge at Bill Black's place just outside the town. Bill emerged to help them tie down the helicopter in the storm, shaking his head out of concern and disbelief.

Few people questioned Tim's ability to navigate across rough country in rough conditions: they realised he knew the lie of land as well as any pilot; he knew its ins and out. In the early 1980s, Tim was the star of an American television documentary that described the capture of red deer live in the mountains of Mount Aspiring National Park. *Wild Kingdom* reporter Jim Fowler was clearly impressed by Tim's approach to flying.

'Tim knows a shortcut,' was a memorable line in the film.

A few years earlier, piloting the company Cessna 210 to the Waikato on deer business, Tim set out for home from Tokoroa into a forecast southerly front. The plane was soon swallowed up in cloud. Instead of retreating, Tim diverted away to the east of the country, out to sea, to try to avoid the worst of the storm. He used beacons at the Chatham Islands and Kaikoura to keep track of his progress, and made landfall again away to the south, off the North Canterbury coast. Later he found out that his Cessna had shown up on Wellington Airport's radar as an unexpected sort of contact – slow moving and removed from the usual flightpaths around New Zealand. The air traffic controllers advised the Air Force base at Ohakea near Palmerston North. This is the kind of incident that can grow a life of its own, and one version has it that the Air Force scrambled a Skyhawk to check out the unidentified flying object. Tim never saw or heard from a Skyhawk that day and no one followed up with an enquiry. Presumably he ceased to be a scary object in the sky when he resumed a more normal flightpath over Canterbury.

He sometimes pushed limits vertically as well. On a clear summer's day in the late 1960s, he took a Hiller helicopter to an altitude of over 3,500 metres – the height of Aoraki/Mt Cook – just for the experience. He was checking up on the progress being made by a shooter-gutter team in the Shotover area at the time. With a Landrover for support, they were chasing deer on sweltering valley floors, and complaining to each other

Advice to Rotary youth

In 1986, Tim was the guest speaker at an awards ceremony for a Rotary Youth Leadership programme. After giving a summary of his life and achievements, Tim listed a set of business principles to live by:
- Make your first loss your last loss
- Select top people
- Engage the best accountancy advice
- Make employees feel they have a stake in the business
- Don't let mistakes frighten you – they build judgment
- Be honest, keep your word

about the 40-degree heat. Suddenly, Tim called up on the radio, asking them how they were faring.

'Bloody hot!' said the shooter, Gavin Overton. 'Where are you?'

'I'm 12,000 feet above you, freezing!' came the reply.

Sure enough, if they squinted into the bright light they could just make out a dot in the pale-blue sky and the faint buzz of an engine. It was as if Tim was mimicking a skylark, hovering high up for the sheer joy of flying.

Tim would use a helicopter the way many people used a car. He once landed at Pukeuri, north of Oamaru, because he was running low on fuel and knew there was a petrol station there, right on a corner of State Highway 1. He made extensive use of helicopters as recreational transport. There were countless joyrides and trips that had little to do with business, notably holidays aboard *Ranginui* in Fiordland or mushrooming in the autumn around Wanaka Spotting the white buttons in a paddock from the air was a lot easier and quicker than doing it from the ground.

Then there were the flights Tim made out of a mixture of friendship, compassion and a keenness to reward loyalty. One year, a few days before Christmas, he asked his office manager Nola Sims if she had done any Christmas shopping yet. Nola said she had been too busy at the office to go to Dunedin to buy presents. In response, Tim offered to take the four Sims children, whose ages ranged from six to 12 years, to Dunedin in his helicopter. He gave the foursome lunch in the big smoke, did the rounds of the shops with them then flew them home to Luggate in the afternoon. Sometimes Tim would lend money to staff members with families who wanted to buy a house or land to build on, or acquire an expensive household item like a suite of furniture or a television set.

Tim also has an eye for the potential in people. Early on in his association with Jim Faulks, Tim realised his Luggate factory manager was out of sorts and unsettled. Jim had been in and out of a few jobs in the previous few years and seemed far from happy with his lot. Tim called on Jim one day and invited him to have a chat. 'Let's not chat here at the factory,' Tim said. 'Too many interruptions. Let's go for a flight.'

They took off from Wanaka Airport in a Cessna 180 and at about a height of 1,000 metres Tim put the plane into a continuous circuit. For over an hour, he talked with Jim about what a positive outlook on life could do to a man. The advice landed in the right spot. Jim returned to earth with a sense of direction and purpose that has lasted him most of his life. From that moment, Tim became more of a wise and kindly older brother than a boss. He demonstrated a sixth-sense about when and how to cultivate the talents of an employee.

Barbecues were good for this: the perfect way for him to demonstrate friendship and generosity. Donning an apron, he became a mixture of friendly shoulder, culinary entertainer and stately personage holding court around the barbecue.

He also wanted to be a good father, although he knew his business affairs constrained the relationship with his sons. To them, he was an action man, sweeping in at holiday time, when they were home from boarding school, for trips away camping or for some other outdoor adventure. Yet he wanted them to grow up not as the sons of Tim Wallis but with a strong sense of their own self-worth. He taught them to challenge themselves.

Tim cooking crayfish at Martins Bay.

Modesty is also part of Tim's character. The most public expression of this, although he never meant it to turn out the way it did, was his initial gesture to decline the knighthood nomination. He liked to think that, yes, his achievements might be worthy but that they were not created by his efforts alone. As he told *North and South* magazine in 1994, he is 'simply not interested in climbing the social ladder'. When writer Cate Brett phoned his office for some background for the article, and requested the faxing of a curriculum vitae, office manager Nola Sims reacted tersely. 'I have worked for Mr Wallis for 25 years and I have never seen anything remotely resembling a curriculum vitae.' She thought the nearest thing to biographical notes on Tim might be the New Zealand Deer Farmers' Association knighthood nomination itself, which summarised his contributions to aviation, deer farming, nature conservation (through the removal of deer from native habitats), economic activity and community affairs.

Cate Brett got her story in the end. She described Tim as a 'self-made man to end all self-made men', one who was liable to stick his neck out. Tim put it this way: 'I take that margin [of risk] further than other people would take it.' This is something of an understatement when you look back on his flying career, his corporate forays into places like Siberia, and his absolute determination to not let a broken back, a paralysed leg, beady-eyed bankers, a session on Russian vodka, tax reforms or anything else get in the way of a goal.

This character trait began early. Christ's College master, Zane Dalzell, described Tim as a 'nice extroverted personality … he'd give anything a go.' He has given an awful lot a go in his life. He is the original networker, with enthusiasm in abundance.

To current Alpine board chairman Don Spary, Tim's enthusiasm is also his Achilles Heel – and he has 'paid the penalty for taking risks on more than one occasion'. Tim's wife, Prue, told *North and South* in 1994: 'Tim is so determined to achieve he goes into the risk area.' She said she saw a 'ruthless' side in him – 'Ruthless in the sense that he will forsake everything to achieve his goal. He is single-minded and utterly determined.'

At the same time it is not a case of winner-take-all for Tim. He won the respect of many a competitor for his sharing attitude, summed up in the expression, 'Leave something for the next guy.' His Canterbury friend, the late Sir Peter Elworthy, was greatly impressed by this aspect of Tim's approach to business. Peter expressed Tim's style this way: 'Always leave a margin for the next person … recognise there has to be a margin for those either side of you. It's part of that generosity of spirit that really pays off in business.'

Tim's way is decidedly gung-ho. The Chinese expression, adopted by the United States marines in 1942 as a rally cry, literally means to work together. Since then, the expression has been corrupted to some extent in the Western world to illustrate a persistent style of enthusiasm.

Hundreds of people have experienced his impulsive enthusiasm over the years. English vintage aircraft restorer, Tony Ditheridge, was among them. In 1993, Tony was approached by Tim to restore a Hurricane fighter, and Alpine flew him out to Wanaka for talks. The Englishman, like many business associates of Tim's, was struck immediately by Tim's nature. 'You knew you were in the presence of an unusual man. His passion, in this case for aeroplanes, his pure gut feel for a business situation, a deal, an investment. I think Tim must have been the original "shoot from the hip" man.' In that meeting over the Hurricane, Tony explained how he envisaged doing the job and how much he thought it would cost. Tim agreed on the spot, told Tony to get on with it and organised for funds to be sent to England even as Tony was flying home.

Robert Wilson is convinced Tim's 'big advantage' in business dealings has been his personality. 'In situations where there is confrontation, people will often back down because of Tim's personality … people tend to think twice.' Conversely, Tim is able to see the facets and forces bearing on a business deal and try to 'work in' – gung-ho. He lives the concept of

a 'fair go'. His egalitarian sense, his common touch and his humility sit alongside – some might say oddly alongside – his political leanings as a long-standing supporter of the National Party.

Although his personality and work ethic were well formed by the time he married Prue, it is widely acknowledged that Prue has been a strong supporting influence. Around the time of the knighthood, the Wallis boys expressed the view that their mother equally deserved the honour for all the work she performed behind the scenes. She interrupted a promising career in theatre, films and the arts to be with Tim, support his business operations and raise four sons. Her support has ranged from entertaining overseas business partners of Tim's to editing and polishing his speeches. By his own admission, Tim may not be the business world's most articulate speaker but he has got his message across. Prue's supportive role was never more important than when Tim was in hospital in 1996, when a critical rehabilitation pathway was set, and in the years since, when he has needed a duty of care far beyond the imagining of most people.

Of all of the demanding situations Tim has faced, none matches the stringency of recovering from a brain injury. This has required all the grit he can muster. There is a gilt-edged plaque at home – it also used to hang

Tim and Prue at Benfiddich, early 2005. Tim is sitting on his ride-on mower. Neville Peat

in the office – that has become part of the Tim Wallis folklore. It is headed up, 'Persistence'. The words underneath assert that nothing in the world can take its place; persistence will win over any shortcoming of talent or education.

Without this trait, Tim could not have progressed as far as he has since the Spitfire crash. Although he remains 'damaged', as he puts it, he is able to apply himself to his ideas, travel around the country and overseas, and generally enjoy his family, his home and his Wanaka environment, not the least Minaret Station, described by Sir Peter Elworthy around the time Tim was negotiating its purchase, as a 'romantic investment'. These days, if he cashed up all of his assets (his THL shares were all sold by 1998), Tim is worth over $30 million but the accumulation of money, to Tim, is not so much a mark of success as the bringing of an original idea to fruition. That is what has driven him – pursuit of a dream through to a successful conclusion. Money has been a secondary consideration, only of importance to drive the next project.

Notwithstanding the serious side of investment and business, Tim exudes a rare kind of charm, a persuasive, energetic charm that is mixed up with a wild kind of ambition, a love of the new and daring, and a compelling interest in pushing boundaries. Fiercely loyal to his own ideals, he has benefited from the loyalty reciprocated by his associates. Bill Black, his Fiordland flying mate of almost 30 years and an aviation legend in his own right, puts it this way: 'I liked working for Tim. I'd do it all again. Hell I would!'

Tim was a pathfinder in a unique enterprise – the right man in the right place at the right time to capitalise on the extraction of shot deer and later live deer by helicopter from the mountains of southern New Zealand. Hurricane Tim went on to take an inspirational role in New Zealand tourism and the collection and display of vintage warplanes. But what history will remember him for, most of all, are the helicopters and the deer. Out of a weekend hobby, deer-stalking, he built not only a career for himself but also a major industry.

Business Milestones

1965 Luggate Game Packers formed.

1967 First three-year venison recovery licence, Fiordland National Park.

1968 Vessels *Ranginui* and *Hotunui* in service in Fiordland.

1970 New Hebrides (Vanuatu) beef export venture.

1970–75 Peak years of venison recovery (up to 130,000 carcasses processed and exported annually).

1971 Alpine Helicopters Ltd formed.

1974 First live exports of deer – to Taiwan.

Mid-1970s. Luggate factory increases production of velvet and other deer co-products for the oriental medicine market.

1975 First live deer exports to Korea.

1976 Mararoa Station purchased.

1977 World's first large-scale live-deer auction, Criffel Deer Park.

1978 First airfreight of deer by DC3 to the North Island.

1979 Peak live-capture period. Alpine Helicopters and subsidiaries operating 40 helicopters, with many involved in the capture of over 7,000 wild deer for deployment to farms.

1981 First deer imports (Canadian elk) since 1910.

1983 Skid-mounted net gun perfected, pilot able to capture wild deer.

1986 The Helicopter Line is floated publicly on share market.

Alpine Helicopters is renamed Alpine Deer Group.

1987 Mararoa Station sold to Challenge Deer Ltd.

1988 Inaugural Easter Warbirds airshow; red deer farming pioneered in Canada and first live shipment from New Zealand.

1989 Live deer shipment to Australia.

1990 Orr Lake Elk stud and genetics business established in Canada with Mike Bringans.

1991 Altyn Kerl deer breeding/velvet trading venture set up in southern Siberia.

1993 New Zealand Fighter Pilots' Museum and Alpine Fighter Collection Hangar opened at Wanaka Airport during Easter.

1995 Minaret Station purchased.

1996 At the annual meeting of Tourism Holdings Ltd (formerly The Helicopter Line), Sir Tim, retiring from Board of Directors, is appointed to the new position of Company Founder.

2000 Over Easter weekend, the Seventh Warbirds Over Wanaka attracts a record attendance of 108,000.

2001 Laurentian Wildlife Estate hunting camp established in Canada.

2004 Ninth Warbirds Over Wanaka attracts 99,000 people over three days.

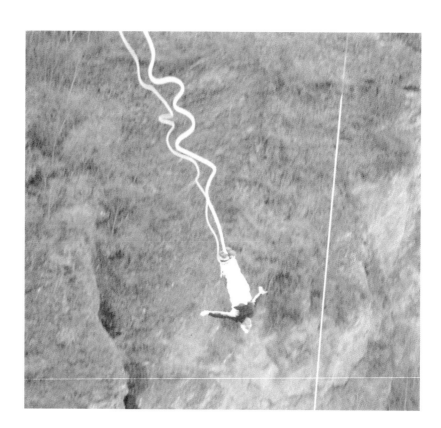

Tim's 50th birthday bungy jump.
Prue Wallis

Honours & Awards

1980 E.A. Gibson Award for services to NZ aviation.

1980 New Mexico Department of Game and Fish, Certificate of Appreciation for helping save New Mexico's endangered population of desert bighorn sheep.

1985 Sir Arthur Ward Award (NZ Society of Animal Production) for achievements in the deer industry.

1989 Aviation Industry Association of NZ Special Award for development of the NZ deer industry by the use of helicopters, for the restoration and collection of vintage war planes and the founding of Warbirds Over Wanaka.

1990 Honorary membership of No. 453 Squadron, Royal Australian Air Force (which flew Tim's Spitfire Mk XVI FUP in operations in Europe in 1945).

1991 New Zealand 1990 Commemorative Medal in recognition of services to New Zealand.

Patron NZ Brain Injury Association; Wanaka St John Ambulance; NZ Wildlife Research Trust; Endangered Species Trust; Upper Clutha Sports Trust; Royal New Zealand Air Force 485 Squadron.

Life member NZ Deer Farmers' Association, NZ Elk and Wapiti Society (founding chairman).

1992 Otago Chamber of Commerce Achievement Award for outstanding contribution to the economy of Wanaka and Otago.

1992 Wanaka Rotary Club's Paul Harris Fellowship plaque for contribution to the community.

1994 Christ's College Honours Tie.

1994 Commemorative Medal (NZ Deer Industry), jointly with Sir Peter Elworthy, for services to the deer industry.

1994 Knight Bachelor.

1994 Melvin Jones Fellow Award (Lions Clubs International Foundation) for dedicated humanitarian services.

1999 Sir Jack Newman Award (NZ Tourism Awards) for outstanding contributions to the NZ tourist industry.

2000 Doctor of Commerce honoris causa, Lincoln University.

2001 Speights Southern Man.

2002 Laureate, NZ Business Hall of Fame (Enterprise NZ Trust and *National Business Review*) for achievements in deer recovery and NZ tourism development, and the founding of Warbirds Over Wanaka.

2006 Royal Aeronautical Society, New Zealand Division, Meritorious Service Award for services to deer farming and the formation of Warbirds Over Wanaka.

The Brietling Fighters in a climb – from left, Spitfire, Corsair (lower), Kittyhawk and Mustang.
Mike Jorgensen

Behind the Scenes at Warbirds

2004

THE HANGAR where Ray Mulqueen and his team of aircraft engineers restored a P40 Kittyhawk years ago now serves as a spacious lunch room-cum-rumpus room behind the Alpine Deer Group office at Wanaka Airport. But at 9 am on Easter Saturday 2004, it took on a different role altogether as the briefing room for pilots, ground crew and the people who run the finest vintage airshow in New Zealand – Warbirds over Wanaka.

Tim Wallis, the airshow's founder, is not here, not yet, but you can feel his presence. 'Tim's Flat' says a sign on the door of a side room, glass-eyed red deer and chamois heads peer down on people helping themselves to coffee, and the back end of a Hughes 500 is mounted overhead wrapped in vegetation to mimic a crash in the bush. Posters of previous Warbirds shows and maps of the Wanaka area surround the space.

Squadron Leader Jim Rankin, flying controller for this event, announces a time check and synchronising of watches. 'Thirty seconds.' There is a pause. Then, 'Ten seconds … five seconds. It's 0900.'

Alpine Chairman Don Spary speaks next. There is a military tone to his welcome. 'All the thrills – none of the spills,' he intones. 'This isn't a competition between pilots. We're here to please our customers.' The pilots take in the advice passively. Seasoned and remarkably square-jawed, they look the part. They have done this before. Some wear leather jackets, others have donned flying suits.

The flying controller is speaking again, describing the runway options. There are three, but only one is sealed. It is 1,200 metres long. As for the weather, there is a front coming through about lunchtime, with hail showers and thunder forecast for late afternoon, between 5 and 7 p.m. For air space the pilots have a radius of five miles from the airfield to work in, to an altitude of 7,500 feet. There will be five hours and 15 minutes of displays, says Jim Rankin, and 57 events all told.

A line-up of campervans on the
terrace overlooking the airport.
Chris Hinch

'Keep it tight – if everyone is 60 seconds over, we won't get the show completed in time. There's no tolerance in the time sched. You'll have to be taking off or landing, many of you, with another display above or below you. Remember, if you're over the sealed runway you're too close [to the crowd], and if you're below the top of the Gold Pass stand, you're too low.'

He describes the alternative airfield, Hawea. He says it is marked by a lone pine and it has a grass runway a kilometre long. Remember the pyrotechnics, too, Jim cautions.

'Questions?' There are none.

'One more thing – quiet times. There'll be an interview with Buzz Aldrin from 10.20 to 10.28, and Buzz and Tim will be driven along the crowd line between 12.15 and 12.25. No engines at those times, please.'

Former American astronaut Buzz Aldrin is the special guest. With Neil Armstrong, he left the first footprints on the moon in 1969.

The briefing is over in 14 minutes and 23 seconds.

Outside, early-comers are reserving places by the netting fence with folding chairs and rugs and chilly bins. From these front-line 'posies' the sealed runway is only 50 metres away, maybe less. Overseas air shows tend to keep spectators much farther away from the action than this. Out on the main road, vehicles queue for kilometres waiting to access the car parks before the 10 am start time. Across the road from the main gate, on Criffel Station, camper vans large and small, and buses transformed into mobile homes, line up along the straight edge of the terrace overlooking the airport, a dress circle – first in, best dressed. There were 20,000 spectators at yesterday's Good Friday practice day. Judging by the numbers coming through the gate so far and the queues of traffic, the crowd is likely to reach over 50,000.

A couple of minutes after 10 a.m., Keith Skilling starts the Vought F4U-1 Corsair's 2,000 hp radial Pratt & Whitney engine. It drives the largest propeller fitted on a Second World War fighter plane. A lot of people know that the Corsair and a P40 Kittyhawk piloted by Ray Hanna will open the show, for a big crowd gathers on the opposite side of the fence to see them fire up. Their pilots are stalwarts of Wanaka Warbirds. Professionals they may be, but that does not mean they skimp on preparation. They meet beforehand to confirm aerobatic and formation flying strategies. The same applies to every combination of pilots for every event involving more than one aircraft. Throughout the day, in various places and at various times, briefings will be happening behind the scenes.

Tim is at the airfield now, dressed in the black Warbirds polar-fleece vest laden with insignia and wearing a red baseball-style Warbirds cap. He has a date with Buzz Aldrin at 10.20, when they will ride together in an open Jeep so the crowd can glimpse the American astronaut. But first, Buzz is introduced to the paying public. In the commentary box, actually the open upper deck of a red double-decker bus parked beside the Gold

Ray Hanna illustrates a manoeuvre at a Breitling Fighters briefing.
Mike Jorgensen

Pass stand, he is interviewed over the public-address system by former television weatherman and pilot Jim Hickey, who asks about the Apollo 11 mission of '69, the moon and other marvels.

Says Buzz: 'You see the lunar horizon curving away, with its rocks and boulders clear-cut on the horizon in the absence of air, and a black sky beyond. Earth is quite huge – four times bigger than what the moon looks like to us – all blue and brown and a long ways away. The only man-made thing we could make out from the moon was a six-lane freeway that ran for miles in a straight line. I once used to look up and see the moon as a stranger; now it's more of a friend. I think of it as magnificent desolation.' Jim Hickey asks about when humans will get back to the moon. By 2020, Buzz is picking. But watch out for the Chinese, he says. 'They'll be doing a lunar orbit soon enough. The Chinese think the Twenty-first Century is their century…'

For a few seconds, his voice is lost as the Corsair roars down the runway – so much for the quiet time the flying controller requested – then the interview resumes, with a question about space tourism.

'Space tourism will come one of these days. I'm encouraging it. But it's going to be an expensive ticket for quite a while. When ordinary people can afford to take a trip into space, that's when we'll really build enthusiasm for pushing on to Mars.' The interview is over as Buzz Aldrin, moonwalker, now 74, offers the command: 'Gentlemen, start your engines!' Some already have.

'Look right,' commentator Jerry Mead urges the crowd as the Kittyhawk scorches out of a cool dry autumn sky, from the Luggate end of the runway, at a speed of about 340 knots (630 kilometres per hour), with the

Buzz Aldrin acknowledges the crowd on a drive-by with Tim and Warbirds general manager Gavin Johnston. Mike Jorgensen

Corsair close behind. Warbirds 2004 has begun. Both aircraft swoop low, seemingly below the level of the top of the Gold Pass stand – something Jim Rankin may have a word to the pilots about.

The Kittyhawk is chased by the Corsair. Glenn Alderton

Englishman Jerry Mead is one of dozens of vintage warplane enthusiasts who have been touched by Tim's Warbirds concept, who know where they will be every other Easter.

In a soft English accent that would not sound out of place in Christchurch, New Zealand, he describes the action as if he were seeing it for the first time. The fact is, though, Jerry is a professional airshow commentator. He encountered Tim at the famous Duxford airshow in England in the mid-1990s when it came to his notice that Tim had been jotting down some of his lines 'to show to the Wanaka boys'. Tim invited Jerry to lead the commentary team at the 1996 Wanaka show and he has been coming back ever since.

Mixing humour with a deep-felt admiration for the pilots and their aircraft, his commentary gels with that of Timaru-based Graeme McLeary, who has participated in all of the Wanaka shows except the inaugural one in 1988. In the days when Tim pirouetted his Hughes 500 the length of the runway, little more than a metre above the seal, Graeme would have

*A formation of PAC Cresco
aircraft approach the airport.*
Rob Neil

no trouble convincing the crowd that this was skill and nerve somewhat above the normal.

The 2004 show produces something that has Jerry Mead spluttering with astonishment – Peter Jackson's Sopwith Camel pursued by a Spitfire. The two classic warplanes, poles apart for speed but whose designs are separated by less than 20 years, do a length of the airfield with the World War I biplane at full speed, tail up and engine crackling, and the Spitfire slewing at the edge of a stall.

The displays run continuously. They run on right through lunchtime. The day's line-up includes Second World War icons of the sky, including a Spitfire, Mustang, Kittyhawk, Corsair and Hawker Hurricane, and a collection of World War I types – a Fokker Dr.1 Triplane, Bristol Freighter biplane, Avro 504K biplane and the Sopwith Camel. There are formation aerobatic displays by Nanchangs, Yak 52s, North American Harvards, and a trio of smoking PAC Cresco top-dressing planes from Wanganui. With picnic lunches out and the sky virtually cloudless – there is no sign of the forecast front, has it gone through already? – the Royal New Zealand Air Force makes a grand entry. Its newly acquired Boeing 757 performs a low-level sweep and climbs steeply away. For its size it is impressively quiet, not to mention manoeuvrable. Then comes a triple treat – a flypast by the 757 jet flanked by a four-engined Orion and C-130 Hercules. The Air Force likes to promote and showcase itself at airshows, especially Warbirds Over Wanaka, the biggest showcase of all. It has been a strong supporter of Tim's show since the inception.

Tim's Polikarpovs are back in number and still noisy. The man who masterminded their restoration watches from the Alpine Deer Group's hospitality area alongside the red bus. He sits at one of several tables laid out in the grass enclosure, and each pilot returning from a display taxies past the Gold Pass stand, taking the applause, and waves to Tim and his Alpine mates in the Alpine hospitality area like proud goggled racetrack jockeys on winning horses. Friends and associates drift in and either sit with him or take a seat in the small stand at the back of the enclosure. Second World War legend Johnny Checketts spends an hour of two there accompanied by his niece. Now retired, he flew more than 50 aircraft types during a long career in the air force. He likes the Wanaka show, calls it the best in the world. Why? 'You get really close to the runway and the planes – at other international shows you'd be a mile away.'

New faces turn up, among them a deer co-products client from North China who is accompanied by Rosanna Yang, manager of Alpine's Hong Kong office. The hospitality area contains a tent where guests browse on finger food and help themselves to wine or juice. Platters of hot food arrive in a rush around lunchtime. Prue has ordered the food and drinks and she makes sure there is a continuous supply. Guests include former Minister of Conservation Denis Marshall and Auckland cereals manufacturer (and soon to be Auckland City Mayor) Dick Hubbard, who are among the trustees of the National Parks and Conservation Foundation, of which Prue is also a trustee. The United States Ambassador Charles Swindells is also a guest, and some of the airshow's pilots also make use of the Alpine hospitality area.

Commentators Jerry Mead (right) and Graeme McLeary. Mike Jorgensen

A section of the crowd, tents and parked aircraft at the 2004 airshow. Chris Hinch

Gung-ho restoration

One of the best examples of the gung-ho behind-the-scenes efforts that characterise Warbirds Over Wanaka occurred on the Easter Saturday of the 2004 show. One of the advertised star acts, a Lavochkin LA-9, the fastest (690 kilometres per hour) piston-engined fighter to appear at Wanaka that year and the only airworthy example in the world, struck a problem just after getting airborne. Pilot John Lamont radioed he was experiencing severe vibration coming from the rudder area and he advised he would have to abandon the display. Before John landed safely, another pilot, Stu Goldspink in the Hurricane, rendezvoused in mid-air with him to cast an eye over the LA-9 and see what might be wrong. It was the rudder all right: it was shuddering so much the paint was flaking off. That evening, despite warnings it might be a waste of time trying to get the aircraft ready for display the next day, the engineers set about restoring the rudder, and Prue Wallis worked until after midnight sewing fabric for it. The final touches involved drying off the paintwork before the start of the Easter Sunday flying – with a hairdryer.

A few pilots have come into the Alpine area to view the show's individual star, Jurgis Kairys, a Lithuanian pilot appearing at Wanaka for the first time. He is no stranger to airshows and aerobatics, however. A world champion, he caught the imagination of news media around the world by flying under a fairly small bridge at 250 kilometres per hour. Upside down. He flies a light-weight silver-and-white Sukhoi SU-31 with a 2.6-metre propeller that becomes a rotor when he brings the aircraft to a hover pointing straight up with the engine at full throttle. He can also make the Sukhoi look like it is having a fit, tumbling out of the sky trailing smoke and seemingly out of control. He lies prone in the cockpit, a pilot at one with his machine, and the crowd can see him clearly as he takes off once more and demonstrates a 'Cobra' manoeuvre. This involves a right-angled movement, with the plane pointing upwards suddenly, 90 degrees to

Seemingly impossible: Jurgis Kairys performs a 'Cobra' on take-off.
Mike Jorgensen

The Air Force 757 on approach.
Ken Chilton

runway, then flattening out, then at right angles again. There is more. In the course of a normal take-off he flips the plane over and continues flying it upside down at low level the length of the airfield, leaving a trail of smoke. Near the end of the display he sideslips along the runway at super-slow speed, defying a stall. Had they not seen for themselves there was someone in the cockpit, more than a few spectators might have assumed this was an aircraft under remote control. To cut down on weight so he can perform these stunts Jurgis strips his aircraft to the bare minimum. Apparently the excess includes a parachute for emergency use.

There are plenty of people in the Alpine hospitality area for Jurgis's performance and one of the pilots is overheard to say, 'He's nuts!'

Keith Skilling is among them, enjoying a break between his three appearances in the Corsair today. He rates the Wanaka show the best in the world for setting, atmosphere, fun and people. He flies at airshows for about half the year and in Air New Zealand Boeing 767s the rest of the time. He has been flying since he left school at Mosgiel, first for the RNZAF, which he joined at the age of 17. In 1972–73 he served two years in Southeast Asia, including time in Vietnam. Since 1998 he has teamed up in England with fellow New Zealander Ray Hanna and two other pilots, Nigel Lamb and Lee Proudfoot, in a class act called the Breitling Fighters (named for the sponsor, Breitling Watches, a 120-year-old Swiss watch-making firm, which supplies the aviation industry).

The Breitling Fighters in close formation – from left, Spitfire, Kittyhawk, Corsair and Mustang. Andy Bennison

What sets the Breitling Fighters apart from most other aerobatic acts is that they fly four different aircraft types (typically Mustang, Spitfire, Kittyhawk and Corsair) in close formation. Warbirds Over Wanaka 2004 is to be their last hurrah, though. They have decided to disband after some 750 displays in 13 countries. Keith Skilling describes those seven years as 'the most enjoyable and exciting chapter of my aviation career'.

Two Mustangs keep clear of a fireball. Glenn Alderton

For one thing, Ray Hanna plans to switch his focus from England, where he formed The Old Flying Machine Company at Duxford in 1980, to Wanaka in the next year or two. He is a master aviator. Born in Takapuna, he joined the Royal Air Force in 1949 and became the leader of the famed Red Arrows team. His formation flying experience spans five decades. Ray rates Wanaka Warbirds as special in the world of airshows – special partly because 'it's more relaxed – there's not as much officialdom involved'.

Put that compliment down to Tim's bent for delivering the goods with the least amount of fuss, although Occupational Health and Safety zeal – the Government's notorious OSH party spoiler – has increased the paperwork and precautionary effort in recent years. Airshow general manager Gavin Johnston knows all about that. Warbirds works wonderfully well because of the huge amount of preparation he and his assistants, surprisingly few in number, have invested in the intervening 24 months. He knows just how much correspondence and negotiation it takes to put together the Breitling Fighters for their last performance along with a line-up of four World War II fighter aircraft. The planes and their pilots are the stars, no question. But the atmosphere Keith Skilling and others talk about is built up by an array of contributions, including the 'warhorses' infantry re-enactments and the displays of vintage machinery, the 100 trade exhibits, the pyrotechnics that produce explosions massive enough to rattle rib cages, and fireballs whose heat is clearly felt by the crowd behind the fence a couple of hundred metres away.

For the two days of Warbirds 2004, the official crowd figure was 99,000. WOW had worked its magic again.

References

Books

Allan, Vivienne, *A New Way of Living: The history of the Spinal Injuries Unit in Christchurch* (Christchurch: Canterbury District Health Board, 2004)

Banwell, Bruce, *Wapiti in New Zealand: The story of the Fiordland Herd* (Wellington: Reed, 1966)

Banwell, Bruce, *The Highland Stags of Otago* (Wellington: Reed, 1968)

Brodie, Ian *The Alpine Fighter Collection's Hurricane Mark IIA* (Auckland: Reed Books, 2000)

Brodie, Ian, *The Best of Warbirds Over Wanaka* (Auckland: Reed Books, 2002)

Brodie, Ian, *Warbirds Over Wanaka: The Official Record of the 2004 Airshow,* (Auckland: Reed Books, 2004)

Brown, Jackson H., *A Father's Book of Wisdom* (Melbourne: Bookman Press, 1988)

Caughley, Graeme, *The Deer Wars* (Auckland: Heinemann, 1983)

Forrester, Rex, *The Chopper Boys* (Christchurch: Whitcoulls, 1982)

Forrester, Rex and Neil Illingworth, *Hunting in New Zealand* (Wellington: Reed, 1979)

Harthoorn, A.M., *The Flying Syringe* (London: Geoffrey Bles, 1970)

Holden, Philip, *The Deerstalkers: A History of the New Zealand Deerstalkers' Association* (Auckland: Hodder & Stoughton, 1985)

Holden, Philip, *Hunt South* (Auckland: Hodder & Stoughton,1989)

McDowall, R.M., *Gamekeepers for the Nation* (Christchurch: University of Canterbury Press, 1995)

Pascoe, John, *The Haast is in South Westland* (Auckland: Reed, 1966)

Price, Alfred, *The Spitfire Story* (London: Jane's, 1982)

Wallis, Prue (ed.) *The Ranginui Book* (editor's private collection, 2000)

Yerex, David, *Deer: The New Zealand Story* (Christchurch: University of Canterbury Press, 2001)

Articles, Reports and Papers

Alpine Deer Group, Report on Minaret Station, 2002.

Alpine Helicopters Ltd, Final Submission to Fiordland National Park Board, Fiordland National Park game recovery licence proceedings, 1976.

Alpine Helicopters / The Helicopter Line, *Alpine Helicopters Ltd*, published for the New Zealand Deer Farmers' Conference at Queenstown, June/July 1985.

Brett, Cate, 'Wallis Over Wanaka: The rise of Sir Tim', *North and South* (April 1994).

Brett, Cate, 'Never Say Die', *North and South* (November 1996).

Bottcher, Sharon A., 'Cognitive Retraining: A Nursing Approach to Rehabilitation of the Brain Injured', *Nursing Clinics of North America* Vol 24 No. 1 (March 1989).

Challies, C.N., 'Establishment, control and commercial exploitation of wild deer in New Zealand', *Biology of Deer Production* (eds P.F. Fennessy and K.R. Drew), The Royal Society of New Zealand Bulletin, 22 (1985).

Deer Industry News, 8 (March 2004).

Hutchings, Brendan, 'The life and times of Johnny Wang', *The Deer Farmer*, 140 (1997).

Kong, Y.C. and P.P.H. But, 'Deer – the ultimate medicinal animal (antler and deer parts in medicine)', *Biology of Deer Production* (eds P.F. Fennessy and K.R. Drew), The Royal Society of New Zealand Bulletin, 22 (1985).

Transport Accident Investigation Commission, Vickers Armstrong Supermarine Spitfire Mark XIV ZK-XIV, Wanaka Aerodrome, 2 January 1996, Report 96-001, 1996.

Wright, Raymond, 'A.R. Wallis, First Secretary for Agriculture, Victoria, 1872–82', research paper, Victoria Department of Agriculture, Melbourne, 1982.

Documentary films

New Zealand Deer, Dir. Jim Fowler. Wild Kingdom (USA) Films. 1983.

Tim Wallis, Helicopters and Deer, Dir. Tony Benny. Country Calendar, Television New Zealand. 1987.

Minaret Station, Dir. Tony Benny. Country Calendar, Television New Zealand. 2003.

Beating the Odds, Dir. Melanie Reid. Insight, TV3. 1997.

Tim Wallis, Dir. Caroline Harker. Inside Out, Television New Zealand. 2004.

ACKNOWLEDGEMENTS

Through his aviation and business enterprises, his deer farming, shipping interests and community links, and his numerous adventures, Tim Wallis has made an impression on tens of thousands of people in New Zealand and overseas. A good number of his colleagues, friends and family members assisted me in my research. Wherever I went for information, I found people only too willing to give me their 'spin on Tim'. Often this took the form of anecdotes that spanned the gamut of human experience. Drama, humour, fear, shock and amazement were common themes.

Through a series of events in early 2004, I found myself immersed in the world of Tim Wallis, his interests and social connections. His second son Jonathan's wedding in January 2004 put me in touch with Tim's brothers, George and Adrian, and his sister, Josephine. A few weeks later I met a cross-section of Tim's former colleagues and business associates, spanning four decades. They were attending a Luggate Game Packers/Alpine Deer Group company reunion at Wanaka Airport, where the nostalgia and camaraderie was as thick in the air as the barbecue smoke. Come Easter 2004 and I encountered a modern dimension of Tim's life – the pulsating Warbirds Over Wanaka airshow.

From the outset of the research I was armed with file boxes of information. Of immediate interest were the transcripts of about 30 interviews with Tim's deer, business and aviation associates, friends and family. The interviews were conducted by writer Cate Brett in 1997. They set me up with a wonderful baseload of anecdotes and information which I supplemented with about 70 further interviews of my own on farms and at other workplaces, in homes and pubs, and at events such as Warbirds. Of special value among the interviews Cate Brett conducted were the impressions and views of two people who died before I began the research – Tim's mother, Janice, and his aunt and godmother, Betsy Anderson (a sister of Janice's). Another important transcript available to me was that of Sir Peter Elworthy, whose untimely death occurred in Wanaka the weekend Jonathan and Annabel were wed and just before I planned to meet him.

I am especially grateful to Tim's close friends Mark Acland (Mt Somers Station) and Robert Wilson (Wanaka), who each agreed to contribute a foreword for this book. Christ's College contemporaries of Tim's, they have supported Tim throughout his working life and were most helpful to me. I thank Alpine Deer Group executive director Graeme Ramshaw for backing the project, providing business and operational information and reviewing the manuscript. ADG directors Don Spary and

Graham Sinclair provided information and comment, and Tim's personal assistant, Annie Trengrove, helped in all kinds of ways with communications and logistics and the sourcing of the bulk of the illustrations – a massive job.

I am indebted to Ken Drew, who provided me with extensive notes and advice on the history of deer in New Zealand, deer research and the development of deer farming. Helicopter pilot Richard Hayes toured me around Tim's favourite Fiordland haunts and we surprised a few deer that day, too. For stories about deer recovery and tales about Tim I am also grateful to a swag of other pilots – Bill Black, Alan Duncan, Doug Maxwell, Dick Deaker, Rex Dovey, Russell Gutschlag (transcript), Gary Cruickshank, Ken Tustin, Denis Egerton, Jeff Sly and Keith Wakeman (transcript). Graeme Gale and Peter Dean of Helicopters Otago and Toby Wallis of Alpine Helicopters helped me understand how choppers fly. More anecdotes on the venison and live-deer recovery days came from a large team of shooters, gutters and support crew, including Gavin Overton, Evan Waby, Charlie Emmerson, Max Street, Charles Jelley, Peter Stephens, John Muir, Duncan Boyd and Tim's Te Anau stalwarts, Errol and Carol Brown. Ann Waby gave me an insight into life in the field camps. Several Fiordland National Park rangers of the era provided information – Harold Jacobs, John Ward, Ray Slater, Wally Sanders and Paddy Gordon. I also thank John von Tunzelman, who worked for the New Zealand Forest Service at the time, for his inputs. Dave Crouchley and Murray Willans of the Department of Conservation at Te Anau briefed me on the situation with deer today and Don Merton told me about Tim's support for saving kakapo.

Bruce Gaffikin and Mike Bringans went out of their way to help me describe Tim's experience of Russia and Canada, respectively, and I thank them most sincerely. Information for the Russia chapter also came from Graeme Ramshaw, Ray Mulqueen, Robin and Noeline Biddulph and Svetlana Grebenkina, Tim's interpreter, now based in Christchurch, who gave me advice on the Russian way of life. I also acknowledge the assistance of the following people associated with Tim's deer farming and business interests now or in the past: Murray Hamer, Peter Hamer, Jim Faulks, Nola Sims, Geoff Taylor, Keith Blanc, Jeff Niederer, Graeme Gosney, Murray Valentine, Steve Dyet, Rosanna Yang, Gilbert van Reenan, Colin Macintish, Simon Bartlett, Les Smith, Adrienne Reid, Russell Knight, Pat Jones, Alison Haig and Geoff Erskine. Trevor Walton and Tony Pearse also provided information on the deer industry. Pilot John Gardiner told me about the illustrious 'Stagliner' operation.

The chapter on Tim's childhood and school days was enhanced by information from Tim's brothers, George and Adrian, and his sister Josephine, his uncle Peter Blunden, Mark Acland, Robert Wilson and (through interview transcripts) Rob Johnson, Richard and John Coates, Trevor Hutton, Zane Dalzell and Ron Hartill. Richard Bromley and Sam Mannering introduced me to Christ's College.

It was a pleasure to talk to New Zealand helicopter pioneer, John Reid, who taught Tim to fly. Other information on aviation matters came from Grant Bisset, Tim Johnston, John Penno and Bill Sommer of the Civil Aviation Authority.

When it came to describing the Warbirds experience, I was ably assisted by Ray Mulqueen and Ian Brodie, and thank them both for their time and expertise. Gavin Johnston, George Wallis and John Cross provided organisational information, and pilots Keith Skilling, Ray Hanna and Johnny Checketts gave me an idea of the flying side. Commentators Jerry Mead, Graeme McLeary and Jim Hickey provided colourful impressions. For supplying a spectacular array of Warbirds images I thank Ewan Fallow and Ian Brodie, and all of the contributing photographers. The *Otago Daily Times* and *Southland Times* kindly allowed the use of a number of photographs, and I thank Tom Scott for the use of his cartoon about Tim's Spitfire crash at Waipukurau.

My thanks also to Arnold and Isabelle Middleton, of Queenstown Hill, for helping me describe Tim's 1968 crash, and to Allan Bean and Bill Utley (transcript) for information about Tim's recovery from that crash. Vivienne Allan, Margot Henderson and Julian Verkaaik provided information about the Burwood Spinal Unit.

For helping me describe Tim's 1996 crash I am grateful to pilot Brian Hore, of Nokomai Station, and to the following who were at the scene: Grant Bisset, Ian Brodie, Barrie McHaffie, Jeff McHaffie, Toby Wallis, Prue Wilson and Ray Mulqueen. Among those involved with the subsequent hospital and rehabilitation phases I thank, in particular, Michael Lucas, Dennis Pezaro, Alan Clarke, Mariann Fairbairn, Sharon Mackie, Annie Trengrove, Nola Sims, Judy Hamilton and Jon Turnbull. Being at the very heart of the rehabilitation effort, this chapter is as much Prue Wallis's story as it is her husband's. Cate Brett's *North and South* article about this episode in Tim's life set a platform for further research. Tim's nurses, including Sharon Mackie, Alison Walker, Christine Sinclair, Suzanne Mannering and Sara Churchill, have been particularly helpful to me. Shirl Rowley (nee Flynn), who was a nanny and home help in earlier years, also assisted with information.

Prue and her four sons, Toby, Jonathan, Matthew and Nicholas, provided considerable information for the chapter about the 1996 crash and generally for the later chapters in the book. Their support has been critical. I am grateful, too, for the hospitality Prue and Tim extended to me at the new Benfiddich. Especially pleasurable were the breakfast interviews with Tim, fresh from his morning swim, as we looked out over the lake and mountain views stretching all the way to Mt Aspiring. I was also warmly hosted on one occasion by Jonathan and Annabel at Minaret Station, where I talked to the four brothers for several hours about their experiences as children, as boarders following a family tradition at Christ's College and their work today. I thank Toby and Nick for getting me there.

Tim put his heart and soul into this project. In numerous interviews, up to two hours at a time, we worked our way systematically through his life. Tim lives to communicate, and a flood of phone calls, faxes and letters from him, together with his prompt comments on the draft manuscript, helped me craft his story as efficiently and accurately as possible. I was aided, too, by Tim's exceptional memory of the early days. I am grateful also to the many informants who replied by email and fax to my requests for checks on sections of the text.

Tim and Prue entrusted me with a large amount of precious records, memorabilia and personal letters. This material included all of Tim's Christ's College term reports and most of his weekly letters from boarding school, all kept safe by his mother. Of special value to the research was Tim's library of Super 8 cine films. He has been an assiduous recorder of everyday activities, events and travels over the years. With Annie Trengrove's support, Tim did an outstanding job identifying the photographs shortlisted for this book, more than 800 in all. I also thank Dave Asher for his documentary films on the deer recovery days and Alpine's involvement in that era.

The Longacre Press team were a delight to work with. Publisher Barbara Larson has been supportive throughout the project, editor Emma Neale provided astute advice and the book's design reflects the skill of Christine Buess.

On a personal front, I thank Robert Steiner and Ian Farquhar for their advice on computers and shipping respectively, and Ray Mitchell for providing vehicles for my numerous research journeys. Because at times I felt something of a hurricane myself as I researched Tim's world, I thank my wife, Mary, and our daughter, Sophie, for their tolerance, support and love.

NEVILLE PEAT